LEARNING MICROSOFT OFFICE 2013

Other Titles by the Same Authors

- PageMaker 7
- 3D Max
- Computer Fundamentals
- Java 7
- Internet & E-mail
- HTML 5
- JavaScript with HTML 5
- Visual Basic 6
- SQL
- Web Designing
- Multimedia
- Networking
- PC Hardware
- Desk Top Publishing
- C
- C++
- Windows XP
- Windows Vista
- Windows 7
- Windows XP, Vista, Office 2007 & Internet & E-mail
- MS Office XP
- MS Access 2013
- MS Excel 2013
- MS Word 2013
- MS Office 2013
- MS Access 2007
- MS Excel 2007
- MS Word 2007
- MS Office 2007
- Tally 9.0 with ERP
- Dreamweaver CS4
- CorelDRAW X4
- Photoshop CS4
- Flash CS4
- Illustrator CS4
- Microsoft Access 2010
- Microsoft Excel 2010
- Microsoft Word 2010
- Microsoft Office 2010
- AutoCAD 2010
- Dreamweaver CS5
- CorelDraw X5
- Flash CS5
- Illustrator CS5
- Photoshop CS5
- ASP.Net 4.0
- C# 4.0
- ASP.Net and C#.Net
- Tally 9.0 (Hindi)
- Internet & E-mail (Hindi)
- Desk Top Publishing (Hindi)

LEARNING MICROSOFT OFFICE 2013

Ramesh Bangia
B.Sc., Dip. Comp. Sc.

Formerly Managing Editor, Software Today
Formerly Incharge Computer Centre, Hindustan Copper Ltd., New Delhi

KHANNA BOOK PUBLISHING CO. (P) LTD.

Publisher of Engineering and Computer Books

4C/4344, Ansari Road, Darya Ganj, New Delhi-110002
Phone : 011-23244447-48 **Mobile:** +91-9910909320
E-mail : contact@khannabooks.com
Website : www.khannabooks.com

Dear Readers,

To prevent the piracy, this book is secured with HIGH SECURITY HOLOGRAM on the front title cover. In case you don't find the hologram on the front cover title, please write us to at contact@khannabooks.com or whatsapp us at +91-99109 09320 and avail special gift voucher for yourself.

Specimen of Hologram on front Cover title:

Moreover, there is a SPECIAL DISCOUNT COUPON for you with EVERY HOLOGRAM.

How to avail this SPECIAL DISCOUNT:

Step 1: Scratch the hologram
Step 2: Under the scratch area, your "coupon code" is available
Step 3: Logon to www.khannabooks.com
Step 4: Use your "coupon code" in the shopping cart and get your copy at a special discount
Step 5: Enjoy your reading!

Thanks,
Khanna Publishing House

Price: ₹295.00

ISBN: 978-93-82609-34-6

Learning MICROSOFT OFFICE 2013
by **Ramesh Bangia**

First Edition: 2014
Reprint: 2024

To view complete list of books, please scan the QR Code:

Published by:
Khanna Book Publishing Co. (P) Ltd.
CIN: U22110DL1998PTC095547

Visit us at: www.khannabooks.com
Write us at: contact@khannabooks.com

Printed in India.

PREFACE

Learning of a software is both easy and difficult. It depends upto what level you are planning to learn. If you are learning only for the working use, then it is very easy. But, when you try to go deep into it, then you realise how difficult it is to master it.

This book has been written in mind to make you aware of the options available in the software and how they can be used. It is like telling the child about the steps and stairs. You are the one who is to climb the stair. This book will just guide you how to use the stairs.

I am indeed debited to my publishers Khanna Book Publishing Co. Pvt. Ltd. for their suggestions and encouragement given in producing this book.

Suggestions for improvement of the book are indeed welcome.

Author

CONTENTS

CHAPTER 1

Introducing Windows 8

In this chapter you will read about:

- What is Windows 8?
- Online Features of Windows 8.
- Windows 8 Features.
- Upgrading to Windows 8.
- Windows 8 Requirements

What is Windows 8?

Windows 8 is the most recent operating system designed by Microsoft. It introduces a lot of new changes, so if you're thinking of upgrading from a previous version of Windows, you should carefully look at these changes to decide whether upgrading is a good idea.

There have been many different versions of Windows over the years, including Windows 7 (released in 2009) Windows Vista (2006) and Windows XP (2001). While previous versions of Windows mainly ran on desktop and laptop computers, Windows 8 is also designed to run on tablets. Because of this, the interface has been simplified so that it will work with touchscreens.

An operating system manages all of the hardware and software on a computer. Without it, the computer would be useless. To learn more about how operating systems work, check out Understanding Operating Systems and Getting to Know the OS in our Computer Basics tutorial.

How is Windows 8 Different From Earlier Versions?

There are many new features and changes in Windows 8, both small and large. These changes include a redesigned interface, online features, improved security, and more.

Interface Changes

The first thing that you'll notice about Windows 8 is that it looks totally different from previous versions of Windows. The all-new interface includes features like the Start screen, live tiles, and hot corners.

- **Start screen:** The main screen that you'll use is called the Start screen, and it displays all of your apps as tiles. You can personalize your Start screen by changing the color scheme, choosing a background image, and rearranging your tiles.
- **Live tiles:** Some apps use live tiles, which let you see information without even clicking on the app. For example, the Weather app displays the current weather on its tile, and you can click on it to see more details.
- **Hot corners:** You'll navigate through Windows 8 by using hot corners. To use a hot corner, just hover the mouse in the corner of the screen, and it will open a toolbar or tile that you can click. For example, to switch to another open app, you can hover the mouse in the top-left corner and then click. If you're using a tablet, you'll swipe from the left or right instead of using hot corners.
- **Charms bar:** Many of your computer's settings are now found in a toolbar called the Charms bar. You can access it by hovering in the top-right or bottom-right corner of the screen. If you're using a tablet, you can swipe from the right to open the Charms bar.

Online Features in Windows 8

Many people are starting to save their files and other information online (also known as the cloud). One way to do this is with Microsoft's SkyDrive service. Windows 8 is designed to connect seamlessly to SkyDrive, as well as other online services like Facebook and Twitter.

- **Sign in with Microsoft account:** Instead of creating an account on your computer, you can sign in with your free Microsoft account. This will bring all of your SkyDrive files, contacts, and more into your Start screen. You can even sign in to a different computer that has Windows 8, and all of your important files will be there.
- **Social networking features:** You can connect your Facebook, Twitter, and Flickr accounts to Windows 8, allowing you to see your friends' updates directly from your Start screen or from the built-in People app.

Apps on the Start screen

Live tiles

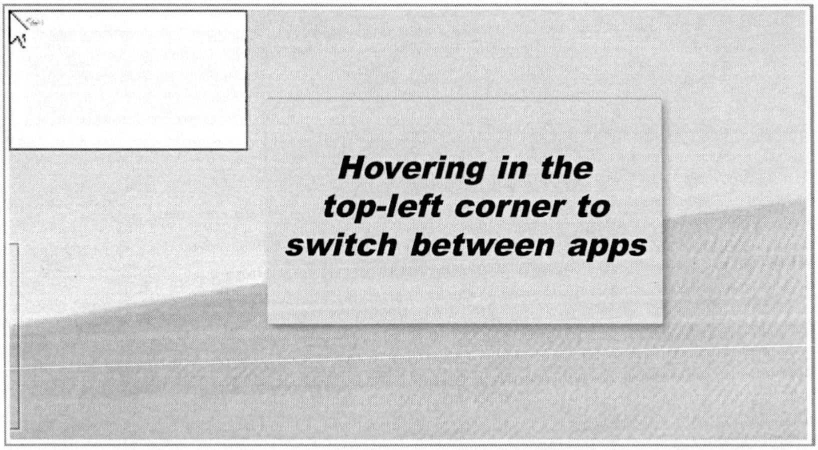

Hot corners

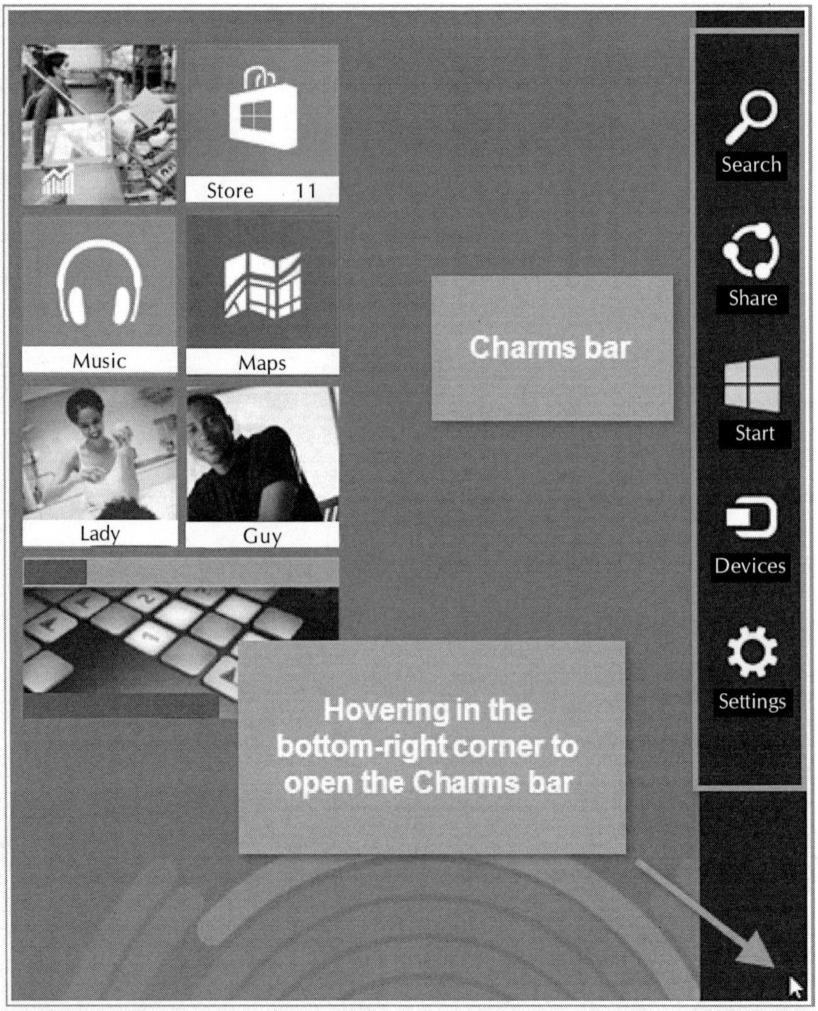

The Charms bar

Other Windows 8 Features

- **Simplified Desktop for increased speed:** Microsoft hasn't removed the Desktop, and you can still use it to manage your files or open many of your existing programs. However, it has removed some of the transparency effects that often caused Windows 7 and Vista to run slowly. The new Desktop should run more smoothly on most computers.

Signing in with a Microsoft account

- **No Start button:** The biggest change to the Desktop is that there is no Start button. In previous versions, the Start button was a very common place to go to launch apps, access settings, or search the computer. Although these features are now accessible from the Start screen, many people may find it disorienting to use Windows without the Start button.

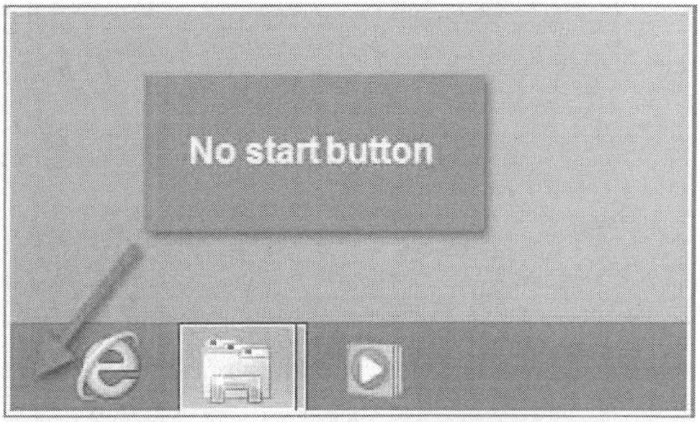

The Desktop no longer has a Start button

- **Improved security:** Windows 8 has a built-in antivirus program called Windows Defender, which can also protect you from other types of malware such as spyware. The built-in Windows Store also helps to keep you and your computer safe by showing you what information each app will have access to. For example, some apps have access to your location, so if you're uncomfortable sharing your location you can decide not to download those apps.

How Will You Use Windows 8?

Since Windows 8 is so different, it will probably change the way you use your computer. This may take a while to get used to, but keep in mind that these changes are designed to make your computing experience easier and smoother.

For example, if you've used previous versions of Windows, you may be accustomed to launching programs by clicking on the Start button.

In Windows 8, you'll use the Start screen instead. On the other hand, you'll still be able to use the Desktop view to organize your files and folders, and to open older programs.

The People app

Most people will have to use both the Start screen and the Desktop, depending on the task. You'll probably have to switch back and forth, which may be disorienting at first.

However, if you mainly use your computer to browse the web, you may spend almost all of your time in the Start screen.

Should You Upgrade to Windows 8?

As you can see, Windows 8 is a big change from previous versions of Windows. It's not just a new version with new features — in many ways, it's a different operating system.

If you don't like the idea of changing the way you use your computer, you may prefer to stick with your current version, or upgrade to Windows 7. But if you like

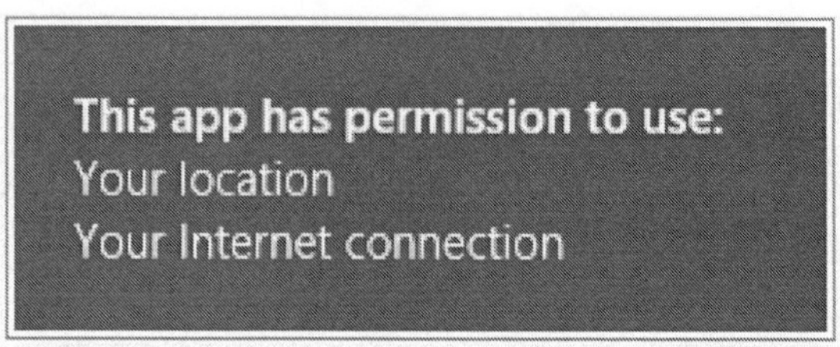

An app that has access to your location and internet connection

the new features that you've seen so far, then you may find that Windows 8 offers an easier and more enjoyable experience.

In the next lesson, we'll cover some of the information you'll need to know before you upgrade, including different editions of Windows 8 and the hardware requirements.

Launching an app from the Start screen

Upgrading to Windows 8

Now that you've seen some of the new features that Windows 8 has to offer, you'll need to decide whether you should upgrade an existing computer, or buy a new computer or tablet that has Windows 8 pre-installed.

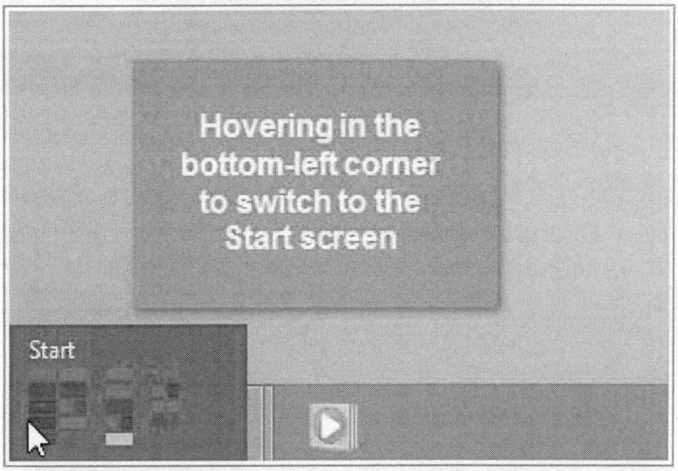

Switching from the Desktop to the Start screen

Windows 8 Editions and Pricing

There are three main editions of Windows 8:

- **Windows 8:** This is the standard edition, and it will run on desktops, laptops, and some tablets.
- **Windows 8 Pro:** This gives you all of the features of Windows 8, as well as some extra features intended for advanced users and businesses. For example, people who need more security can use BitLocker to encrypt their files.
- **Windows RT:** This is the edition that most tablets will have. It may also be used by some budget laptops and netbooks. Windows RT comes pre-installed with a version of Microsoft Office that is optimized for touchscreens.

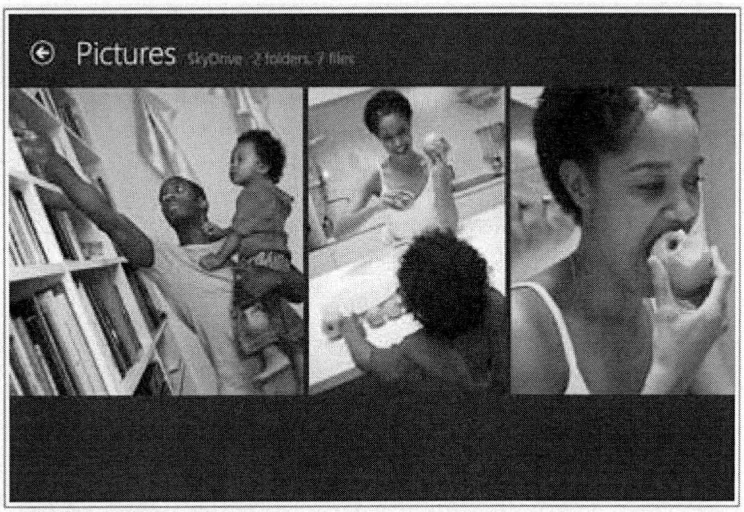

Windows 8

Windows 8 Tablets

If you want to use Windows 8 on a tablet, you'll need to buy a tablet that has Windows 8 pre-installed, such as the Microsoft Surface. The Surface comes in two versions: A cheaper version that runs Windows RT, and a more powerful version that runs Windows 8 Pro. Other companies are expected to release Windows 8 tablets over the next few months.

Microsoft Surface

Windows 8 Requirements

Before you upgrade to Windows 8, it's important to make sure your computer meets the minimum hardware requirements. Below are the requirements that Microsoft has given:

- 1 GHz (gigahertz) processor or faster. Your processor will either be 32 bits or 64 bits, and 64-bit processors will have stricter hardware requirements (see below).
- 1 GB (gigabyte) RAM (32-bit), or 2 GB RAM (64-bit).
- 16 GB available hard disk space (32-bit) or 20 GB (64-bit).
- DirectX 9 graphics device with WDDM 1.0 or higher driver.
- A screen resolution of at least 1024x768 pixels.

Note that these are the minimum requirements. If you use your computer for gaming or other demanding apps, you may need a faster processor, more RAM, or a more powerful graphics card.

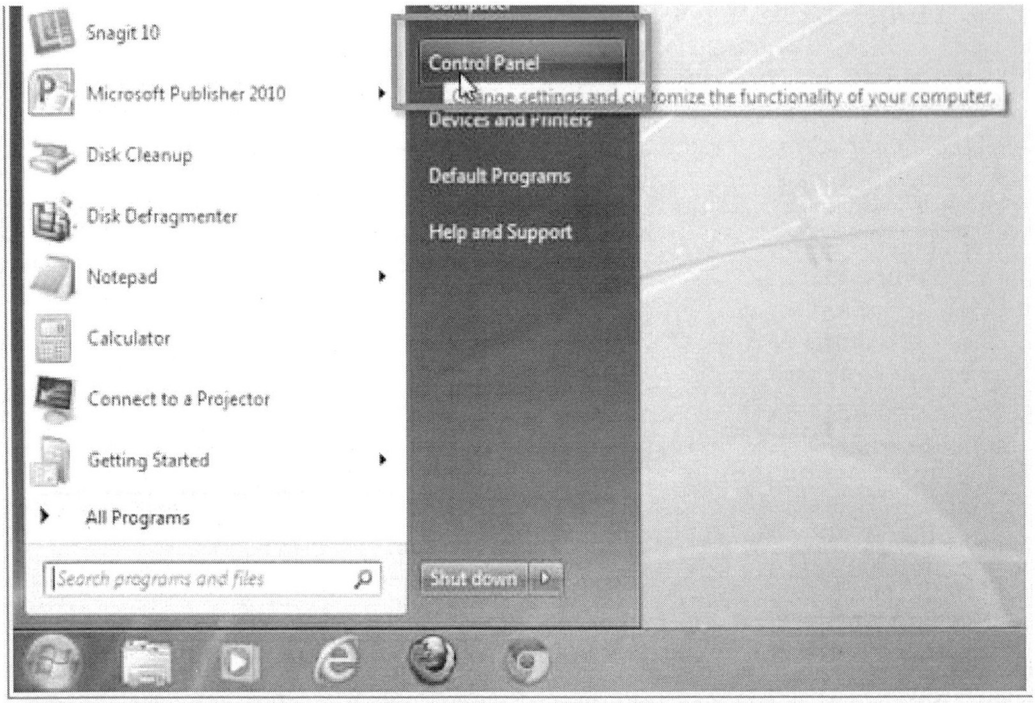

Opening the Control Panel in Windows 7

The good news is that Windows 8 has the same requirements as Windows 7, so if you're upgrading from Windows 7, you'll probably have no problems with Windows 8. On the other hand, if you want to upgrade from Vista or XP, you should check your computer's system information to see if it meets the requirements.

To View Information About Your Computer:

To see if your computer meets the requirements for Windows 8, you can view information about your computer by going to the Control Panel.

- Click on the Start button and select Control Panel.
- Click System and Security.
- Click System.
- You will now be able to see information about your computer's processor, RAM, and more.

Software Compatibility

In order for software to work, it has to be compatible with the operating system. Therefore, you may not be able to use all of your existing software if you switch to a different operating system. Before you upgrade to Windows 8, ask yourself if there is any software on your computer that you can't do without - and then do some research to find out if it is compatible.

If you are upgrading from Windows 7 or Vista, most of your apps should still work. However, if you're using an older version like Windows XP, there's a good chance some of your apps will not be compatible with Windows 8. A simple Google search will often be enough to tell if an app will be compatible in Windows 8.

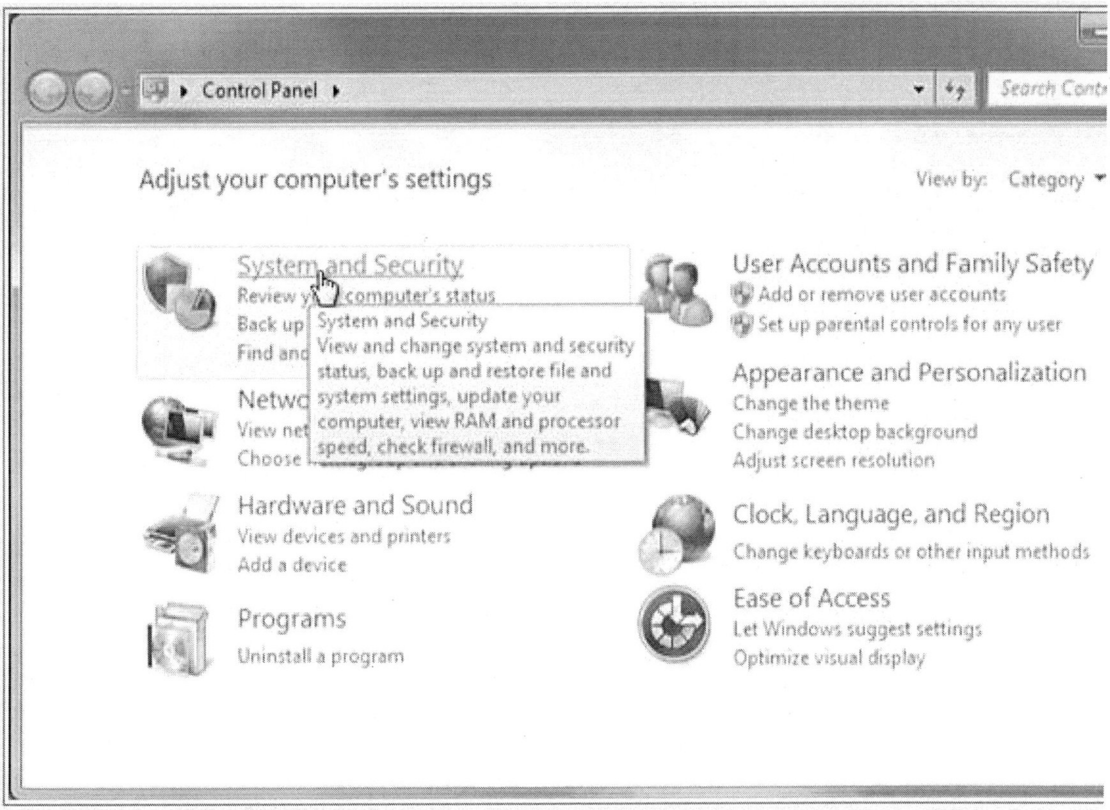

Clicking System and Security

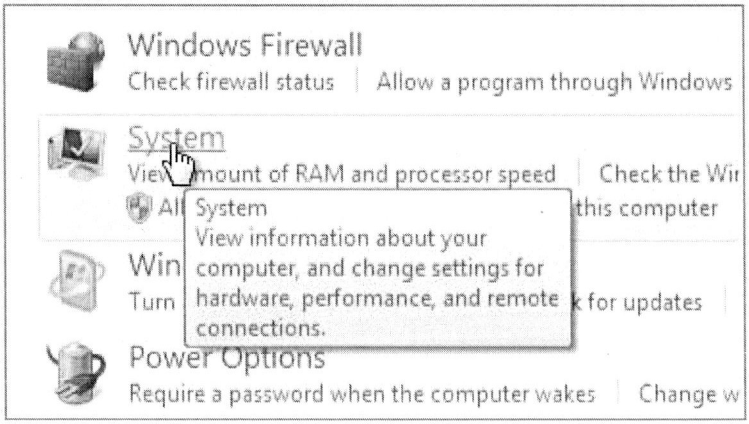

Clicking System

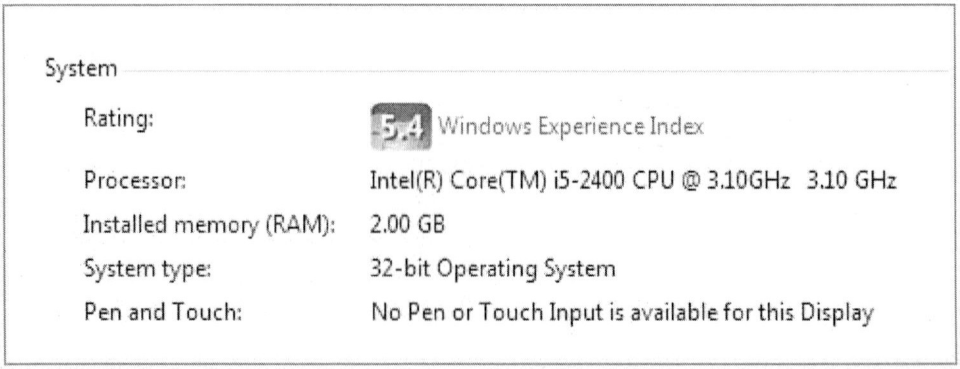

Viewing system info

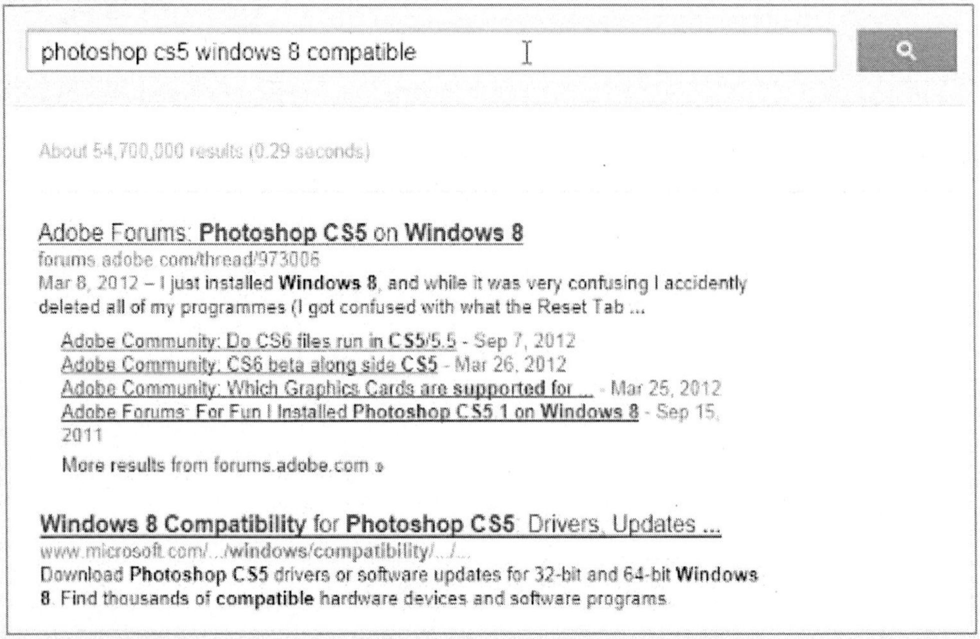

Searching the web for compatibility info

Getting Started with Windows 8

Windows 8 can be confusing at first, since the interface has changed so much. You'll need to know how to navigate the Start screen as well as the Desktop. Although the Desktop looks very similar to previous versions of Windows, it has one major change: The Start menu has been removed.

To Sign In to Windows 8:

When you're setting up Windows 8, it will require you to create an account name and password that you will use to sign in. You can also create additional accounts, and you'll have the option of associating each one with a Microsoft account.

- Click anywhere on the lock screen to unlock the computer.
- Your user account name and picture will appear. Type your password and then press Enter to sign in. Alternatively, you can press the back arrow to select a different user.
- The Start screen will appear.

Clicking the lock screen

Navigating Windows 8

There are several ways to navigate through Windows 8, including hot corners, keyboard shortcuts, and gestures if you're using a tablet.

Using Hot Corners

Whether you're in the Start screen or the Desktop, you can navigate through Windows 8 by using hot corners. To use a hot corner, just hover the mouse in the corner of the screen, and it will open a toolbar or tile that you can click. Each corner performs a different task:

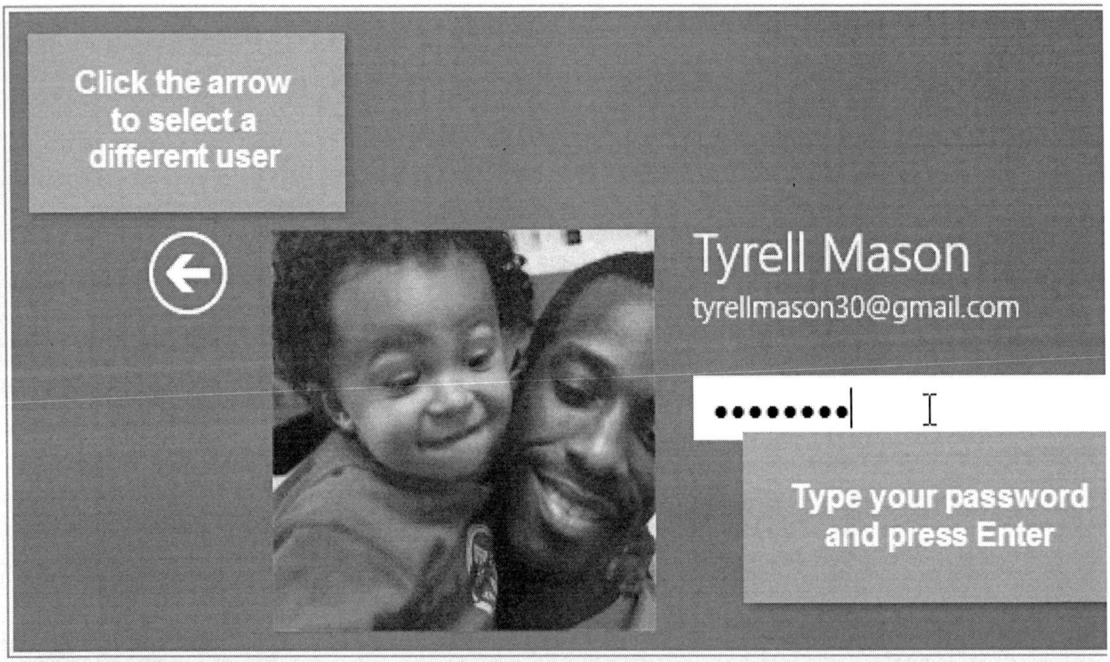

The sign-in screen

The Start screen

- Lower left: When you're using an app, you can click in the lower-left corner to switch back to the Start screen.

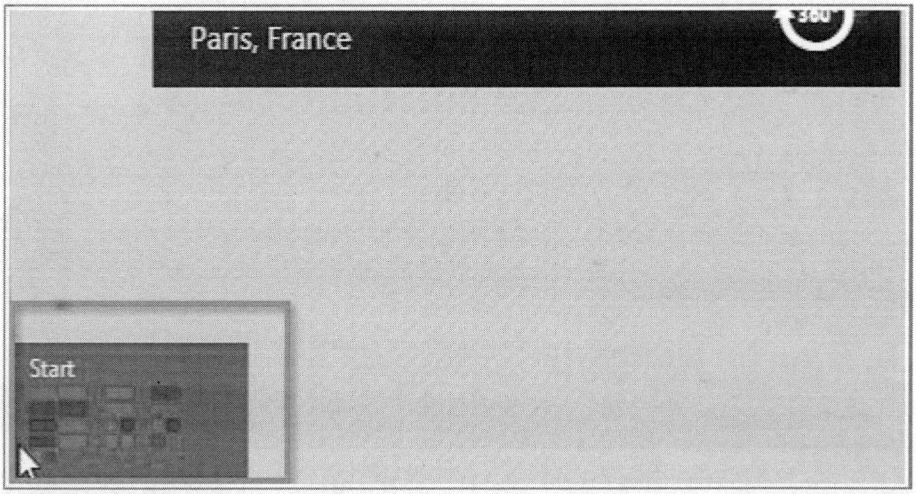

Clicking in the lower-left corner

- Upper left: If you click in the upper-left corner, it will switch to the previous app that you were using.

Clicking in the upper-left corner

- Upper right or lower right: You can hover the mouse in the upper-right or lower-right corner to open the Charms bar, which you'll use to adjust your computer's settings, manage printers, and more.

If you have several apps open, you can switch between them by hovering the mouse in the upper-left corner and then moving the mouse down. This displays a list of all of your open apps, and you can click the desired app to switch to it.

Navigating on a Tablet

If you have a Windows 8 tablet, you can navigate by using swipe gestures instead of hot corners:

- Swipe in from left edge lets you switch to a different open app.
- Swipe in from right edge opens the Charms bar.

Switching to a different app

Using Keyboard Shortcuts to Navigate

Windows 8 has several keyboard shortcuts that you can use to navigate more easily:

- **Alt + Tab:** You can hold down the Alt key and then press Tab one or more times to switch between your open apps. This feature is called Flip, and it works in both Desktop view and the Start screen.
- **Windows:** When you have an app open, you can press the Windows key to switch to the Start screen. This shortcut also lets you switch back to the Start screen when you are in Desktop view.

Alt+Tab

- **Windows+D:** You can hold down the Windows key and press D to switch to Desktop view.

Windows key

The Charms Bar

The Charms bar is a toolbar that lets you access your computer's settings, along with other options. You can access the Charms bar by hovering the mouse in the top-right or bottom-right corner.

Charms

The Charms bar contains several icons, which are called charms, and each one contains different options:

Windows+D

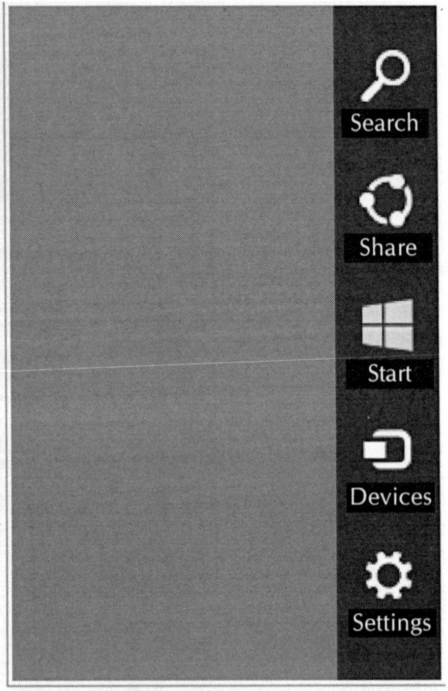

The Charms bar

- **Search charm Search:** The Search charm lets you find apps, files, or settings on your computer. However, a simpler way to search is to go to the Start screen and type the name of the file or app that you're looking for.
- **Search charm Share:** The Share charm is basically a copy and paste feature that is designed to be as convenient as possible. It allows you to "copy" information (such as a photo or web address) and "paste" it into another app. For example, if you're viewing a photo in the Photos app, you can share it with the SkyDrive app, which will upload the photo to your SkyDrive. If you're reading an article online, you can share the address with the Email app, which lets you email the article to a friend.

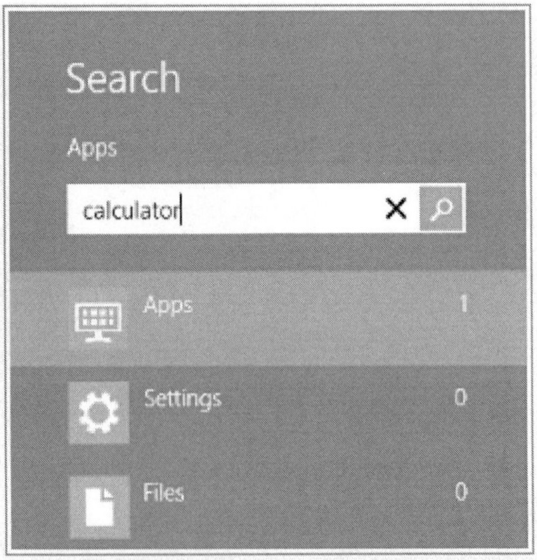

Searching for an app

- **Search charm Start:** This switches to the Start screen. If you're already on the Start screen, it will open the most recent app.
- **Search charm Devices:** This shows any hardware devices that are connected to your computer, such as printers or monitors.
- **Search charm Settings:** This lets you access general settings for your computer, as well as settings for the app you're currently viewing. For example, if you're in Internet Explorer, you can go to the Settings charm to access your Internet Options.

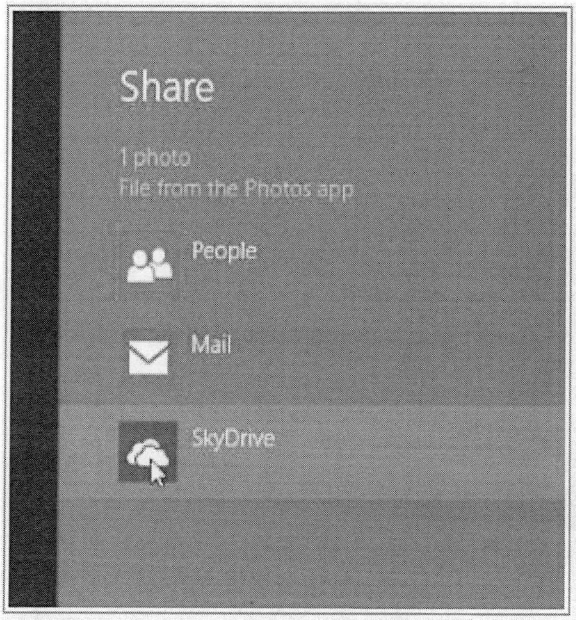

Using the Share charm to upload a photo to SkyDrive

Coping Without the Start Menu

One of the biggest complaints about Windows 8 is that it doesn't have a Start menu. The Start menu was a very important feature in previous versions of Windows, as it was used to launch apps, search for files, open the Control Panel, and shut down the computer. You can still do all of these things in Windows 8, but they're now found in different places.

To Launch an App:

There are several ways to open an app in Windows 8:

- Click the app icon on the taskbar.
- Double-click the app shortcut on the Desktop.
- Click the app tile in the Start screen.

To view all of your apps, right-click the Start screen background and select All apps.

Opening an app from the taskbar

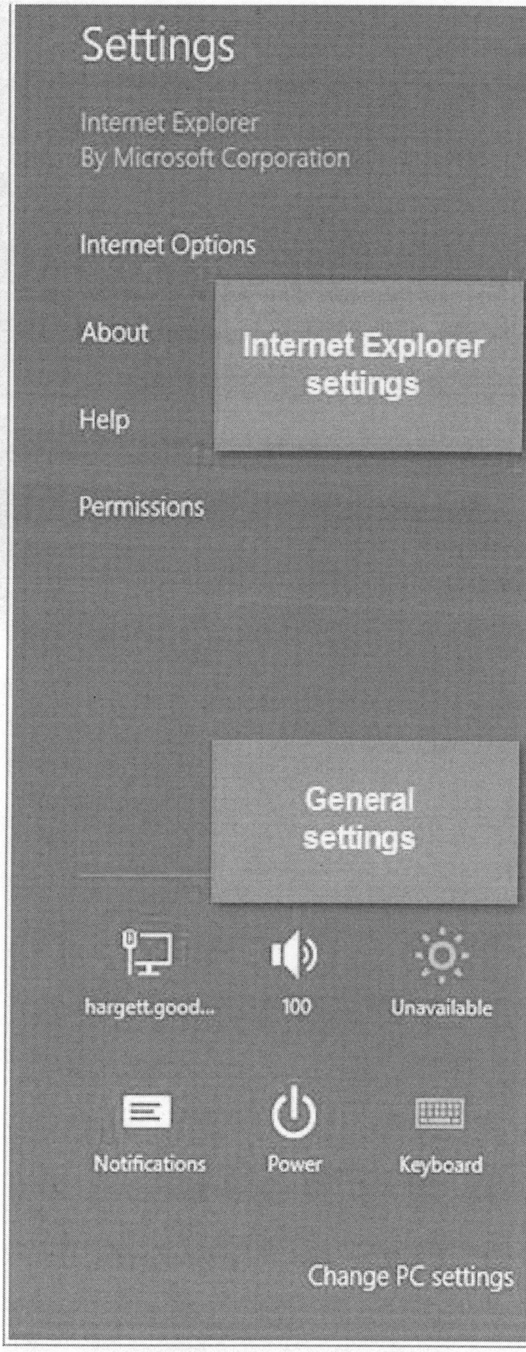

Viewing settings in Internet Explorer

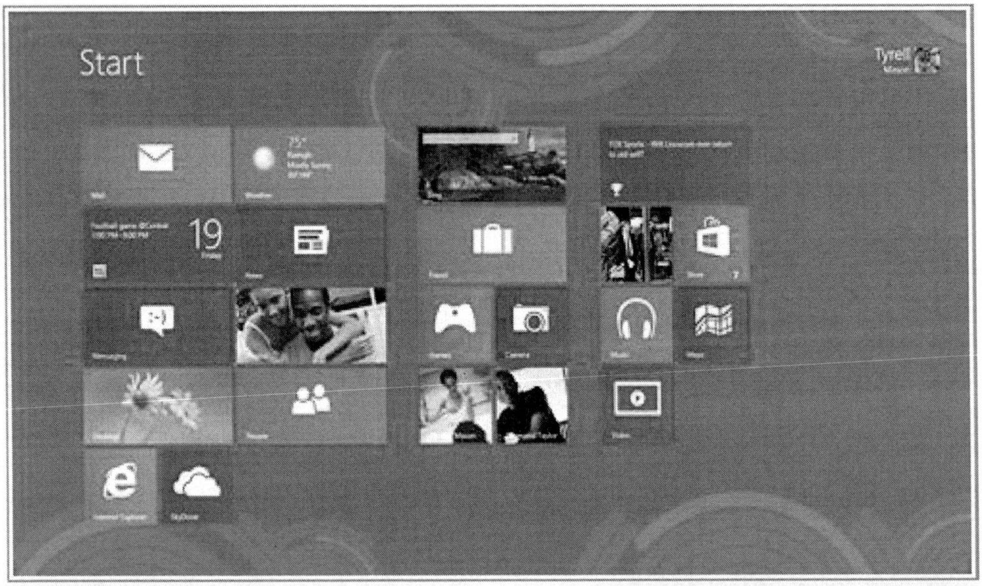

The Start screen

Opening an app from a shortcut

Opening an app from the Start scre

Clicking the All apps button

To Search for a File or App:

- Press the Windows key to switch to the Start screen, and then type what you're looking for. Your search results will instantly appear on the left side of the screen, and search options will appear on the right.

To Open the Control Panel:

- From the Desktop view, hover the mouse in the lower-right corner to access the Charms bar, then select Settings.
- Locate and select Control Panel from the Settings Pane.

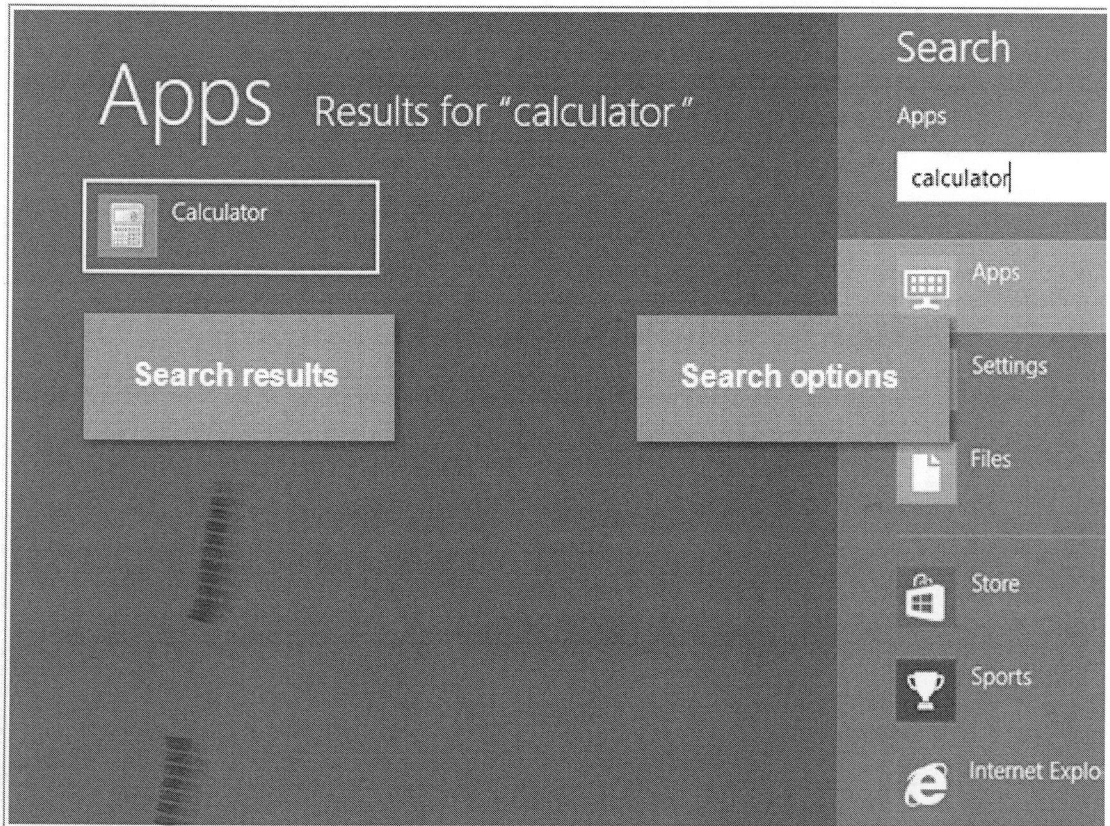

Searching for the Calculator app

- The Control Panel will appear. You can then select the desired setting to change it.

To Shut Down Your Computer:

- Hover the mouse in the lower-right corner to access the Charms bar, then select Settings.
- Click Power and select Shut down.

The Settings charm

Working with Start Screen Apps

Start screen apps are different from the "classic" Windows apps you may be used to. Apps fill the entire screen instead of opening in a window. However, you can still multitask by opening two apps side-by-side.

To Open an App:

- On the Start screen, locate and click the app that you want to open.
- The app will open and fill the entire screen.

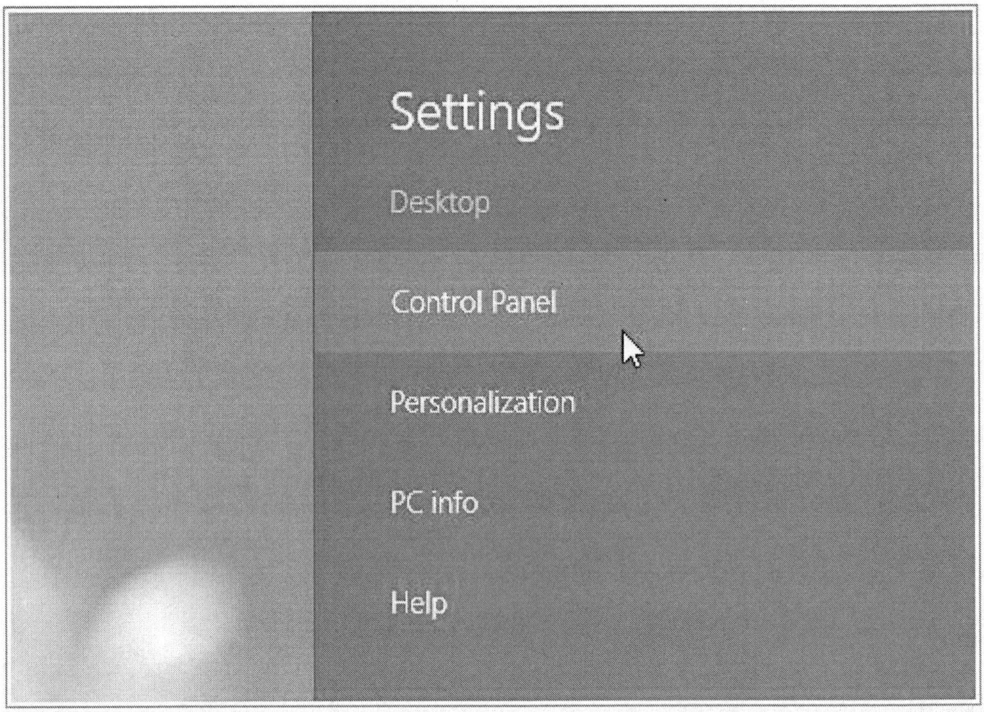

Clicking Control Panel

The Control Panel

The Settings charm

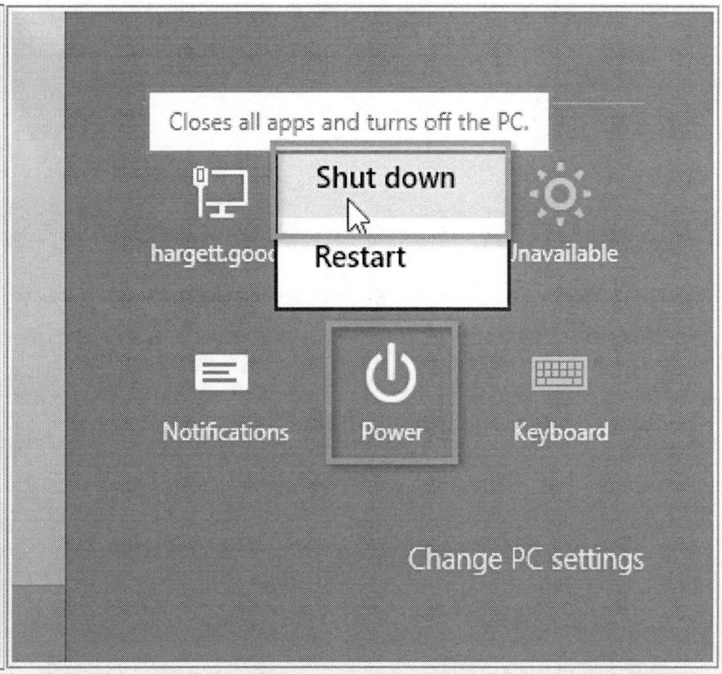

Shutting down the computer

To Close an App:

- Hover the mouse at the top of the app. The cursor will change to a hand icon.
- Click, hold, and drag the top of the app all the way down to the bottom of the screen and then release. The app will close, and you'll return to the Start screen.

When dragging the app down, it may look like it's "stuck." However, just keep moving the mouse down until the cursor gets to the bottom of the screen, and the app will then close.

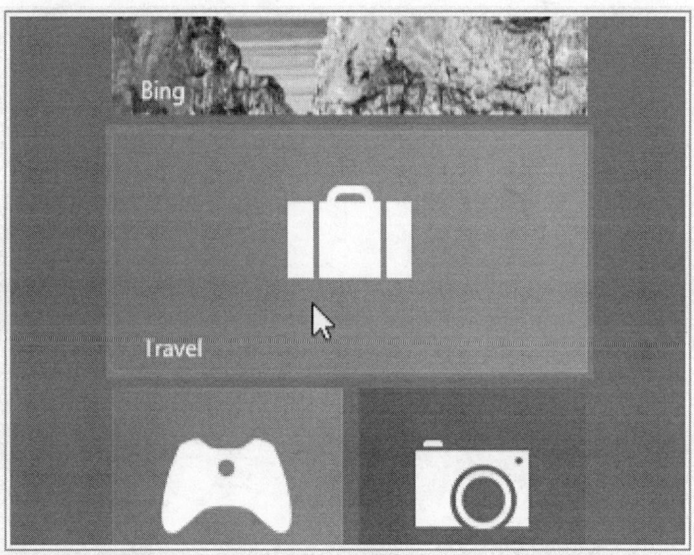

Opening the Travel app

Viewing Two Apps Side-By-Side

Although apps usually fill up the entire screen, Windows 8 lets you snap an app to the left or right side and then open a second app. For example, you might want to keep your calendar visible while you're using another app.

The Travel app

The hand icon

To View Two Apps Side-By-Side:

- From the Start screen, click on the first app to open it.

Closing an app

- Click, hold, and drag the top of the app all the way to the right or left side of the screen.
- Release the mouse, and the app will snap to the side of the screen. You cannot change the size of the snapped app.
- Click anywhere in the empty part of the screen to return to the Start screen.
- Click the second app to open it
- Both apps will now appear side-by-side.

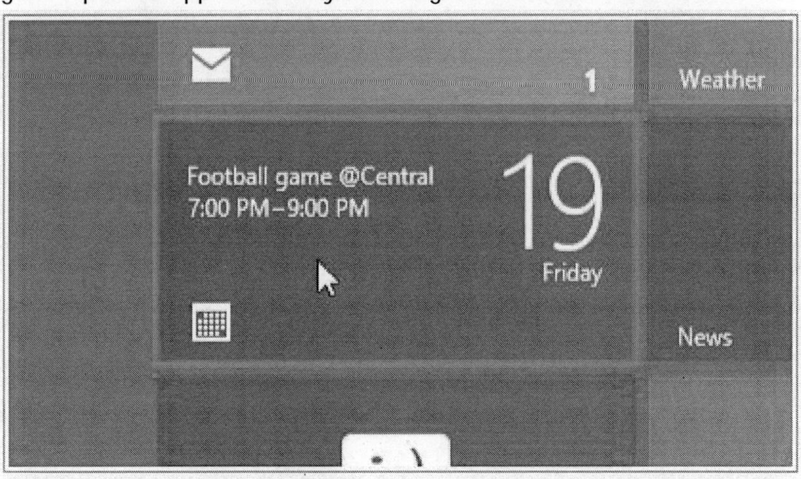

Opening the Calendar app

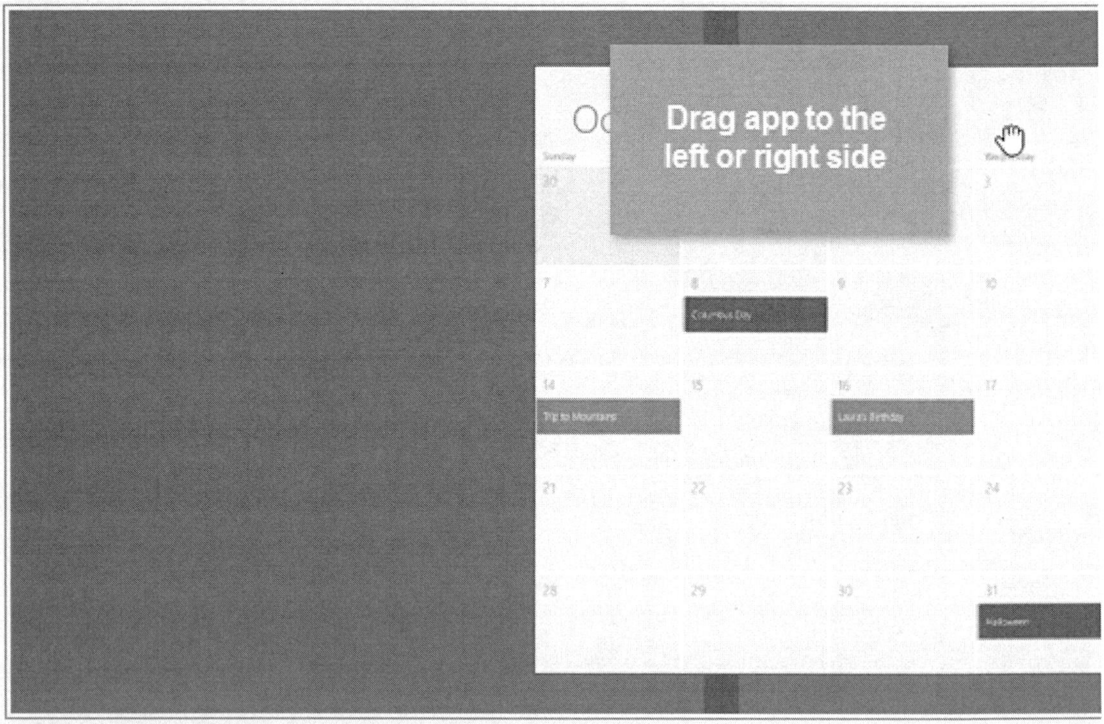

Snapping to the right side of the screen

The snapped app

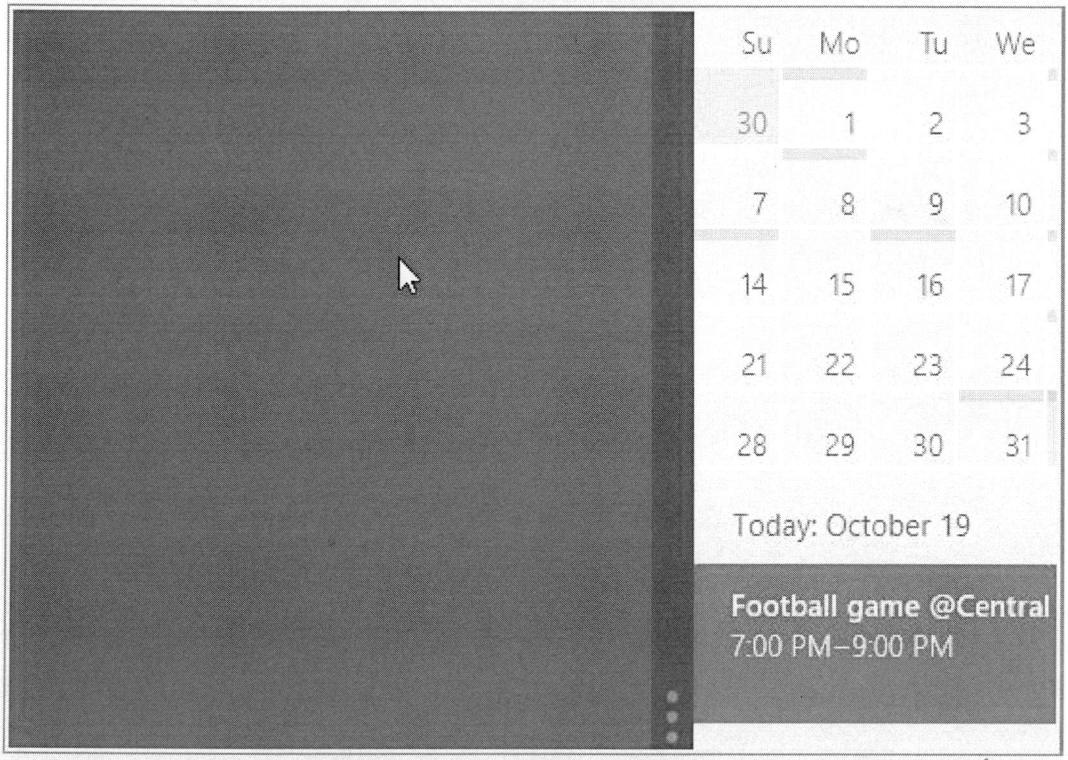

Clicking in the empty part of the screen

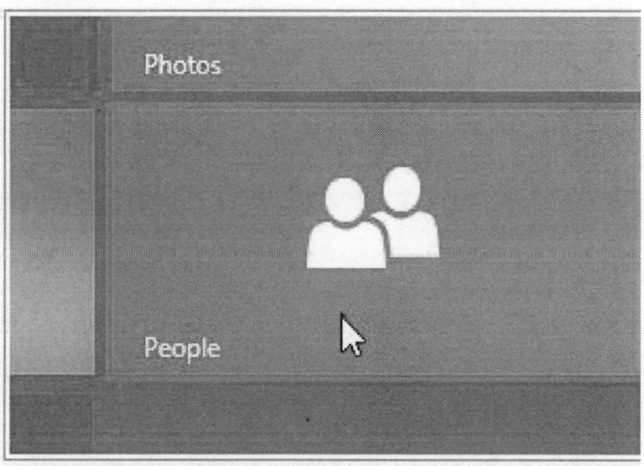

Opening the People app

Snapping is designed to work with wide-screen monitors. You will need a screen resolution of at least 1366x768 pixels to use this feature.

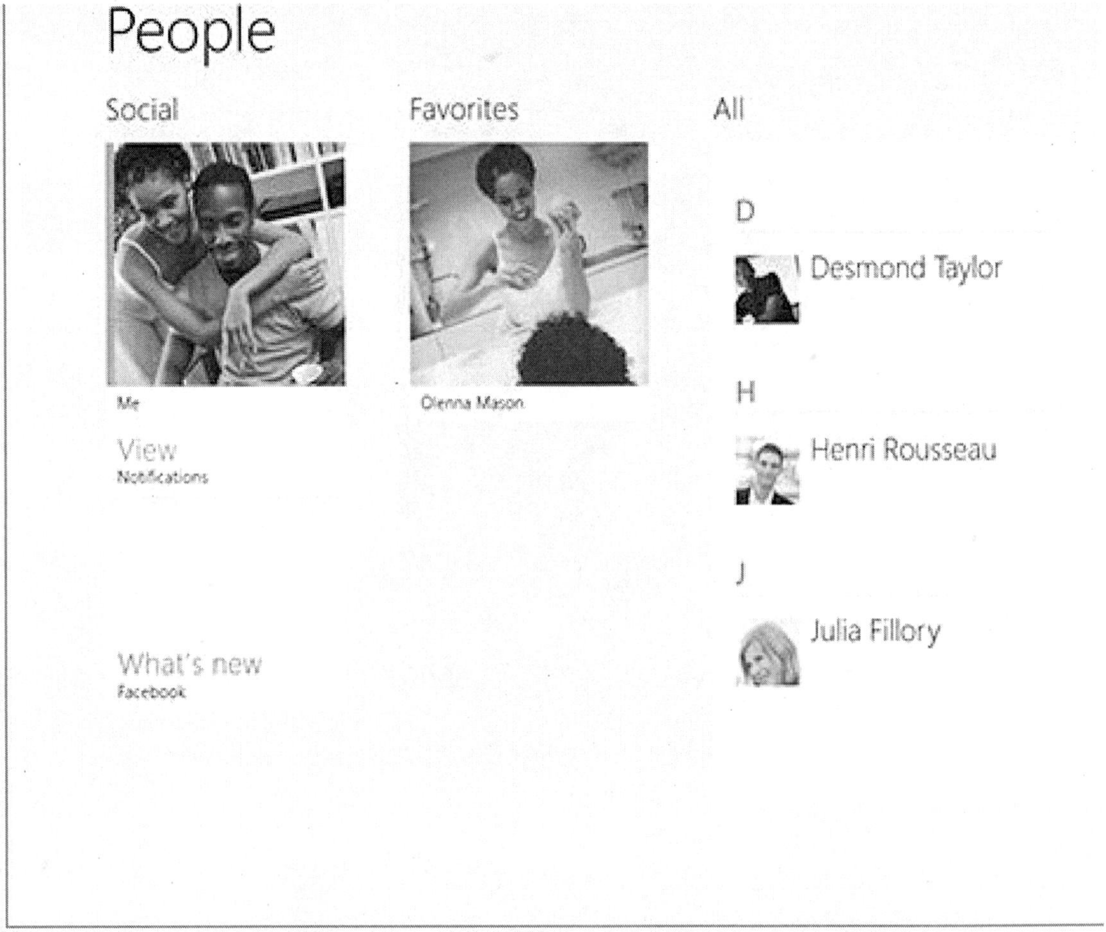

Two apps side-by-side

CHAPTER 2

Introduction to Microsoft Office 2013

Introduction

Microsoft Office 2013 comes in twelve different editions, including three editions for retail outlets, two editions for volume licensing channel, five subscription-based editions available through Microsoft Office 365 program, the web application edition known as Office Web Apps and the Office RT edition made for tablets and mobile devices. Office Web Apps are available free of charge on the web although enterprises may obtain for on-premises installation for a price.

What is Microsoft Office?

There are software and software. But, when you come to using the computer and a single software which can do everything for you, the choice mostly is Microsoft Office. This is not a software but a combination of software which can perform various aspects of your office routines. It can be writing letters, maintaining accounts, keeping databases, making a presentation, etc. This Microsoft Office has a solution for everything.

Microsoft Office 2013 (formerly Office 15) is a version of Microsoft Office, a productivity suite for Microsoft Windows. It is the successor of Microsoft Office 2013 and includes extended file format support, user interface updates and support for touch among its new features. Office 2013 is suitable for IA-32 and x64 systems and requires Windows 7, Windows Server 2008 R2 or later version of either. A version of Office 2013 comes included on Windows RT devices.

Development on this version of Microsoft Office was started in 2013 and ended on October 11, 2012 when Microsoft Office 2013 was released to manufacturing. Microsoft released Office 2013 to general availability on 29 January 2013. This version includes new features such as integration support for online services (including SkyDrive, Outlook.com, Hotmail, Skype, Yammer and Flickr), improved format support for Office Open XML (OOXML), OpenDocument (ODF) and Portable Document Format (PDF) and support for multi-touch interfaces.

Microsoft Office applications may be obtained individually; this includes Microsoft Visio, Microsoft Project and Microsoft SharePoint Designer which are not included in any of the twelve editions.

Let us take a look at the various constituents which are there in Microsoft Office 2013.

Microsoft Office Word 2013

A word processing software which allows you to write letters, edit them and print them after formatting it according to your needs. It has all the possible options of a word processor in the form of font style and size; indents; line spacing; margins; spell checking and grammar checkers to name a few.

Microsoft Office Excel 2013

This spreadsheet program allows you to manipulate and present your data in almost any way you choose. It allows you to work on a tabular pad consisting of columns and rows where you can perform all your mathematical, financial and statistical calculations. These calculations can be as simple as totalling a row or column of values or as complex as figuring the rate of return on an investment under varying circumstances. It also allows you to make a graphical representation of all your data in the form of 2-dimensional or 3-dimensional graph or pie chart.

Microsoft Office Access 2013

A software to take care of most of your database requirements. It allows you to store and organize information in sets of tables, which can be displayed in the form of columns and rows to look like a table or an index card. What's more it allows you to perform calculations and find for you simple statistics like totals and averages. It allows you to sort the data in any form and extract the required information based on the key given by you.

Lineup of Microsoft Office 2013 icons, from left to right: Word, Excel, PowerPoint, Outlook, Access, OneNote, Publisher, Lync and InfoPath. Absent in this lineup: Visio, Project, SharePoint Designer and SkyDrive Pro

Microsoft Office PowerPoint 2013

Want to make a presentation in a hurry! This is an ideal program of the same. Make sophisticated slide shows and professional looking electronic presentations. It also allows you to add charts, tables and pictures for make the presentation look alive.

Microsoft Office Outlook 2013

It is an electronic tool for managing appointments, addresses, e-mail, and notes. With lots of stress being given to the e-mail these days, it is an ideal software for sending and receiving e-mail.

Microsoft Office Publisher 2013

It is Microsoft's answer to the various other publishing software available in the market like PageMaker. It allows you to create invitations, design business-cards, and letter-heads, make your own calenders, produce newsletter, etc.

Microsoft Office OneNote 2013

It is used to gather information during meetings, brainstorming sessions, interviews, and more. The notes you create can include text, drawings, images, and audio recordings. OneNote uses a freeform page layout, so you can place and move information wherever you want.

Microsoft Office InfoPath Designer 2013/InfoPath Filler 2013

Microsoft Office InfoPath is a software application for designing, distributing, filling and submitting electronic forms containing structured data. According to one of its inventors, a key architectural design decision was "to adhere to the XML paradigm of separating the data in a document from the formatting." Thus the product features a WYSIWYG form design area in which the various controls (dropdowns, text boxes, etc.) are bound to data fields represented separately as a hierarchical tree view of folders and data fields.

Microsoft Office Lync 2013

Microsoft Lync (formerly Microsoft Office Communicator) and Microsoft Lync for Mac are instant messaging clients used with Microsoft Lync Server or Lync Online available with Microsoft Office 365 and Live@Edu. They are replacements for Windows Messenger which was used with Microsoft Exchange Server.

Both Microsoft Lync and Microsoft Lync for Mac are enterprise software; unlike Windows Live Messenger, they have a different feature set that is targeted toward corporate environments.

Microsoft Office SkyDrivePro 2013

SkyDrive (officially Microsoft SkyDrive, previously Windows Live SkyDrive and Windows Live Folders) is a file hosting service that allows users to upload and sync files to a cloud storage and then access them from a Web browser or their local device. It is part of the Windows Live range of online services and allows users to keep the files private, share them with contacts, or make the files public. Publicly shared files do not require a Microsoft account to access.

The service offers 7 GB of free storage for new users. Additional storage is available for purchase. Users who signed up to SkyDrive prior to April 22, 2012 could opt-in for a limited time offer of 25 GB of free storage upgrade. The service is built using HTML5 technologies, and files up to 300 MB can be uploaded via drag and drop into the web browser, or up to 2 GB via the SkyDrive desktop application for Microsoft Windows and OS X.

Starting Above Software

You can start any of the above mentioned software by one of the following methods:

From Start Button

Click at Start button to access the various commands. Click on All Programs to get the various programs. From here click at the program called Microsoft Office 2013 group and then the required program

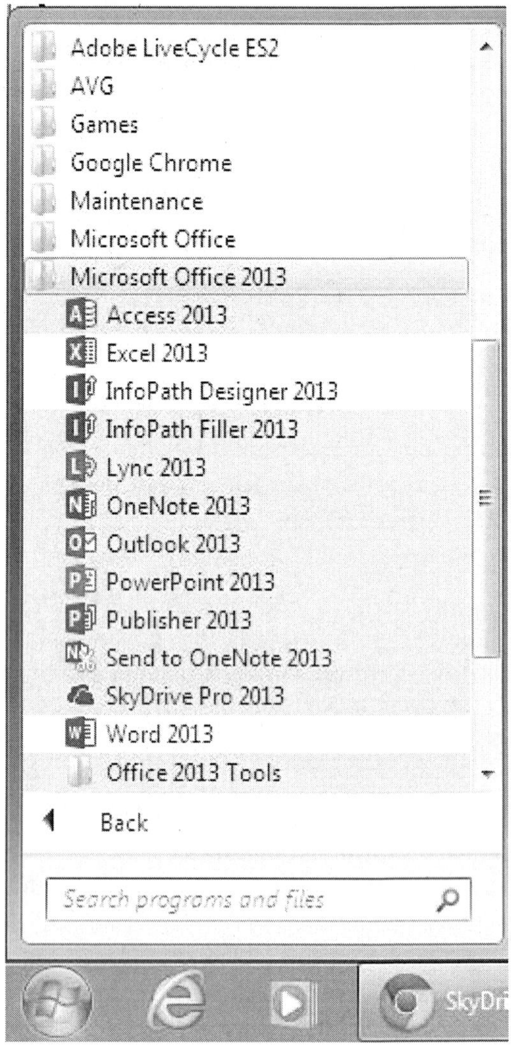

From Icon or Shortcut

You can choose to have an icon of the software on your desktop. This icon can be created by using the feature of Creating Shortcut.

Working with Various Constituents of Microsoft Office 2013

Let me give you here the tips for working under various constituents of Office 2013.

Microsoft Word 2013

As you know that Word is used for creating a document. So in simple terms, follow the following procedure to create a document.

1. Open Word 2013.
2. Click at Blank Document.
3. A new blank slate for writing would be opened for you.
4. Type the text as you would otherwise too.
5. Do not bother about any formatting or spelling.
6. Save the document at this stage to avoid loosing the text, if the lights go out.
7. Now format the text of the document according to your needs, i.e., Bold, Italics, etc.
8. If required, change the alignment of the text or part of it.
9. Save again.
10. Close the document from Info button.
11. Now open the same document again.
12. Spell check the whole document, correcting the wrong words.
13. Your document is ready.
14. Print it on the attached printer.
15. See the result of your effort.

If you follow these steps for creating a document in Word 2013, I am sure that you would never fail.

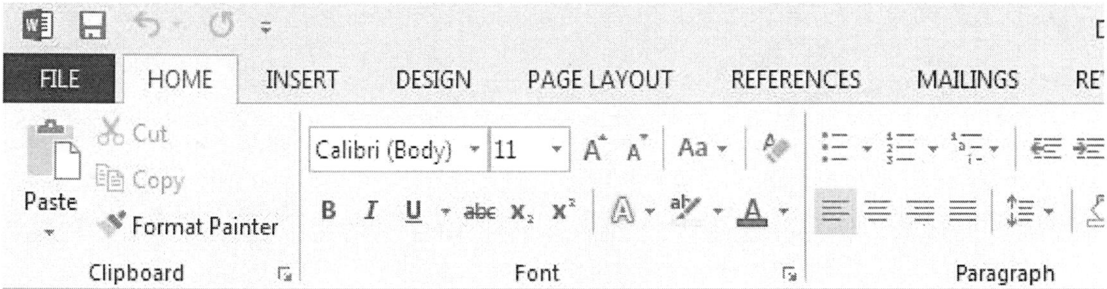

Microsoft Excel 2013

As you know that Excel is used for creating a spreadsheet. So in simple terms, follow the following procedure to create a spreadsheet.

1. Open Excel 2013.
2. Click at Blank Worksheet.
3. A new blank spreadsheet would be opened for you.
4. Type the number, text, formula, as the case may be.
5. Do not bother about any formatting at this stage.
6. Save the document at this stage to avoid loosing the typing, if the lights go out.
7. Now format the spreadsheet according to your needs, i.e., Bold, Italics, etc.
8. If required, change the alignment of the cells.
9. Save again.
10. Close the spreadsheet from Info button.
11. Now open the same spreadsheet again.
12. Spell check the whole spreadsheet, correcting the wrong words.
13. Your spreadsheet is ready.

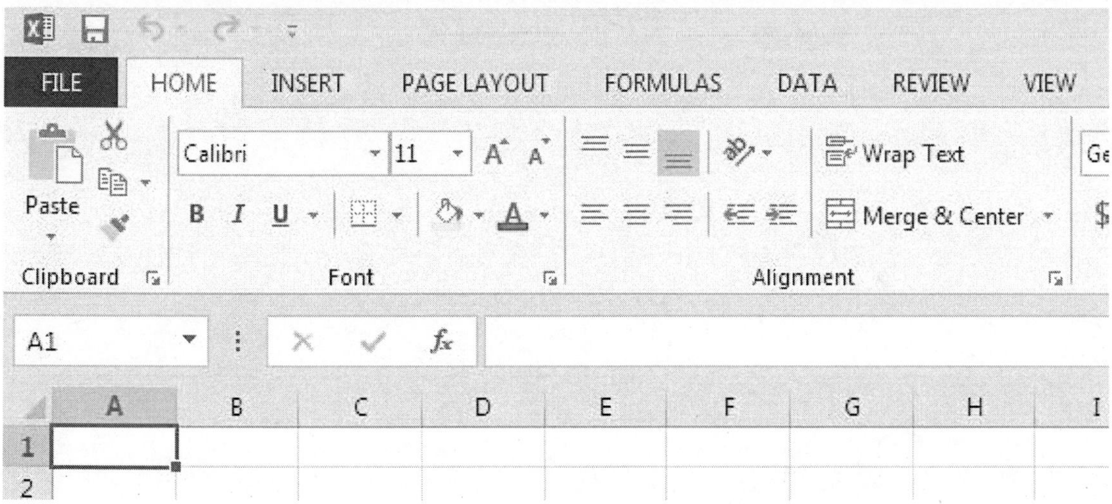

14. Print it on the attached printer.
15. See the result of your effort.

Microsoft PowerPoint 2013

As you know that PowerPoint is used for creating a presentation. So in simple terms, follow the following procedure to create a presentation.

1. Open PowerPoint 2013.
2. Click at Black Presentation from the Office button.
3. A new blank presentation would be opened for you.
4. Select the type of slide you want to create.
5. Type the text and other details, as the case may be.
6. Save the slide/presentation.
7. Now format the slide according to your needs, i.e., Bold, Italics, etc.
8. If required, change the alignment of the text within presentation.
9. Save again.
10. Add a new slide, if the need be.
11. Close the slide from Info button.
12. Now open the same presentation again.
13. Create a slide show of the slides.
14. Run the slide show to see the effect.

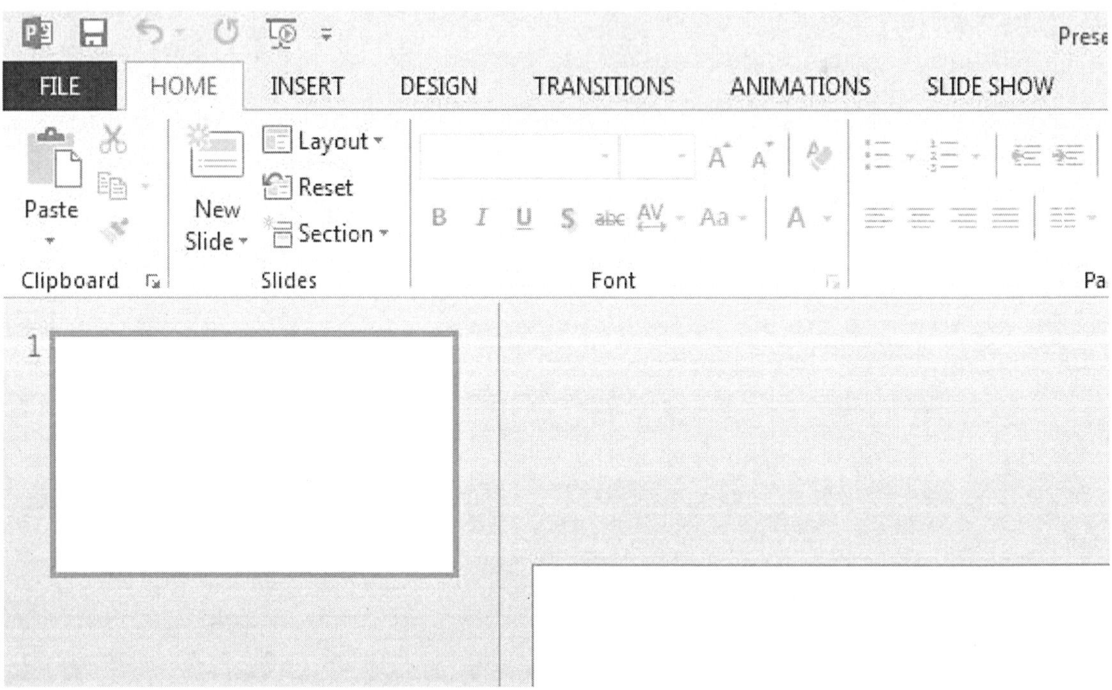

In similar way, you can run the other software of Microsoft Office 2013.

Using the Mouse

Since most of the activities in Microsoft Office are done using the mouse, it is very important to have the complete knowledge of working of mouse while using the constituents of Microsoft Office.

To click

Position the pointer on a menu, a button, or an icon and click the left mouse once.

To double-click

Position the pointer on an item and click the left mouse button twice in quick succession.

To select

1. Position the pointer on the first item to select.
2. Click and hold down the mouse button.
3. Move the mouse pointer across the items to select.
4. Release the mouse button.

To drag

1. Position the pointer on an item.
2. Click and hold down the left mouse button.
3. Move the mouse.
4. Release the mouse button.

To scroll

Drag the scroll button in the scroll bar up or down.

Or

Click a scroll arrow at either end of the scroll bar.

To choose from a menu

1. Click a menu name.
2. Click an item on a menu.

   Or

   If the item is followed by an arrow, position the mouse pointer on the item to open the submenu and then click an item on the submenu.

To move a window

Position the pointer on the window's title bar and press and hold the mouse button as your drag the window.

To resize a window

Position the pointer on the window's corner and, when you see the diagonal pointer, drag to resize the window.

To minimize a window

Click the Minimize button.

To restore a minimized window

Click the button for the window on the taskbar.

To maximize a window

Click the Maximize button.

To switch windows

Click any visible part of the window

Or

Click the button for the window on the taskbar.

To close a window

1. Click the Close button on the window

   Or

   Right click the button for the window on the taskbar and choose Close from the shortcut menu.

Remember

1. Menus in Office programs might be collapsed to show only frequently used items. To view the complete menu, click the More icon at the bottom of the menu or pause with the pointer on any menu option.
2. Menu items that are grayed out are not currently available.
3. To display a tooltip, which is a description of a toolbar button, position the pointer on the button and pause for a moment without clicking.
4. To minimize all windows, you can rightclick the taskbar and then click Minimize All Windows from the shortcut menu.
5. If one window fills the screen, you might have to click its Restore button to return it to a partial-screen window. You will then be able to see and click other windows.

Common Keyboard Commands

Ctrl + N	Open a new document
Ctrl + O	Opens a existing document
Ctrl + S	Saves the current document
Ctrl + W	Close the current document
Ctrl + P	Prints the current document
Ctrl + C	Copies the highlighted matter to store it in clipboard
Ctrl + X	Cuts the highlighted matter to store it in clipboard
Ctrl + V	Pastes the matter available on the clipboard
F1	Call for help
Shift + F1	Use the What's This? Button
Ctrl + F6	Switch between open documents
Ctrl + Z	Undo an action
Ctrl + Y	Redo an action

CHAPTER 3

Introduction to Microsoft Word 2013

Introduction

Microsoft Word 2013 is a word processing software which allows you to write letters, edit them and print them after formatting it according to your needs. It has all the possible options of a word processor in the form of font style and size; indents; line spacing; margins; spell checking and grammar checkers to name a few.

What's New in Microsoft Office Word 2013

Do more with your docs: Pop in an online video, open a PDF and edit the content, align pictures and diagrams with minimal fuss. The new Read Mode is clean and distraction-free—and it works great on tablets. Teaming-up is better too, with direct connections to your online spaces and streamlined review features like Simple Markup and comments.

Tip To get started creating your first Word document, see Basic tasks in Word 2013.

Enjoy the read

Get absorbed in Word documents right from your screen with a new clean, comfortable reading view.

New Read Mode

Enjoy reading with a view that displays your documents in easy-to-read columns on the screen.

Editing tools are removed to minimize distractions, but you still have access to the tools that are always handy for reading such as Define, Translate, and Search on Web.

Object zoom

Double-tap with your finger or double-click with your mouse to zoom in and make tables, charts and images in your document fill the screen. Focus on and take in the information, then tap or click again outside the object to zoom out and continue reading.

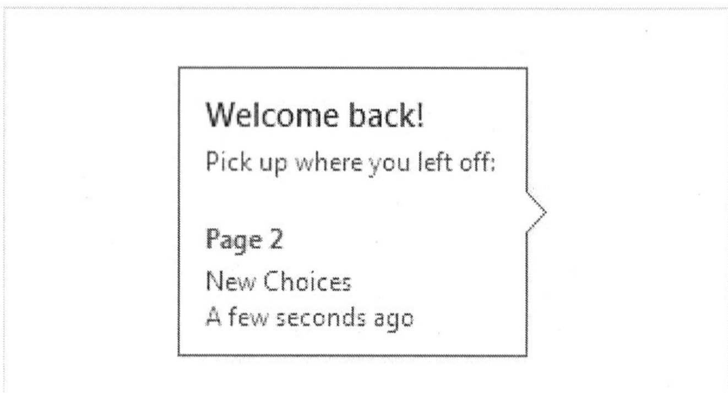

Resume reading

Reopen a document and keep reading right where you left off. Word remembers where you were—even when you reopen an online document from a different computer!

Online video

Insert online videos you can watch right in Word, without having to leave the document, so you can stay focused on the content.

Expand and collapse

Collapse or expand parts of a document with just a tap or click. Put summaries in headings and leave it to readers to open the section and read the details if they want.

Work together

Work with others with streamlined collaboration tools.

Save and share files in the cloud

The cloud is like file storage in the sky. You can get to it anytime you're online. Now it's easy to share a document using SharePoint or SkyDrive. From there you can access and share your Word docs, Excel spreadsheets, and other Office files. You can even work together with your colleagues on the same file at the same time.

Simple markup

A new revision view, Simple Markup, provides a clean, uncomplicated view of your document, but you still see indicators where tracked changes have been made.

Reply to comments and mark them as done

Comments now have a reply button. You can debate and easily track comments right next to the relevant text. And when a comment is addressed and no longer requires attention, you can mark it as done. It will be greyed out to keep out of your way, but the conversation will still be there if you need to revisit it later.

Add polish and style

With Word 2013 you can create more beautiful and engaging documents, and you can work with more media types—like online videos and pictures. You can even open PDFs.

Start with a template

When you open Word 2013, you're offered a choice of great new templates to help get you started along with a list your recently viewed documents so you can get back to where you left off in no time.

If you'd rather not use a template, click the Blank document.

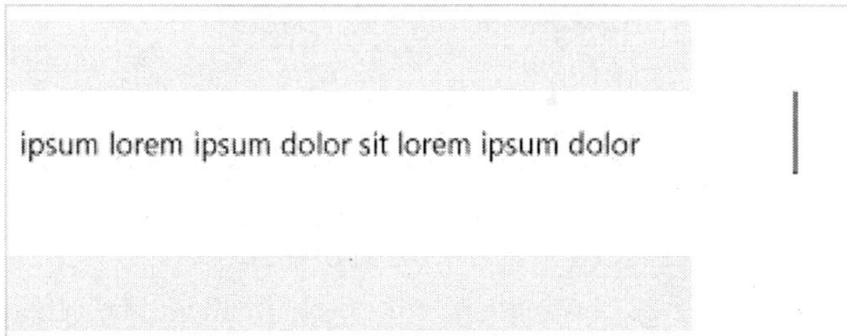

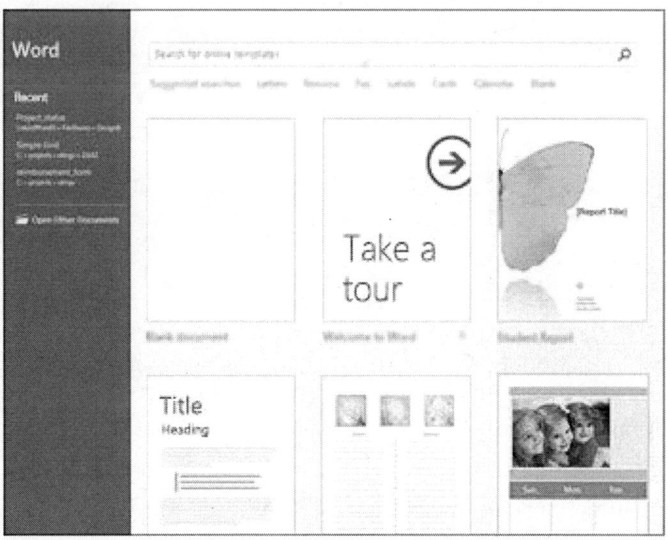

Open and edit PDFs

Open PDFs and edit the content in Word. Edit paragraphs, lists, and tables just like familiar Word documents. Take the content and make it look great.

Insert online pictures and video

Add online videos directly to your documents that readers can watch right in Word. Add your pictures from online photo services without having to save them first to your computer.

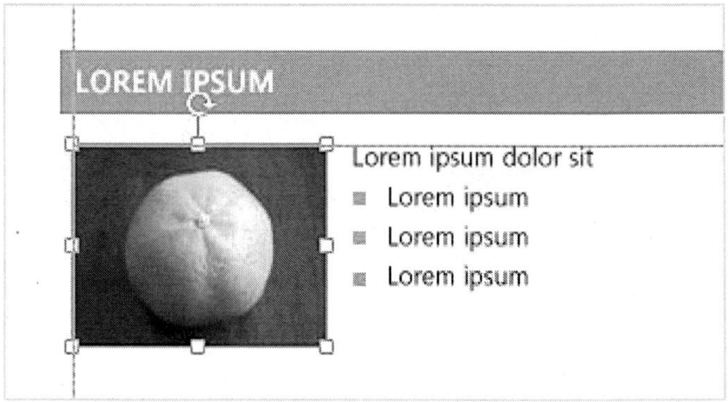

Live layout and alignment guides

Get a live preview as you resize and move photos and shapes in your document. The new alignment guides make it easy to line up charts, photos, and diagrams with your text

Opening Screen of Microsoft Word Screen

Gone are the days of Menu, for example, File menu, Edit menu, etc. Now everything is there on the screen. You have to just click it and presto, you have the command available to you. But, first have a look at the opening screen, which is shown next. There are some main Tabs, which are basic substitutions for the menus. They are: File, Home, Insert, Design, Page Layout, References, Mailings, Review, and View. Let us see what each one of them contains.

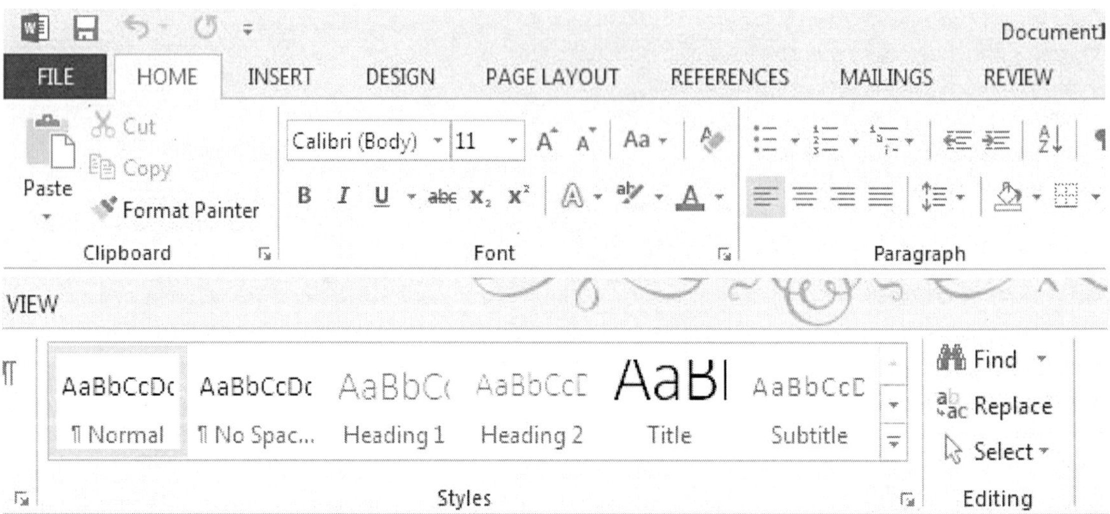

Home Panel

It has the various options of changing the style and type of text. Among the various important features are: Clipboard, Font, Paragraph, Styles, and Editing. Let us look at them one by one.

Clipboard

Most important commands here are: Cut, Copy, Paste and Format Painter.

The Format Painer is used for copying formattting from one place and applying it to another. Paste includes options like, Paste Special and Paste as Hyperlink.

Font

Various options of the font dialog box are all here. You can choose Font, Font size, Grow font, Lower font, Clear formatting in the first row. The second row contains options for Bold, Italics, Underline, Strikethrough, Subscript, Superscript, Change case, Text highlighting, and Text colour. The underlining option contains options for different type of lines which can be chosen for underlining and then choosing the colour of the same too. In Change case you have the option of changing the case to Sentence case, lowercase, UPPERCASE, Captalize Each Word and tOGGLE cASE. Text highlighting and colours have various options too.

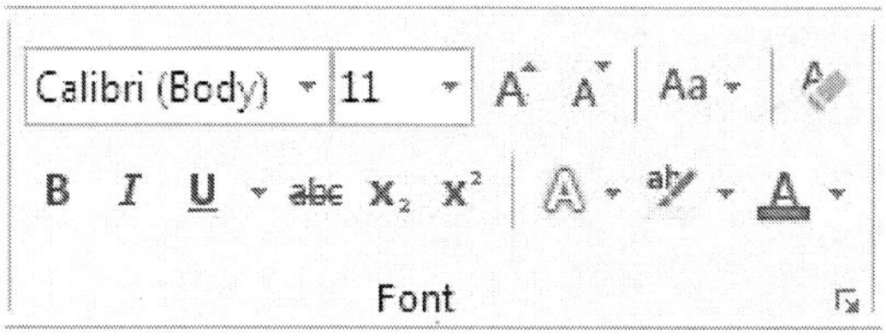

Paragraph

It has options for paragraph styling. The first row contains options for Bullets, Numbering, Multilevel numbering, Shifting text to left, Shifting text to right, Sort, Show/hide non printing characters. In the second row you have the options of making paragraph, Left aligned, Centrally aligned, Right aligned, Box aligned, Line spacing, Shading, and Bottom border. Bullets have different options. Numering can be done in different styles too. So can be done in the case of Multilevel numbering.

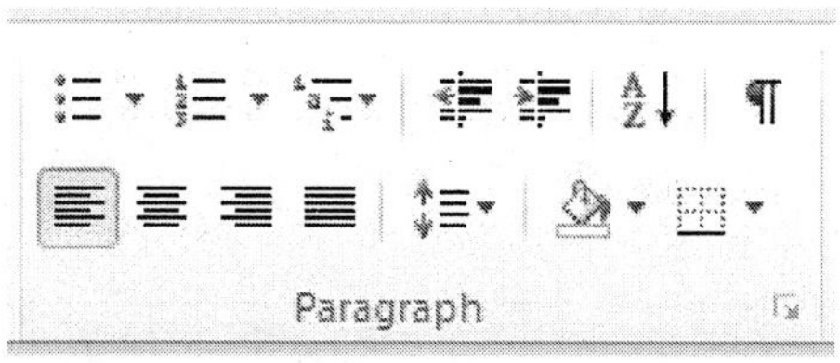

Styles

It displays the various styles which you have created. Just click at the one you want to apply to your text and it will be done. You can also Change Styles and create your own style from it.

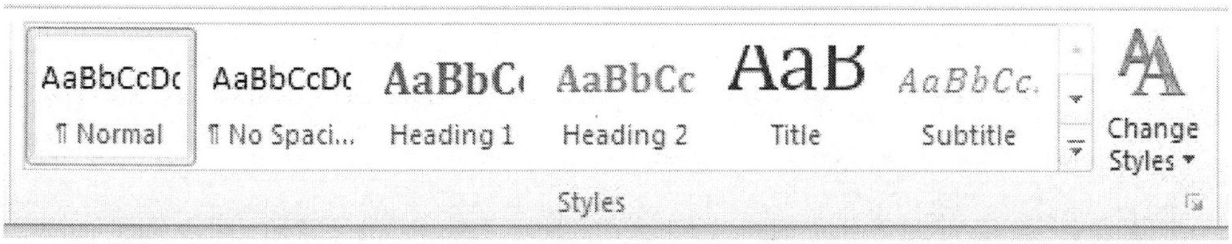

Editing

It has various other editing options, like, Find, Replace, and Select. Find allows you to find a particular word in the text. Replace allows you to find the word and replace it with another one. Select allows you to select text, select objects or the text with similar formatting.

The next panel is Insert.

Insert Panel

It has options like: Pages, Tables, Illustrations, Links, Header & Footer, Text, and Symbols.

Pages

It has options of Cover Page, Blank Page, Page Break. Blank page inserts a blank page in the text. Page break puts a page break in the text.

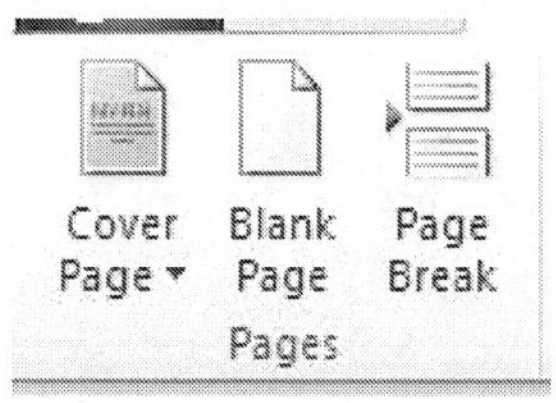

Tables

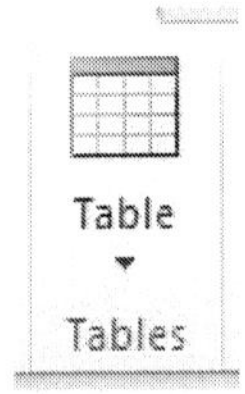

Inserts table format in the text. If you click at the arrow, you will see the options shown here, which not only describe the type of table you are choosing but also draws the table in the text simultaneously. You can also insert as a table, an Excel Spreadsheet. There is option of Quick Tables too, which allows you to save a table format, which can be called later for quickly creating a table.

Illustrations

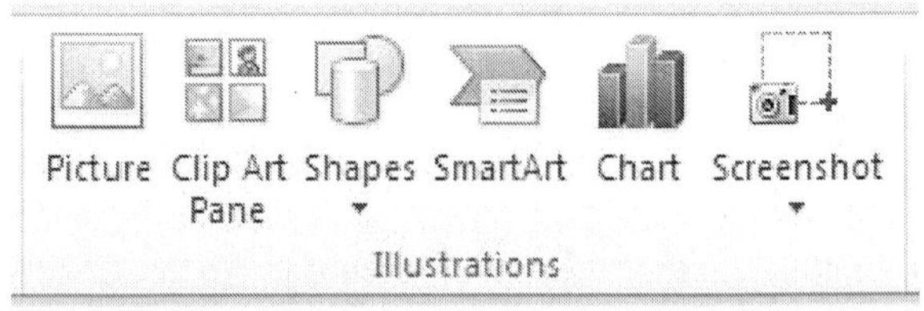

The various type of illustrations which can be inserted into the text of the document are: Picture, Clip Art, Shapes, SmartArt, and Charts. All of these have options, which are shown here.

Links

Among the various options which are here are: Hyperlink, Bookmark, and Cross-reference. These can be used in inserting these links into the text of the document.

Header & Footer

You can insert from here, Header, Footer and Page Numbers. Header appears on the top of each printed page. The content of the Footer appears at the bottom of the printed page. Header and Footer both of options of Editing and Removing them. Page number options are Top of Page, Bottom of Page, Page Margins, Current Position, Format Page Numbers and Remove Page Numbers.

Text

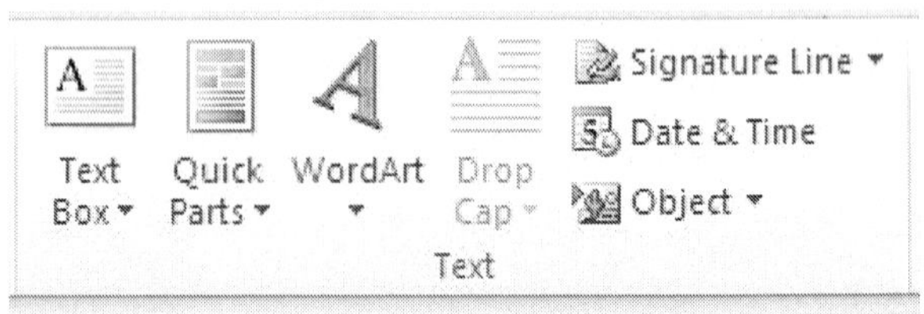

Various options here are: Text Box, Quick Parts, Word Art, Drop Cap, Signature Line, Date and Time, and Object. Text box creates a box which can be filled up with the text and is independent of the document text.

Quick Parts has the options of Document Property, Field, Building Blocks Organizer, Get More on Office Online, and Save Selection to Quick Part Gallery.

WordArt is an independent program which allows you to create and insert an independent text.

Drop Cap allows you to put a capital letter in the beginning of the text. It can cover 2-3 lines of the text to highlight the alphabet.

Signature Line allows you to insert a signature line.

Date and Time would insert date and time in the text, in the format selected by you.

Object allows you to insert objects in the text. It also allows you to insert text from another file.

Symbols

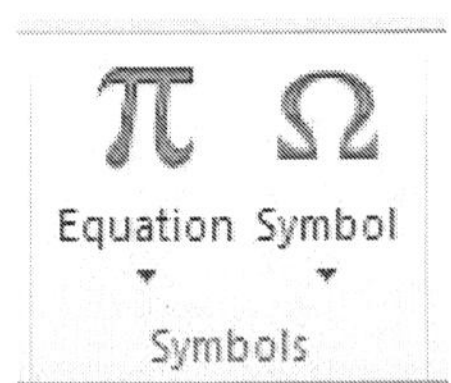

It has two options: Equation and Symbol. Equation allows you to enter equations in the text, after creating it using the various symbols available under it. It is quite a big topic and can be discussed in an advanced book. Symbol button allows you insert a symbol from the list shown here.

Now we come to Design.

Design Panel

It has the various options of changing the design of the text. Among the various important features are: Themes, Colors, Fonts, Paragraph Spacing, Effects, Set as Default, Watermark, Page Colours, Page Borders. Let us look at them one by one.

Themes

Pick a new theme to give your document instant style and just the right personality. Each theme uses a unique set of colors, fonts and effects to create a consistent look and feel.

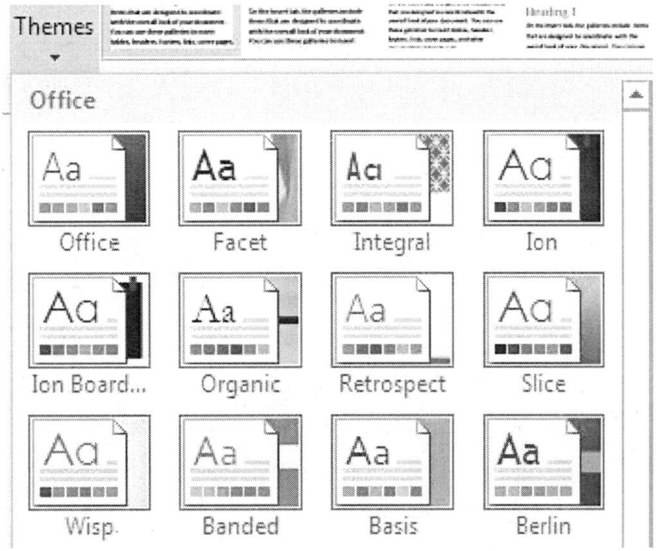

Document Formatting

You can choose any of the document formatting which are shown here. You can browse to have more options.

Colors

Quickly change all the colors used in your document by picking a different color palette. This will update the colors available to you in the color picker along with any theme color in your document. No matter what palette you choose, your document will look perfectly coordinated.

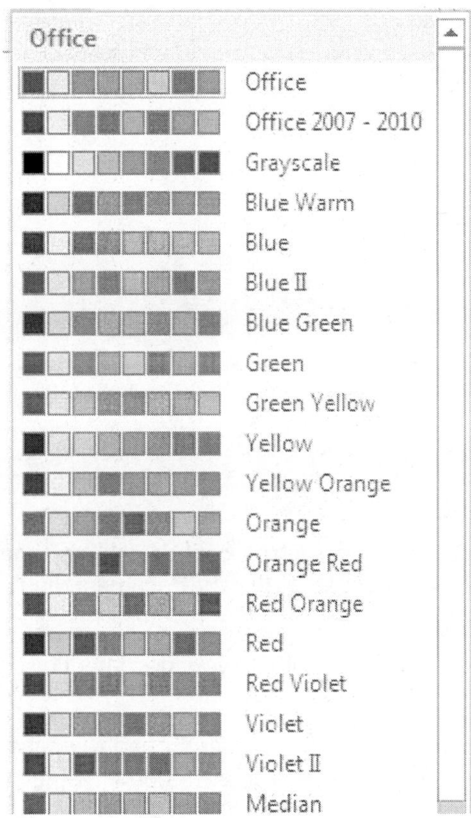

Fonts

Quickly change the text in your document by picking a new font set. This is an easy way to change all of your text at once. For this to work your text at once. For this to work, your text must be formatted using the 'body' and 'heading' fonts.

Paragraph Spacing

Quickly change the line and paragraph spacing of your document. This option will change the spacing of your entire document including new paragraphs. You can choose between predefined values or specify your own.

Effects

Quickly change the general look of objects in your document. Each option uses various borders and visual effects, such as shading and shadow, to give your objects a different look.

Set as Default

Use this look for all new documents. Save your current settings so that every time you create a blank document it will be formatted just the way you like. This is pefect if you have a favorite font or always want specific paragraph spacing.

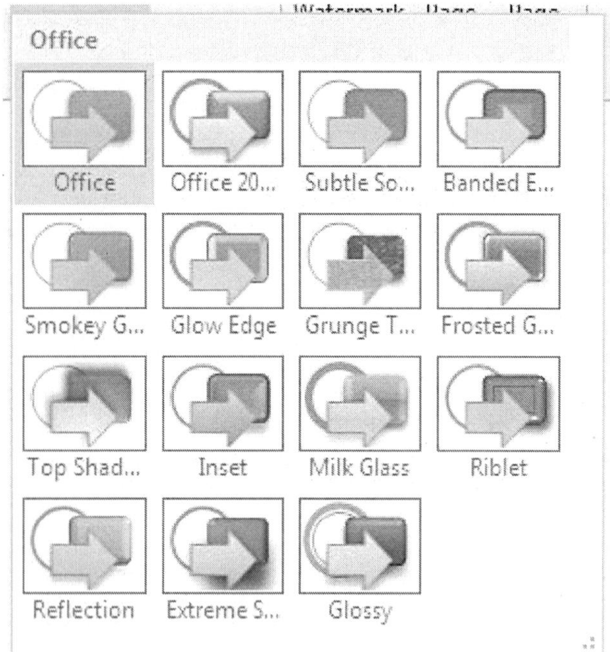

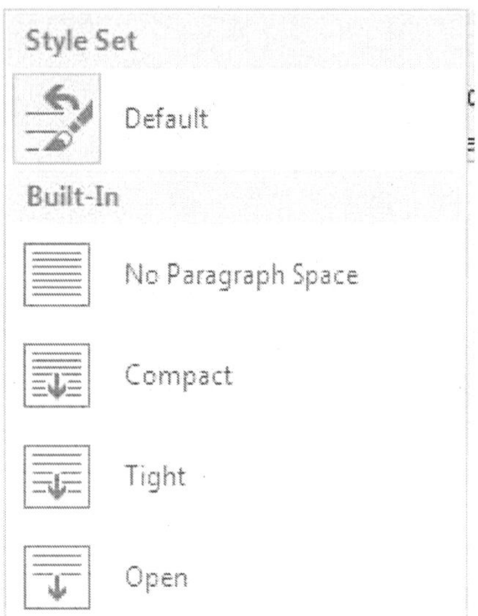

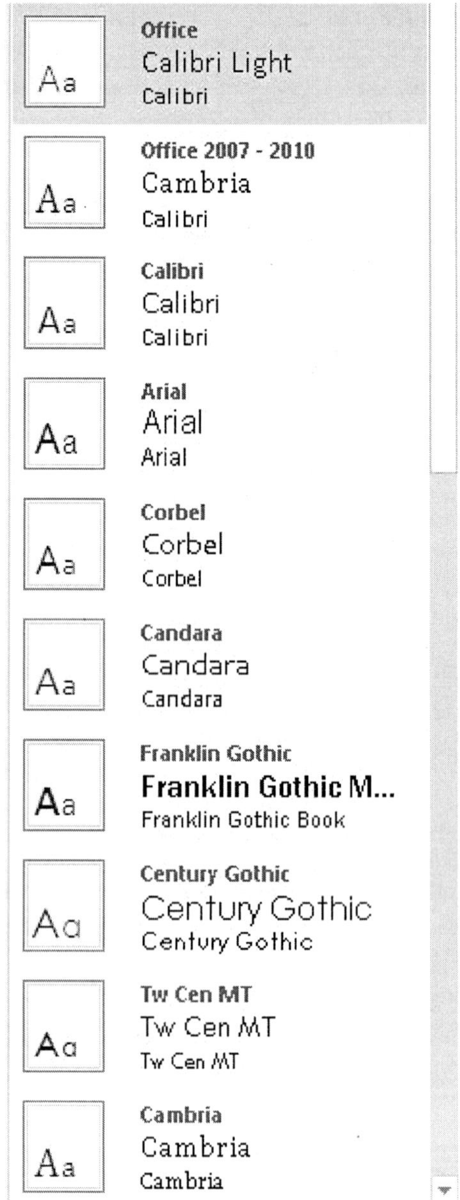

Watermark

Add ghost text, such as "confidential" or "urgent" behind the content on the page. The faint watermark is a great way to show that the document requires special treatment without distracting from the contents.

Page Color

Add a splash of color to your document by changing the color of the page.

Page Borders

Add or change the border around the page. A border draws focus and adds a stylish touch to your document. You can create a border using a variety of line styles, widths and colors, or choose an art border with a fun theme..

Page Layout Panel

It has the following options: Themes, Page Setup, Page Background, Paragraph, and Arrange.

Page Setup

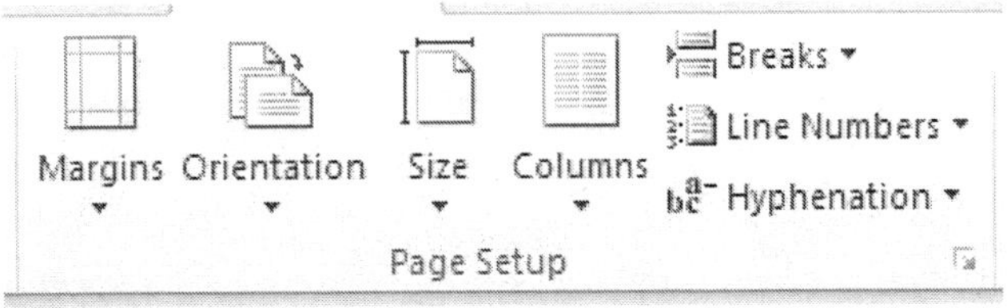

Among the various options available here are: Margins, Orientation, Size, Columns, Breaks, Line Numbers and Hyphenation.

Margins allows you to set margins of the page, i.e., margins from the left and right of the page.

Orientation has two options: Portrait and Landscape.

Size allows you to choose from the various size of the paper normally used globally.

Columns allow you to set the page into various columns with line in-between or not.

Breaks inserts break into the text in the form of line, page, etc.

Line Numbers are inserted using this option.

Hyphenation allows to have hyphens in the paragraph or not.

Paragraph

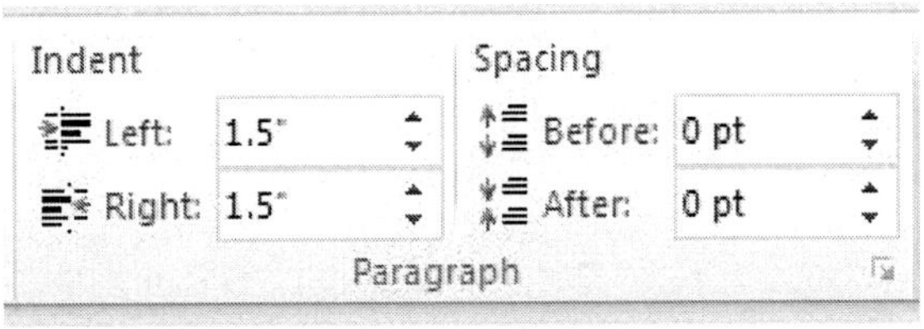

It has two main options: Indent and Spacing.

Indent allows you to set the left and right indent.

Spacing allows you to set the Before and After paragraph space.

Arrange

It has the following options: Position, Bring to Front, Send to Back, Text Wrapping, Align, Group and Rotate.

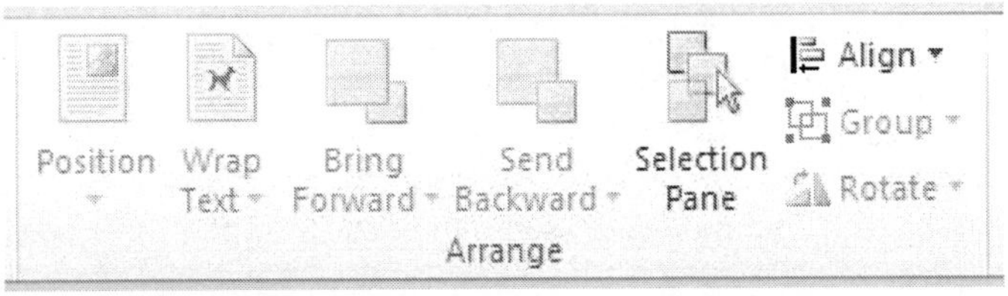

Position allows you to position the picture/object as per the options available.

Bring to Front and Send to Back are used when you have to rearrange the picture/object with respect to the text.

Align allows you to align the text, as per the options shown here.

Group allows you to group two or more objects together.

Rotate allows you to rotate the inserted object as per the options shown here.

References Panel

It has the following options: Table of Contents, Footnotes, Citations and Bibliography, Captions, Index, and Table of Authorities.

Table of Contents

It has the options: Table of Contents, Add Test and Update Table. Table of Contents allows you create table of contents of the text. Add Text allows you to set levels of the text. Update Table updates an existing table of contents.

Footnotes

It has the options: Insert Footnote, Insert Endnote, Next Footnote, and Show Notes. Insert Footnote allows you to insert a footnote in the text. Insert Endnote allows you to insert endnote. Next footnote allows to insert the next or prev footnote, endnote. Show notes shows all the notes in the text.

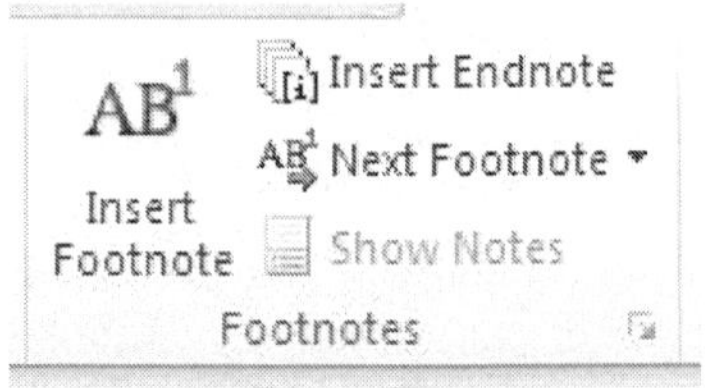

Citations & Bibliography

It has the options of Inserting a Citation, Managing Sources, Style, and Bibliography. Citation allows you to cite a book, journal article, or other periodical as the source for a piece of information in the document. Choose from the list of sources you have created or enter information for a new source. Word formats the citation according to the style you have selected. Manage Sources allow you to look into the source manager and manage it. Style allows you to choose from the various styles given. Bibliography allows you to maintain the various references.

Captions

This has the following options: Insert Caption, Insert Table of Figures, Update Table, and Cross-reference. Insert Caption allows you to add a caption to a picture or other image. A caption is a line of text that appears below an object to describe it.

Insert Table of Figures inserts a Table of Figures into the document. A Table of Figures includes a list of all of the figures, table, or equations in the document.

Cross-reference refers to items such as headings, figures, and tables by inserting a cross reference such as, "See Table 6 below" or "Turn to page 8." Cross references are automatically updated if the content is moved to another location. By default, cross references are inserted as hyperlinks.

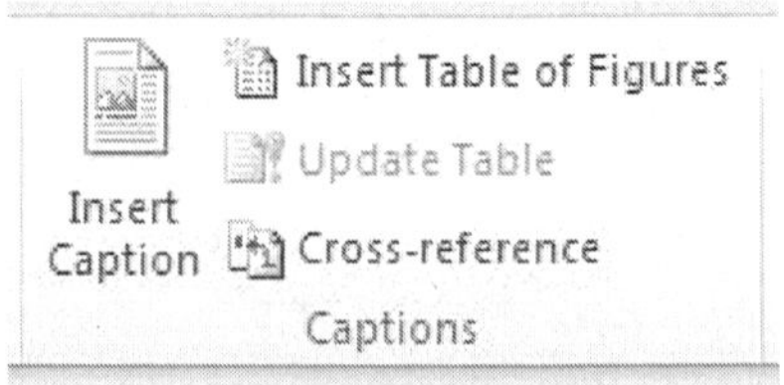

Index

It has the following commands: Mark Entry, Insert Index, and Update Index.

Mark Entry allows you to include the selected text in the index of the document.

Insert Index inserts an index into the document. An index is a list of keywords found in the document along with the page numbers the words appear on.

Table of Authorities

It has the option called Mark Citation, Insert Table of Authorities, and Update Table of Authorities. Mark Citation adds the selected text as an entry in the Table of Authorities.

Mailings Panel

It has the following options: Create, Start Mail Merge, Write & Insert Fields, Preview Results, and Finish.

Create

It has the following options: Envelopes, and Labels. Each one of them gives rise to a dialog box, which allows you to create envelopes and labels.

Start Mail Merge

It has options to Start Mail Merge, Select Recipients and Edit Recipients List.

Start Mail Merge allows you to select the options of Letters, E-Mail Messages, Evelopes, Labels, Directory or start the Step by Step Mail Merge Wizard.

Select Recipients allows you to choose the list of people you intend to send the letter to. You can type you own list, use your Outlook contacts, or connect to a database. It also has options to Type New List, Use Existing List or Select from Outlook Contacts.

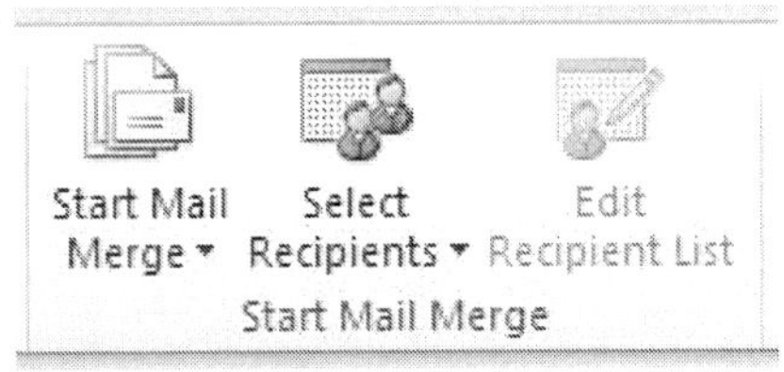

Write & Insert Fields

It has the options to Highlight Merge Fields, Address Block, Greeting Line, Insert Merge Field, Rules, Match Fields, and Update Labels.

Highlight Merge Fields highlights the fields you have inserted into the document. This makes it easy to see what part of your form letter will be replaced by information from the recipient list you have chosen.

Addresss Block adds an address to your letter. You specify the formatting and location, and Word will replace it with actual addresses from your recipient list when you finish the mail merge.

Greeting Line adds a greeting line such as "Dear< <First Name> >", to your document.

Insert Merge Field adds any field from your recipient list to the document, such as "Last Name," "Home Phone," "Company Name," or any other field.

When you finish the mail merge, Word will replace these fields with the actual information from the recipient list.

Rules specifies rules to be added decision-making ability to the mail merge. For instance, you could use If...Then...Else to check the address of recipient and show a local phone number to recipients near you and an international phone number for recipients outside of your country.

Match Fields allows you to tell Word the meaning of different fields in your recipient list. For example, you can indicate that your custom field "Home" is equivalent to normal built-in field "Home Phone."

Update Labels allow you to create labels, update all the labels in the document to use information from the recipient list. For a mail merge to a printed letter or e-mail, this command is not necessary.

Preview Results

It has the options to Preview Results, Find Recipient, and Auto Check for Errors.

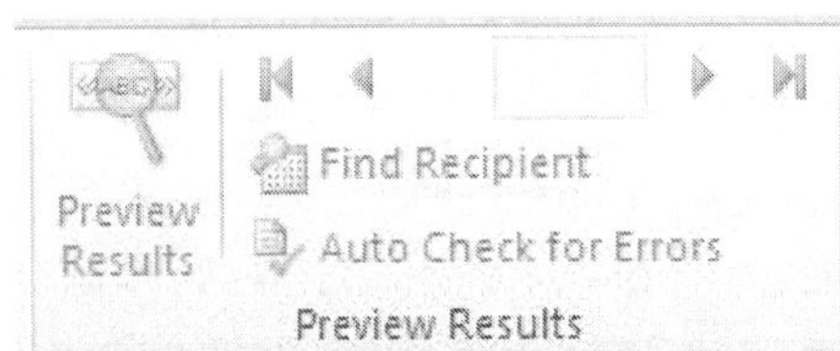

Preview Results replaces the merge fields in your document with acutal data from your recipient list so you can see what it looks like.

Find Recipient finds and previews a specific record in the recipient list by searching for text.

Auto Check for Errors specifies how to handle errors that occur when completing the mail merge. You also have the option of simulating the mail merge to see if any errors would occur.

Finish

It has the options to Finish & Merge. It completes the mail merge. You can create separate documents for each copy of the letter, send them all directly to the printer, or send them via e-mail.

Review Panel

It has the following options: Proofing, Comments, Tracking, Changes, Compare, and Protect.

Proofing

It has the following options: Spelling & Grammer, Research, Thesaurus, and Word Count.

Spelling & Grammar checks the spelling and grammar of text in the document.

Research opens the Research Task Pane to search through reference materials, such as dictionaries, encyclopedias, and translation services.

Thesaurus suggests other words with a similar meaning to the word you have selected.

Word Count finds out the number of words, characters, paragraphs, and lines in the document. You can also find the word count in the status bar at the bottom of the window.

Language

Translates the selected text into a different language. Translation ScreenTip enables a ScreenTip that translates words you pause your cursor over into another language.

Editing Language sets the language used to check the spelling and grammar of the selected text.

Comments

This has the following options: New Comment, Delete, Previous, and Next.

New Commnet adds a selection over the selection.

Delete command deletes an existing comment.

Previous locates the previous comment.

Tracking

This has the following options: Track Changes, Balloons, Final Showing Markup, Show Markup, and Reviewing Pane.

Track Changes trackes all changes made to the document, including insertions, deletions, and formatting changes. Change Tracking Options allows you to change the tracking options. Change User Name would allow you to change the user name.

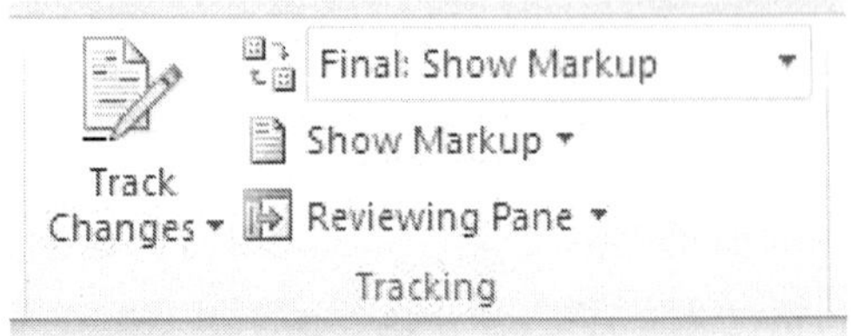

Balloons allow you to choose how to show revisions to the document. You can show revisions as balloons in the margins of the coument or show them directly within the document itself.

Display for Review allows you to choose how to view the proposed changes to the document. Final shows the document with all proposed changes included; Original shows the document before any changes were made. The markup shows what changes have been proposed.

Show Markup allows you to choose what kind of markup to show in the document. You can hide or show comments, insertions and deletions, formatting changes, and other kinds of markup.

Reviewing Pane shows revisions in a separate window.

Changes

This has the following options: Accept, Reject, Previous, and Next.

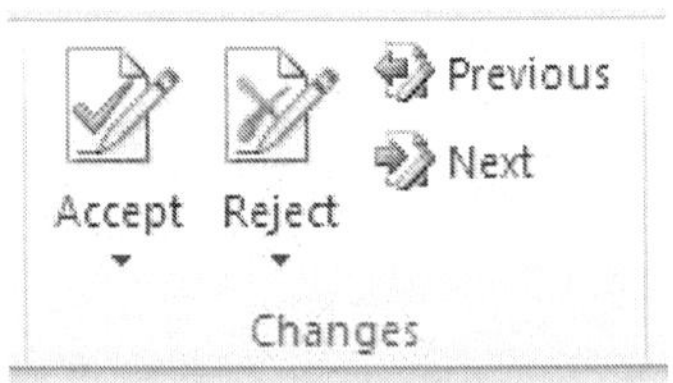

Accept and Move to Next allows you to access other options such as accepting all changes in the document.

Reject and Move to Next allows you to access other options such as rejecting all changes in the document.

Previous Change allows you to navigate to the previous revision in the document so that you can accept or reject it.

Next Change allows you to navigate to the next revision in the document so that you can accept or reject it.

Compare

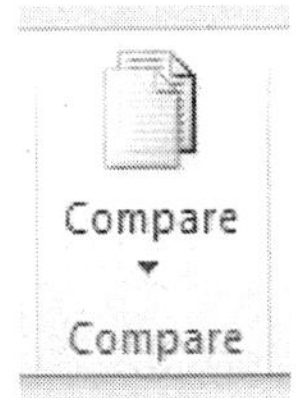

This has the following options: Compare, and Show Source Documents.

Compare compares or combines multiple versions of a document.

Show Source Documents allows you to choose which source documents to show. You can show the original document, the revised document, or booth.

Protect

This has only one option: Protect Document.

It restricts how people can access the document.

View Panel

It has the following options: Document Views, Show/Hide, Zoom, Window, and Macros.

Views

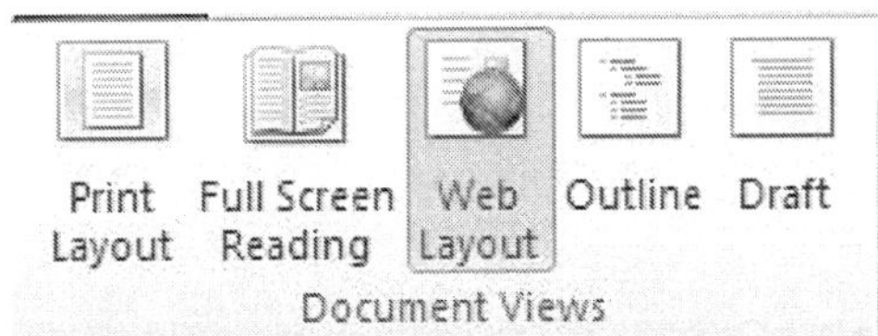

It has the following options: Print Layout, Full Screen Reading, Web Layout, Outline, and Draft.

Print Layout views the document as it will appear on the printed page.

Full Screen Reading allows you to view the document in full screen Reading View in order to maximize the space available for reading or commenting on the document.

Web Layout allows you to view the document as it would look as a Web page.

Outline View allows you to view the document as an outline and show the outlining tools.

Draft View allows you to view the document as a draft to quickly edit the text.

Show

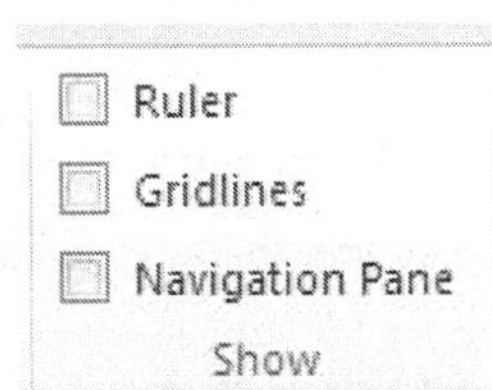

It has the following options: Ruler, Gridlines, Message Bar, Document Map, and Thumbnails.

Ruler allows you to view the rulers, used to measure and line up objects in the document.

Gridlines turns on gridlines to which you can align objects in the document.

Message Bar opens the Message Bar to complete any required actions on the document.

Document Map opens the Document Map, which allows you to navigate through a structural view of the document.

Thumbnails opens the Thumbnails pane, which you can use to navigate a long document through small pictures of each page.

Zoom

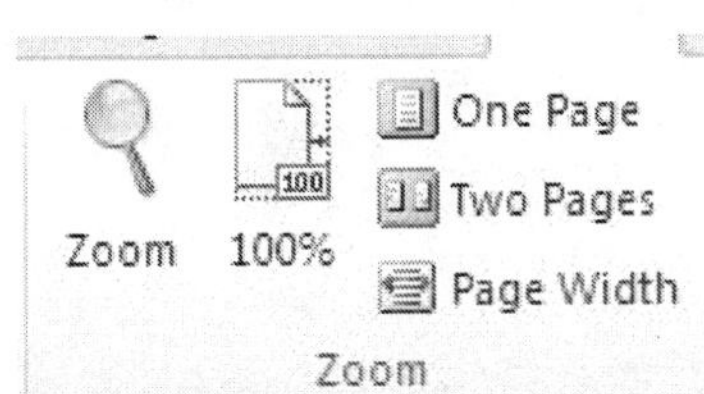

It has the following options: Zoom, 100%, One Page, Two Pages, and Page Width.

Zoom opens the Zoom dialog box to specify the zoom level of the document. In most cases, you can alos use the zoom controls in the status bar at the bottom of the window to quickly zoom the document.

100% zooms the document to 100% of the normal size.

One Page zooms the document so that an entire page fits in the window.

Two Pages zooms the document so that two pages fit in the window.

Page Width zooms the document so that the width of the page matches the width of the window.

Window

It has the following options: New Window, Arrange All, Split, View Side by Side, Synchronous Scrolling, Reset Window Position, and Switch Windows.

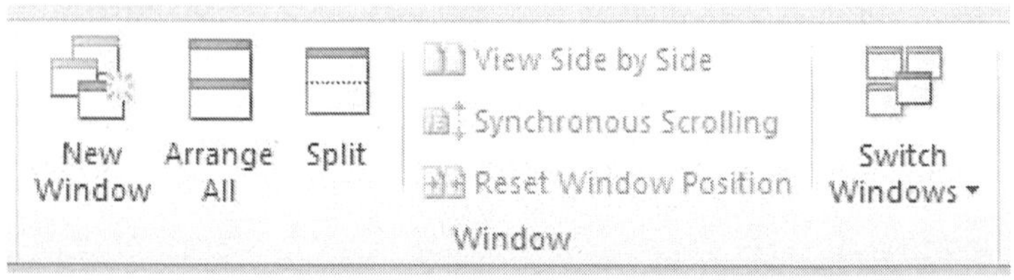

New Window allows you to open a new window containing a view of the current document.

Arrange All tiles all open program windows side-by-side on the screen.

Split Window splits the current window into two parts so that you can view different sections of the document at the same time.

View Side by Side allows you to view two documents side-by-side so that you can compare their contents. Synchronous Scrolling synchronizes the scrolling of two documents so that they scroll together. To enable this feature, turn View Side by Side.

Reset Window Position resets the window position of the documents being compared side-by-side so that they share the screen equally. To enable this feature, turn on View Side by Side.

Switch Windows allows you to switch to a different currently open window.

Macros

It has only one option, i.e., Macros.

Macros command allows you to view macros. Click here to record a macro or to access other macro options.

File Button

Besides, the commands mentioned till now, we have a set of commands, under the so called File Button. These are the commands which can be used just by a clik. Given below are the various options available.

They are: Info, New, Open, Save, Save As, Print, Share, Export, Close, Account and Options. Want to see what is there in each one of them. Go through the pages next to see them.

Working with Documents in Microsoft Word 2013

The best way to learn about a new software is to use it. It is like jumping into the swimming pool to learn swimming. What we will do here is that we will type our document and learn the various commands side by side. Starting Word 2013 is easy so I am not discussing that here. Let us start a new document here. This can again be done from the Start button. After you have opened Word 2013 you can either click at New from the Office button.

Supposing we have to create a document in the form of a letter written to the General Manager of Telephones complaining him of the inflated bills. The text of the letter is shown next. Now that you have opened a new document, do not worry about any typing mistakes or any formatting, just type the text as it is.

Text of the document follows:

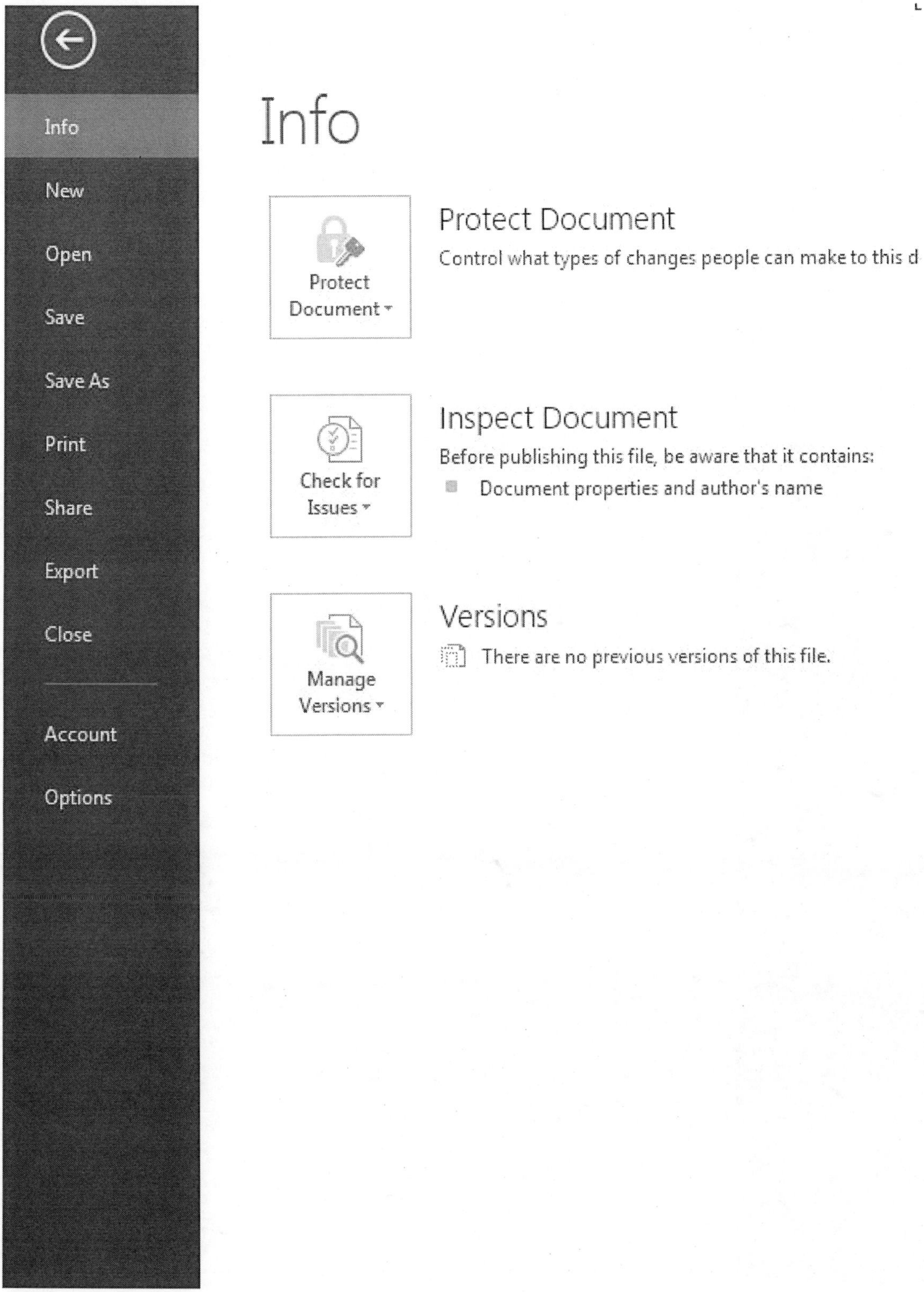
Info
New
Open
Save
Save As
Print
Share
Export
Close
Account
Options
Info
Protect Document
Protect Document
Control what types of changes people can make to this d
Check for Issues
Inspect Document
Before publishing this file, be aware that it contains:
Document properties and author's name
Manage Versions
Versions
There are no previous versions of this file.

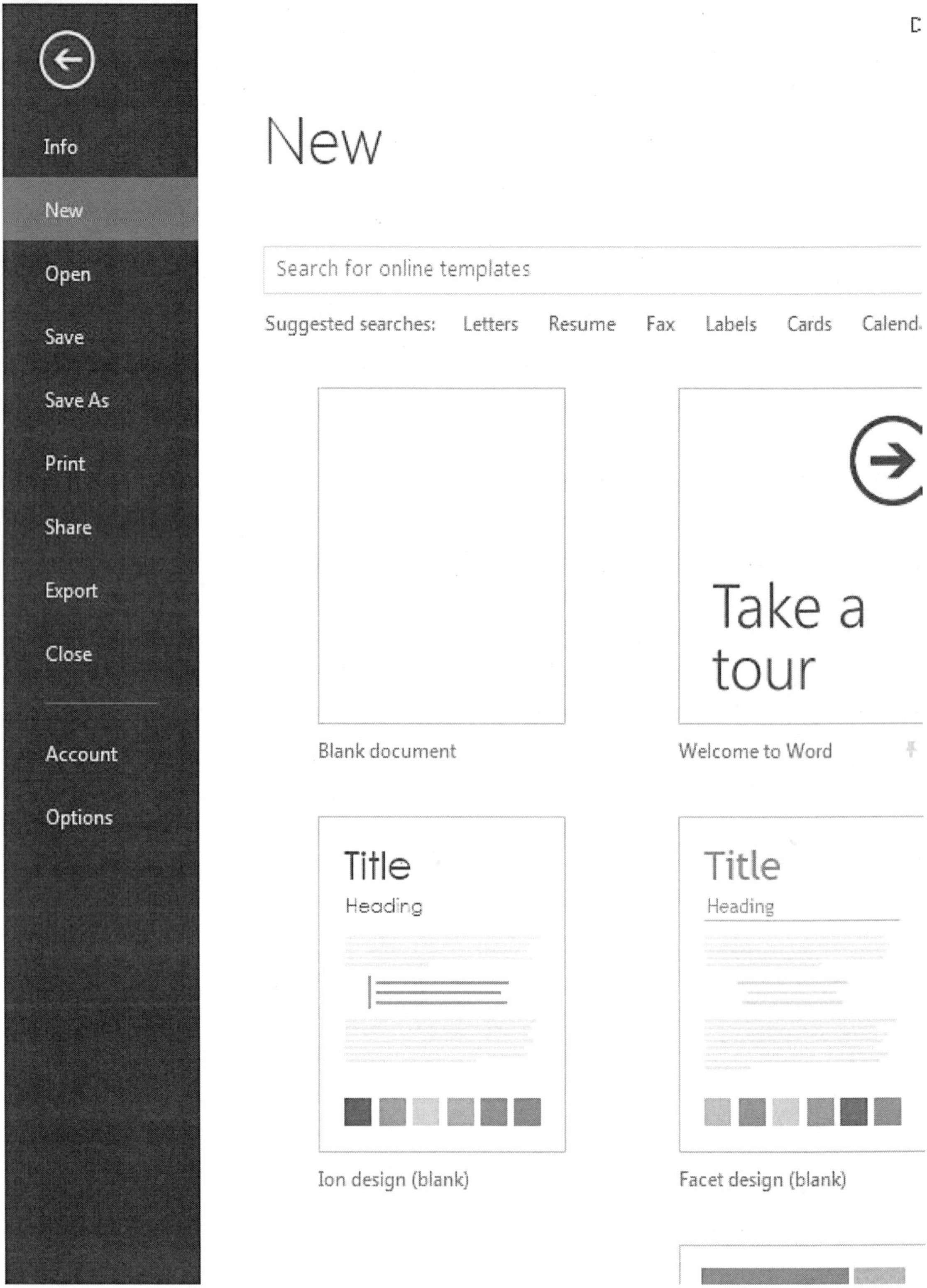
Info
New
Open
Save
Save As
Print
Share
Export
Close
Account
Options
New
Search for online templates
Suggested searches: Letters Resume Fax Labels Cards Calend.
Take a tour
Blank document
Welcome to Word
Title
Heading
Title
Heading
Ion design (blank)
Facet design (blank)

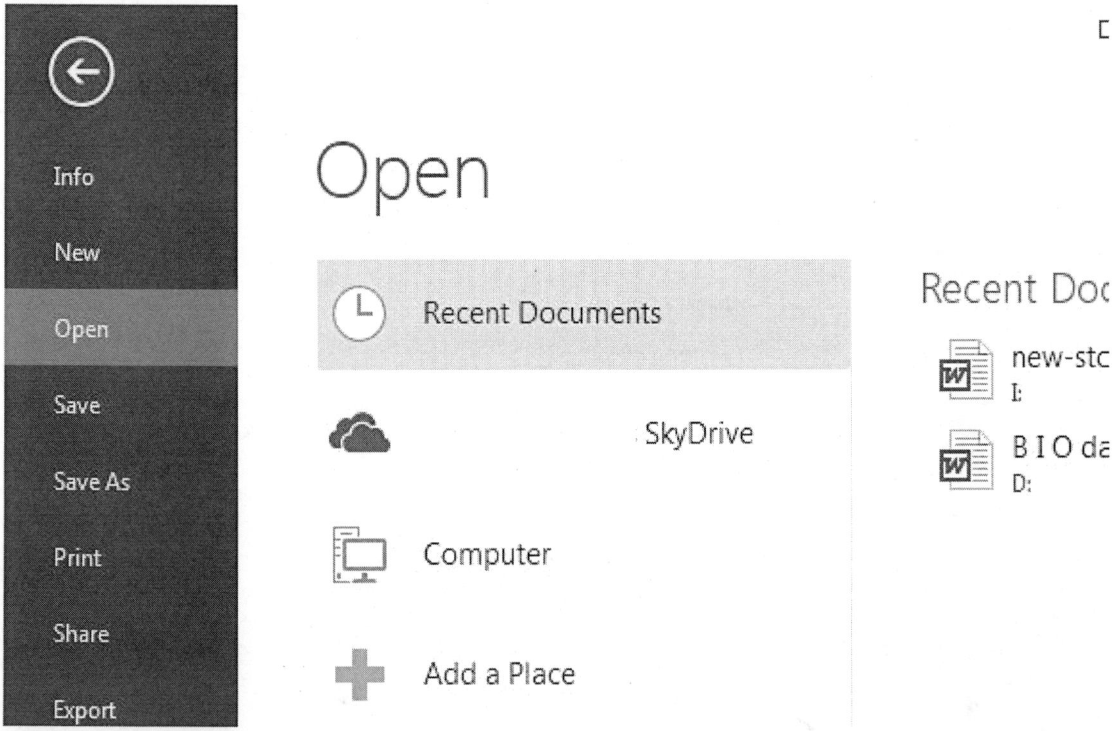
Info
New
Open
Save
Save As
Print
Share
Export
Open
Recent Documents
SkyDrive
Computer
Add a Place
Recent Doc
new-stc
B I O da

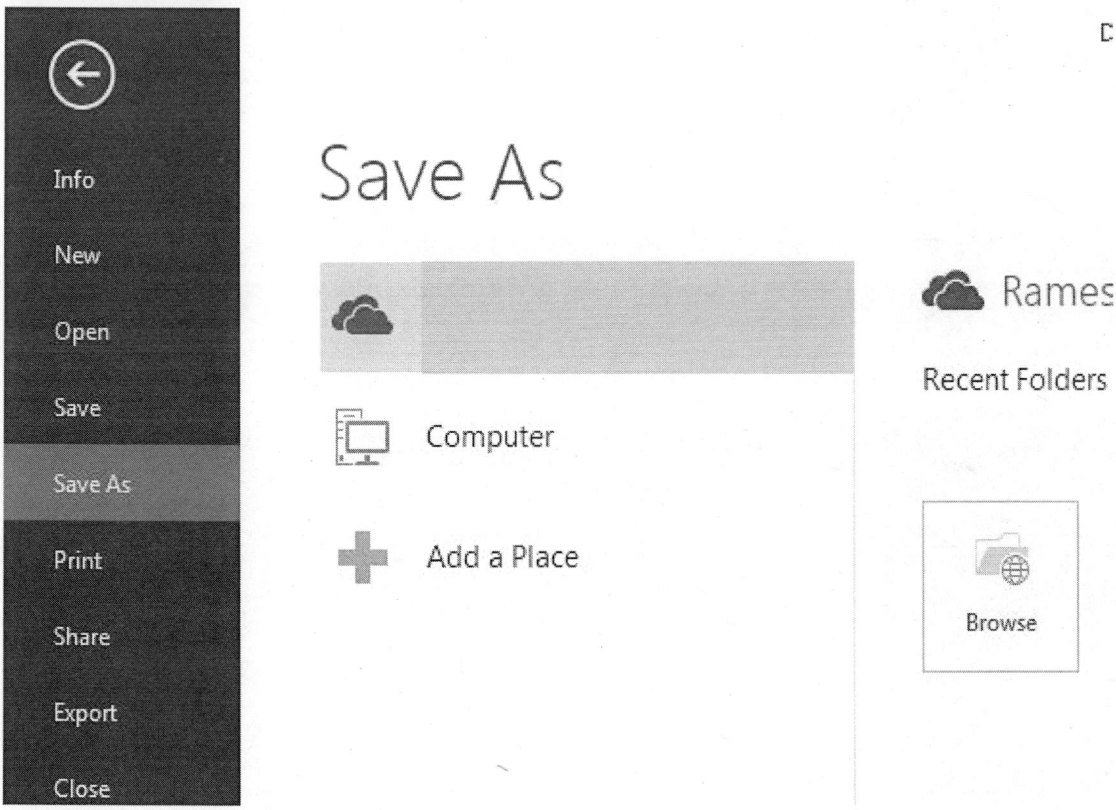
Info
New
Open
Save
Save As
Print
Share
Export
Close
Save As
Computer
Add a Place
Rames
Recent Folders
Browse

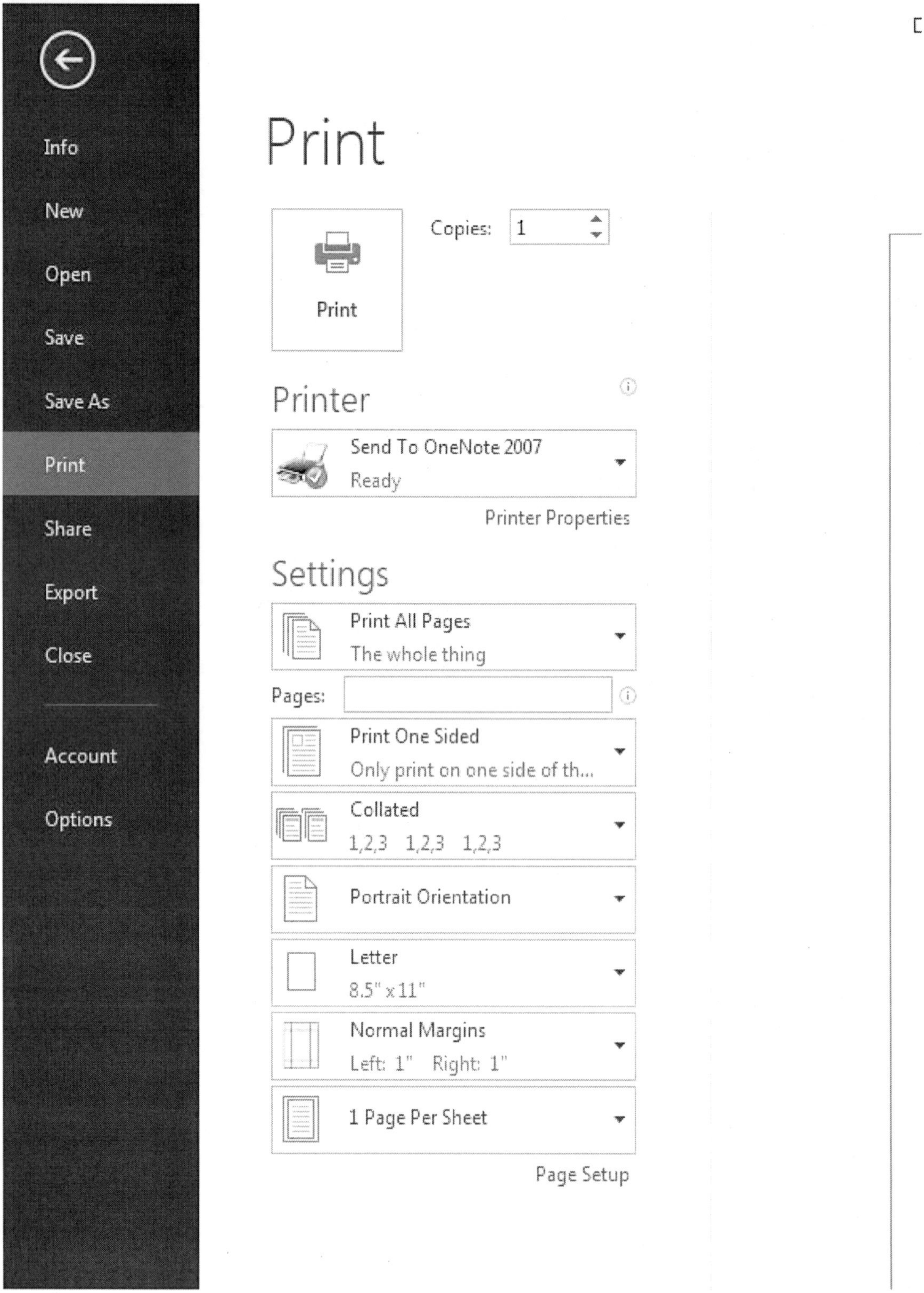
Info
New
Open
Save
Save As
Print
Share
Export
Close
Account
Options
Print
Copies: 1
Print
Printer
Send To OneNote 2007
Ready
Printer Properties
Settings
Print All Pages
The whole thing
Pages:
Print One Sided
Only print on one side of th...
Collated
1,2,3 1,2,3 1,2,3
Portrait Orientation
Letter
8.5" x 11"
Normal Margins
Left: 1" Right: 1"
1 Page Per Sheet
Page Setup

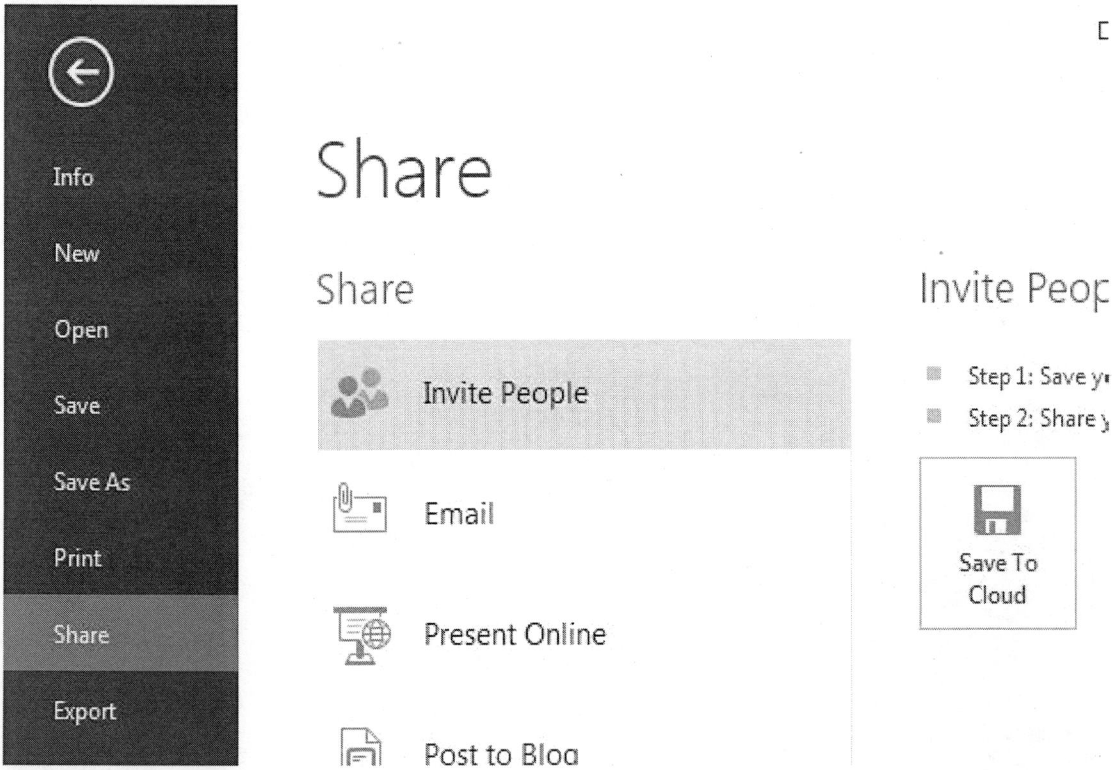
Info
New
Open
Save
Save As
Print
Share
Export
Share
Share
Invite People
Email
Present Online
Post to Blog
Invite Peop
Step 1: Save y
Step 2: Share y
Save To
Cloud

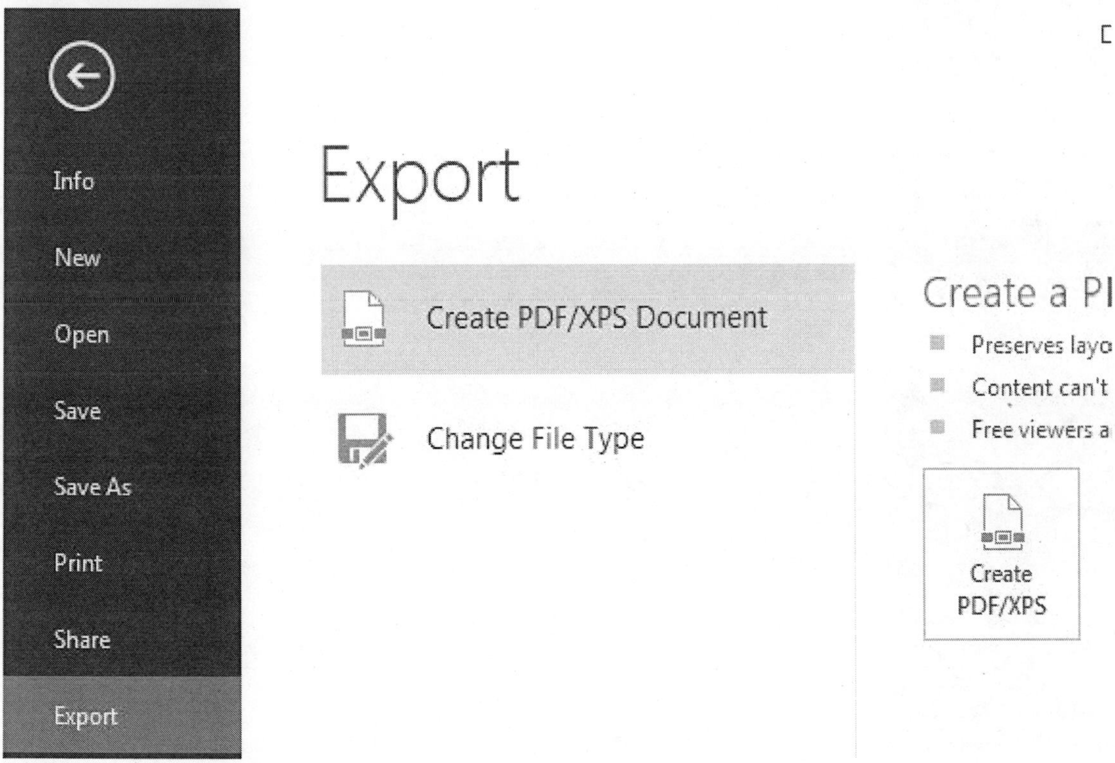
Info
New
Open
Save
Save As
Print
Share
Export
Export
Create PDF/XPS Document
Change File Type
Create a PI
Preserves layo
Content can't
Free viewers a
Create
PDF/XPS

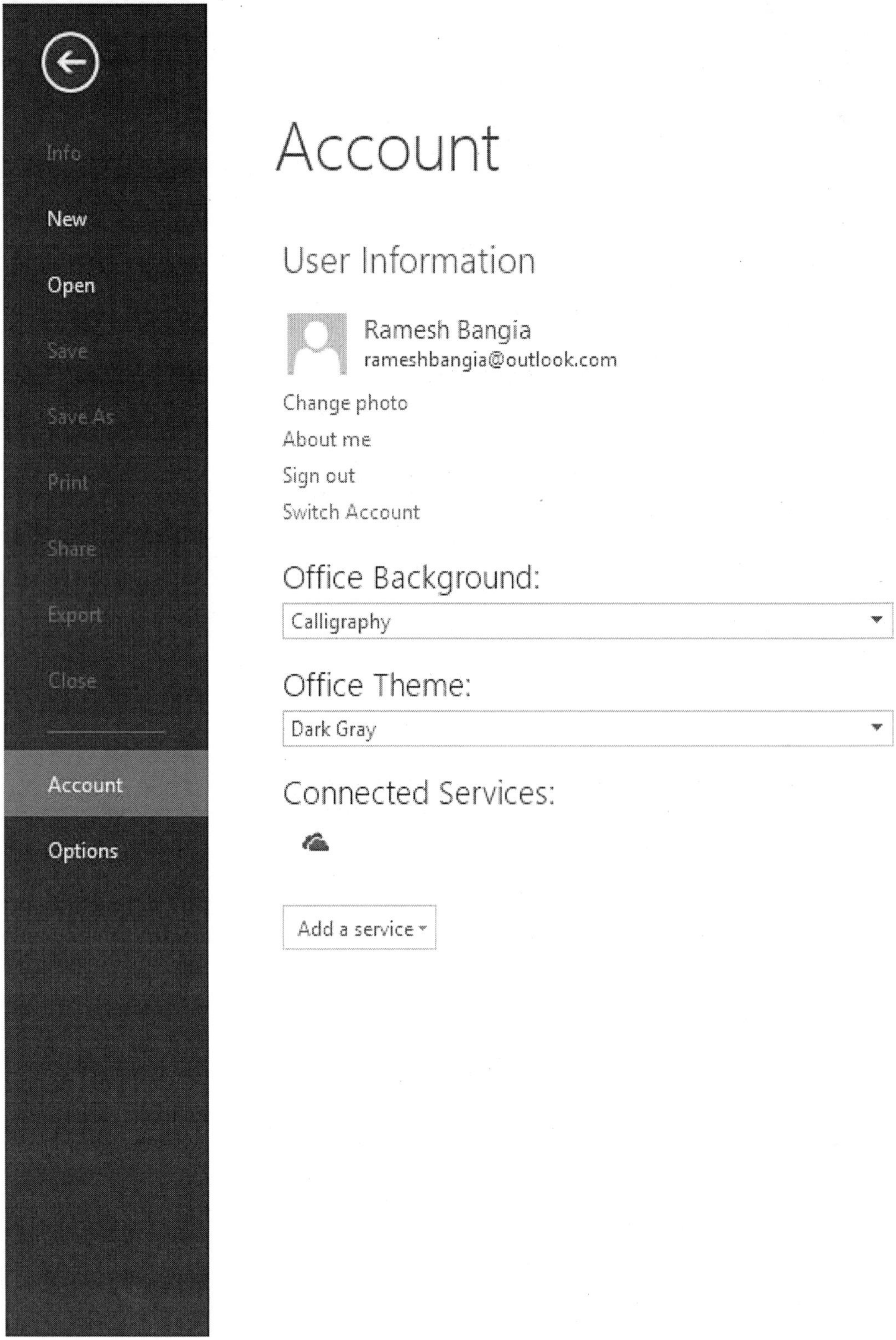
Info
New
Open
Save
Save As
Print
Share
Export
Close
Account
Options
Account
User Information
Ramesh Bangia
rameshbangia@outlook.com
Change photo
About me
Sign out
Switch Account
Office Background:
Calligraphy
Office Theme:
Dark Gray
Connected Services:
Add a service

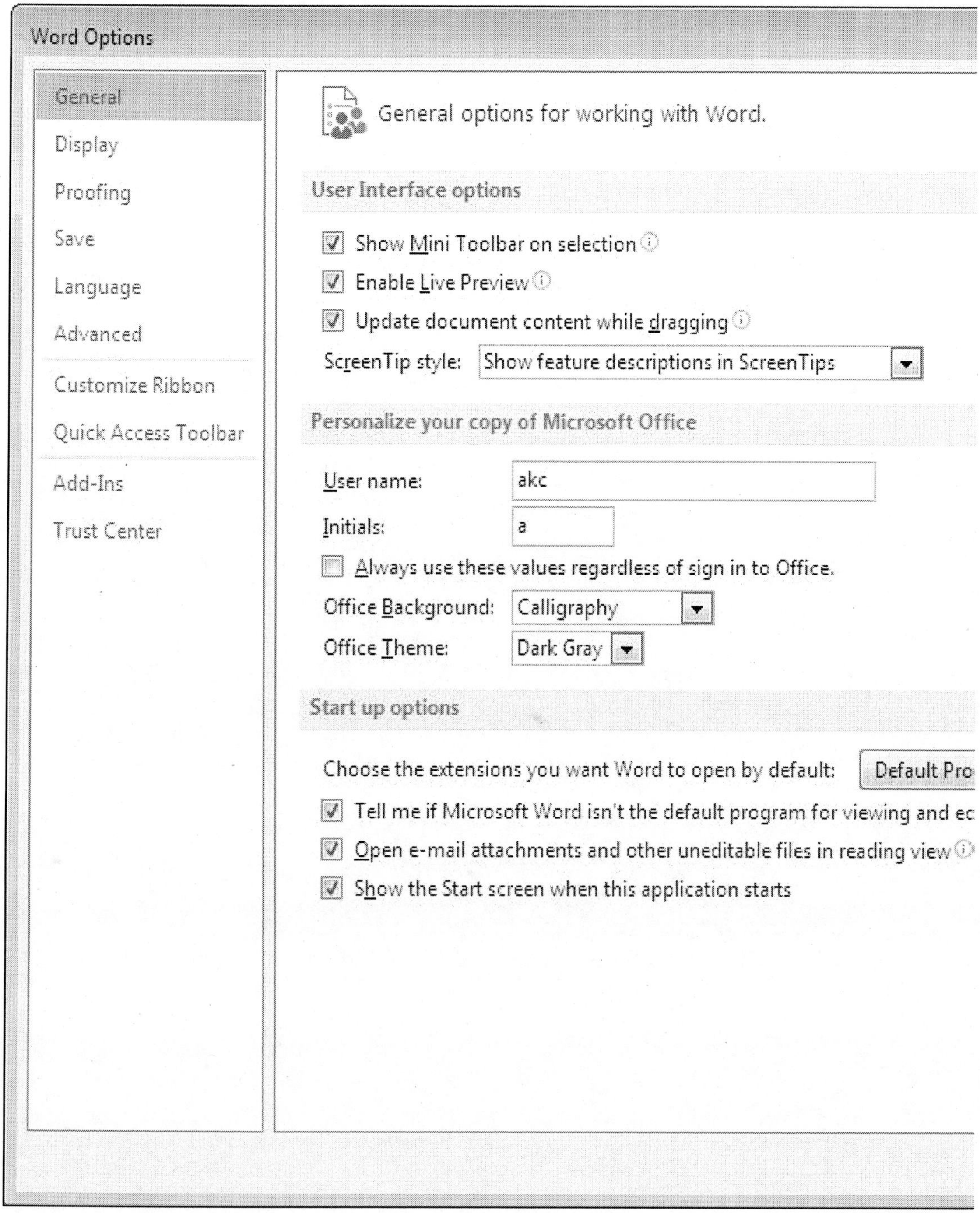
Word Options
General
Display
Proofing
Save
Language
Advanced
Customize Ribbon
Quick Access Toolbar
Add-Ins
Trust Center
General options for working with Word.
User Interface options
Show Mini Toolbar on selection
Enable Live Preview
Update document content while dragging
ScreenTip style:
Show feature descriptions in ScreenTips
Personalize your copy of Microsoft Office
User name:
akc
Initials:
a
Always use these values regardless of sign in to Office.
Office Background:
Calligraphy
Office Theme:
Dark Gray
Start up options
Choose the extensions you want Word to open by default:
Default Pro
Tell me if Microsoft Word isn't the default program for viewing and ec
Open e-mail attachments and other uneditable files in reading view
Show the Start screen when this application starts

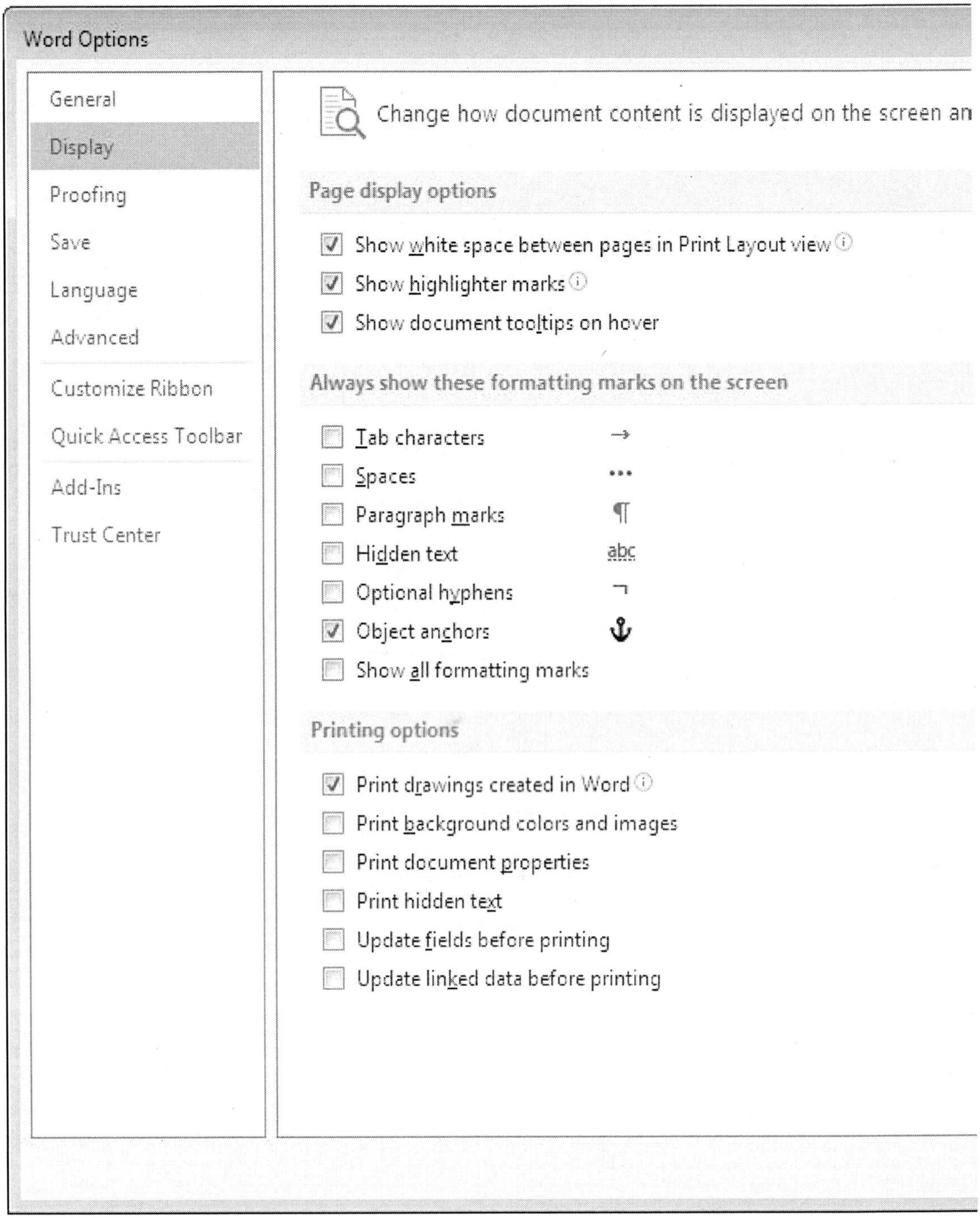
Word Options
General
Display
Proofing
Save
Language
Advanced
Customize Ribbon
Quick Access Toolbar
Add-Ins
Trust Center
Change how document content is displayed on the screen an
Page display options
Show white space between pages in Print Layout view
Show highlighter marks
Show document tooltips on hover
Always show these formatting marks on the screen
Tab characters →
Spaces •••
Paragraph marks ¶
Hidden text abc
Optional hyphens ¬
Object anchors
Show all formatting marks
Printing options
Print drawings created in Word
Print background colors and images
Print document properties
Print hidden text
Update fields before printing
Update linked data before printing

13th April, 2013

To,

The General Manager
Mahanagar Telephones Nigam Limited
Khurshid Lal Bhawan
New Delhi - 110 001

Ref: Telephone No. 4611098

Sir,

I am in receipt of bill for the above telephone number dated 1.10.2010 for an amount of Rs. 4,678.90. This bill is to be paid by 21.10.2010. While going through the bill, I notice that I have been charged at two accounts for the calls which have not been made by me. These enteries are:

Called Id	***Duration***	***Amount***
0017249873769	120	1,008.00
0013245934234	60	675.90

As you can notice that both these entries pertain to **International calls** and since my phone does not have this facility, these calls could not have been made from my phone.

I hope that you would look into and send me the revised bill, so that I can make the payment in time.

Hoping for an early action,

Thanking you,

Yours faithfully,
Amitabh Bachan

3695 Ballimaran, Delhi - 110 006

As you may notice that there are few red and green wavy lines. The red lines, show that the word is incorrectly typed as per the dictionary available with the system and the word/words under whom the green line is, show that the words are grammatically wrong. This is the opinion of the software, you may beg to differ from it. Since most of the proper names like Shah Rukh Khan, are shown as wrong.

This is just the raw text which has been typed. Now we have to do the formatting. But, before that, lest the file gets tangled in power failure or something, we must save the file.

Saving the file

It is the process by which you give the name to the file and save under that name. Since our letter pertains to the inflated bill, we will call our file as Bill. For saving, just select the Save option under Office button. You will get the following dialog box. Just type the name Bill in the space provided for typing the filename and click Save. Your file will be saved under this name and automatically the title bar will show the name of the file on the top of the Word 2013 screen.

Now we come to other fomatting tools.

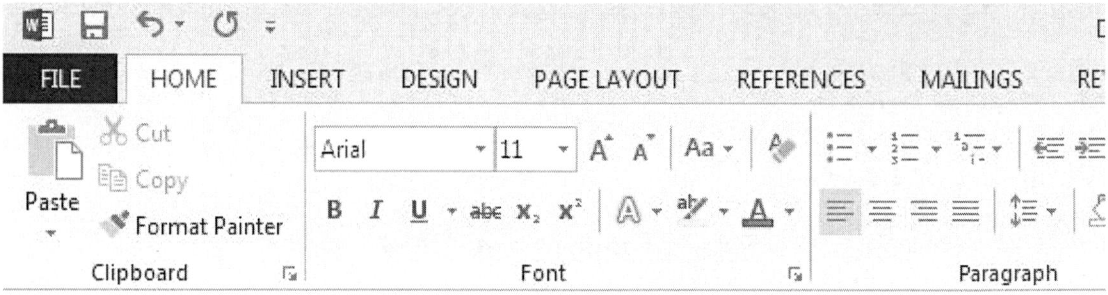

Yours faithfully, 13th April, 2013

To,

The General Manager
Mahanagar Telephones Nigam Limited
Khurshid Lal Bhawan
New Delhi - 110 001
Ref: Telephone No. 4611098

Sir,

I am in receipt of bill for the above telephone number dated 1.10.2010 for an amour
have been charged at two accounts for the calls which have not been made by me.

Called Id	*Duration*	*Amount*
0017249873769	120	1,008.00
0013245934234	60	675.90

As you can notice that both these entries pertain to International calls and since my

I hope that you would look into and send me the revised bill, so that I can make the

Hoping for an early action,

Thanking you,

Amitabh Bachan
3695 Ballimaran, Delhi - 110 006

Formatting the text

Let us now start our formatting from the top. The first line containing address has nothing to be done. The second line containing To, has to be *italized.*

For this do the following:

1. Click the mouse button at the left of T of To.
2. Now drag the mouse, still having it pressed to the right so that the next character o also gets highlighted. At this stage both T and o are highlighted.
3. Now leave the mouse with To highlighted.
4. With the mouse, click at I in the formatting toolbar to make To as *To.*

5. See how To looks in the next figure.

Now we come to the line having The General Manager. This line has to be made bold. This is how we do it.

1. Click the mouse button at the left of T of The General Manager.
2. Since we had highlighted the matter using mouse in the case of To, we will use a different approach here. Press Shift key and start pressing right arrow key ⇨. You will see that as the right arrow key is pressed the matter on the right gets highlighted. So highlight the matter till the point you want it to highlight. In this case highlight till r of Manager.
3. Now leave the shift key.
4. With the mouse, click at B in the formatting toolbar to make the highlighted text as **Bold**.

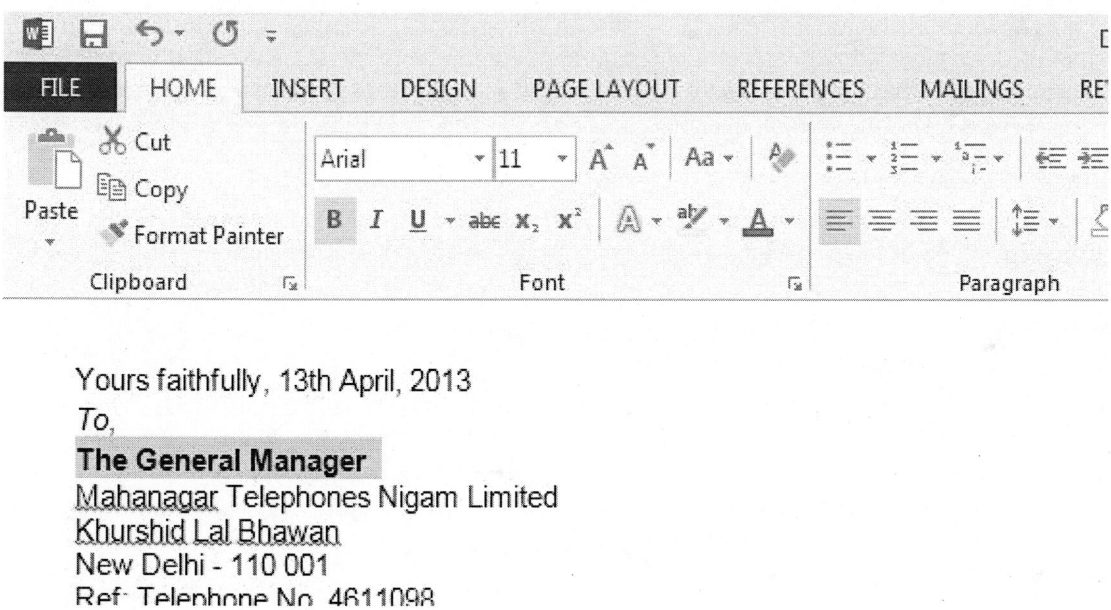

5. In the figure next, see how the text looks now.

Next in the line is the address, whose last line New Delhi - 110 001 has to be underlined. Word 2013 allows you the option of underlining the word with one or more lines. This option is available under Font. But for the time being, we will stick to single underline.

For this do the following:

1. Click the mouse button at the left of N of New Delhi - 110 001.
2. Using any of the two methods described above, highlight the text to be underlined.
3. With the mouse, click at U in the formatting toolbar to make the highlighted text **Underlined**.

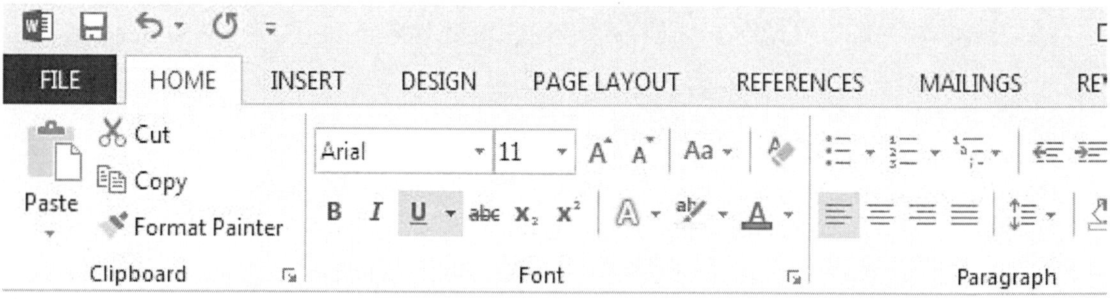

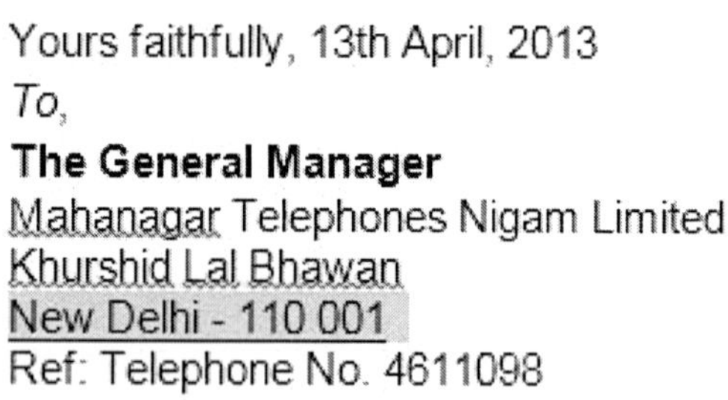

Yours faithfully, 13th April, 2013

To,

The General Manager

Mahanagar Telephones Nigam Limited

Khurshid Lal Bhawan

New Delhi - 110 001

Ref: Telephone No. 4611098

4. You can see the text underlined next.

Coming down now you see the line containing the telephone number. This line has to be underlined and centralized. I am not describing here the method to underline this line since it is similar to the one followed by you in the above case. I am sure you can do it yourself. Let us now concentrate on alignment. Let us see how it is done in Word 2013.

Alignment of Text

Word 2013 gives you the option of placing the text in four different alignments. These are:

Left aligned This line is left aligned.

Right aligned This line is right aligned.

Centralized This line is centrally aligned.

Justified This line has been justified.

You will not notice much of a difference here in left aligned text and justified text. This is so because the matter is small. Just notice the whole text of this book, it is justified, i.e., it aligns to the left and right both. Whereas this particular paragraph is left aligned and see the difference for yourself.

All the four alignments are there on the formatting toolbar. You can choose any one of them. (If you do not have all 4 of them, click at Add and Remove button on the right of the toolbar to add the missing alignment to the formatting toolbar.

Coming back to our text. We have to centrally align the line containing the telephone number.

For that do the following:

1. Click the mouse button at the left of R of Reference: Telephone No. 4611098.
2. Click at the icon which shows the centralized alignment.
3. Notice here that you do not have to highlight the text for alignment. This is so since the whole matter of the paragraph has to be aligned to the same alignment. It is not possible to align one word to one alignment and another word to another alignment.

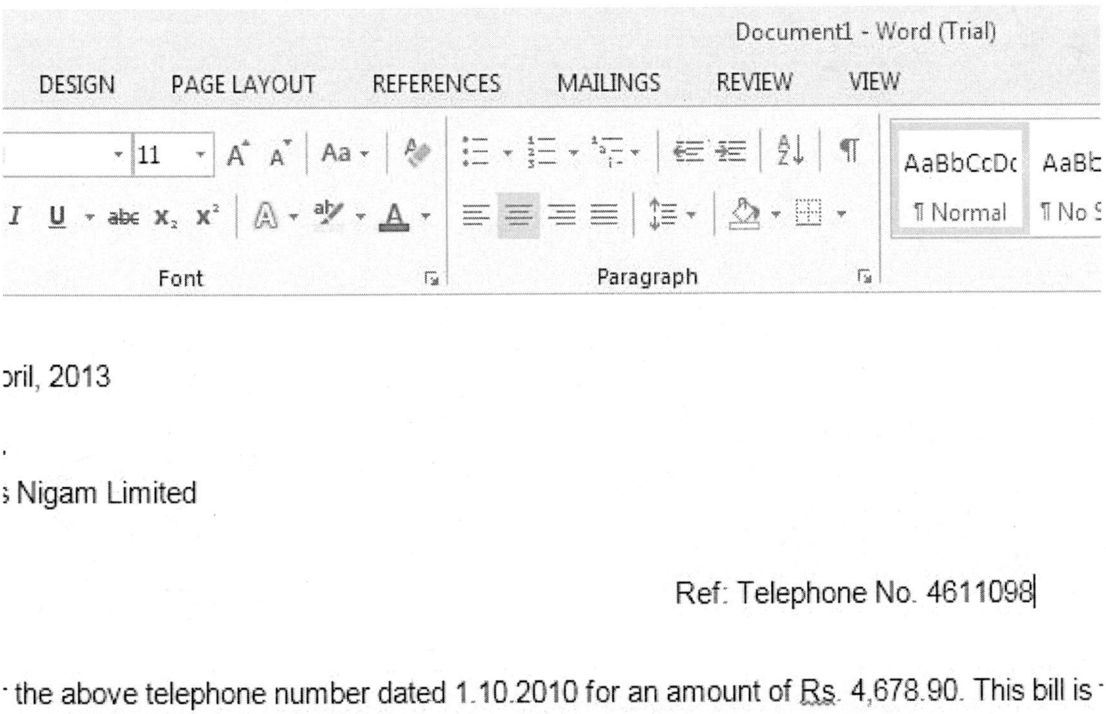

4. You can see the text underlined and centralized aligned in the figure next.

Now that the next lines have nothing much to be done, expect that International calls and Amitabh Bachan have to be made bold. This I presume you will be able to do without any difficulty.

It is time to save the document again so as to make sure that the changes made by you are stored in the hard disk.

Next, let us try to put some fancy things on the text. First among them is Font.

Applying fonts

It is upto you to select the same font for the whole text or have different fonts for different paragraphs. Let us see how it is done.

1. Click at any place in the text with the mouse.
2. Click at Select All in the Edit menu or simply press Ctrl and then A. This will highlight the whole text in the document.
3. Now you can select the font of your liking in the whole text. You can also change the size of the font too.
4. Select Arial for font and size 12 for the whole text in the Formatting toolbar.

5. This will make the whole text 12 points and will have Arial as the font.
6. The previous changes made by you in terms of **Bold**, *Italics* will remain intact and will not be disturbed by doing this.
7. Now if you want you can change the font of particular items like address, etc., to make it more decorative.

Now that our letter is ready, we can just print it, but before that we must check the spelling in the document so as no typological errors remain in the document.

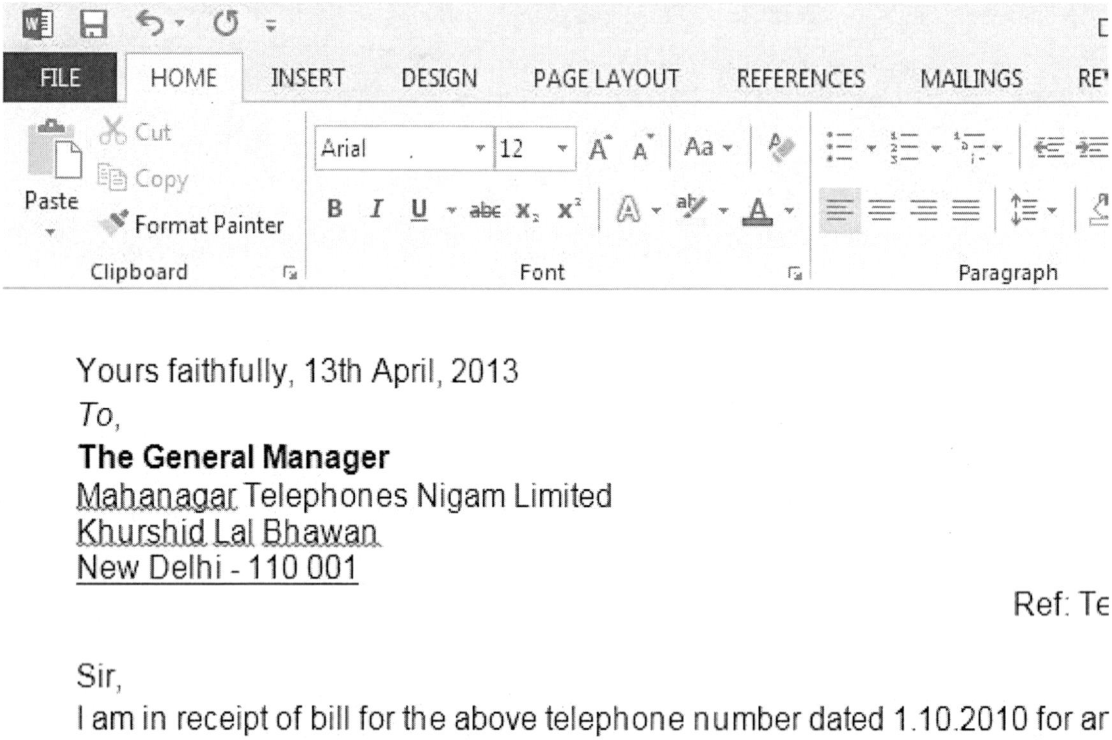

Spell Checking

As was mentioned in the options, Word 2013 points out the spelling errors by underling the word/words with red wavy line. Since our document is just one page long. It is not difficult to pin point the errors.

There are two methods of correcting these errors. One method is to correct these errors one by one, picking them up. Secondly, you spell check the whole document. Let us do both on our document.

Looking from top to bottom of the text in the document file Bill, you will see few of the words underlined by wavy red line. Few of them are the proper words and thus cannot be corrected.

Words like Mahanagar is basically a *Hindi* word, so it cannot be in the dictionary of Word 2013 and that is why it has been shown as an error. Similar is the case with enteries which is wrong and needs to be corrected. For this follow the following procedure:

1. Click with the mouse at any place within the word to be corrected, in this case enteries.
2. Now right click the mouse button.
3. A pop-menu will pop-up as shown next.
4. Among the various options are:

Alternative words: Word 2013 displays few words which are similar to the word in question with a hope that these may had been word in your mind while typing this word wrongly. You can choose any one of them, which you feel is the right word by just clicking and selecting that and leaving the mouse. The word will stand corrected with the new word and will replace the wrong word.

Ignore: It is like over ruling the dictionary and saying that whatever you have typed is right and would like the dictionary to ignore this not only at this place but also at all other places within the document.

Ignore All: This will allow you to ignore this error thoughout the document.

Add to Dictionary: You feel that this word is right and would like this word to be added to the dictionary so that it is not shown as an error in the future.

AutoCorrect: You will learn about AutoCorrect later. But, only thing to understand here is that it is a list of mostly misplaced word which can be corrected without referring to the dictionary. For example, you may have the bad habit of typing *the* as *teh*. You can add this to AutoCorrect to correct *teh* to *the* always without even telling you.

Language: You feel that this particular word which has been pointed as wrong by the current dictionary would be available in other language dictionary. So mention here the name of the other dictionary where this word could be found. If you do not have a second dictionary loaded, just ignore this.

Spelling: By clicking at this, you can start the spell checking of the whole document from this point onward.

Look Up: It looks for an alternative word in the Thesaurus.

Cut, Copy and Paste: These can be used for transferring the word to some other place in the document by cutting or copying it at this place and pasting it there.

5. In our case we will accept entries as the correct substitute for the wrong word enteries.

Since there is no other word which is to be corrected here. The corrected text would now look like the one shown next. Now we come to the second way of spell checking which is checking the whole document. In this case place the cursor at the beginning of the text in the document. In our case we will place the cursor at the left of 1 of 11th January.

From here do either of the following to start the spell checking.

1. Select Spelling and Grammar from the Tools menu.

   Or

2. Press F7

   Or

3. Click at Spell Grammar in Proofing panel of Review.

This will initiate the spell checking process and will start the spell checking of the document with each word of the document being searched with the similar word with the words available in the dictionary. If not found it will point out.

In our case it will select *Mahanagar* of **Mahanagar Telephones Nigam Limited**. As was mentioned before it is a proper *Hindi* word, so it cannot be corrected. Ignore it to proceed further. Other words in the document are also correct. So keep clicking Ignore for all of them till you reach the end of the document and it stops checking the spelling of the document. After this there is no other word to correct and the spell checking ends with a dialog box, saying that the spelling checking is complete.

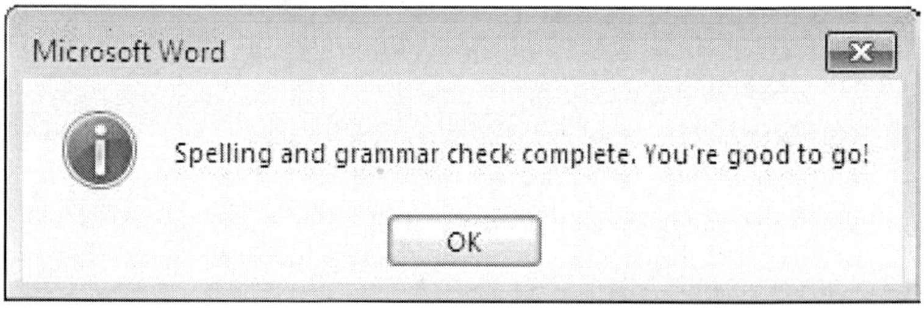

Remember, you can spell check a portion of the text or a word by just highlighting it and then clicking at Spell Checking Icon.

Then there is another option called Thesaurus.

Consulting Thesaurus

Thesaurus is there to help you find Synonym, words with similar meanings and Antonym, words with opposite meanings. Using the thesaurus not only helps your vocabulary, but gives you alternatives to using the same word over and over again throughout your text.

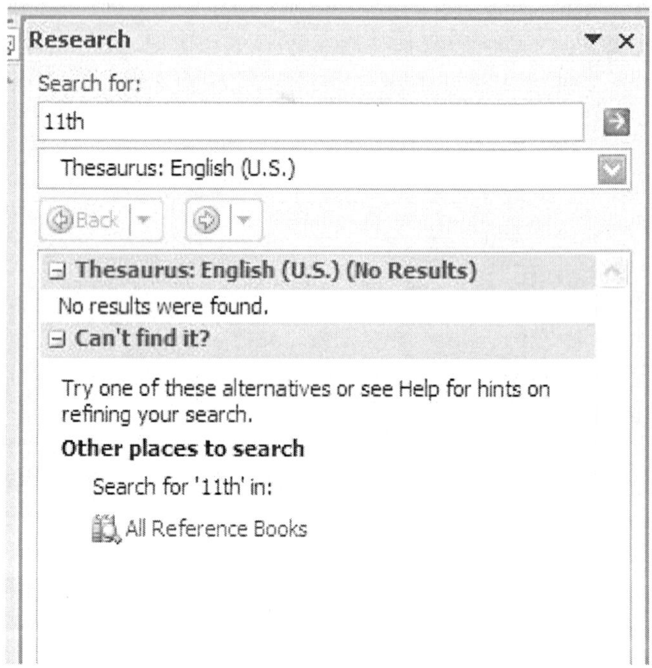

Let us try to use this option in our text. We would like to see the alternatives to the word Bill. For this we do the following:

1. Select the word bill in the second line of the paragraph.
2. Now select Thesaurus from the Proofing panel.
3. You will get the dialog box as shown here.
4. The options given here are Invoice as the main. But there are others too like statement, check, etc.
5. You have the option to select a new word Invoice or other or let the bill remain as it is.

Borders and Shading

Word 2013 allows you to highlight headlines, captions, and other text of importance by applying a border or shading to that text. You can apply it to a piece of text or to the full text.

Apply Borders and Shading

1. Select the text on which you want to apply Borders or Shading. Basically the rules to follow this are:

- If no text is selected, the paragraph where the cursor is, will be taken as the starting point.
- If you select text within a single paragraph, but the paragraph mark itself is not included in the selection, the results affect only the selected text.
- If you select text included in more than one paragraph (so that at lease one paragraph mark is included in the selection), the results affect all the paragraphs in which any of the selected text resides.

2. Open the Design Panel, and select Page Border.
3. Click Borders to work with options available under it.

- Under Setting, click one of the preset border options.
- Select None to remove all borders from the selected paragraph(s), Box to insert a box border around the selected paragraph(s), and Shadow to insert a box border around the selected paragraph(s) and apply preset shadow formatting to the border.
- Select 3-D to insert a box border around the selection and apply preset 3D border formatting. Choose Custom to create a border using the options you click in the Preview window. When you choose any of these settings, the current selections in Style, Colour, and Width apply to the borders.
- From the Style list, select the type of line you want to use for the border, including *dotted, dashed*, and *wavy lines.*
- Click the Color drop-down list to select a colour to apply to the border.

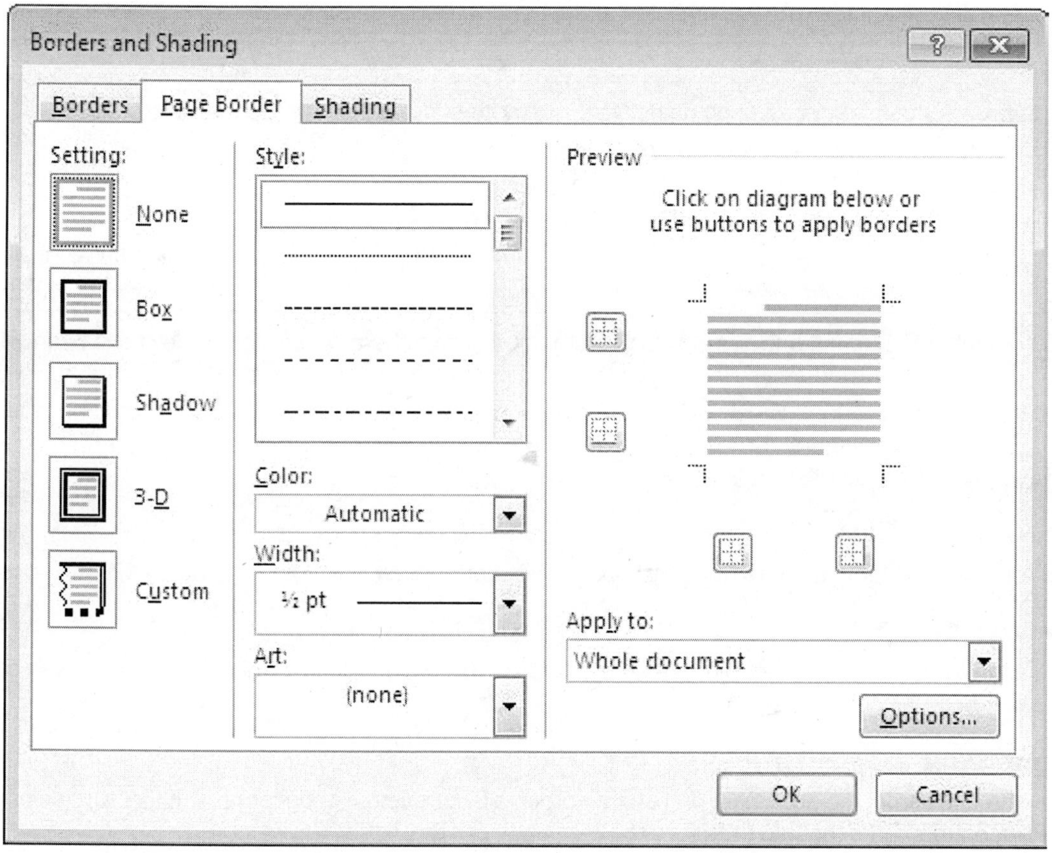

- From the Width drop-down list, choose the thickness of the border line from ¼ point to 6 points.
- In the Preview box, click the individual border lines or use the border line buttons to apply or remove borders or change the attributes of a particular border (select the attributes first and then add the border).
- From the Apply To drop-down list, select whether to apply the border to just the selected text or to the whole paragraph(s).

4. Select Shading to choose shading options.

- Under Fill, select the colour or shade of gray with which you want to fill the selection. Click More Colors to see a larger selection of colours.
- From the Patterns Style drop-down list, choose a shading percentage for the colour you selected under Fill or a pattern of lines such as Lt Horizontal or Dk Trellis.
- If you selected a pattern of lines, select the Color of the lines from the drop-down list. The Fill colour then becomes the background colour for the pattern.
- From the Apply To drop-down list select whether to apply the shading options to just the selected text or to the whole paragraph(s).

5. Click Ok.

You can use all these options of Borders and Shading from the Tables and Border toolbar, which can be called from toolbar options. This will allow you to select shading colours, border line styles, border line colours, and border line widths, etc.

Following are the button on the toolbar that apply to borders and shading.

Button	***Description***
Line Style	Sets the style of the border lines (dotted, dashed, wavy, double, and so on)
Line Weight	Sets the thickness of the border lines
Border Color	Sets the colour of the border lines
Borders	Specifies where the border appears (top, bottom, left, right, or box)
Shading Color	Sets the colour of the background shading for the paragraph (you cannot specify the percentage)

Since our letter is a formal one, we would not like to use any of these decorations. They have been told here so that they can be used at a later stage in another document.

Now that our letter is final. What we would do now is that we will close the file and then reopen and finally print. This is deliberately done so as to learn the concept of closing and opening of the file. If you want you can print the file as it is.

Closing of the File

As mentioned earlier in the Info Button, there is close option on it.

Save as option

Unlike the earlier options of Save As, this time in Word 2013 has different options for Save As. These can be seen here in the Info Button.

Printing Your Document

As mentioned earlier, no document preparation process is complete without printing it. For this we have the Print option under the Info Button.

Once clicked it gives rise to a dialog box as shown here. The various options, which can differ depending upon the printer, which you are working on, of the dialog box are as follows:

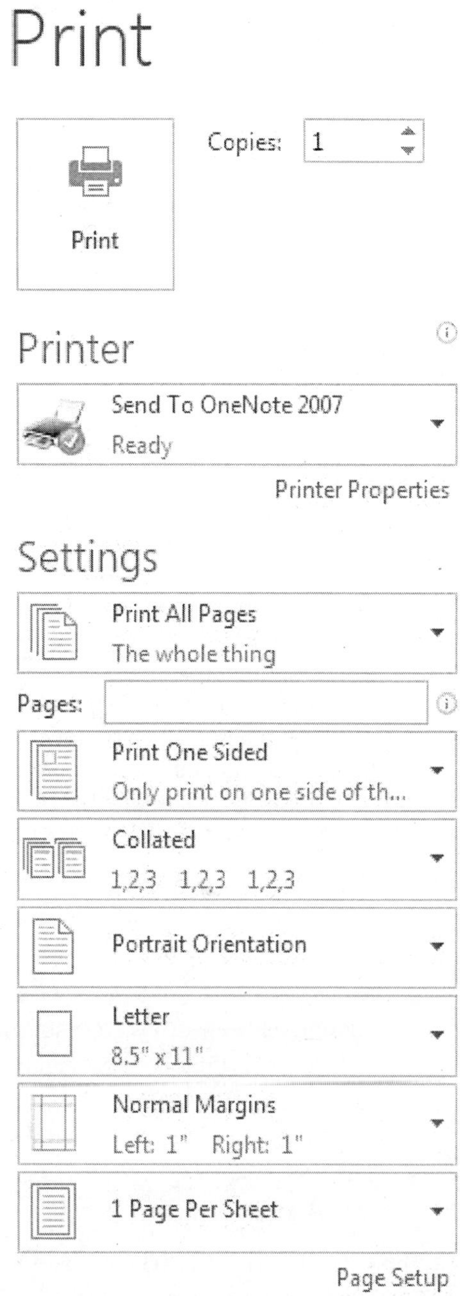

Print All Pages: Select to print all pages in the file.

Print One Sided: Select to print one side of the paper or on both sides of the paper.

Collated: Yoy can select to have the pages collated in case of multiple copies being printed.

Orientation: You may select from Portrait or Landscape.

Page Size: Select the page size from the various page sizes options available.

Normal Margins: You can choose to have normal margins or set up your own margins as required.

Page Per Sheet: You can choose to print multiple pages printed on the sheet.

Zoom: Pages per sheet allows you to print 1 to 16 pages of the document on one sheet. Scaling allows you to scale your document to the various sizes of the paper.

Once you are sure that you have selected all the options required by you, just click Ok to for document to start printing. However, do not forget to have the Printer ON before giving the final print command.

Editing the Document

Now that you have printed the document, you may want to either correct few words which you have realized that they do not look good in the letter. Even otherwise you may want to enhance the overall look of the letter. Besides this you would also learn how to do the tailor's job, i.e., Cut, Copy and Paste. There are other options too which may not be used in this letter but are quite useful overall for editing. Let us start with the proofing tools.

Editing Tools

Many editing functions are performed on selected text, such as cut, copy, move, and delete. There are various tools provided by Word to help you edit text:

Cut, Copy: Cutting and copying items places them on the Clipboard and you can paste these items anywhere in the document, wherever required. These items can be text, graphics, tables and any other object which is there in the word document. Cut and Copy can be performed using mouse and key strokes.

Paste: It is the command used to paste whatever is available on the Clipboard to paste it in the document. This is also done by the use of mouse and key strokes.

Move: It is an action associated with the mouse. However, if you cut and paste from one place to another, it can also be called move.

Insert Mode: It is the feature that adjusts spacing when you add new text to the document.

Overtype Mode: This option replaces the existing text with your new text.

Delete: It is an action you should reserve for text you want to permanently remove. Deleted text is not placed in the Clipboard. You can delete text with either mouse or key strokes.

Undo and Redo: Using these commands you can reverse the tasks performed earlier.

All these commands are available on the toolbar in the Home menu.

For either cutting or copying, you have to highlight the part of the text on which you want to perform this operation. All these commands have their keyboard strokes associated with them too.

Let us now learn few options of Word 2013 which help us in correcting our document with minimum efforts.

AutoCorrect

It is a handy feature of Word 2013 which automatically corrects common typing, capitalization, and spelling errors for you, as you type. It also enables you to type shortcuts that AutoCorrect replaces with the full text, such as typing BOMBAY and having AutoCorrect replace it with MUMBAI. This has been neccesiated due to the fact that the name of the city has been changed as thus. Although Word 2013 has a number of default AutoCorrect entries, you can add your own common misspellings and shortcuts.

It only checks whole words, so if you type TEH, Word won't replace it with THE until your press the spacebar, period, or some other key that indicates that the word is complete. It is also useful tool for applying formatting options. In a business letter, for example, you might want your company name to always appear in a certain font and size, regardless of the font you are using for the letter. By creating an AutoCorrect entry of your company name with formatting options, you eliminate the need to format while you type, or to run search and replace when you are finished with the letter.

Add AutoCorrect Entries Without Formatting

1. From the Info button, select Options, and then Proofing, AutoCorrect options.
2. Click Replace Text as You Type to place a check mark there, if it isn't already checked.
3. In the replace box, enter the text you want AutoCorrect to automatically replace for you, such as your initials or a word you commonly misspell.
4. Click Plain Text if it is not selected to inserted text without formatting options.
5. Choose Add. If the text in the Replace box is already listed, choose Replace to replace the existing replacement text with the text you entered in the With box.
6. Click Ok.

Text your new AutoCorrect entry by typing the word in a document and pressing the Spacebar.

Add New AutoCorrect Entries with Formatting

1. Type the text in your document and format it.
2. Select the text. To store paragraph formatting with your entry, include the paragraph mark at the end of the text, in your selection.
3. From the Info button, select Options and Proofing and AutoCorrect Options. The AutoCorrect dialog box appears.
4. In the Replace text box, type a name for the AutoCorrect entry (an abbreviation, or the entire word or phrase).
5. Click Formatted Text.

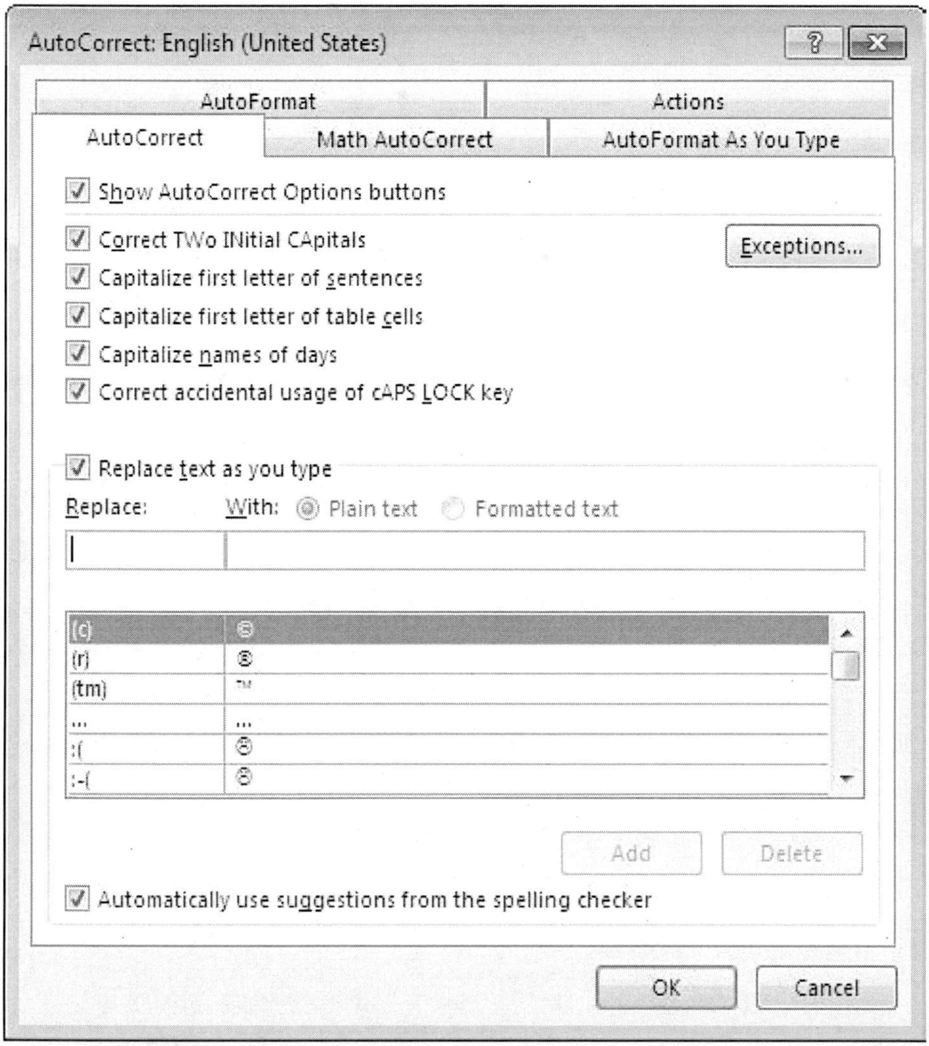

6. To save the entry and close the dialog box, click Add.

Here you have an option for Math AutoCorrect tool, which allows you to create mathematical characters, by just writing the english word for it.

AutoFormat

Word 2013 has automated a lot of small, tedious chores that we had to do manually in older word processing programs. Many of these are formatting chores, and Word collects them under the term AutoFormat. You can control what formatting chores Word 2013 performs automatically in the AutoFormat panels of the AutoCorrect dialog box. The benefit of using AutoFormat is that you can concentrate more on the content of your document and less on the details of formatting.

AutoFormat works on two different ways—as you type or on command.

AutoFormat as You Type

Automatically formats headings, bulleted and numbered lists, borders, numbers, symbols, and so on, as you type.

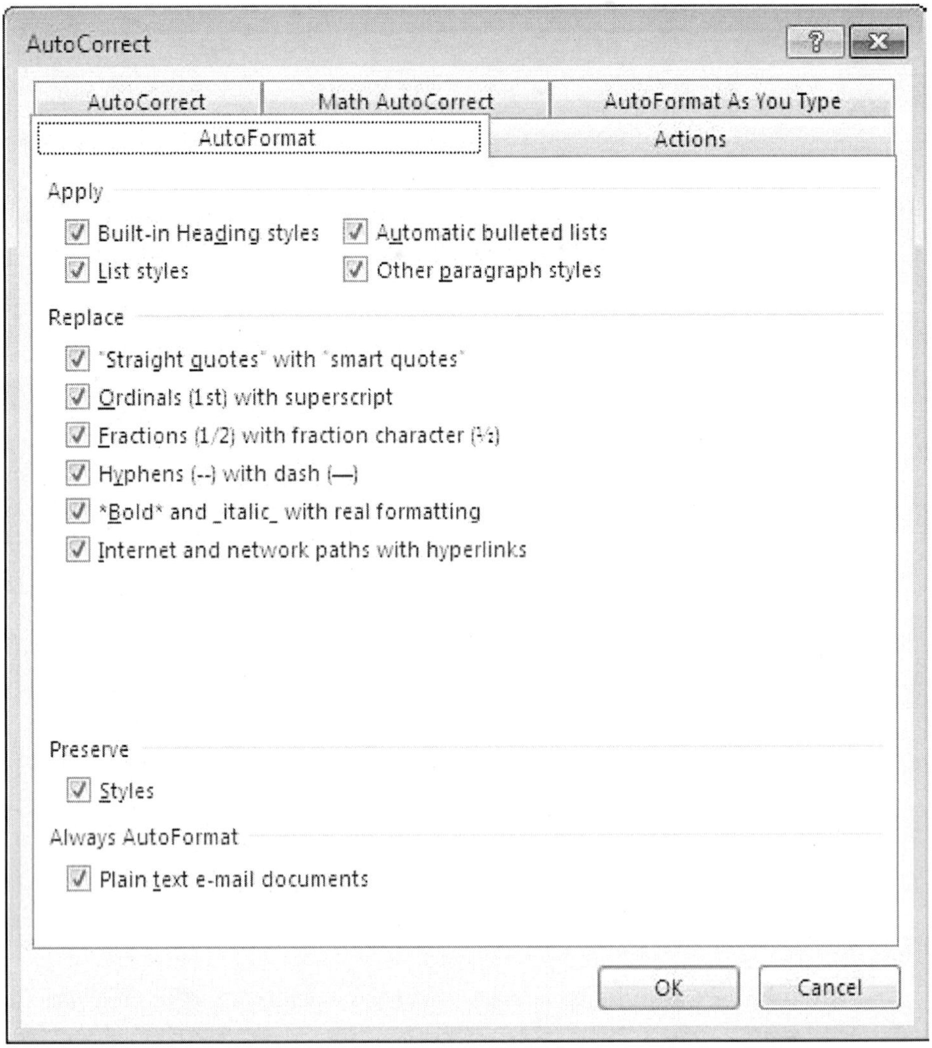

AutoFormat on Command

Automatically formats selected text or the entire document in one pass. You don't have to do anything to activate AutoFormat. By default, AutoFormat as You Type is enabled—you just enter text and Word formats it as you go. You can change the default to AutoFormat on Command, which allows you to manually run AutoFormat. This is similar to the way in which you can spell check a document—as you type, or manually, using the menu commands or toolbar icons.

AutoFormatting Text

1. To AutoFormat a block of text, select it. To AutoFormat the entire document, make sure that no text is selected.
2. From the Office button, select Word Options followed by Proofing options. From here click at AutoCorrect options to get the dialog box.
3. Click AutoFormat.
4. Click AutoFormat and Review Each Change if you want the opportunity to accept or reject each change proposed by Word.

5. Choose the type of document you have created in the drop-down list labelled Please Select a Document Type to Help Improve the Formatting Process. This helps Word to AutoFormat the document properly.
6. If you want to limit the types of formatting Word does, choose the Options button to display the AutoFormat panel of the AutoCorrect dialog box. Make your selections and then click Ok to return to the AutoFormat dialog box.
7. Click Ok to begin the AutoFormat process.

If you choose AutoFormat Now, Word 2013 formats the document, and that's that. If you choose AutoFormat and Review Each Change, Word 2013 formats the document and then presents a new AutoFormat dialog box. This version of the document looks very different from the first version.

Find and Replace

Supposing you had prepared a thesis on the working of middle level managers in the city of Bombay. Naturally the word Bombay must have come in it quite a number of times. Then you hear that the Government of that State has decided to change the name of city from **Bombay** to **Mumbai**. What will you do? Will you be able to locate each occurrence of Bombay and physically change it to Mumbai? No! For this Word 2013 has an excellent option called Find and Replace. Once you give this command, Word 2013 will automatically search for Bombay and replace it with Mumbai.

You can use Find and Replace to do the following:

Text strings: Either strings of text embedded in words, or discrete words or whole phrases.

Text strings with formatting: Strings of text that are formatted a particular way, such as Bold.

Formatting: Font formatting options, such as underlining and bold, that are not necessarily associated with words or text.

Styles: Find all instances of a named style or replace one named style with another.

Special characters: Tab markers, forced line breaks, non-breaking spaces, non-breaking hyphens, whitespace, and so on.

This command is actually divided into 2 parts, Find and Replace. Let us see how the find command works first.

Find

This command will find for you the exact text which is mentioned in its box and will stop for further

action. Normally the finding of the text starts from the position where the cursor is. If you have selected some text, the finding will be restricted to that block of text only. So if you have to select the entire text, then it is advised to put the cursor at the beginning of the text in the document.

To start the Find command, click at Find in the Home menu.

Find and Replace dialog box, as shown here will appear.

This is how you will use the Find command.

1. Type the text that you are seeking in the Find What? text box. This word or phrase is also referred to as the search string.
2. Choose the More button (if necessary) to specify search options.
3. Choose Find Next. Find looks through the document for text that matches your search strings. When it finds matching text, Word highlights the text in the document and stops. The Find and Replace dialog box remains on screen.
4. Choose Find Next if you want to continue the search for another instance of the search string. Click Cancel or press Esc to close the dialog box and return to the document. The text in the document is still highlighted.

When Word finishes the entire document, or if it could not find the search string in the document, a dialog box displays a message to that effect. Choose Ok to continue working in the document.

Replace Text

Next step after finding the required text is to replace it with some other text. For this we would call the command called Replace. To get the replace command click at Replace in the Home menu.

Now on the Find and Replace dialog box click at the Replace panel and do the following:

1. Type the text you want to replace in the Find What text box (in this case, *Bombay*). You can leave this field blank if you have to search for a formatting only. However, you have to search for something.
2. Type the text you want to replace it with in the Replace With text box (in this case, *Mumbai*). If you search for text and leave this field blank, you are in effect telling Word to delete all instances of the search strings, because they would be replaced by a blank.
3. Choose the More button (if necessary) to specify search options.
4. Choose Find Next to locate and highlight the first occurence of text that matches your search string.

5. Then do one of the following:
- Choose Replace to replace the text matching the search string with the replacement text and then locate the next occurrence of the search string in your document.
- Choose Find Next to leave the text matching the search string unchanged and to locate the next occurence of the search string.
- Choose Replace All to replace text in the entire document that matches the search string with the replacement text.
6. Choose Cancel. Alternatively, press Esc to close the Find and Replace dialog box and return to the your document.

When Word has finished searching through the document and has replaced all occurrences of the search text or can't find any further occurrences, a message box appears. Click Ok to return to your document.

Word Count

Printed documents longer than one page should have page numbers. You can set up page numbering in two ways. Either insert a page number code while editing headers and footers, or insert page numbers from the Insert menu. Both methods insert a page number code in you documents' header or footer, but there are two differences.

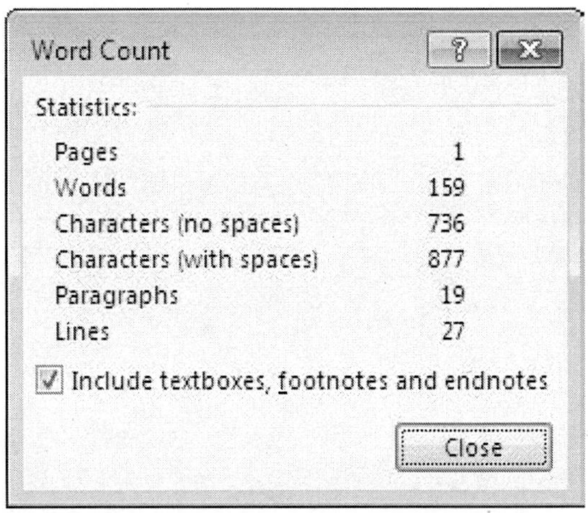

1. Click the Insert panel and select Page Numbers to open the Page Numbers dialog box.
2. From the Position drop-down list, select the position on the page where you want your page numbers to appear. The options are:

   Top of the Page (Header)

   Bottom of the Page (Footer)
3. From the alignment drop-down list, select Left, Center, or Right to specify the horizontal position of the page number in relation to the right or left margins.
4. If you want the page number to appear on the first page, Show number on first page to place check mark there. Deselecting this option creates a separate header or footer for the first page.
5. Click Ok.

When you insert a page number, Word automatically switches you to Print Layout view so you can scroll to the portion of the page where the page number appears to check its appearance.

Header and Footer

As you must be knowing that Header appears on the top of the page and Footer appears on the bottom of the page. Word 2013 allows you to put both of them on the document pages. Once clicked they give you the options to choose from.

Headers and footers can vary within a document. Choices include:

1. The same header and footer on every page.
2. A different header and footer for the first page only
3. Different headers and footers for odd numbered pages than those on even numbered pages.
4. Different headers and footers for each section of the document.

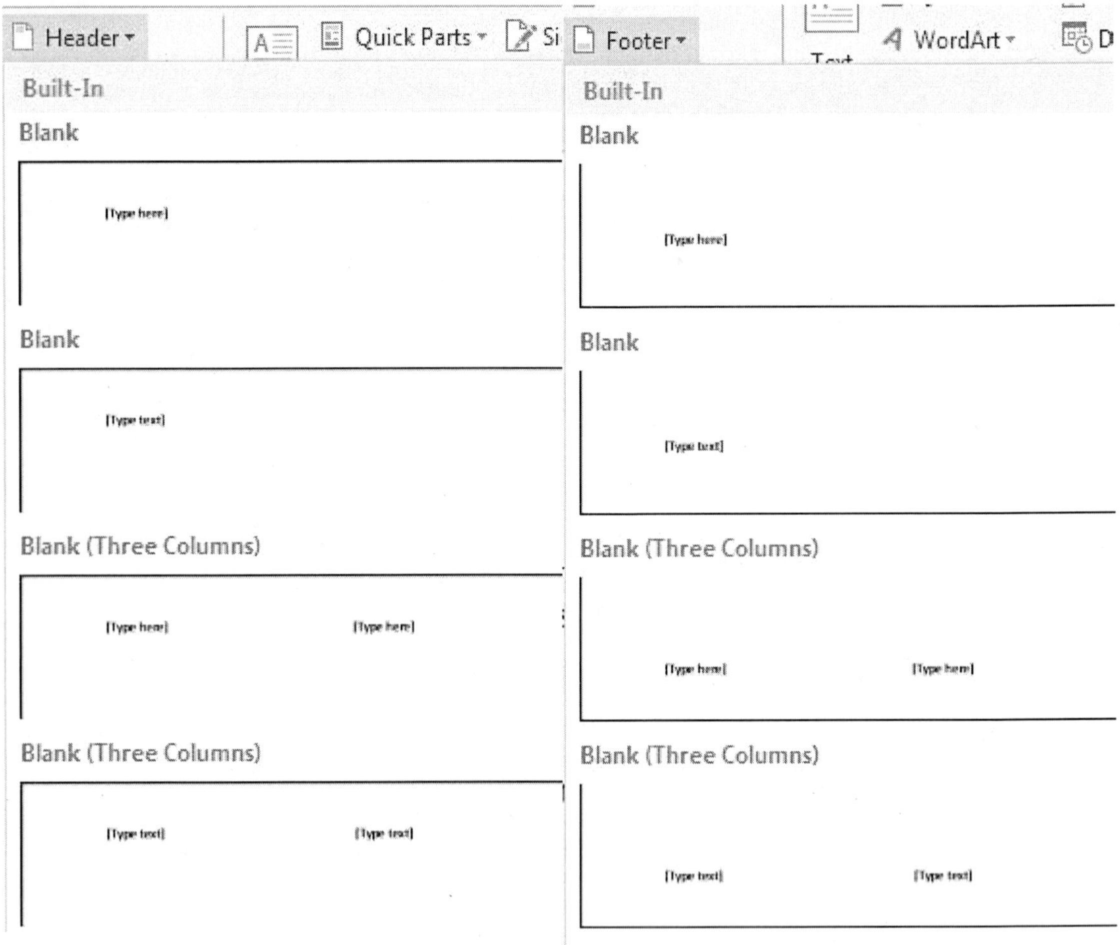

Footnotes and Endnotes

These are used in the documents to provide references to the source documents for the document text, to provide more detailed explanations and definitions that might otherwise distract the reader if left in the main body of the document.

The two parts to each footnote or endnote are the reference mark—a number, character, or combination of characters appearing in the body of the document—and the note text. You may automatically number the marks or create your own custom marks. If you use the automatic numbering, Word renumbers the note reference marks if you add, delete, or move notes. The note can be of any length and format, and you can format the line that separates the notes from the body of the document.

To view the note text, rest the mouse pointer on the note reference mark. The note text appears in a pop-up box above the mark. Double-click the note reference mark to display the note text in a note pane at the bottom of the screen. If you are using Print Layout view, footnotes display at the bottom of the page, endnotes at the end of the document.

Add a Footnote or Endnote

1. Place curosr where you want the note reference mark to appear.
2. Choose the Reference menu and select Insert Footnote. The Footnote dialog box appears.

3. Select Footnote or Endnote.
4. Under Numbering, select AutoNumber or Custom Mark. If you choose Custom Mark, insert the symbol or symbols for the reference mark or choose Symbol to open the Symbol dialog box. Choose a font, click the symbol you want to use, and then click Ok.
5. Choose Ok to close the Footnote and Endnote dialog box.
6. Type the note text in the footnote pane. Apply formatting as desired or, better yet, reformat the Footnote text style (which automatically appears in the Style list when you insert your first footnote).
7. Choose Close to close the footnote pane or click in the document to continue typing.

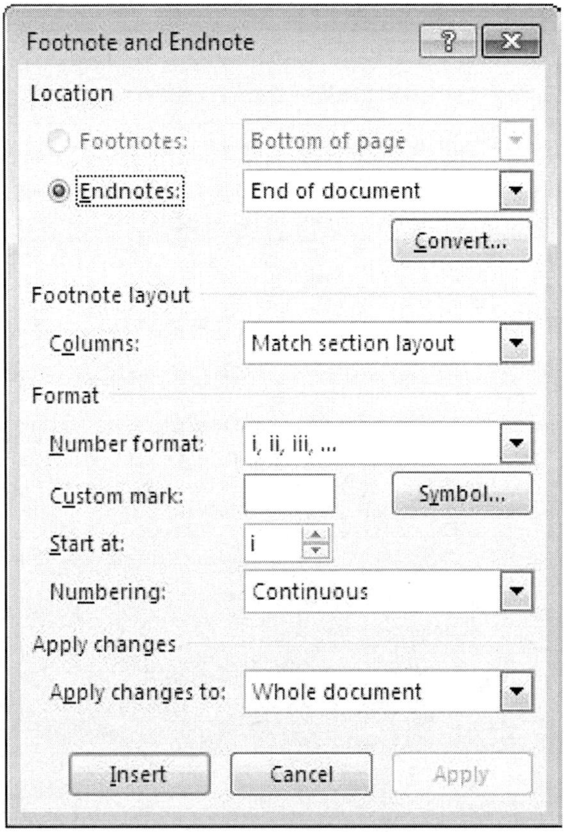

Splitting Panes

You can split a document window into two panes. Then, you can display different portions of the same document at the same time. This lets you compare two portions of a single document. It also makes it easier for you to move or copy text from one portion of a document to another. When you make a change to the document from either pane, the change is applied to the same document. As a result, the change can be found in both panes.

Splitting Document into Two Panes

1. Choose the New window command from the View panel, drag the separator bar to where you want to split the window, and click the left mouse button.
2. Use Remove Split to remove the split.

Tiling of the Documents

With tiling you can display two or more different documents at the same time. This makes it easy for you to compare two or more documents, or to move and copy text from one document to another. However, this works best when only two documents are open. Otherwise, the windows get too small for effective use. To return the display so only one window shows, just maximize the window that you want dispalyed.

To Tile Open Document Window

1. Choose the Arrange All command from the View menu.
2. The Arrange All command sizes the open documents windows so they are all the same height and so they are as wide as possible within Word's application window.
3. You can use standard Windows techniques to move, size and maximize the document windows and to switch between them.

Using MailMerge in Word 2013

MailMerge is one of the very important application of any word processing software. It has been given an important panel in the Word 2013. Word has indeed made it very easy to operate. In MailMerge you have the variable data coming from a data source which can be either a database file, spreadsheet, or even a text file with fields marked in it. Then you have the document file whose text remains the same for all the subsequent merged files changing only the data which has been received from the source. So in fact you create multiple documents having the same text but having different fields depending upon the source.

Well, one can think of various usages of the MailMerge. The most important being sending the same letter to various parties. Sending the same invitation to various guests. Sending payment reminders to various creditors. Calling all the directors to the same board meeting. In all these cases, the text would remain more or less the same but the name and address of the receiver would change. You can even change the salutation too, for example, Dear Mr. so and so, picking the name from the data source.

MailMerge in Word is done in steps. Creating document (text), data source and then merging them before printing. Let us see how it is done. For your information, here I am creating a appreciation letter for the various members of the victories Indian Cricket Team. So, lets start.

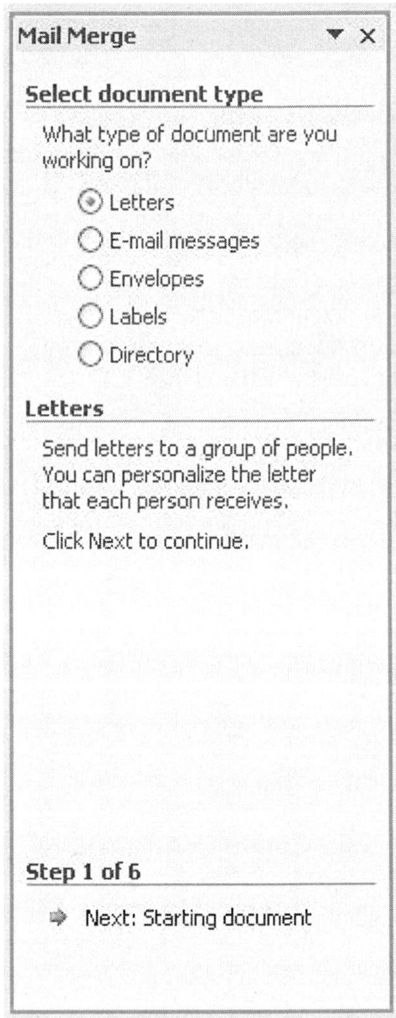

1. Start Word 2013.
2. On the Panels menu, select Mailings.
3. From here on the Start Mail Merge, click at Step by Step Mail Merge Wizard.
4. As shown here, the first step is to select the document type.
5. Select Letters as shown here.
6. Click at Next to start document.
7. The second step as mentioned is to select the document.
8. You have the option of using the current document, starting from an existing document or from a template.
9. Step 3 asks you to type your letter.
10. We have written a letter to various people inviting them to the marriage.
11. As shown next the letter for the same has been type.
12. Now comes the part of selecting the recipients of the letter.
13. In the top portion of the Wizard, choose the Type a new list option and click at Create.
14. You would be given a blank dialog box to create a New Address Book. Here various options of filling the name, address, company's name, etc are given. Type the ones you want to use and ignore others. When you have types one, click at New Entry to go for the next entry.
15. Once you have typed all the entries, click at Ok. You would be asked to save the address list with a name.
16. Once again the same list would be shown to you for making the last minute correction, addition, deletion, etc. You can even change the sequence by sorting it.
17. In the next step, you would insert the field name at the

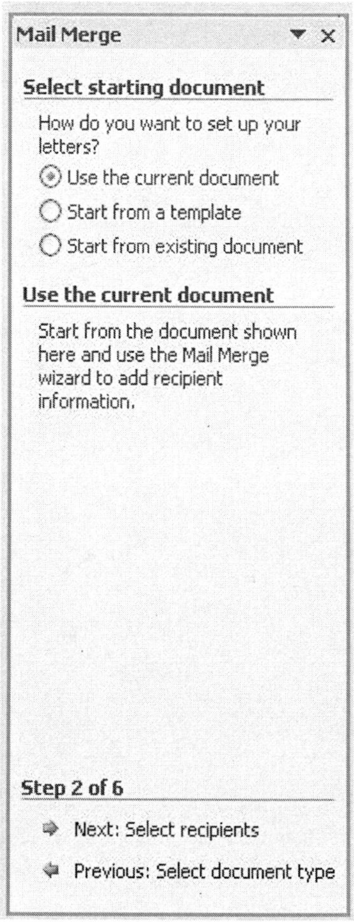
Mail Merge
Select starting document
How do you want to set up your letters?
Use the current document
Start from a template
Start from existing document
Use the current document
Start from the document shown here and use the Mail Merge wizard to add recipient information.
Step 2 of 6
Next: Select recipients
Previous: Select document type

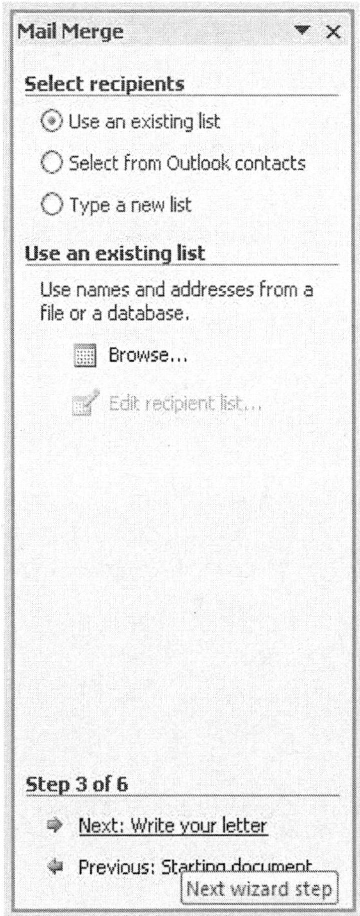
Mail Merge
Select recipients
Use an existing list
Select from Outlook contacts
Type a new list
Use an existing list
Use names and addresses from a file or a database.
Browse...
Edit recipient list...
Step 3 of 6
Next: Write your letter
Previous: Starting document
Next wizard step

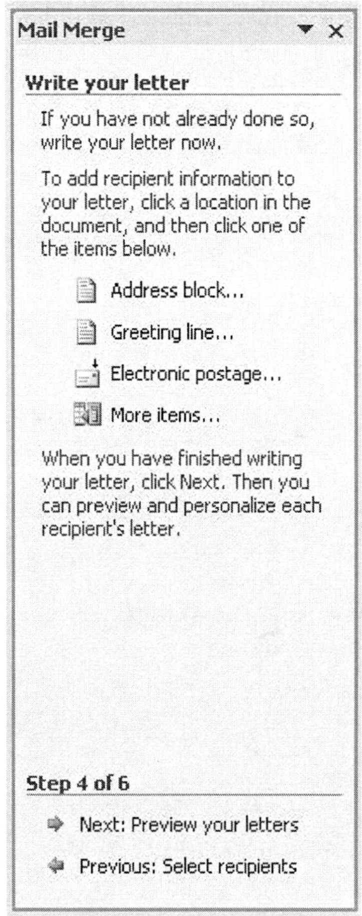
Mail Merge
Write your letter
If you have not already done so, write your letter now.
To add recipient information to your letter, click a location in the document, and then click one of the items below.
Address block...
Greeting line...
Electronic postage...
More items...
When you have finished writing your letter, click Next. Then you can preview and personalize each recipient's letter.
Step 4 of 6
Next: Preview your letters
Previous: Select recipients

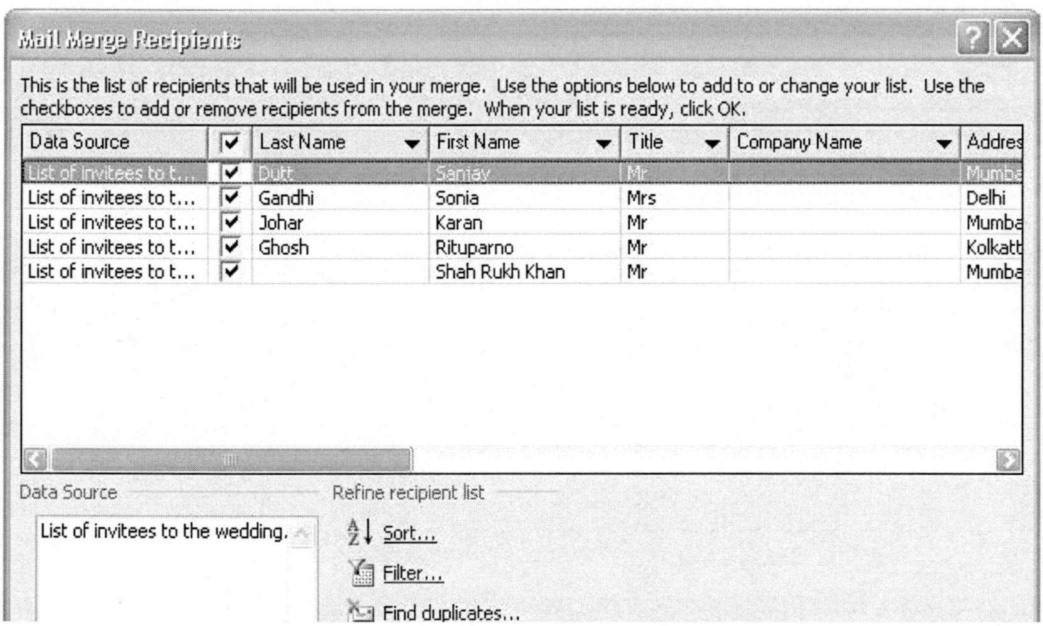
Mail Merge Recipients
This is the list of recipients that will be used in your merge. Use the options below to add to or change your list. Use the checkboxes to add or remove recipients from the merge. When your list is ready, click OK.
Data Source | Last Name | First Name | Title | Company Name | Addres
List of invitees to t... | Dutt | Sanjay | Mr | | Mumba
List of invitees to t... | Gandhi | Sonia | Mrs | | Delhi
List of invitees to t... | Johar | Karan | Mr | | Mumba
List of invitees to t... | Ghosh | Rituparno | Mr | | Kolkat
List of invitees to t... | | Shah Rukh Khan | Mr | | Mumba
Data Source
List of invitees to the wedding.
Refine recipient list
Sort...
Filter...
Find duplicates...

place where it would be displayed. For this choose the option of Insert Merge Field, and then the field name, where it would be replaced with the actual data.

18. You will notice that the fields are shown within < < and > >.
19. Next step would show you the preview of the letter by inserting the actual data from first entry into the letter.
20. Next step is to complete the merge.
21. This will create a file of all letters to be sent, one by one.

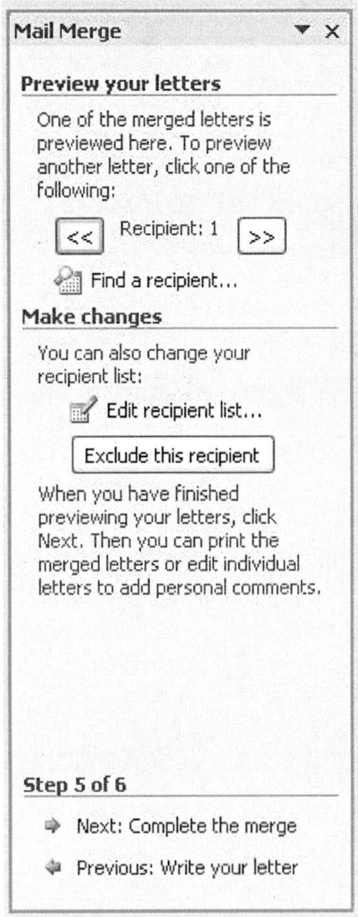

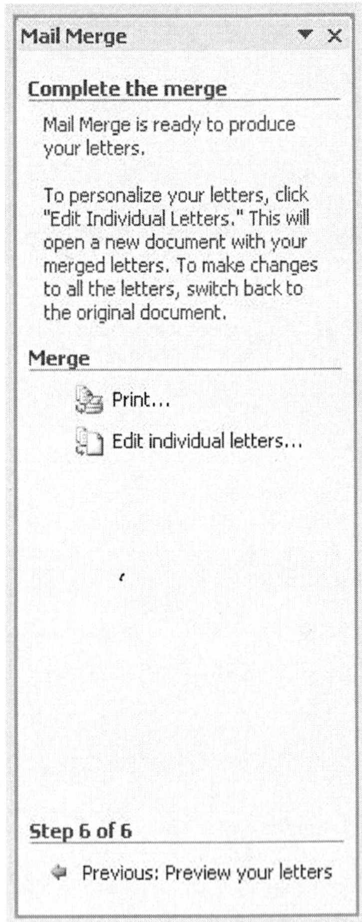

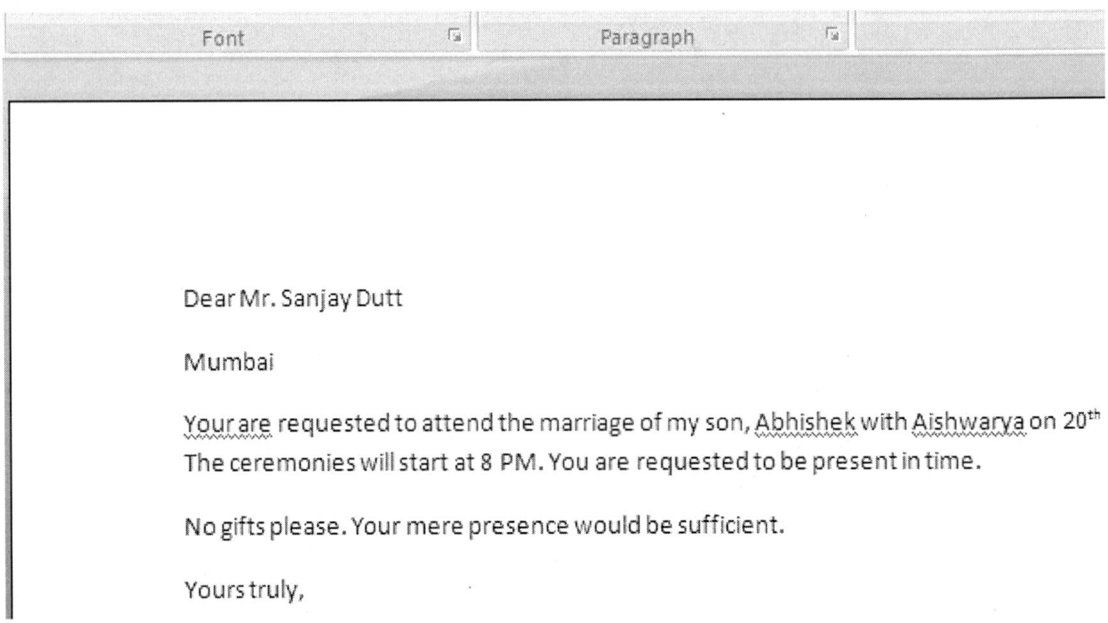

CHAPTER 4

Introduction to Microsoft Excel 2013

Introduction

This spreadsheet program allows you to manipulate and present your data in almost any way you choose. It allows you to work on a tabular pad consisting of columns and rows where you can perform all your mathematical, financial and statistical calculations. These calculations can be as simple as totalling a row or column of values or as complex as figuring the rate of return on an investment under varying circumstances. It also allows you to make a graphical representation of all your data in the form of 2-dimensional or 3-dimensional graph or pie chart.

Understanding Spreadsheets

Before we go into understanding the various commands of Excel, let us first understand the working of a spreadsheet. A spreadsheet as the name suggests is a sheet which is spread in such a way that it divides itself into the various horizontal rows and vertical columns. Rows are numbered from 1 onwards and Columns are numbered from A onwards. Graphically they can be represented as:

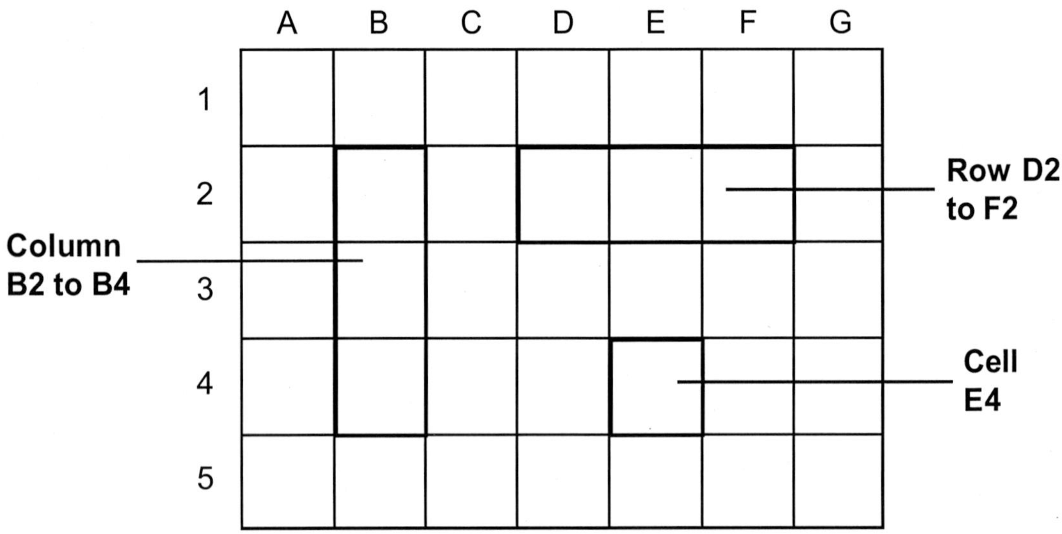

When we take this to the computer and see it electronically using our software Excel, this becomes Electronic Spreadsheet, also called Worksheet. The main features of the worksheets are:

Rows	These are the horizontal cells which can contain any information.
Columns	These are vertical cells which can also contain information.
Cell	It is the interaction of a row with a column. Each cell is identified with its position.

Naming Conventions

It is not that I have named rows from 1 onwards and columns A onwards on my own but they are so numbered by the software itself. These are the standard way of expressing these columns and rows.

If we have to name a large number of cell or columns, for that too we have the convention which asks us to call them with starting cell address and last cell address with colon in between. For example, see the following addressed cells, shown below.

Another convention is of the sheets in the worksheet.

Sheets

These are like pages in a book. Initially there are 16 worksheets in the file. But, you can add more. However, there may be only 6 of them visible on the screen. These sheets are independent but you can transfer data from one sheet to another. These sheets are very helpful. For example, for a salary spreadsheet, one sheet may belong to one month and there may be a sheet for the total of the year.

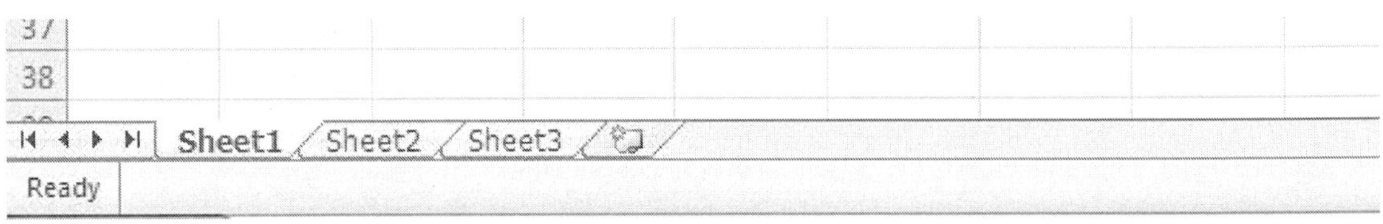

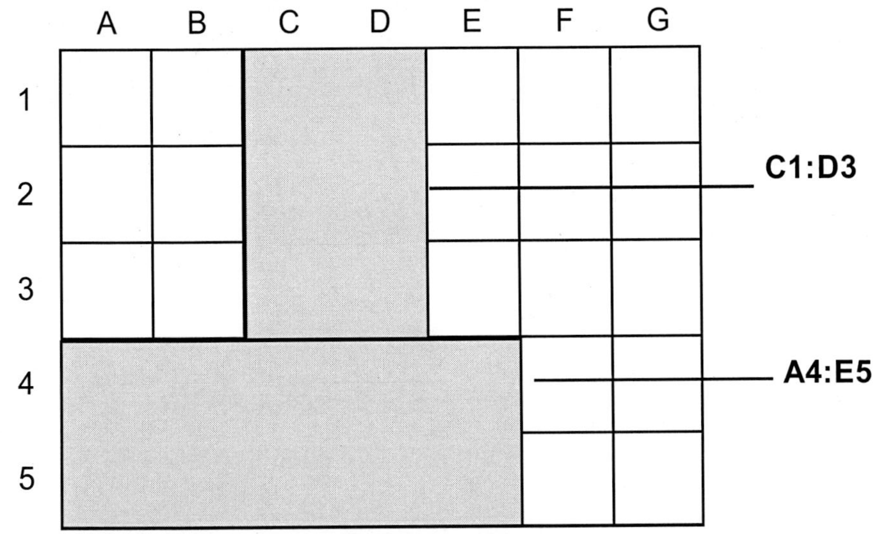

To understand the software better, let us create a worksheet in Excel 2013 and apply the various options/ commands on it to see the working of the software. This will give you an idea about creating a workshett and applying the commands.

Creating a Worksheet in Excel 2013

We have learnt quite a number of commands and naturally would like to use them in a worksheet. So let us create a worksheet and use these commands side-by-side to see how they work out. Supposing we have the financial highlights of a company as given below:

Year	Total Income (A)	Interest Paid (B)	Profit (C)	Tax (D)	Profit After Tax (E)
1999	4,500	To be	To be	To be	To be
2000	5,500	Calculated	Calculated	Calculated	Calculated
2001	7,000	as 15%	as Income	as 12% of	as Profit
2002	8,000	of the	minus	the Profit	minus Tax
2003	9,000	Total	Interest		(C) - (D)
2004	12,000	Income	(A) - (B)		
2005	15,000				
2006	20,000				

As you can see that there are quite a number of fields which have to be calculated. This will act as a good exercise for you to do. Let us start from the very beginning, i.e., start the software Microsoft Excel 2003. You will end up with a blank worksheet, ready for you to take action, with the first cell **A1**, totally at your command to do something, as shown in the figure next.

So what we have to do here. We have to type "Year". So just type the word Year and press **Enter**. You will see the word being shown in the formula bar too. This will also take you to the cell **A2**. But, for typing the next heading, you have to go to the cell **B1**. So use the arrow keys right and up to reach **B1**. Next we have to type "Total Income". (Please note that for the sake of convenience I had shown this

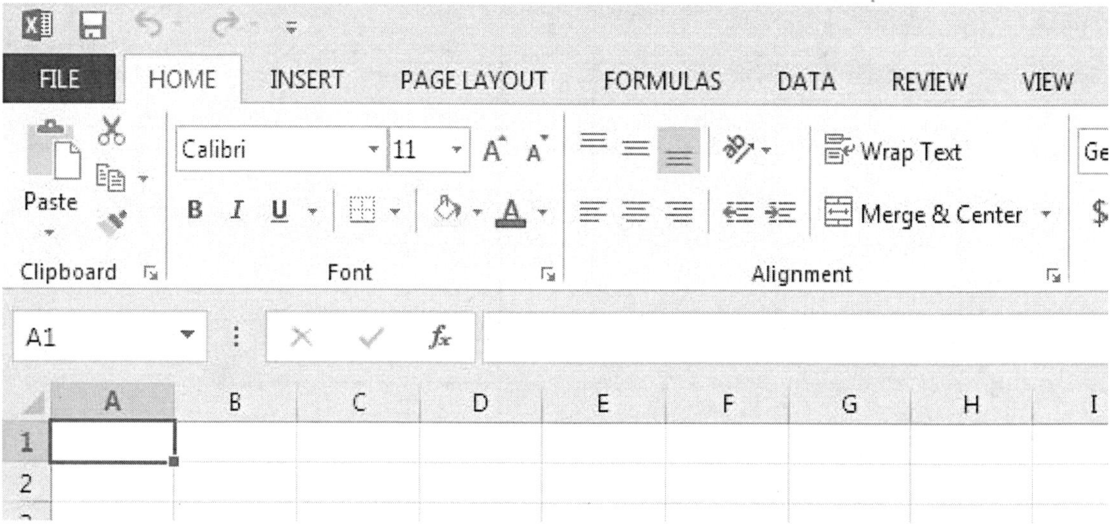

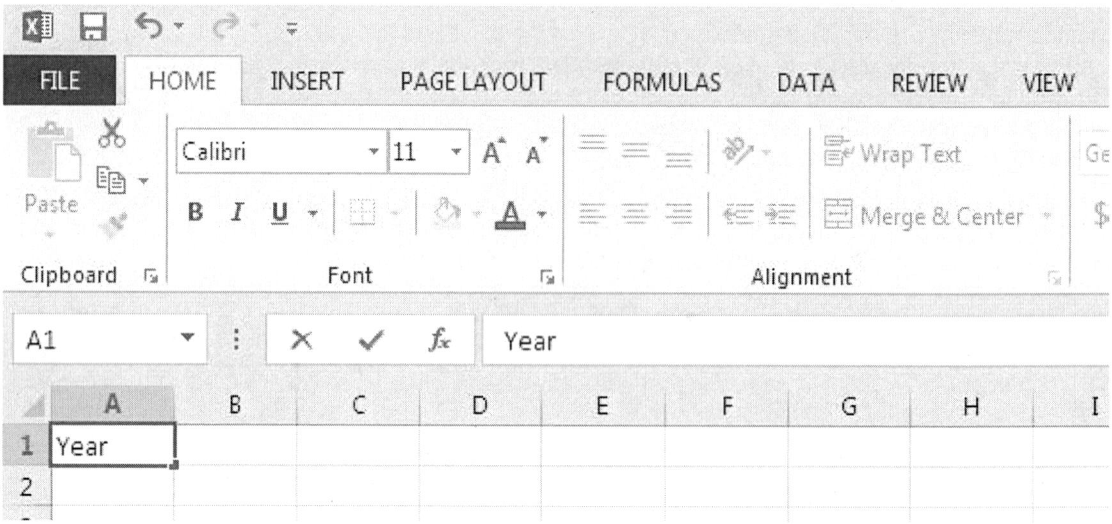

heading in 2 lines, but, if permitted we will type it in one line. Also (A), (B), etc., in the table are just symbolic and are not to be typed).

So for type the next heading, "Total Income" in the cell **B1**, as shown next.

Did you notice anything wrong here? Well, the cell is not big enough to carry your heading. So what will we do? We will increase the width of the column **B**, by using one of the methods mentioned earlier in the chapter, i.e., by using the Cells command under Tools.

This way now we will type the complete headings, i.e., all of them, as shown next.

But, since these are headings, and are to be highlighted. We will make them **Bold** and put them in the centre of the cells. This way they will look good.

Highlight all the cells by just clicking at cell **A1** and then while pressing **Shift** key click mouse in the cell **F1**, the whole row gets highlighted.

Now click at B in the formatting bar to make the whole text as Bold.

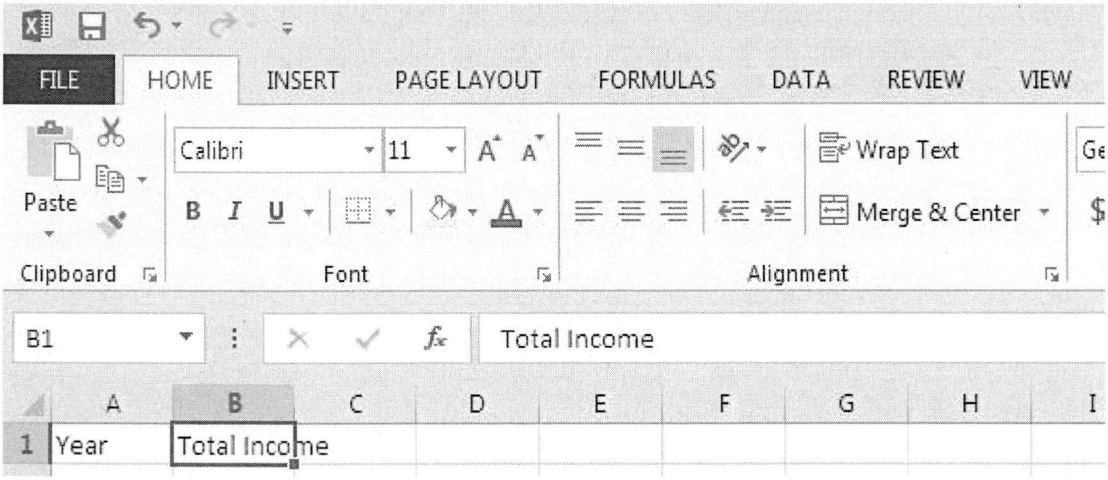
FILE
HOME
INSERT
PAGE LAYOUT
FORMULAS
DATA
REVIEW
VIEW
Calibri
11
Wrap Text
Merge & Center
Paste
Clipboard
Font
Alignment
B1
Total Income
Year
Total Income

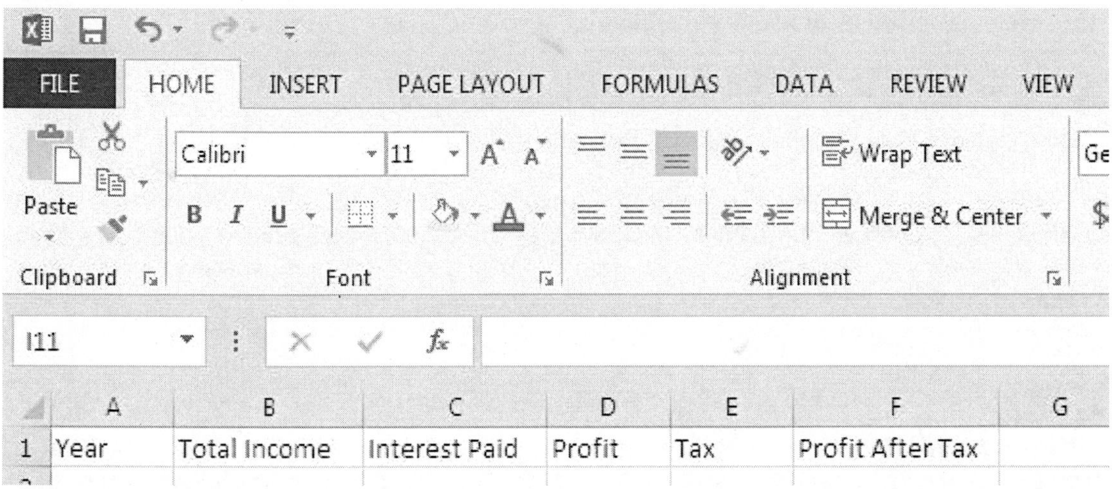
FILE
HOME
INSERT
PAGE LAYOUT
FORMULAS
DATA
REVIEW
VIEW
Calibri
11
Wrap Text
Merge & Center
Paste
Clipboard
Font
Alignment
I11
Year
Total Income
Interest Paid
Profit
Tax
Profit After Tax

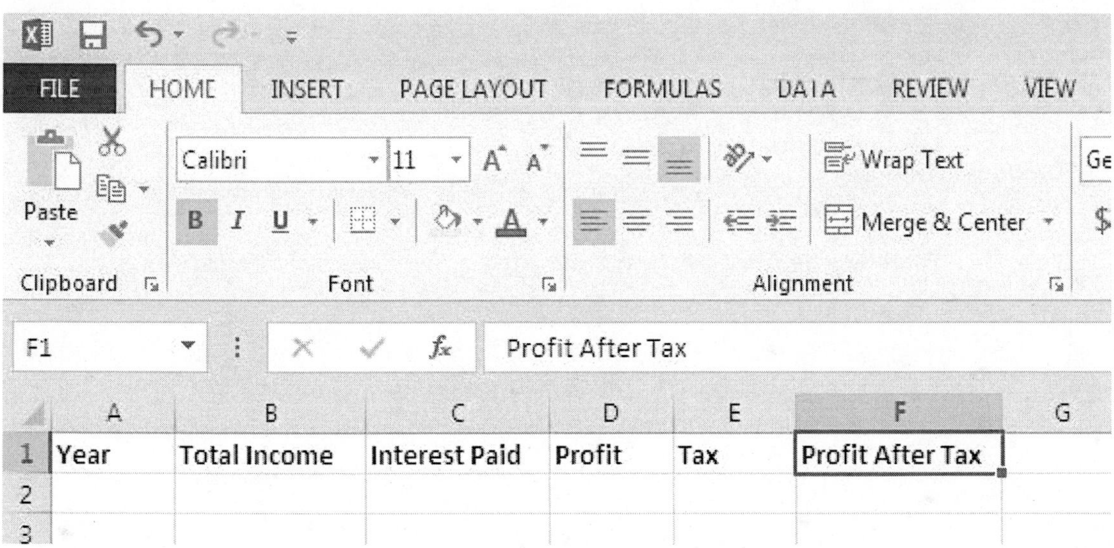
FILE
HOME
INSERT
PAGE LAYOUT
FORMULAS
DATA
REVIEW
VIEW
Calibri
11
Wrap Text
Merge & Center
Paste
Clipboard
Font
Alignment
F1
Profit After Tax
Year
Total Income
Interest Paid
Profit
Tax
Profit After Tax

With the text in the cells remaining highlighted, click at [icon] in the alignment panel of Home menu. This will make the text in the cells centralized in all the cells. This is shown in the figure shown next.

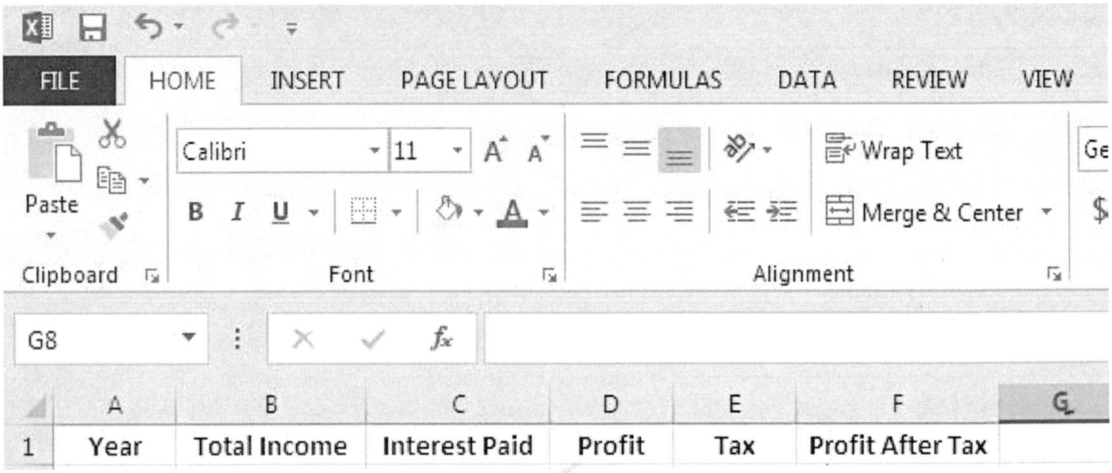

So now we have the headings ready. It was not very difficult, was it? Now all we have is the numeric data. Let us type them too. First of all we will type the various years.

By using the arrow keys, reach the cell **A2**. This is here that we have to type the first year, i.e., **1999**. Type it and press **Enter** to see the data getting aligned to the right. Remember, Excel aligns the numeric data to the right as a default. By pressing **Enter** you must have reached **A3** and this is where you wanted to be for typing the next year, i.e., **2000**. So now type one year and press **Enter** to reach the next cell for typing the next year, till you reach the last year, i.e., **2006**. At this stage your worksheet will look like the one shown next .

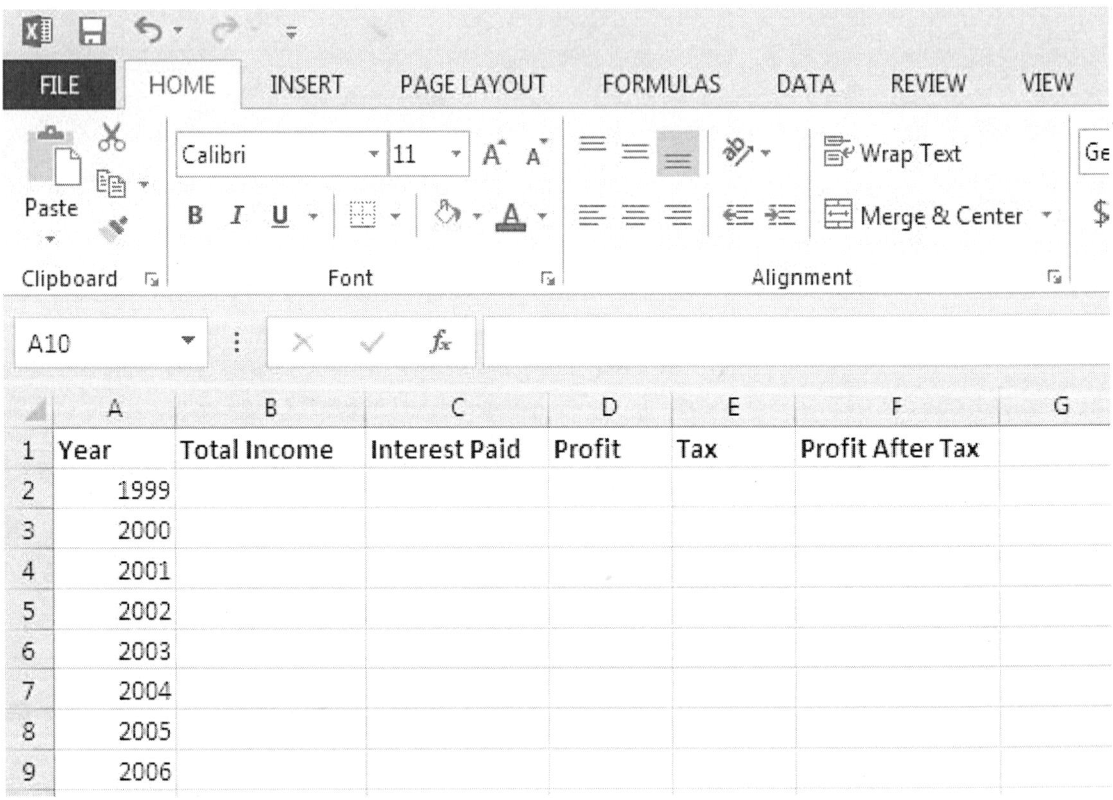

Next step is also easy. You have to just type the numbers in the cells **B2** to **B9**. All these figures are available with you. Just type one figure and press **Enter** to reach the next cell and so on till you reach the last cell in the column. After doing this your worksheet will look like the one shown next.

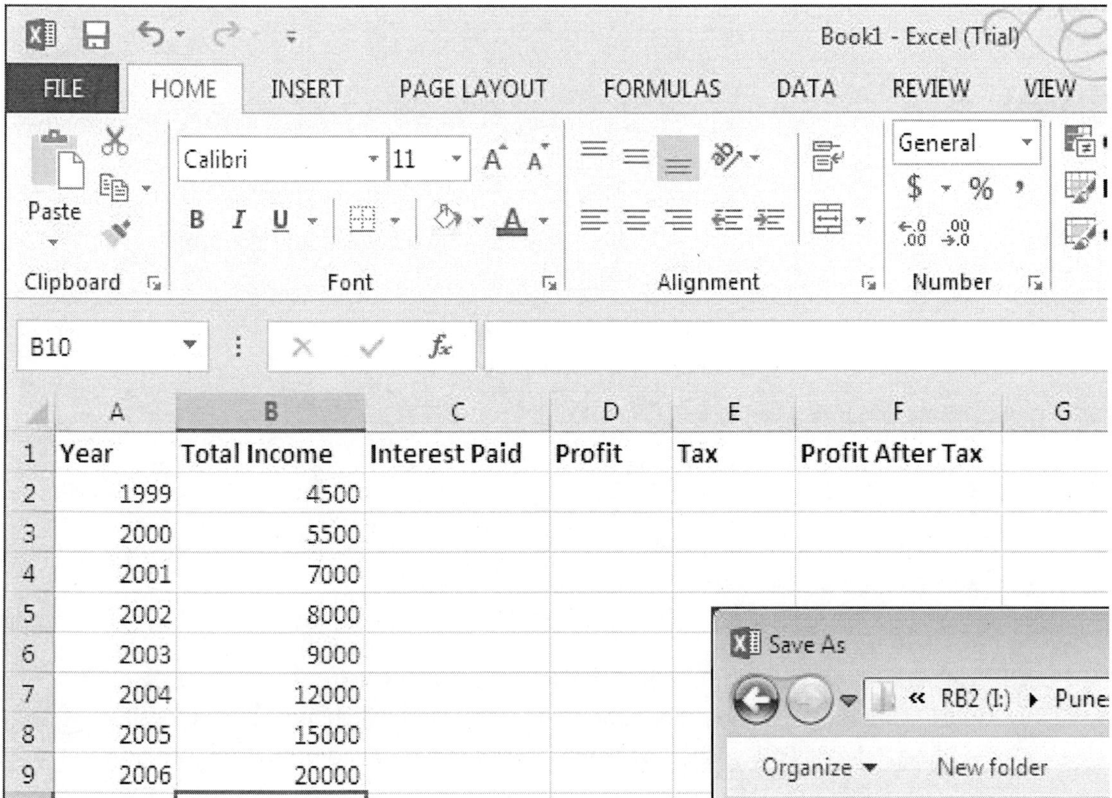

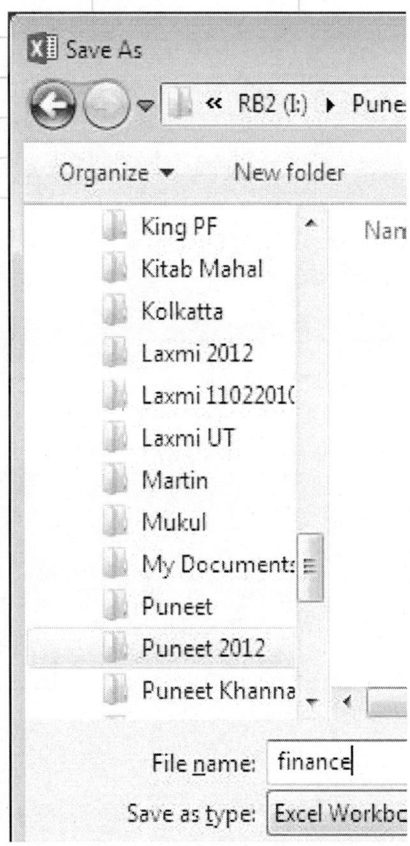

It would not be a bad idea to save this worksheet at this stage. For god forbid, if something happens, like power cut or so. So just press **Ctrl+S** to give the save command, as you would give in any other software. Now all you have to do it to give it a name and decide where you want to save this worksheet. Let us give the name **Finance** to it.

Now we come to the interesting part of this worksheet. So far we have typed whatever was available. Now we have to generate the figures. The column **C** is of Interest Paid which is to be calculated by using the formula.

$$\text{Interest Paid} = \frac{\text{Total Income} \times 15}{100}$$

Transformed to the computer language it will become:

Interest Paid = (Total Income x 15)/100

If we put this in Cell **C2**, it will become:

C2 = SUM(B2*15/100)

Try putting this in the cell **C2** and see the result. It will be as shown below. It has given a figure of 675. Calculate the amount manually to see whether the result is Ok or not. It is correct, isn't it? Now we have to apply this formula to all the cells from **C3** to **C9**. Do you have to put the formula for each cell or there is a method in Excel which allows you to copy the formula in each of the cell.

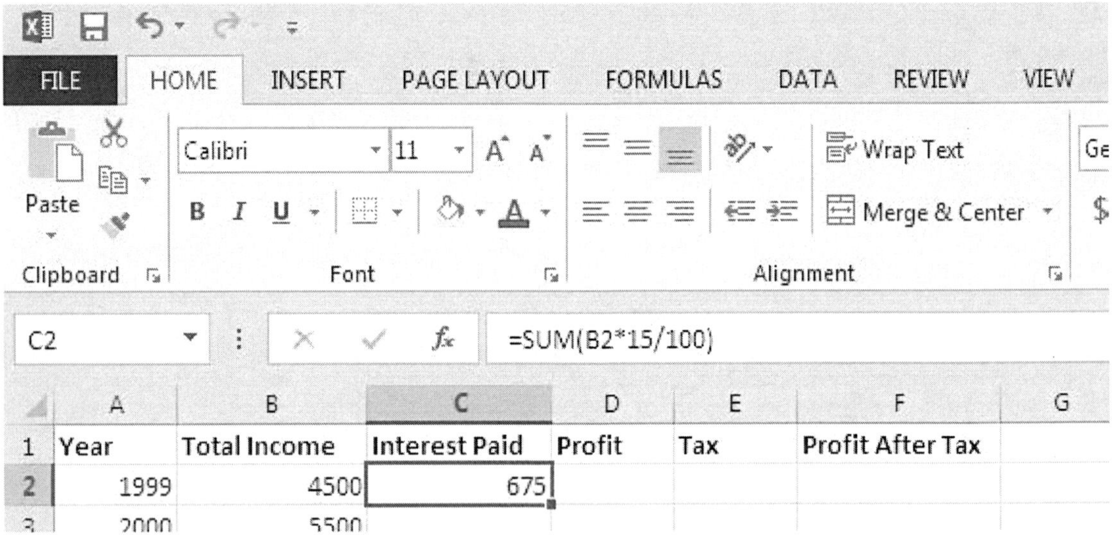

Well, fortunately there is. So this is how you will do it.

Copying Formula

1. Click at cell C2 to have the formula displayed in the formula bar.
2. Now with your mouse having clicked at cell C2, press the right button of the mouse.
3. You will get a dialog box, as shown below, which has various commands at your disposal.

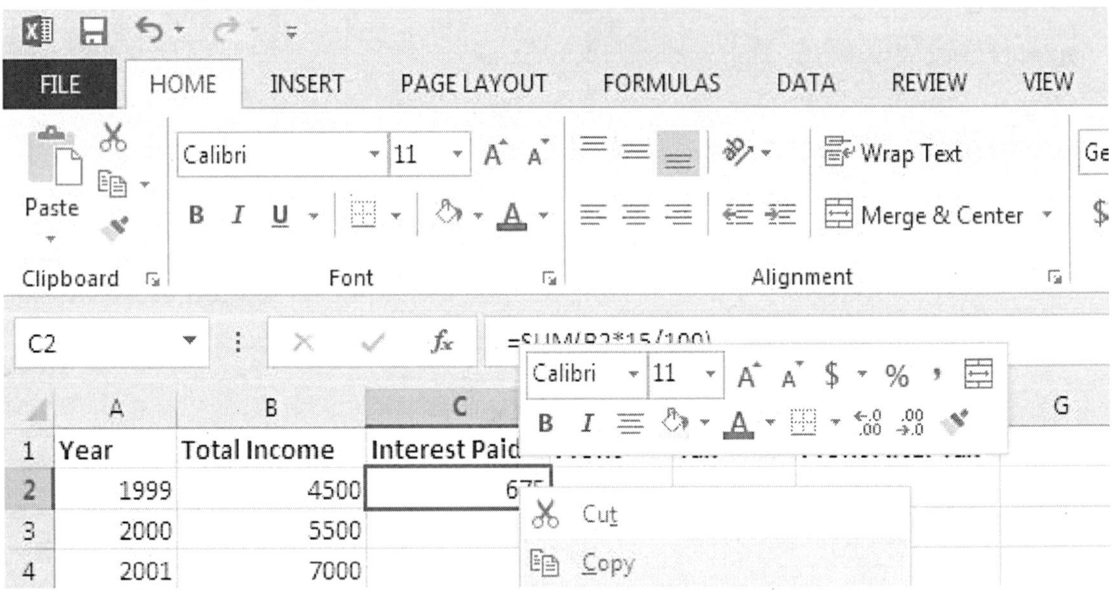

4. Choose copy, as shown here, to copy the formula.
5. Next step now is to paste the formula in their respective cells.

6. Now click at cell C3 with the mouse (left button).
7. Click the right button again to get the dialog box.
8. This time click at Paste instead, as shown next.

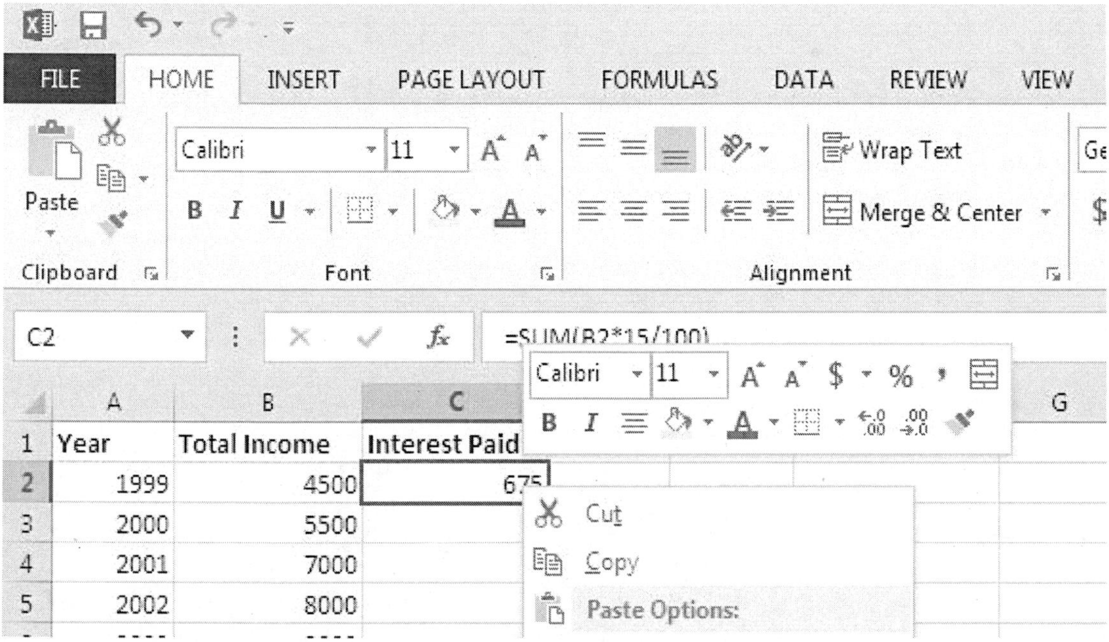

9. Immediately you will get the figure in cell C3.

   This calculation has been based on B3 (see the formula bar) and not B2 which had been copied in our formula. Is it not great? Excel has changed the cell address for you. This is called relative addressing and is a very useful feature of Excel.
10. Similar pasting in the cells from C4 to C9 can also be done.
11. Once done your worksheet should look like the one shown next.

Remember

1. You can take out the dotted lines blinking around the cell C2 by pressing the Esc key.

One look at the worksheet and you will notice that something is wrong. Some figures have no decimals and some have one. This does not look good. So what will you do? You will make them uniform. This is how:

1. Highlight all the cells from C2 to C9.
2. From the Home menu, click at General in Number panel.
3. Choose the category of Number to make all the cell data into 2 digits of numbers.
4. All your cells now have 2 places of decimals, as shown below.

Now that we have all the figures of Column **C** ready, we can proceed ahead to the next column, i.e., **D**. This column has "Profit", which is nothing but the difference of "Income" and "Interest". So let us calculate that.

Click at cell **D2** and put the formula

=SUM(B2 – C2)

This will give you the figure for **D2**. Calculate it manually to make sure that the formula is right.

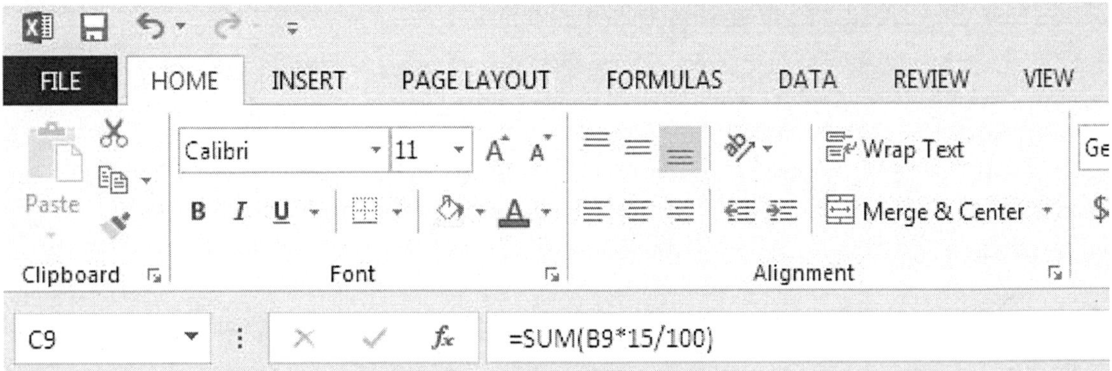

	A	B	C	D	E	F	G
1	Year	Total Income	Interest Paid	Profit	Tax	Profit After Tax	
2	1999	4500	675				
3	2000	5500	825				
4	2001	7000	1050				
5	2002	8000	1200				
6	2003	9000	1350				
7	2004	12000	1800				
8	2005	15000	2250				
9	2006	20000	3000				

Now, as we had done in the earlier case of Interest Paid, we will copy the formula and paste it in other cell, as shown below. One by one you would be able to calculate all the figures of Profit and would be able to fill up the whole column **D**. After you have done so, your worksheet would look like the one shown below. These figures have been corrected to 2 places of decimals as was done in the earlier case.

Next in line is the column called Tax. This is as said earlier, 12% of the Profit. So this can be calculated as below:

$$\text{Tax} = \frac{\text{Profit} \times 12}{100}$$

Transformed to the computer language it will become:

Tax= (Profit x 12)/100

If we put this in Cell **E2**, it will become:

E2 = SUM(D2*12/100)

Let us apply this formula in **E2** and see what happens. It gives you the result as 459. Copying this formula to the other cells, i.e., from **E3** to **E9**, you can fill up the whole column and make the worksheet look like the one shown next.

The last column in this case is the "Profit After Tax", which can be calculated after subtracting "Tax" from the "Profit". This calculation I am not showing here, since I assume that you should be able to do this easily. However, your resultant worksheet should look like the one shown next.

You think the worksheet is complete. No. You still have to do the column totals without which the whole worksheet looks incomplete.

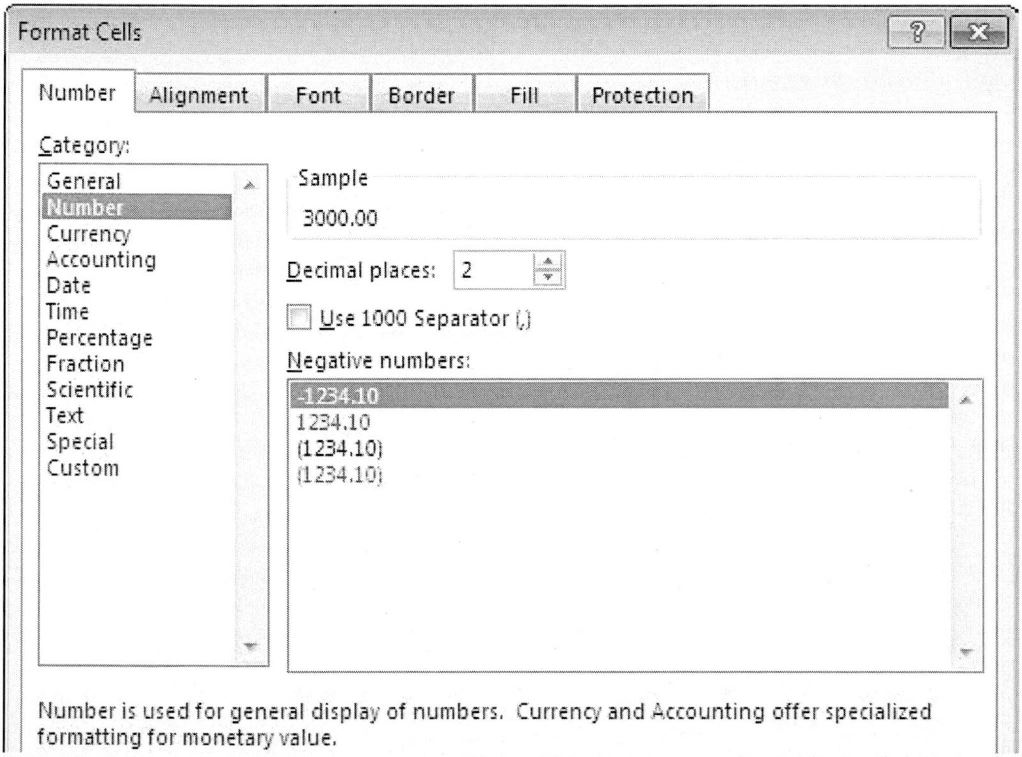
Format Cells
Number
Alignment
Font
Border
Fill
Protection
Category:
General
Number
Currency
Accounting
Date
Time
Percentage
Fraction
Scientific
Text
Special
Custom
Sample
3000.00
Decimal places: 2
Use 1000 Separator (,)
Negative numbers:
-1234.10
1234.10
(1234.10)
(1234.10)
Number is used for general display of numbers. Currency and Accounting offer specialized formatting for monetary value.

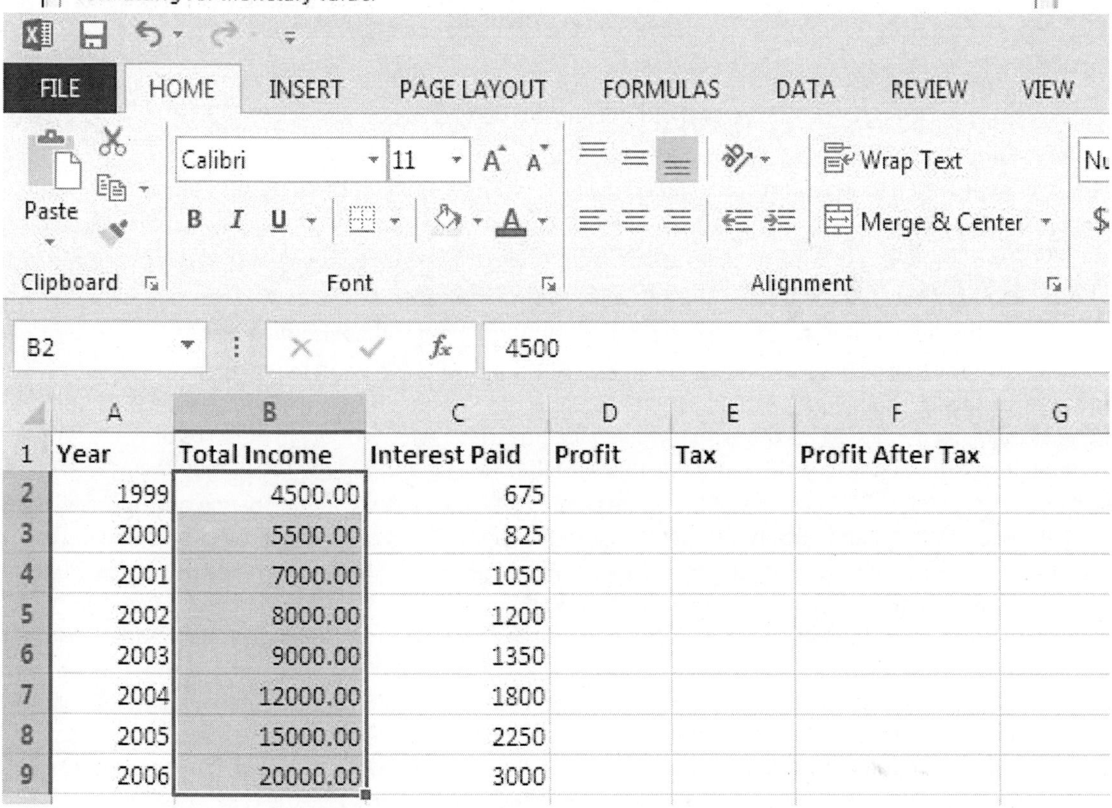
FILE
HOME
INSERT
PAGE LAYOUT
FORMULAS
DATA
REVIEW
VIEW
Paste
Calibri
11
Wrap Text
Merge & Center
Clipboard
Font
Alignment
B2
4500
A
B
C
D
E
F
G
1 Year
Total Income
Interest Paid
Profit
Tax
Profit After Tax
2 1999 4500.00 675
3 2000 5500.00 825
4 2001 7000.00 1050
5 2002 8000.00 1200
6 2003 9000.00 1350
7 2004 12000.00 1800
8 2005 15000.00 2250
9 2006 20000.00 3000

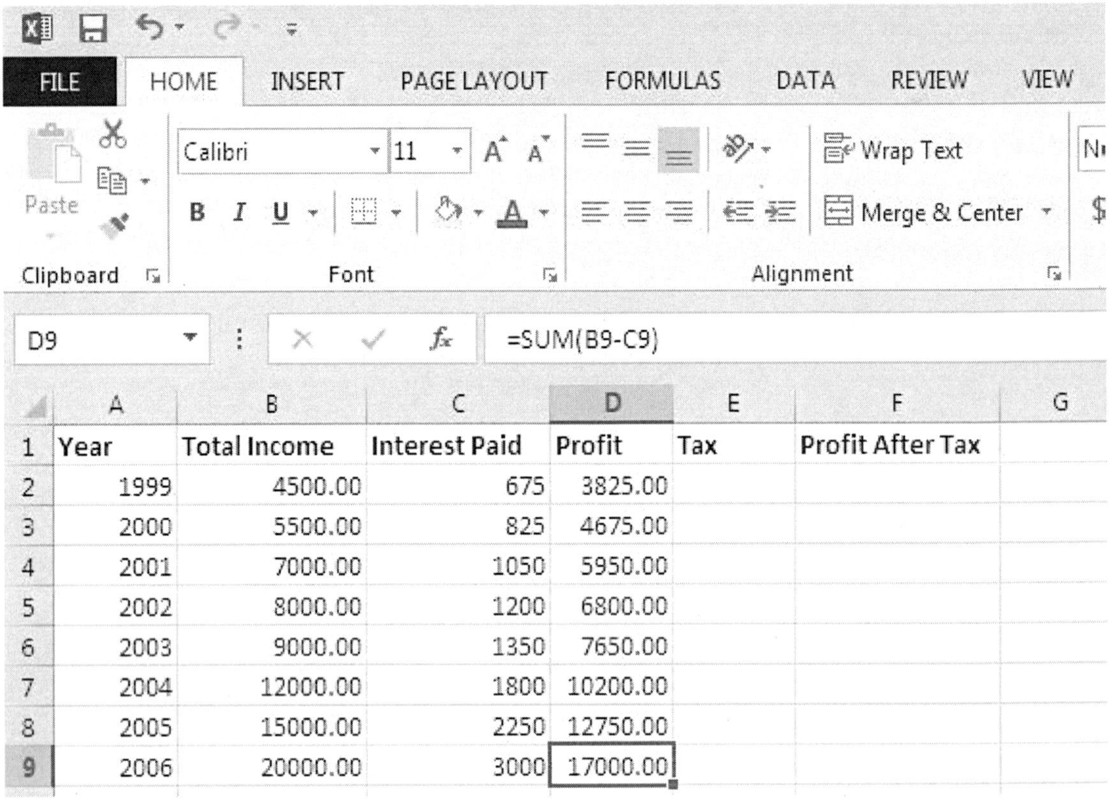

	A	B	C	D	E	F	G
1	Year	Total Income	Interest Paid	Profit	Tax	Profit After Tax	
2	1999	4500.00	675	3825.00			
3	2000	5500.00	825	4675.00			
4	2001	7000.00	1050	5950.00			
5	2002	8000.00	1200	6800.00			
6	2003	9000.00	1350	7650.00			
7	2004	12000.00	1800	10200.00			
8	2005	15000.00	2250	12750.00			
9	2006	20000.00	3000	17000.00			

For this follow the following steps.

1. Click at cell B10 to get the total of figures from B2 to B9.
2. Now click at Σ symbol in the Home menu.
3. It will search for the numeric cells above and put the formula for the same and highlight the cells it has selected.
4. It will wait for your Ok in the form of Enter to put the result.
5. Press Enter to get the total in the cell B10, as shown below.

Similarly all the other columns can be summed up showing the result as shown next.

Now you can say that your worksheet is complete. But, supposing we want to make any change. This is done delibrately to show you the main advantage of Excel software. Supposing, we change the figure of the year 2003 from 9,000 to 9,200, which we can assume that it was wrongly given to us or was a typing mistake. It is shown next. Try changing this figure in the cell **B6** and see the resultant effect.

What have you noticed? Well since all the figures are mostly inter-linked, if you change one figure all the relative figures change automatically. This is the main advantage of Excel or for that an electronic spreadsheet.

Now if you apply this to the accounting department and assume that these figures relate to actual working of the finance department. Try changing the figures of one voucher and the poor accountant would have to sit probably the whole night to recalculate all the totals in the Balance Sheet. But, now with this kind of spreadsheet, this can be done in a flash. Coming back to our worksheet. There are 3 things more to be done. Firstly, we will decorate it using the options available in Excel 2013. After seeing a preview of our worksheet and we will print it on our printer. For decorating in Excel 2013, we have the command called Conditional Formatting, which is on the Home menu. It has various options which can be used. I have gone for the one which is of color scales and have applied one of them. See the result next.

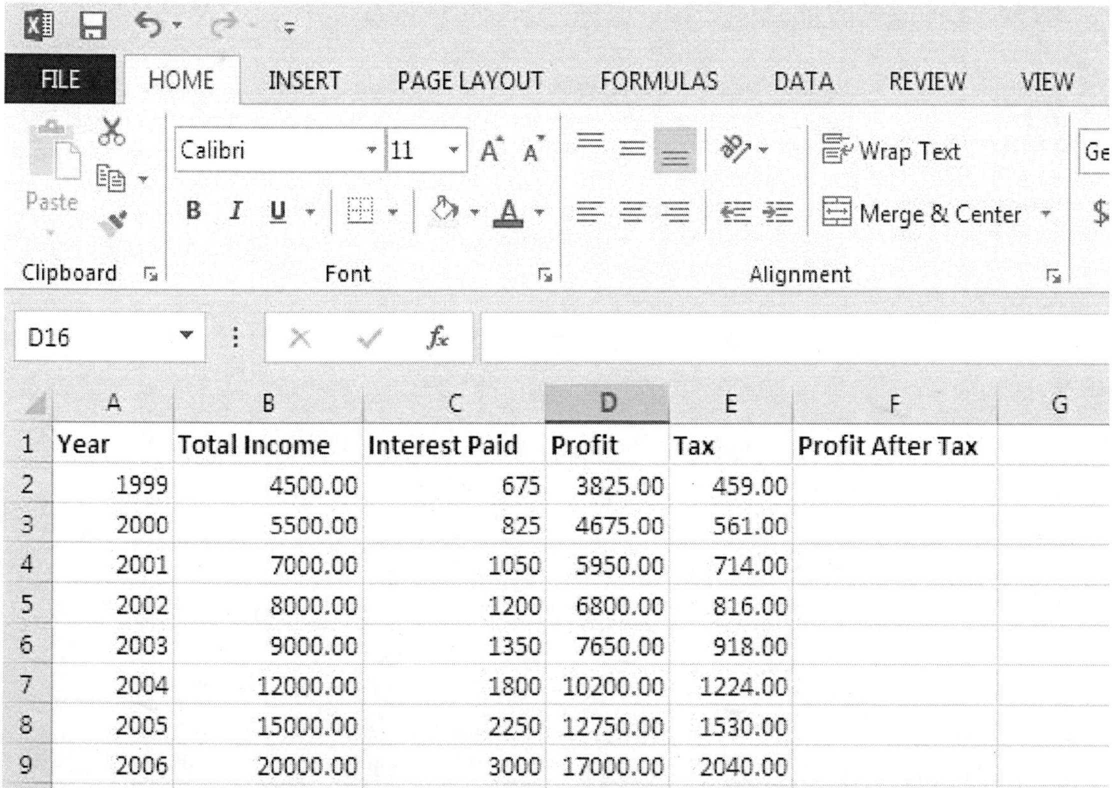
FILE HOME INSERT PAGE LAYOUT FORMULAS DATA REVIEW VIEW
Paste
Calibri 11
Wrap Text
Merge & Center
Clipboard
Font
Alignment
D16
A B C D E F G
1 Year Total Income Interest Paid Profit Tax Profit After Tax
2 1999 4500.00 675 3825.00 459.00
3 2000 5500.00 825 4675.00 561.00
4 2001 7000.00 1050 5950.00 714.00
5 2002 8000.00 1200 6800.00 816.00
6 2003 9000.00 1350 7650.00 918.00
7 2004 12000.00 1800 10200.00 1224.00
8 2005 15000.00 2250 12750.00 1530.00
9 2006 20000.00 3000 17000.00 2040.00

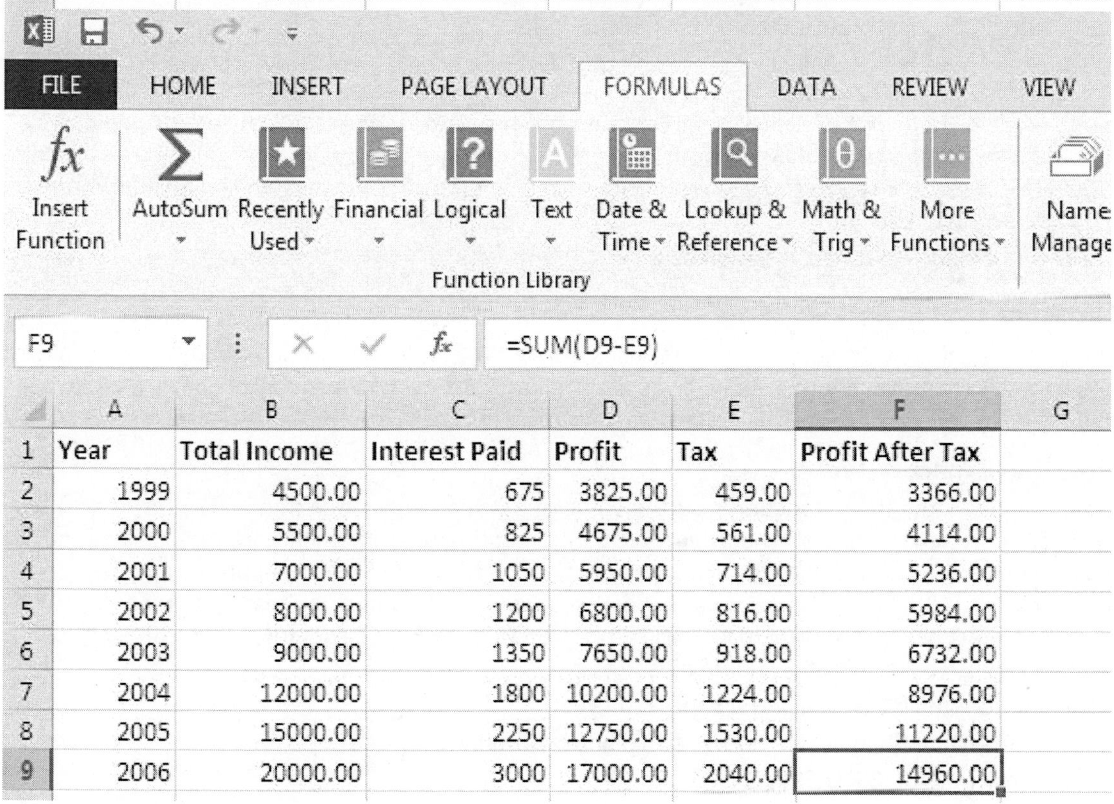
FILE HOME INSERT PAGE LAYOUT FORMULAS DATA REVIEW VIEW
Insert Function
AutoSum
Recently Used
Financial
Logical
Text
Date & Time
Lookup & Reference
Math & Trig
More Functions
Function Library
F9
=SUM(D9-E9)
A B C D E F G
1 Year Total Income Interest Paid Profit Tax Profit After Tax
2 1999 4500.00 675 3825.00 459.00 3366.00
3 2000 5500.00 825 4675.00 561.00 4114.00
4 2001 7000.00 1050 5950.00 714.00 5236.00
5 2002 8000.00 1200 6800.00 816.00 5984.00
6 2003 9000.00 1350 7650.00 918.00 6732.00
7 2004 12000.00 1800 10200.00 1224.00 8976.00
8 2005 15000.00 2250 12750.00 1530.00 11220.00
9 2006 20000.00 3000 17000.00 2040.00 14960.00

You are free to choose any one of them and decorate your worksheet as you wish. As you move your

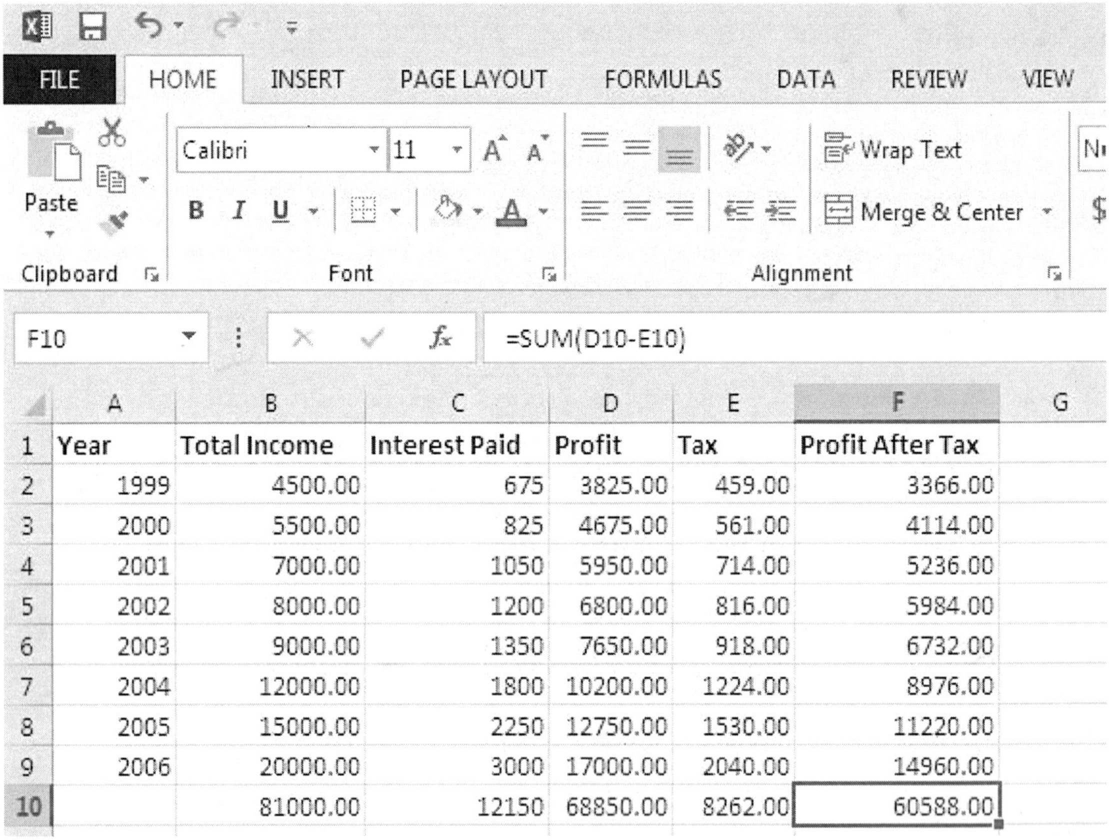

	A	B	C	D	E	F	G
1	Year	Total Income	Interest Paid	Profit	Tax	Profit After Tax	
2	1999	4500.00	675	3825.00	459.00	3366.00	
3	2000	5500.00	825	4675.00	561.00	4114.00	
4	2001	7000.00	1050	5950.00	714.00	5236.00	
5	2002	8000.00	1200	6800.00	816.00	5984.00	
6	2003	9000.00	1350	7650.00	918.00	6732.00	
7	2004	12000.00	1800	10200.00	1224.00	8976.00	
8	2005	15000.00	2250	12750.00	1530.00	11220.00	
9	2006	20000.00	3000	17000.00	2040.00	14960.00	
10		81000.00	12150	68850.00	8262.00	60588.00	

mouse over the options the resultant effect on the worksheet is also shown, which helps you in making the decisions. Now that you have to print it on your printer to see the final result. But, before that we would like to see its **Preview**. This command is part of the **Print** command which is available under the **Options button**.

The preview of the worksheet is shown next.

Formulas That Make Decisions

There will be a time when you want Excel to carry out one task under certain circumstances and another task if those circumstances don't apply. If you are familiar with any programming language, it is the case of IF, WHEN or IF, THEN. You have a similar IF function in Excel.

How the IF function works

In its simplest form, the IF function tests the value of a cell and does one thing if the test is positive (**TRUE**) and another if the test is negative (**FALSE**). It requires three arguments: the test data, the action to perform if the test is TRUE and the action to perform if the test is FALSE. You supply the arguments one after the other within the function's parentheses, separating them with commas (no spaces are to be given). The text which you want to appear as it is, i.e., TRUE or FALSE should be given under quotes, reference of cells like **C5**, etc., should be as it is.

Apply this formula in cell **B6** and see the result:

1. Select cell B6, type the following in place of formula and press Enter:

   = IF(B2=0, TRUE, FALSE)

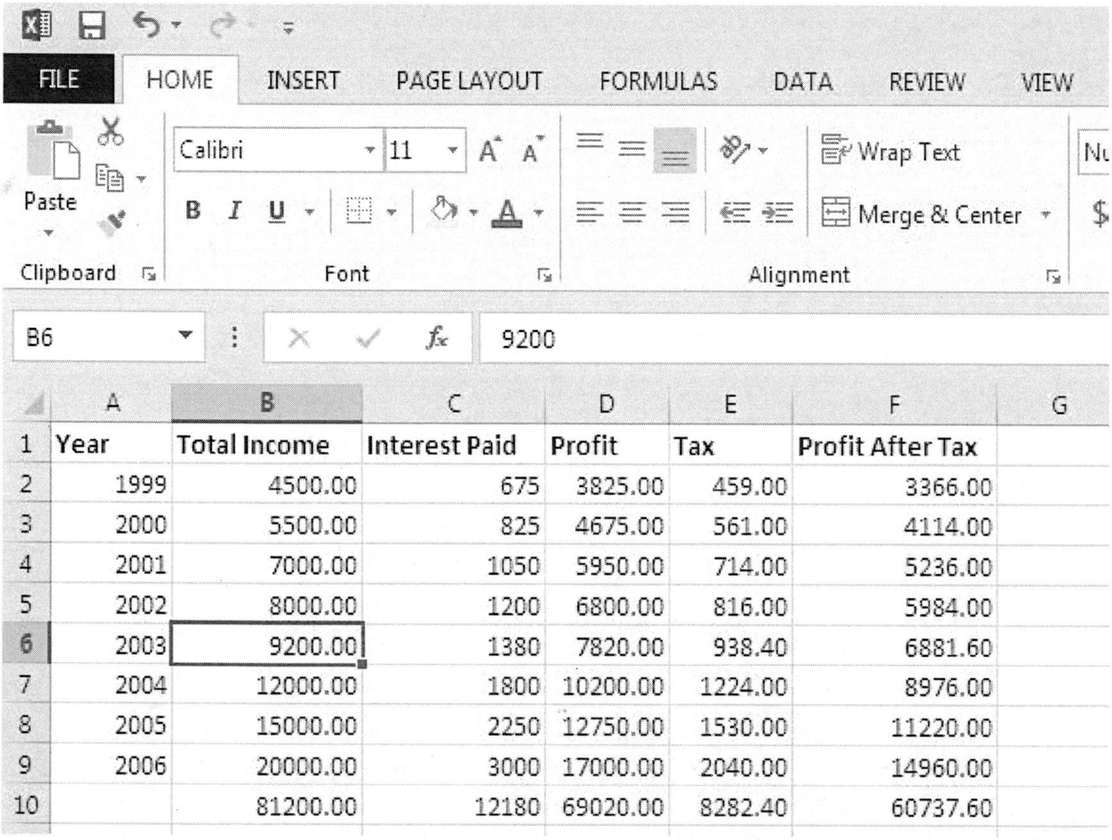

	A	B	C	D	E	F
1	Year	Total Income	Interest Paid	Profit	Tax	Profit After Tax
2	1999	4500.00	675	3825.00	459.00	3366.00
3	2000	5500.00	825	4675.00	561.00	4114.00
4	2001	7000.00	1050	5950.00	714.00	5236.00
5	2002	8000.00	1200	6800.00	816.00	5984.00
6	2003	9200.00	1380	7820.00	938.40	6881.60
7	2004	12000.00	1800	10200.00	1224.00	8976.00
8	2005	15000.00	2250	12750.00	1530.00	11220.00
9	2006	20000.00	3000	17000.00	2040.00	14960.00
10		81200.00	12180	69020.00	8282.40	60737.60

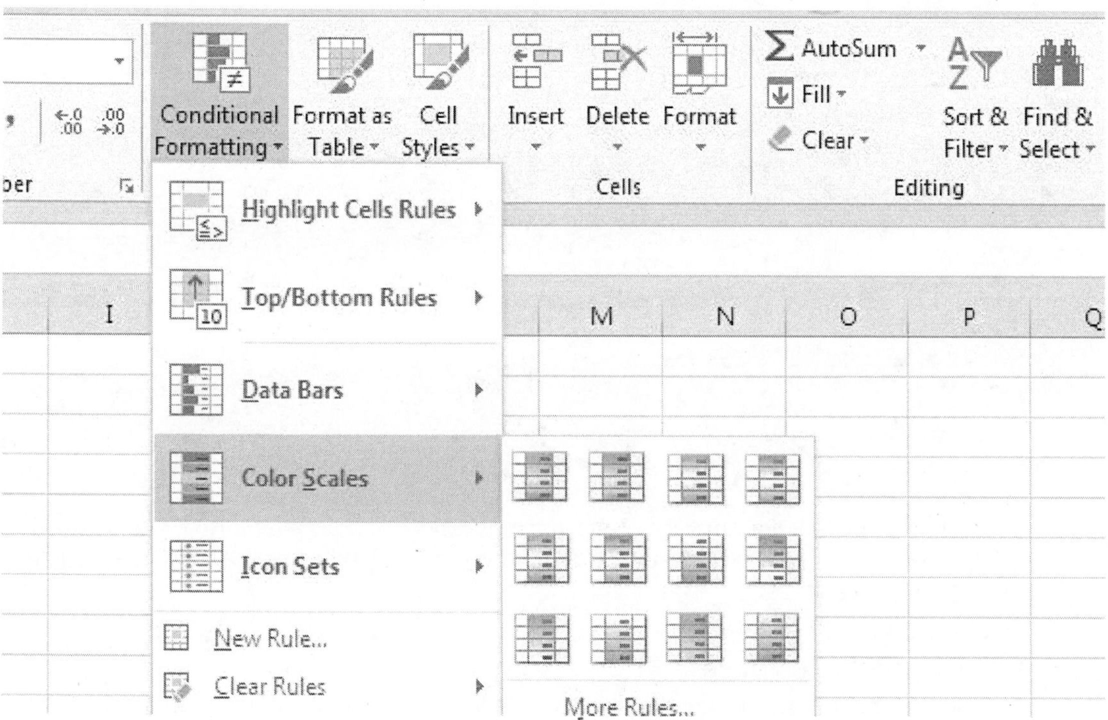

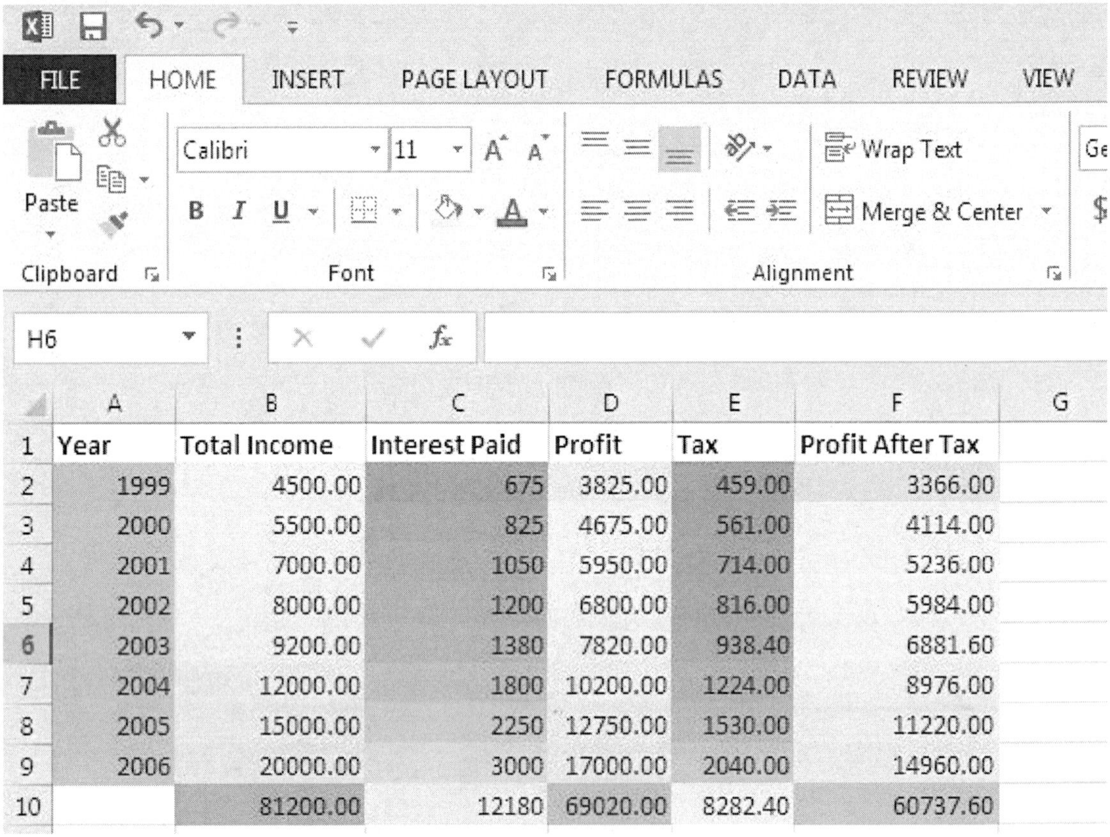

	A	B	C	D	E	F	G
1	Year	Total Income	Interest Paid	Profit	Tax	Profit After Tax	
2	1999	4500.00	675	3825.00	459.00	3366.00	
3	2000	5500.00	825	4675.00	561.00	4114.00	
4	2001	7000.00	1050	5950.00	714.00	5236.00	
5	2002	8000.00	1200	6800.00	816.00	5984.00	
6	2003	9200.00	1380	7820.00	938.40	6881.60	
7	2004	12000.00	1800	10200.00	1224.00	8976.00	
8	2005	15000.00	2250	12750.00	1530.00	11220.00	
9	2006	20000.00	3000	17000.00	2040.00	14960.00	
10		81200.00	12180	69020.00	8282.40	60737.60	

Year	Total Income	Interest Paid	Profit	Tax	Profit After Tax
1999	4,500.00	675.00	3,825.00	459.00	3,366.00
2000	5,500.00	825.00	4,675.00	561.00	4,114.00
2001	7,000.00	1050.00	5,950.00	714.00	5,236.00
2002	8,000.00	1200.00	6,800.00	816.00	5,984.00
2003	9,200.00	1380.00	7,820.00	938.40	6,881.60
2004	12,000.00	1800.00	10,200.00	1,224.00	8,976.00
2005	15,000.00	2250.00	12,750.00	1,530.00	11,220.00
2006	20,000.00	3000.00	17,000.00	2,040.00	14,960.00
	81,200.00	12180.00	69,020.00	8,282.40	60,737.60

Excel checks whether the value in cell B2 is zero (the test), and because it isn't zero, it ignores TRUE (the action to perform if the test is TRUE) and displays FALSE (the action to perform if the test is FALSE) in cell B6.

2. Double-click cell B6, change formula to

   = IF(B2>1000, TRUE, FALSE)

   and press Enter. The entry in cell B6 instantly changes from FALSE to TRUE because the value in cell B2 is greater than one thousand; that is, the test is TRUE.

Both the options can be seen next.

Now this was very simple. Isn't it. However, you can also build tests that involve other functions. Suppose that in our Finance worksheet, we say that the Tax has to be a minimum of 1000, which means that if the Tax is less than 1000 it has to be put as 1000 and if it more that 1000, then the figure will stand as it is.

For this perform the following steps.

1. Click at any entry in E and select to insert a column from Insert Menu.
2. Use the Cut, Paste and Format buttons to restore the entries now in E2:E9 to F2:F9.
3. Click at F2 and apply the formula

   =IF(E2>1000, E2, 1000)

   This means that you are asking the system to check if it is above 1000, One of the two possibilities will arise:

TRUE This means that the figure in cell is more than 1000, then the column will be replaced by the figure in **E2**, which means that it is not changed.

FALSE This means that the figure in the cell **E2** is less than 1000, then the second condition will be met, i.e., figure in cell **F2** will be replaced with the figure of 1000.

Repeat this for all the other cells of column **F**. The easiest way out to repeat the formula in each column.

Next we work with various commands of Excel 2013.

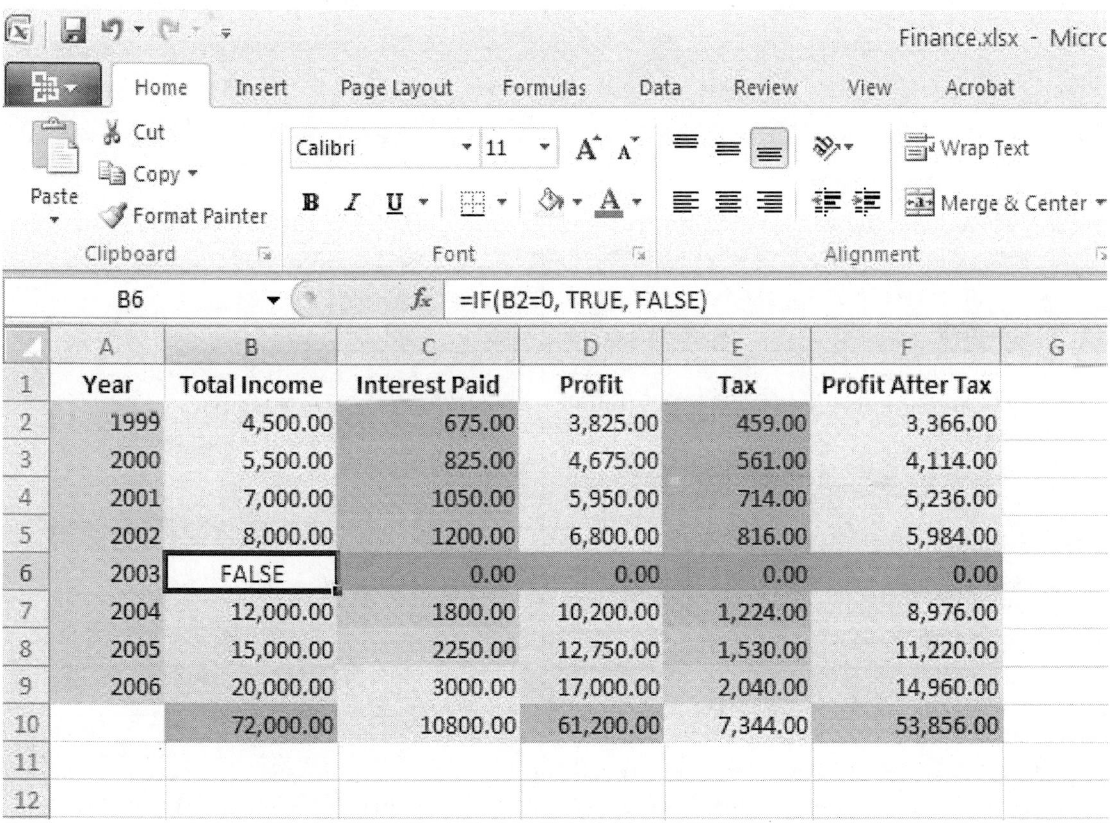

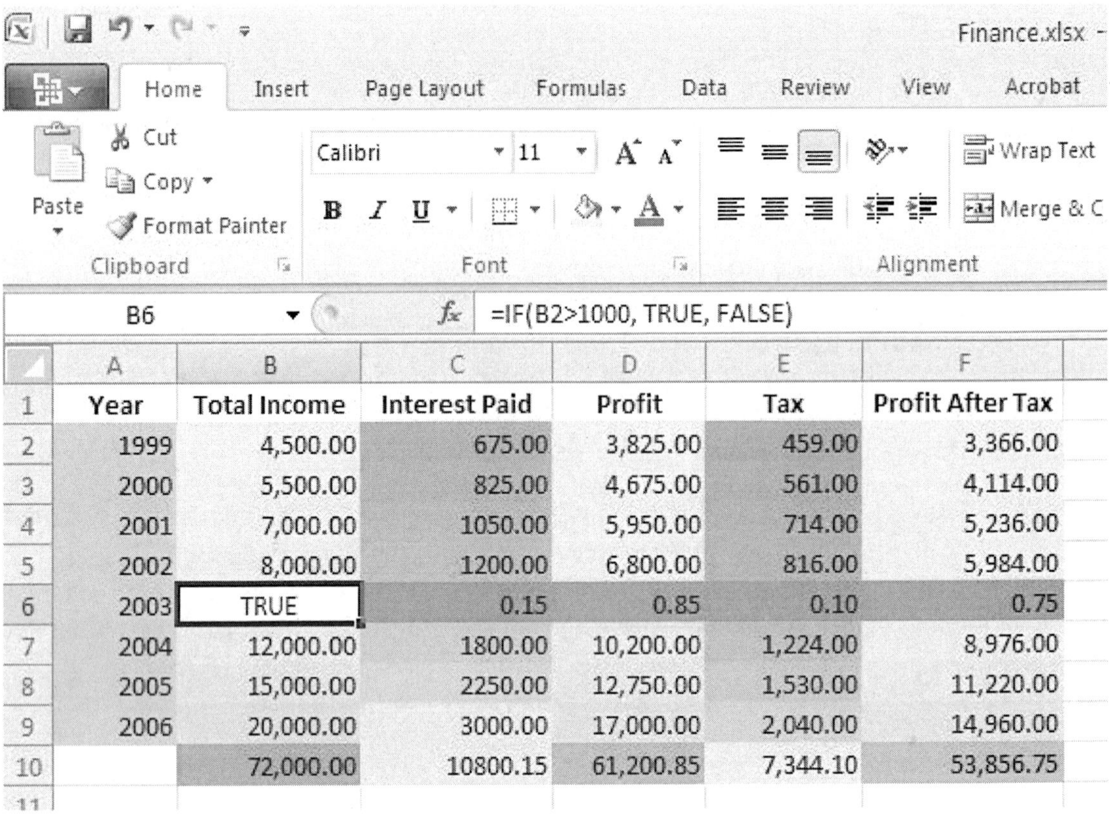

Styles

Create a Style by Example

1. Select cell containing desired formats
2. Click Cell Styles in the Home Panel.
3. It will show the various style sheet options available.
4. In the end there is an option of Create New Style which allows you to create one of your own.
3. Type a name for style in Style Name: The style's formats in Style includes box.

Exclude formats of selected cell from style:

1. Deselect Style Includes (by example) options: Number, Alignment, Font, Border, Fill, Protection
2. Click Ok.

Functions in Excel

They establish relationships between two or more cells.

If you want to add the values in cells A3 and A4 and put the result in cell A5, move to the cell A5 and

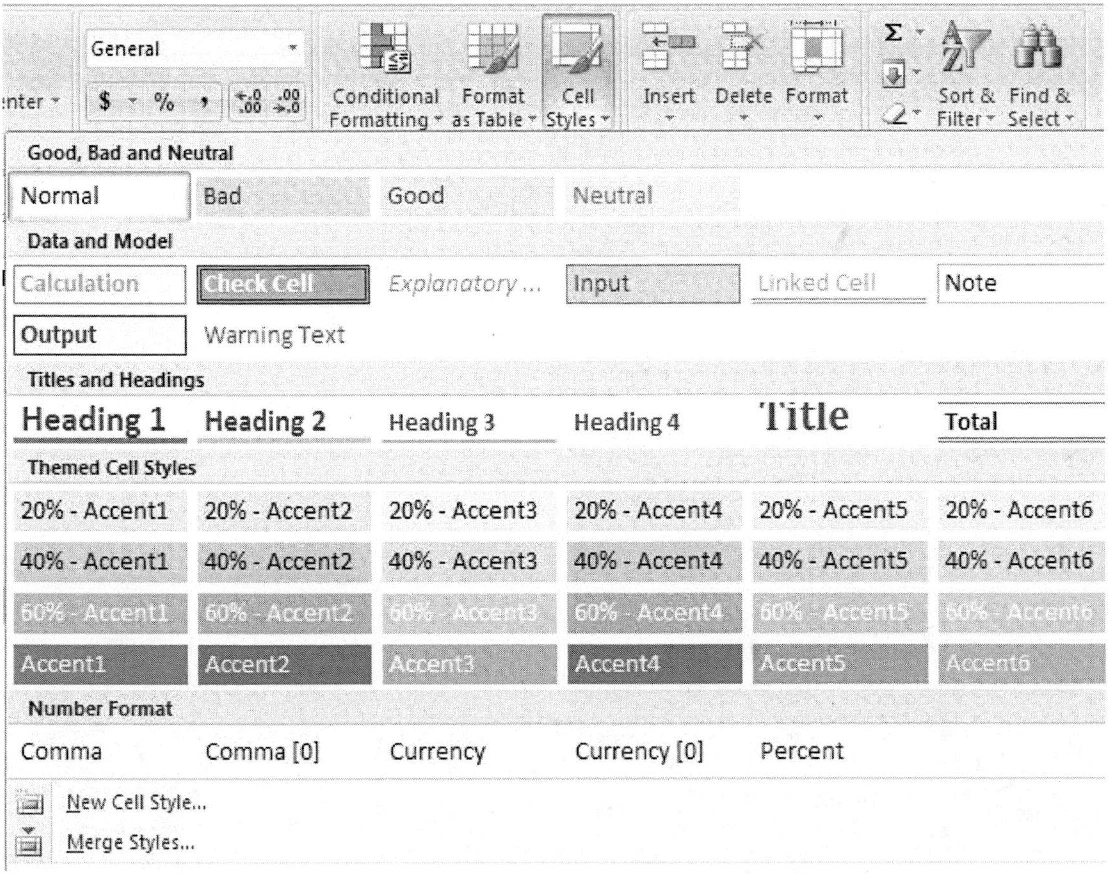

type =A3+A4 and press Enter. The result is displayed immediately in cell A5. Another way to achieve the same result is to move to cell A5 and type +, point to cell A3, type +, then point to A4, and press Enter. The easiest way to achieve this operation is to point to A5, pick up the AutoSum button Σ on the toolbar.

The following symbols have their specific meaning in the formulae which are used in Excel.

Symbol	*Description*	*Symbol*	*Description*
:	Reference operator	,	Argument operator
–	Negation	%	Percentage sign
^	Exponent	*	Multiplication
/	Division	+	Addition
–	Subtraction	&	Text concatenation
>	Greater than	<	Less than
>=	Greater than or equal to	<=	Less than or equal to
< >	Not equal to		

While working with the formulae you would come across the various errors too, which could happen due to wrong use of formula or wrong typing. The following are the common type of errors.

Error Type	Description
# # # #	the column is not wide enough to display the number so either widen the column, or reduce the font size or change the numeric format.
# DIV/0!	Dividing by zero is invalid
# N/A	Data is not available. It happens usually when you refer to a function or value where data is not available
# NAME?	The formula references a name that is unknown to Excel
# NUM !	The formula is using an invalid number
# REF !	A cell reference is not available may be because you deleted that cell or moved another cell onto it.
# VALUE !	The formula contains an invalid operator or argument, for example, adding a text value to a numeric value

Using Autocalculate

It is very useful when you just want to total a number of columns but have the total in a particular field. The result will be displayed in Excel status bar and not in any cell. You can just view the sum. Perform the following steps to see the result.

1. Select the range whose total you want.
2. Right click at Status bar of the worksheet.
3. From the sub menu that appears, click at Sum.
4. The sum total would be displayed on the Status bar alongwith the sub menu, as shown next.

References

By default, Excel uses relative references in its formulae. Relative references refer to cells by their position in relation to the cell containing the formula. So when you copy the formula in cell F5 to cell F6, Excel changes the reference from E5 to E6.

Absolute references

When you don't want a reference to be copied as a relative reference, you need to use an absolute reference. Absolute references refer to cells by their fixed position in the worksheet. To make a reference absolute, you add dollar signs before its column letter and now number. For example, you would enter it as $C$4:$C$9. You could then copy formula that contained this reference anywhere on the worksheet and it would always refer to the range C4:C9.

Mixed references

References can also be partially relative and partially absolute. For example, $C3 has an absolute column reference and a relative row reference and C$3 has a relative column reference and an absolute row reference.

Sum Function

The Sum function is perhaps the most commonly used of the Excel functions that carry out mathematical, statistical, financial, date, time, and other calculations.

1. Click the destination cell for the formula.
2. Type an equal sign to start the formula and then type the word SUM and a left parenthesis.
3. Drag down the column of numbers to sum.
4. Press Enter.

Points to Remember

1. You do not need to type the close (right) parenthesis before you press Enter—Excel will do it for you.
2. Use this technique instead of AutoSum to sum ranges of cells that contain blanks.

Average Function

You can use the Average function to calculate the average of values in cells.

1. Click the cell where you want to place the average function.
2. Type an equal sign (=) and then type the word AVERAGE and a left parenthesis.
3. Drag across the cells whose values you want to average.
4. Press Enter.
5. Blank cells are not counted in average.

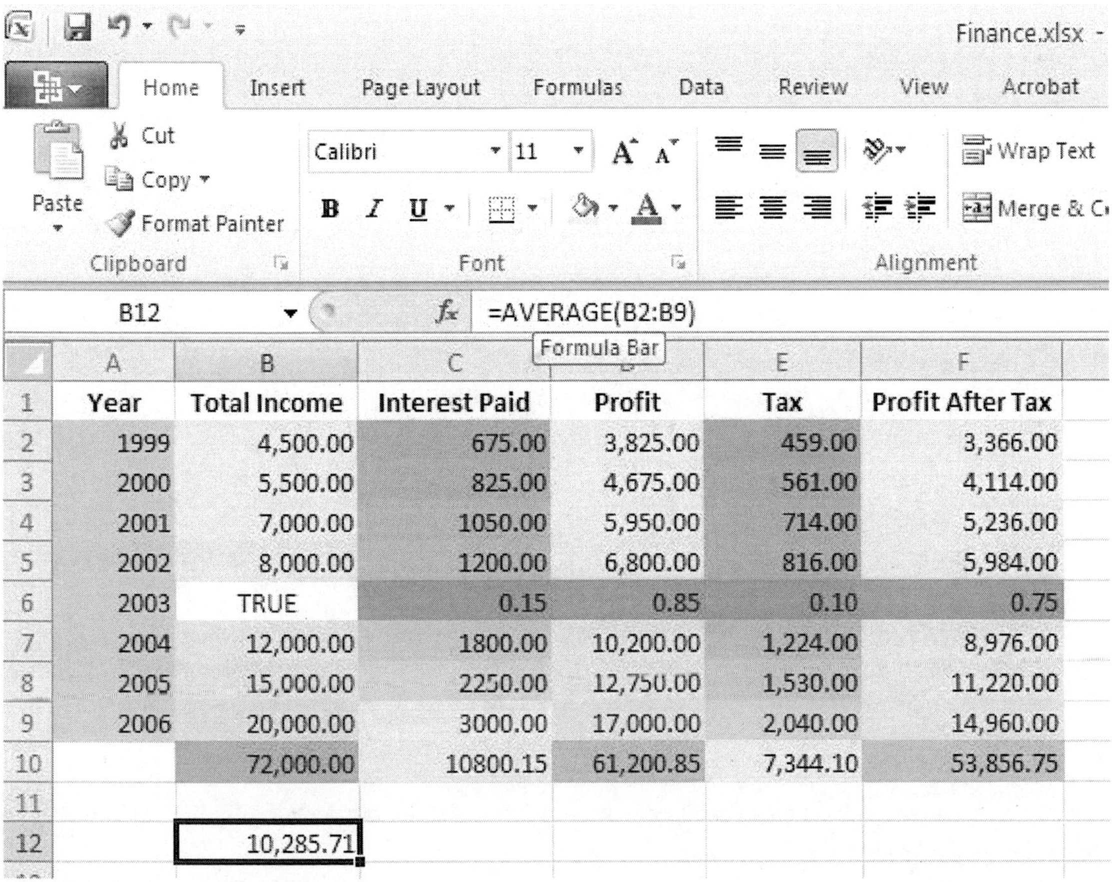

Creating Charts in Excel

In the earlier chapter we had created a worksheet and decorated it. There is another method of presenting this worksheet and that is by converting it into graphics and specially in the form of **Charts** in Excel.

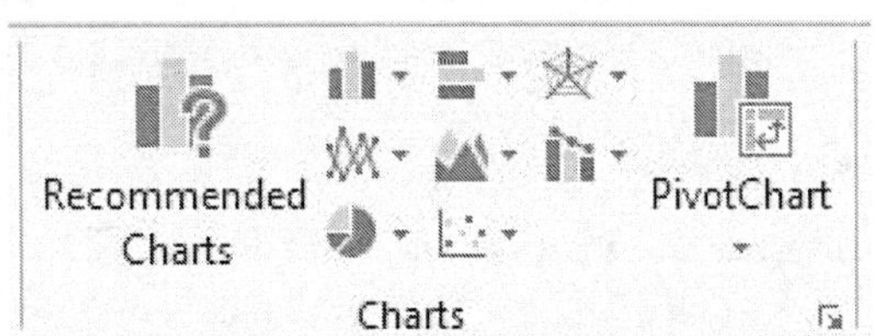

Let us use the same worksheet to make charts of the

same. Different type of charts which can be created using Excel 2013 are shown here. Each one of them has various options underneath which can be chosen. For example, the 3-D column chart of the worksheet created earlier would be as shown below.

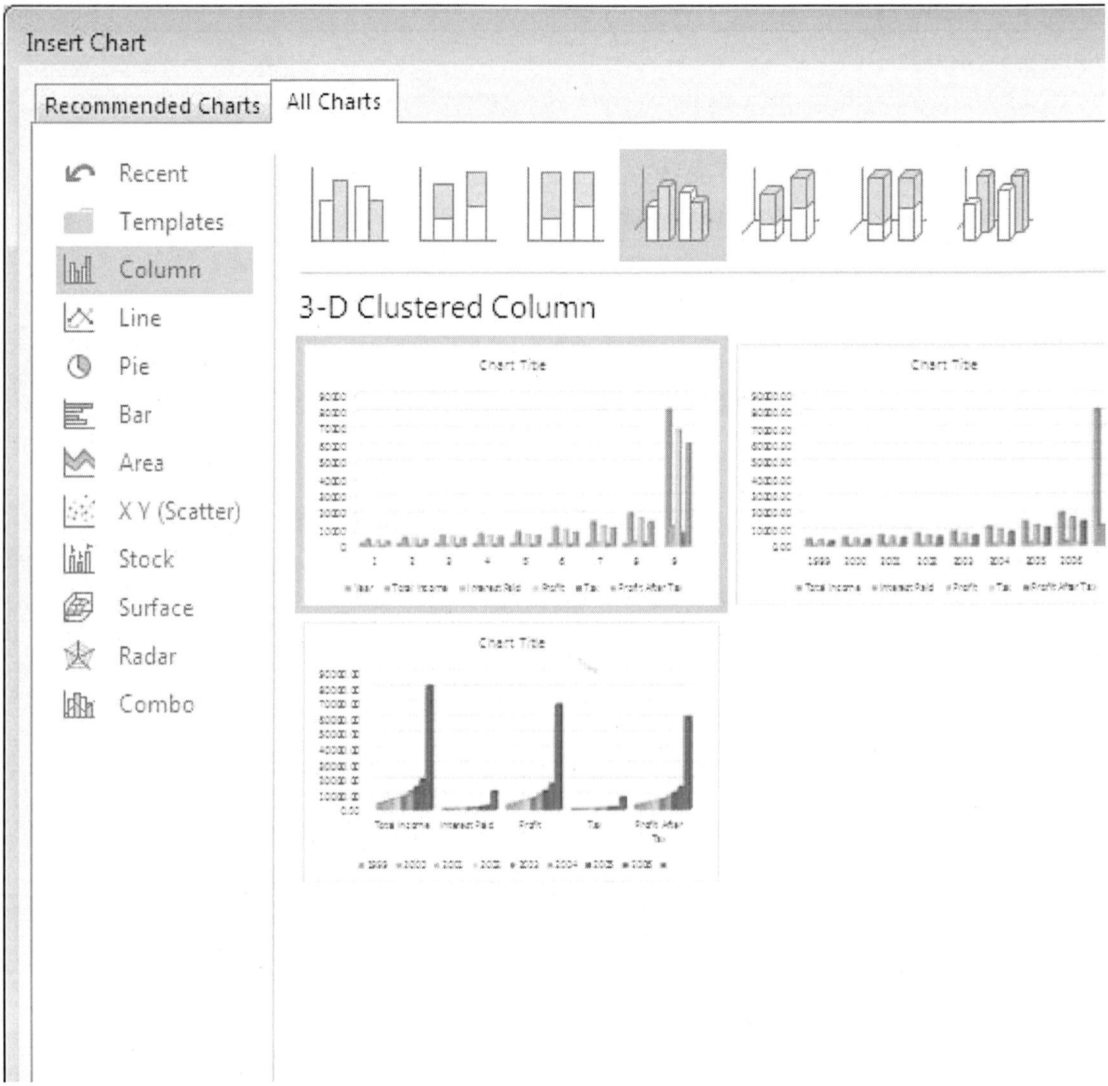

Similary you can create other type of charts. All these charts with their options can also be seen under All Chart Types under Other Charts.

Auditing a Workbook

To avoid bogus results from incorrect formulas, you can have Excel identify the cells that have supplied data for a formula. That way, you can easily see whether all the cells you wanted have been included in the calculation.

To Trace the Precedents for a Formula:

1. Select the cell or cells that contain the formulas.

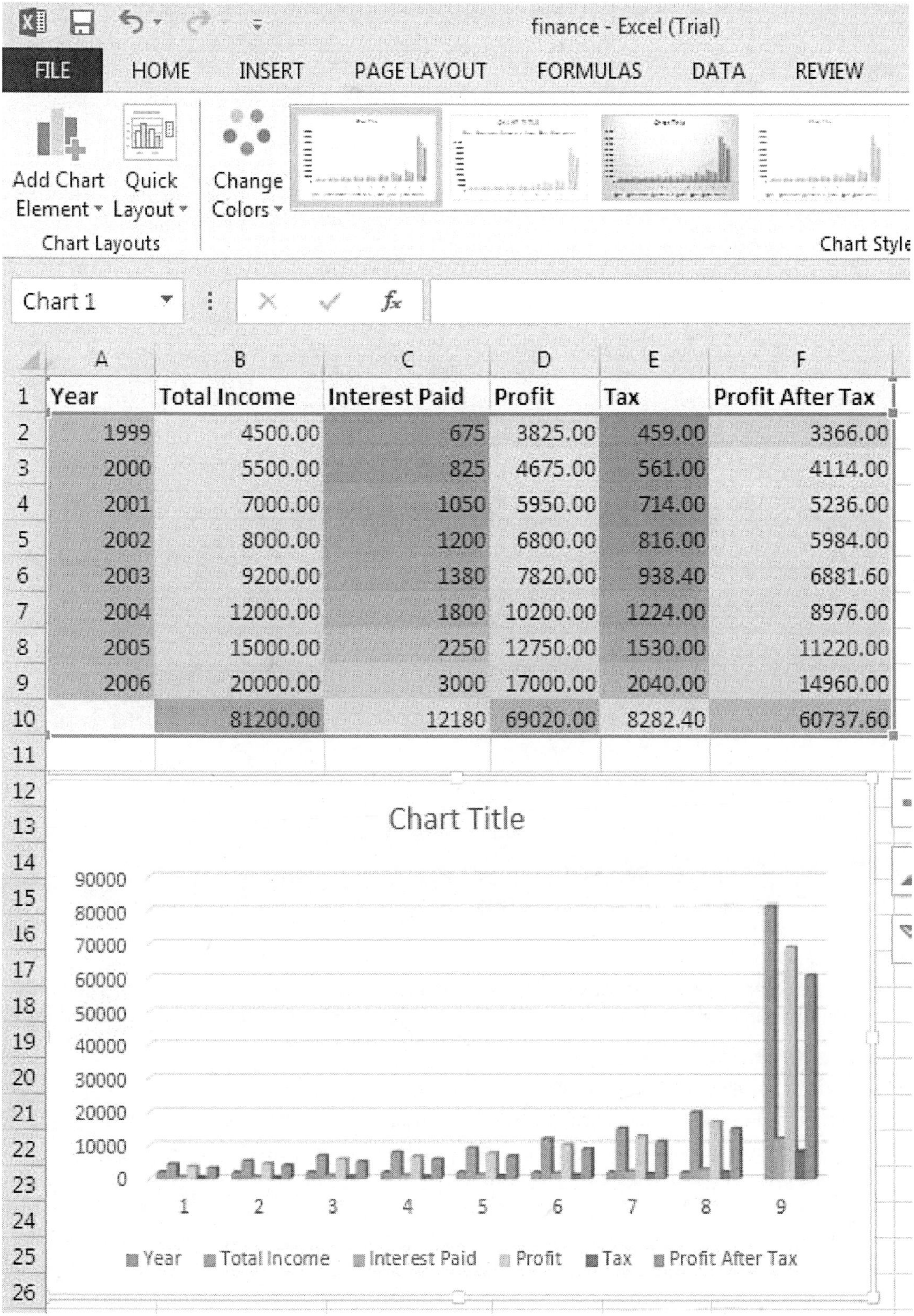

	A	B	C	D	E	F
1	Year	Total Income	Interest Paid	Profit	Tax	Profit After Tax
2	1999	4500.00	675	3825.00	459.00	3366.00
3	2000	5500.00	825	4675.00	561.00	4114.00
4	2001	7000.00	1050	5950.00	714.00	5236.00
5	2002	8000.00	1200	6800.00	816.00	5984.00
6	2003	9200.00	1380	7820.00	938.40	6881.60
7	2004	12000.00	1800	10200.00	1224.00	8976.00
8	2005	15000.00	2250	12750.00	1530.00	11220.00
9	2006	20000.00	3000	17000.00	2040.00	14960.00
10		81200.00	12180	69020.00	8282.40	60737.60

2. From the Formulas panel, choose Trace Precedents from Formula Auditing submenu.
3. Choose Trace Precedents again to view an additional level of precedents, if one exists.
4. This is shown below.

Remember

1. To clear the arrows that have appeared to show the cells that are included in the formula, choose Remove All Arrows from the Auditing submenu menu.
2. The Auditing toolbar contains Trace Precedents and Remove All Arrows buttons. To view the Auditing toolbar, choose Show Auditing Toolbar from the Auditing submenu.

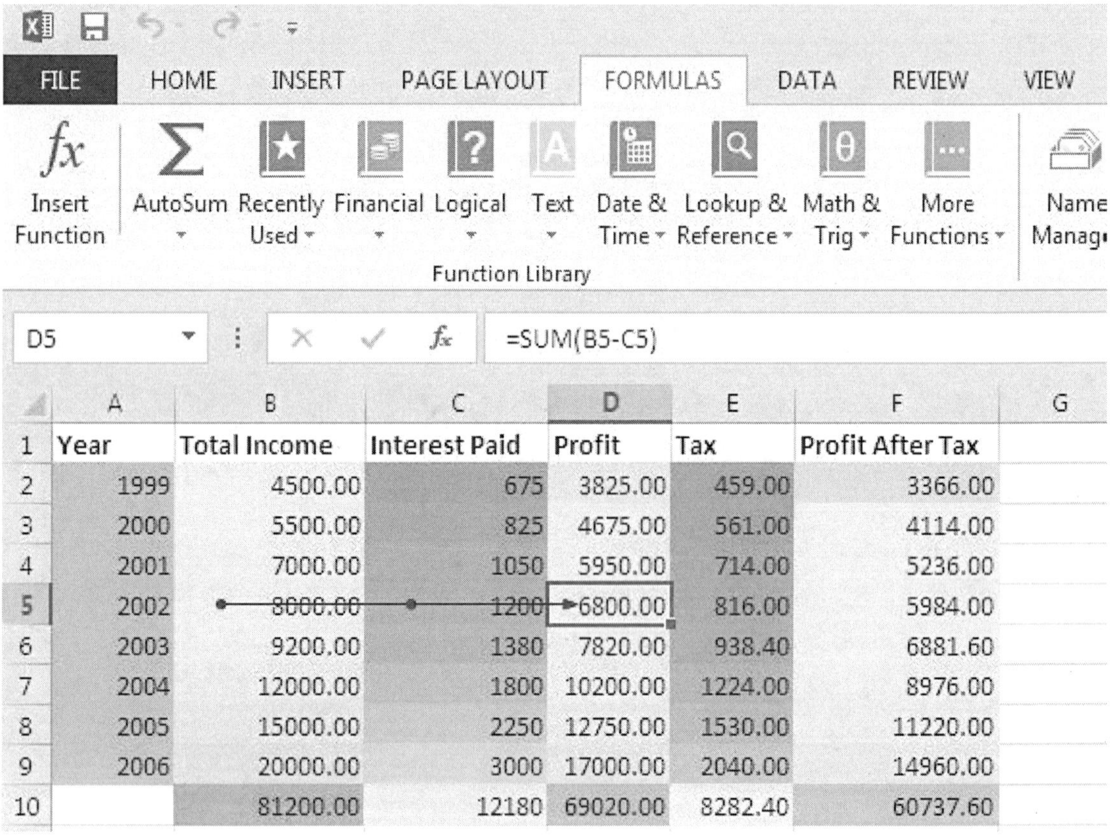

Comments Inserting

A comment is an annotation that you attach to a cell to provide information about the cell's contents. This capability enables several people to review the same worksheet and attach their comments.

To insert a comment:

1. Select the cell to which you want to attach a comment.
2. From the Review menu, choose New Comment from Comments panel.
3. In the yellow text box that opens and displays the text for the comment.
4. Click in another cell to close the text box.

Remember

1. A comment is indicated by a comment marker (a small red triangle) at the upper right corner of the cell. To view the comment, pass the cursor over the cell.

2. To remove a comment, right-click in the cell, and choose Delete Comment from the shortcut menu.

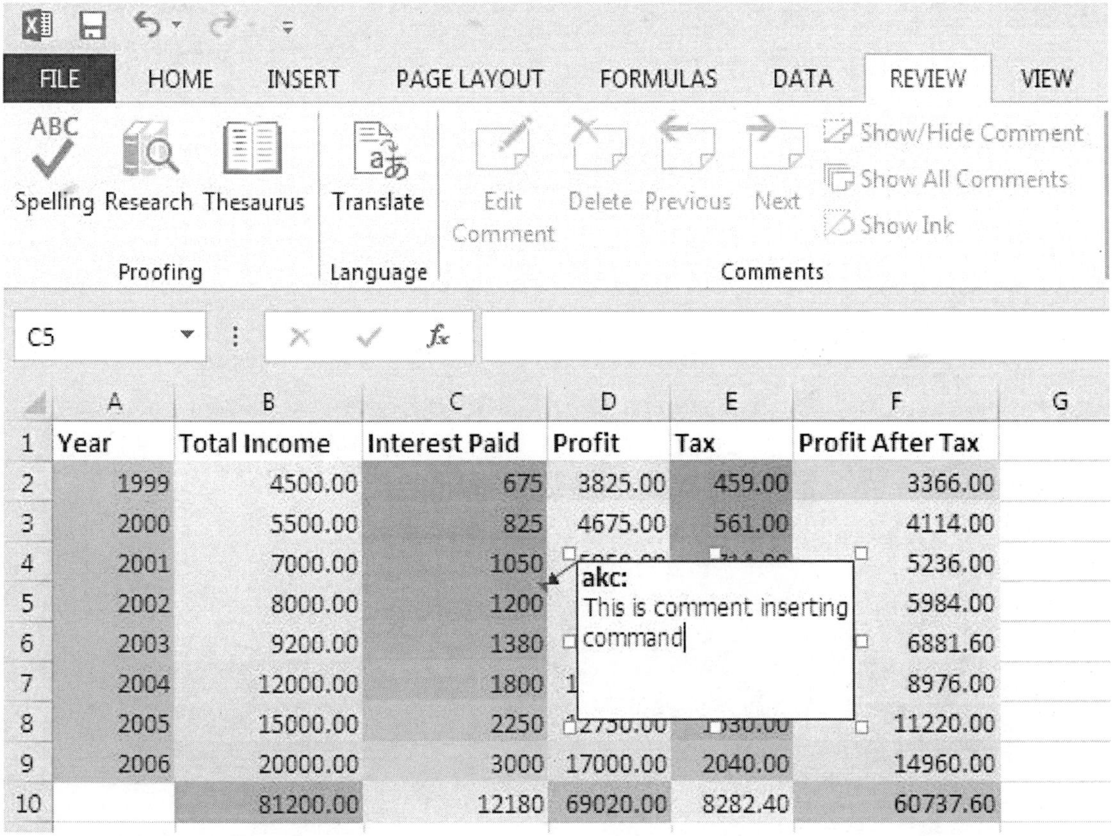

Outlines

Outline a Worksheet Automatically

1. Select a single cell to outline or the entire worksheet
2. Select a range of cells to outline
3. Click Data menu, Group and Outline command, and click at Group.

An outline created with outline symbols to the left of the row heading and/or above column headings.

Clear Entire Outline

1. Select any cell in outline
2. Click at Data menu, Outline and Ungroup command, and Clear Outline.

Worksheet Fitting on a Page

If your worksheet is too large to print on one page even after you change the orientation and margins, you might consider using the Fit to option.

This option shrinks the worksheet to make it fit on the specified number of pages. You can specify the document's width and height.

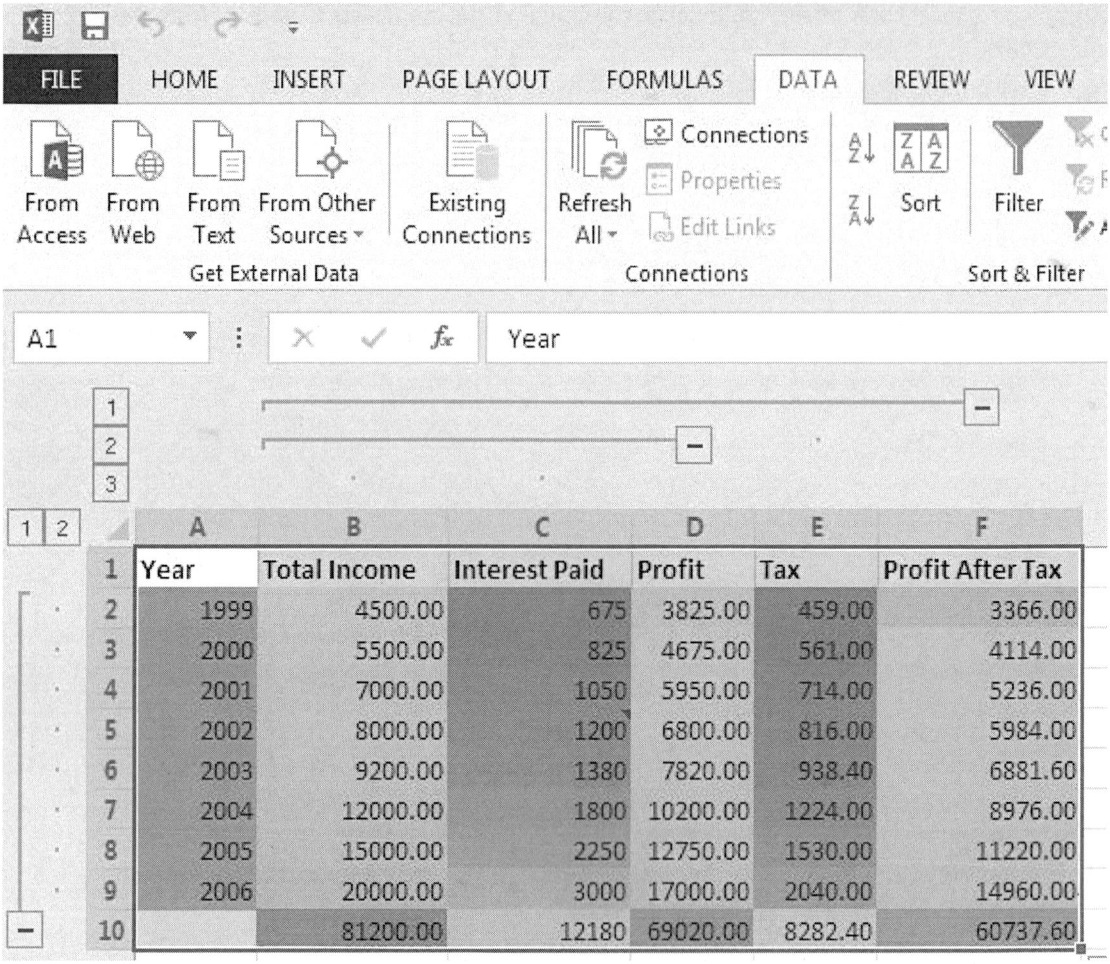

Follow these steps to scale a worksheet to fit on a page:

1. Open the Page Setup menu and choose Page Setup and Print Area. The Page Setup dialog box appears.
2. Click the Page tab to display the Page options.
3. In the Fit to XX page wide by XX tall text boxes, enter the number of pages in which you want Excel to fit your data.
4. Click Ok to close the Page Setup dialog box and return to your worksheet. Or click the Print button in the Page Setup dialog box to display the Print dialog box, and then click Ok to print your worksheet.

Function Wizard

Sum and Average are just two of the most commonly used functions whereas there are lots of them in Excel. You can use them to get the desired results in a flash.

To get them click at the Formulas menu and then Function Library. Here you have the various options of the functions which you can choose from.

Insert Function

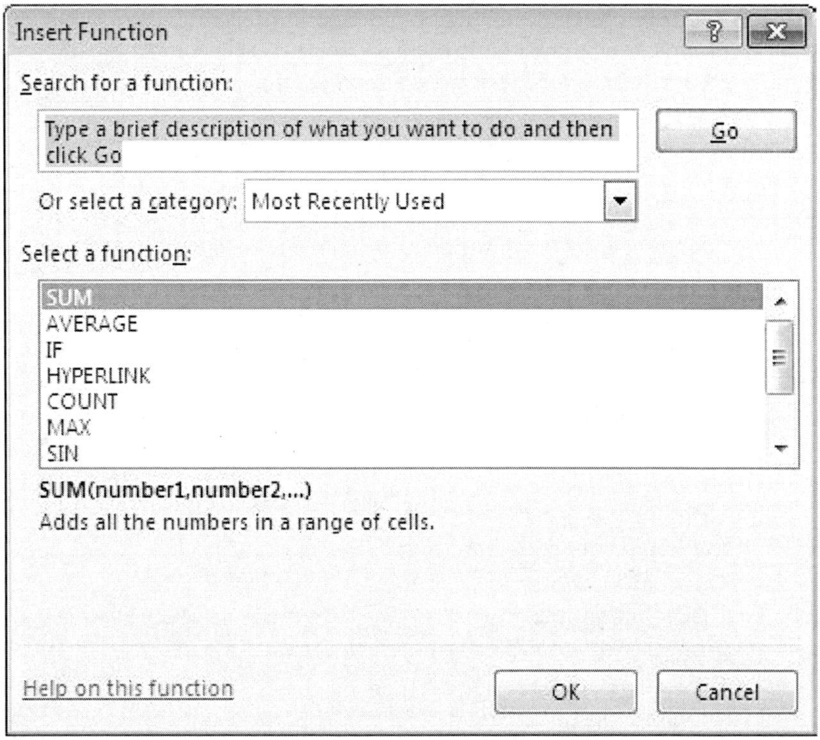

The Insert Function button is the option for building the formula. The Insert Function wizard takes you through the steps of building a formula.

1. Click the destination cell for the formula.
2. Click the Insert Function button.
3. In the Insert Function dialog box, select the category and then the function.
4. Click Ok.
5. Use the Insert Function Wizard to guide you in completing the formula.
6. Click Ok when you have finished.

Goal Seeking

Usually after you create a formula, you can type in new data to see how the formula calculates the new result. However, Excel also offers a feature known as Goal Seeking. With this, you specify the value you want a formula to calculate, and then Excel changes the data in thr formula's cell references to tell you what values you need to achieve that goal.

To use Goal Seeking, follow these steps.

1. Click a the cell that contains a formula.
2. Click the Data tab.
3. Click the What-If Analysis Icon in the Data Tools group.
4. Click Goal Seek.
5. Click in the To Value text box and type a number that you want to appear in the formula stored in the cell that you clicked in Step 1.
6. Click in the By Changing Cell text box and click one cell that contains data used by the formula you choose in Step 1.
7. Click Ok.
8. Click Ok (to keep the changes) or click Cancel (to display the origianl vlaue your spreadsheet had before you choose the Goal Seek command)

Scenarios Manager

Human mind is made of What-if situations. The same what-if can be applied to your worksheet to see if the results of the selection displays the good or bad results.

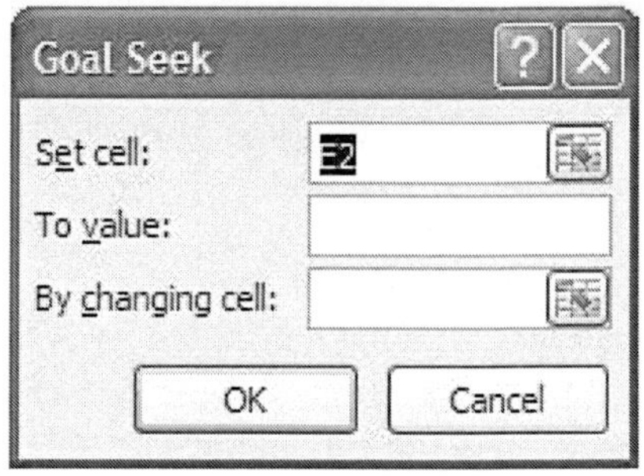

Each time you change the data, the previous solution is lost. To address this limitation, the Scenario Manager helps you keep track of multiple what-if models. Using the Scenarios manager, you can create new forecasting scenarios, view existing scenario, run scenario management commands and display consolidated scenario reports. Let us start with creating a worksheet and then apply the scenario to it.

On the next page a worksheet is shown which has been taken as an example for creating a scenario. Here the figures are very simple and calculated. If you want you can use the constant figures too. Next we perform the following steps to create and view the scenario.

1. Click at Data panel, Data Tools tab and What-If Analysis and then Scenarios manager.
2. A Scenario manager dialog box would appear on the screen, as shown here.
3. As the dialog box says, click at Add to add a scenario.
4. This gives rise to another dialog box, which is called Add scenario.
5. In this dialog box, you have to firstly name the screnario.
6. I have named it as Good.
7. You can type the cell names or choose them by clicking at those cells. I have chosen cells from E2 to E4.
8. Click OK to add your scenario to the Scenario Manager. You'll see the Scenario Values dialog box, which asks you for your model's variables. The default values are the numbers that were already in the cells.
9. Type the various values which you want to see in the scenario.
10. Click Add to create a second scenario. If you do not want another set, just click at Ok.
11. This will return you to the scenario manager with your scenario added to it.
12. As mentioned you can add another scenario to it.
13. Now we will see how this scenario works. For this click at Show.
14. Excel substitutes the values in the scenario for the variables in your worksheet and displays the results in your worksheet, as shown on the next page.
15. Next step is of having the Scenario Reports.
16. For this you choose the button called Summary from the Scenario Manager dialog box.

17. For this you will have to click at a cell where the summary would be placed.
18. You also have to define whether you want the summary or the PivtoTable report. Click any one of the two.
19. I have taken here Scenario summary and have given E9 as the cell for showing the results.
20. The net results is shown here.

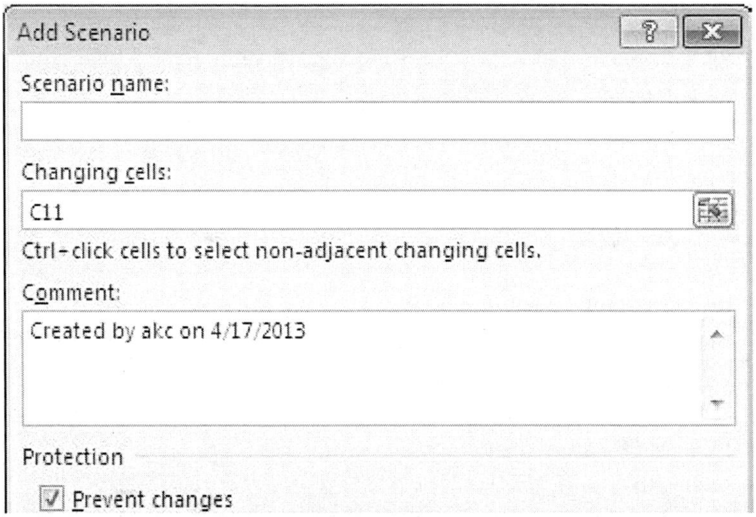

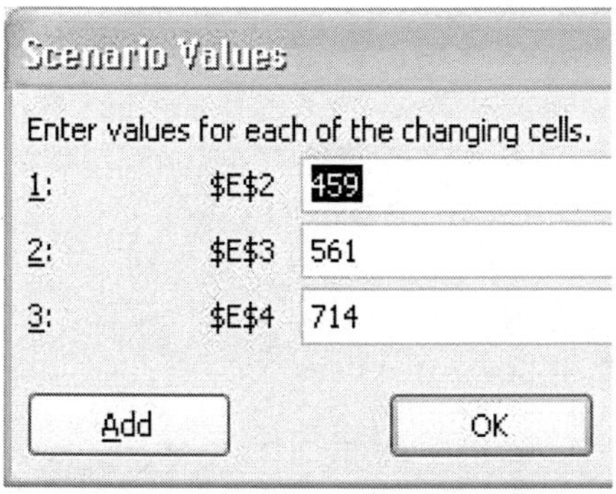

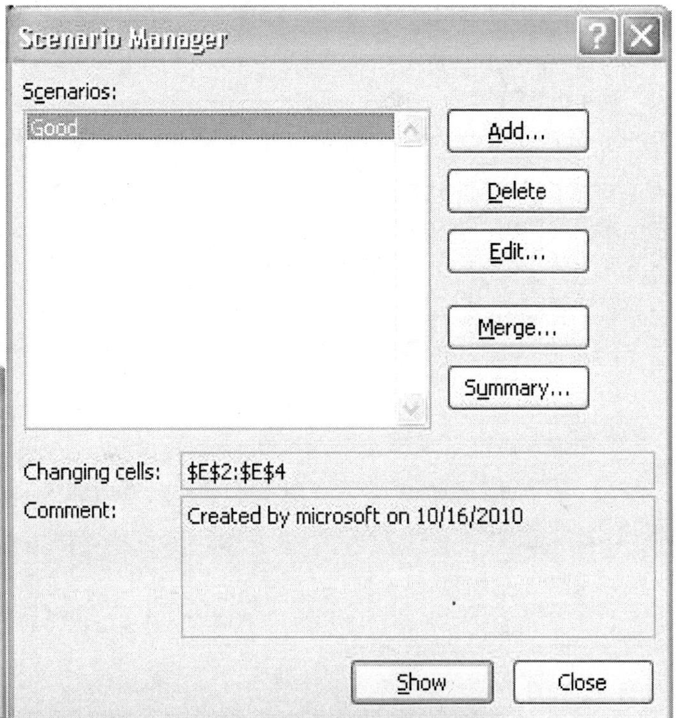

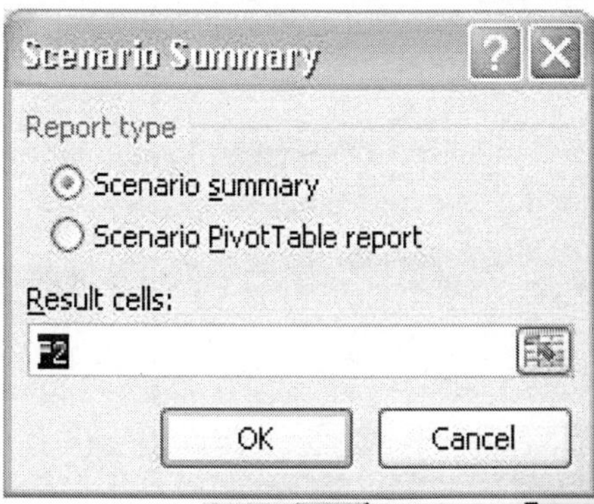

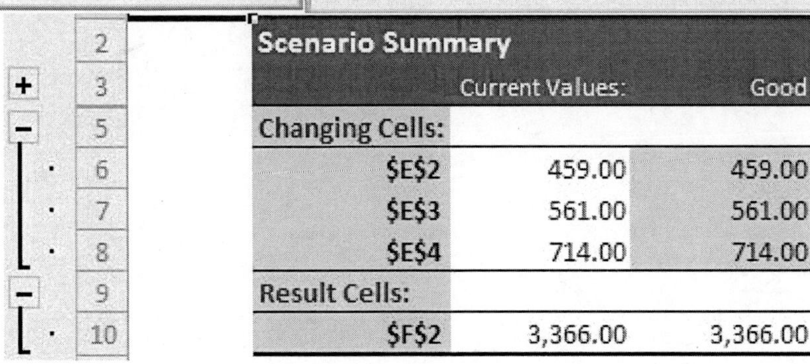

Creating a Pivot Table Report

PivotTable reports can help you look at data in different ways. Once the reports are created, you can swap rows with columns for different views.

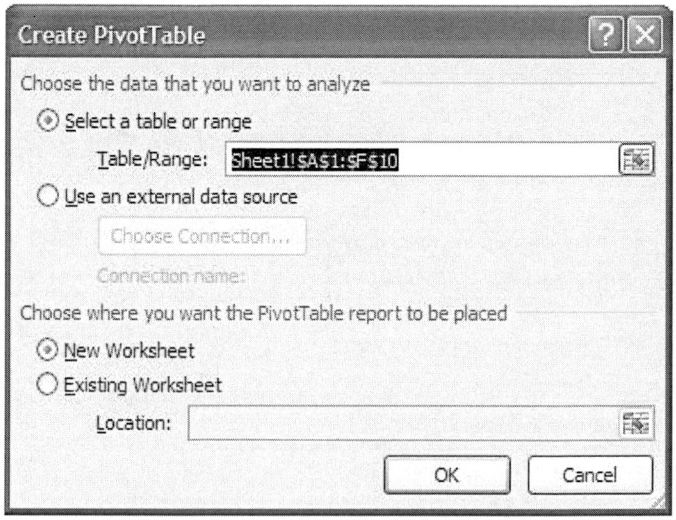

1. Click in the selected data area.
2. From the Insert menu, choose PivotTable in the Tables group.
3. Select the cells that contain the data yu want to use in your pivot table. This is optional.
4. Select one of the following radio buttons:
   - New Worksheet: Puts the pivot table on a new worksheet.
   - Existing Worksheet: Puts the pivot table on an existing worksheet.
5. Click Ok, Excel displays a Pivot Table Fiel List pane.
6. Mark one or more check boxes inside the PivotTable Field List pane.

Rearranging labels in a pivot table

A pivot table organizesdata according to your spreadsheet's columns headings, which appear in a pivot table as row labels. To rearrange column headings in a pivot table, follow these steps:

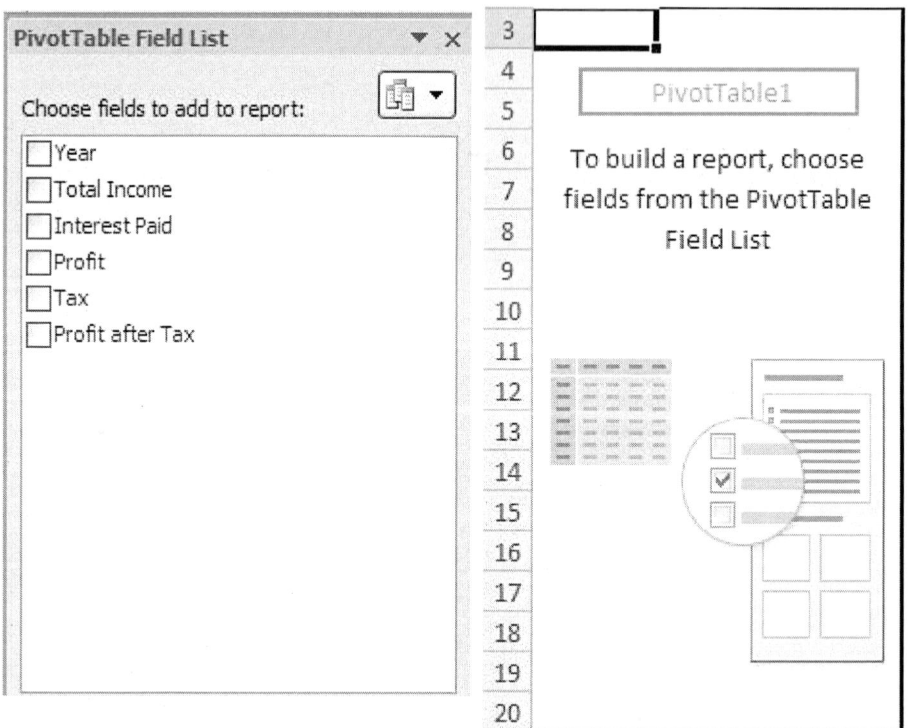

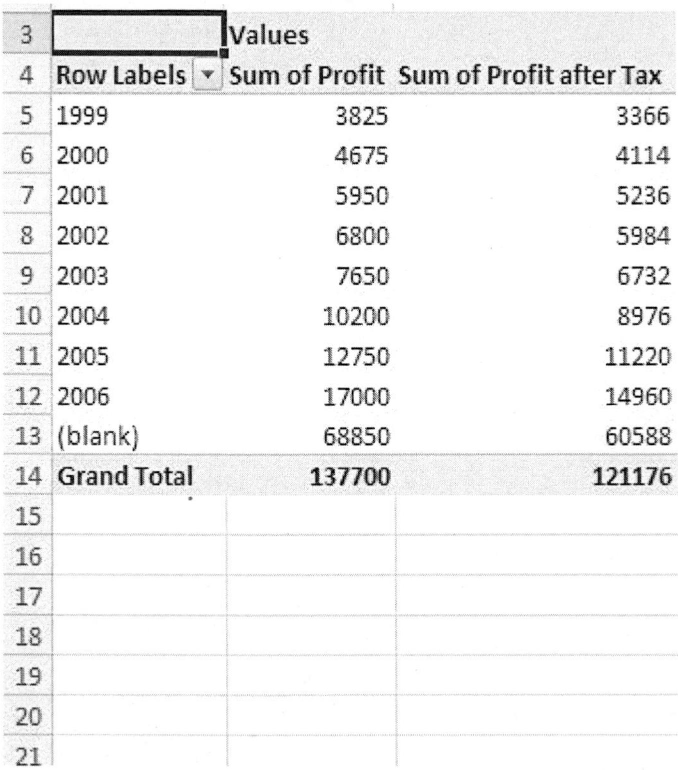

	Values	
Row Labels	Sum of Profit	Sum of Profit after Tax
1999	3825	3366
2000	4675	4114
2001	5950	5236
2002	6800	5984
2003	7650	6732
2004	10200	8976
2005	12750	11220
2006	17000	14960
(blank)	68850	60588
Grand Total	**137700**	**121176**

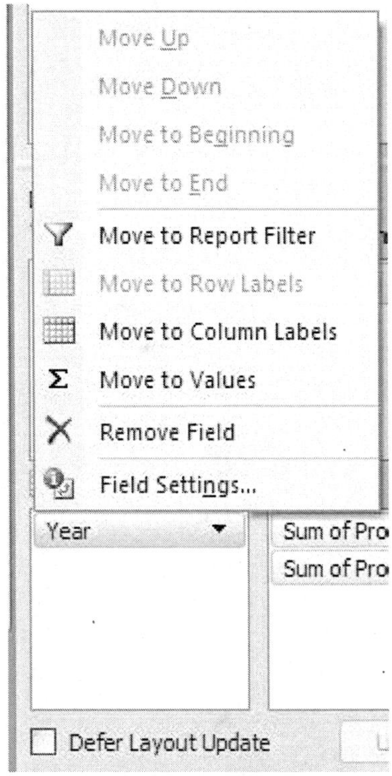

1. Click the pivot table you want to rearrange.
2. Click the downward-pointing arrow of a lable that appears under the Row Labels group.
   Select one of the following:
   Move Up: Moves the lable one level closer to the beginning.
   Move Down: Moves the lable one level down to the end.
   Move to Beginning: Makes the label the dominant criteria for sorting data.
   Move to End: Makes the label the last criteria for sorting data.

Modifying a Pivot Table

Row labels let you organize data according to different criteria, such as sales per region and then by product. For greater flexibility, you can also turn a row label into a column heading.

To turn row labels into column headings in a pivot table (or vice versa), follow these steps:

1. Click the pivot table you want to modify.
2. Click a heading.
3. Choose Move to Column Labels (or Row Labels).

Typing with AutoFill

If you need to type the names of successive months or days in a row or column (such as January, February, February, March and so on). Excel offers a shortcut to save you from typing all the day or month names yourself. With this shortcut, you just type one month or day and them drag the mouse to highlight all the adjacent cell. Then Excel types the rest of the month or day names in those cells automatically.

To use this shortcut, follow these steps:

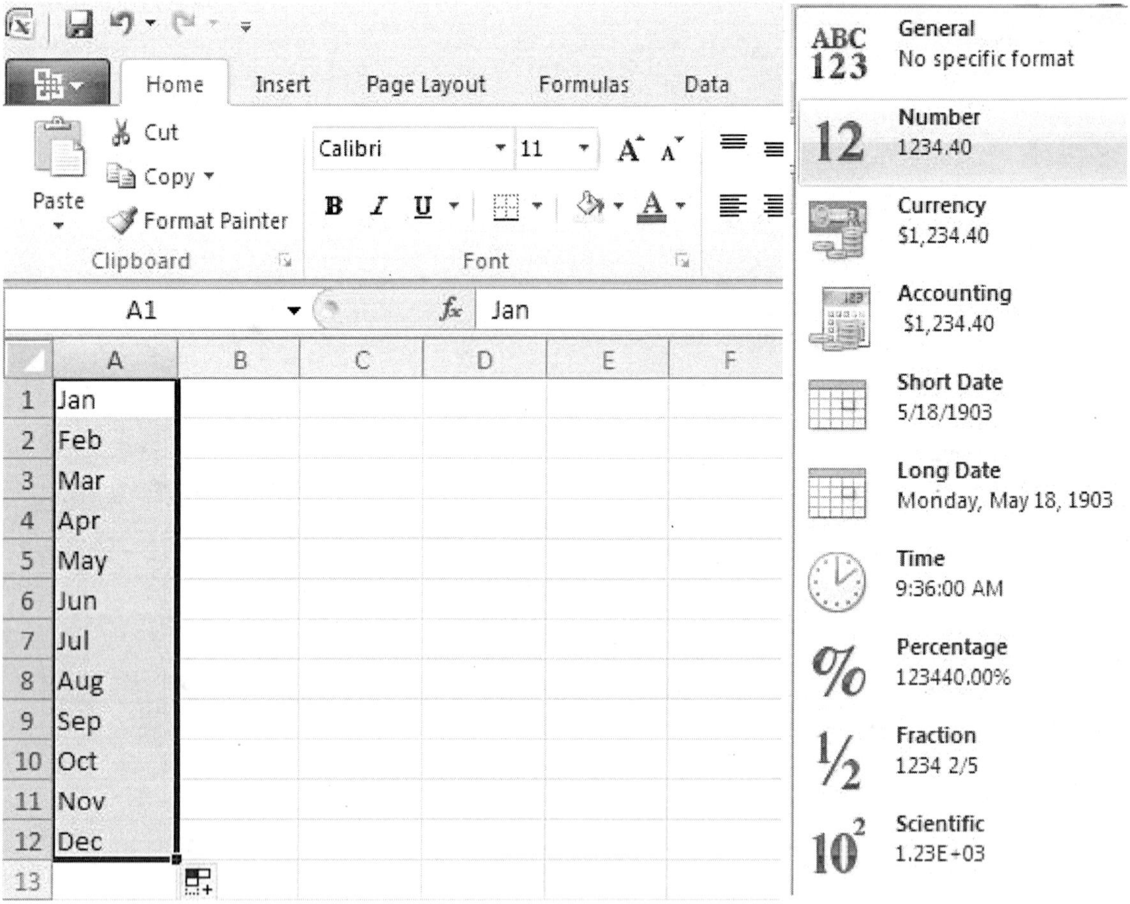

1. Click a cell and type a month (like January or just Jan) or a day (like Monday or just Mon).

   You can also type in a sequence of numbers in Step 1. So if you typed the numbers 2, 4, and 6 in adjacent cells, highlighted all these adjacent cells, and grabbed the Fill Handle, Excel is smart enough to detect the pattern and display the numbers 8, 10, 12 in the next three adjacent cells.
2. Move the mouse pointer over the Fill Handle until the mouse pointer turns into a black corosshair icon.
3. Hold down the left mouse button and drag the mouse down a column or across the row.

   As you drag the mouse, Excel automatically types in the remaining month or day names.

Formatting Numbers and Labels

When you first create a spreadsheet, numbers and labels appear as plain text. Plain labels might look boring, but plain numbers, such as 8495 or 0.29, can be difficult to read and understand it the numbers are supposed to represent currency amounts ($8,495) or percentage (29%). To make labels visually intersesting and numbers appear more description of what they actually represent, you need to format your data after you type it into a spreadsheet.

Formatting Numbers

To format the appearance of numbers, follow these steps:

1. Select one or more cells using the mouse or keyboard.
2. Click the Home tab.
3. Click the Number Format list box in the Number group.

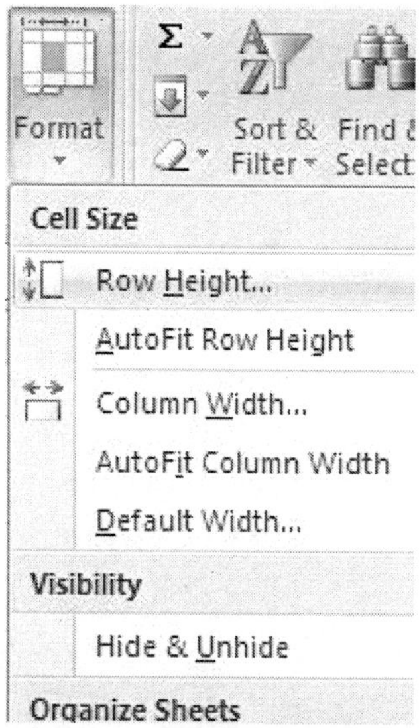

Changing the size of Rows and Columns

If you need to resize a row or columns to a precise value, it's easier to type a specific value into the Row Height or Column Width dialog box instead. To type a value into a Row Height or Column Width dialog box, follow hes steps:

1. Click the Home tab.
2. Click the row or column heading that you want to resize. Excel highlights your entire row or column.
3. Click the Format icon that appears in the Cells group. A pull-down menu appears.
4. Click Height, if you select a row, or Width, if you selected a column.
5. Type a vlaue and then click Ok.

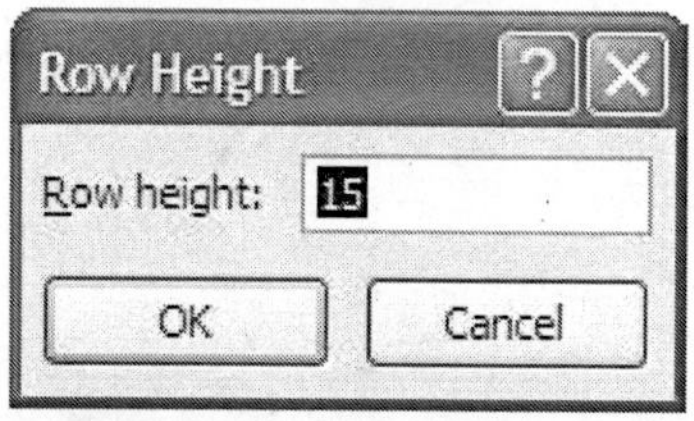

Adding and Deleting Rows and Columns

After you type in labels, numbers, and formulas, you may suddenly realize that you need to add or delete extra rows and columns.

To add a row or column, follow these steps:

1. Click at Home Tab.
2. Click the row or column heading where you want to add another row or column.
3. Click the Insert icon in the Cells group.

   Inserting a row adds a new row above the selected row. Inserting a column adds a new column to the left of the selected column.

To delete a row or column, follow these steps:

1. Click at Home tab.
2. Click the row or column heading that you want to delete.
3. Click the Delete icon in the Cells group.

   Deleting a row or colun deletes any data stored in that row or column.

Inserting (and Removing) Page Breaks

One problem with large spreadsheets is that when you print them out, parts may get cut off when printed on separate pages. To correct this problem, you can tell Excel exactly where page breaks should occur.

To insert page breaks, follow these steps:

1. Move the cursor in the cell to define where the vertical and horizontal page breaks will appear.
2. Click the Page Layout tab.
3. Click the Breaks icon in the Page Setup group.
4. Choose Insert Page Break.

   Excfel inserts a horizontal page directly above the cell you selected in Step 1 and a vertical page break to the left of that cell, too.

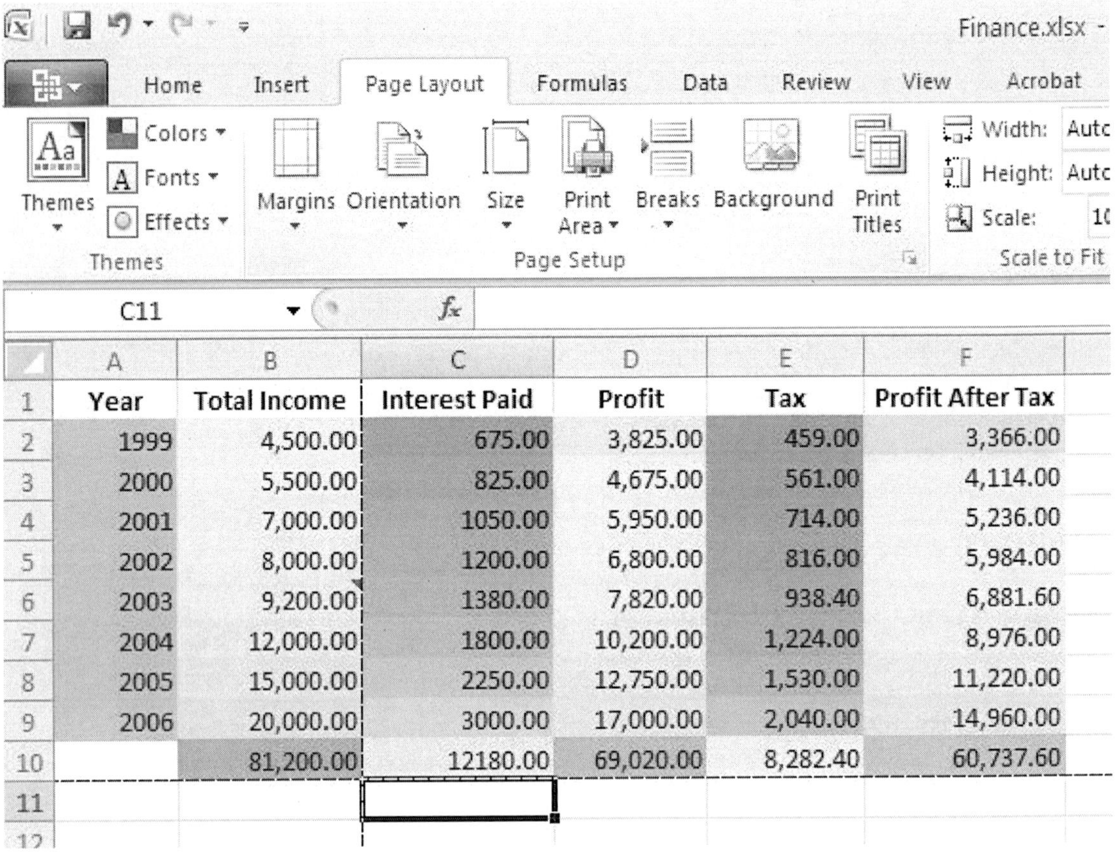

To remove a page break, follow these steps:

1. Choose one of the following:
   - To remove a horizontal page break: Click in any cell that appears directly below that horizontal page break.
   - To remove a vertical page break: Click in any cell that appears directly to the right of the vertical page break and directly underneath the horizontal page break.
   - To remove both a vertical and horizontal page break: Click in the cell that appears to the right of the vertical page break and directly underneath the horizontal page break.
2. Click the Page Layout tab.
3. Click the Breaks icon in the Page Setup group.
4. Choose Remove Page Break. Excel removes your chosen page break.

Applying Themes

You can quickly and easily format an entire document to give it a professional and modern look by applying a document theme. A document theme is a set of formatting choices that include a set of theme colors, a set of theme fonts (including heading and body text fonts), and a set of theme effects (including lines and fill effects).

Apply a Document Theme

You can change the document theme that is applied by default in Office programs, such as Word, Excel, and PowerPoint, by selecting another predefined document theme or a custom document theme. Document themes that you apply immediately affect the styles that you can use in your document.

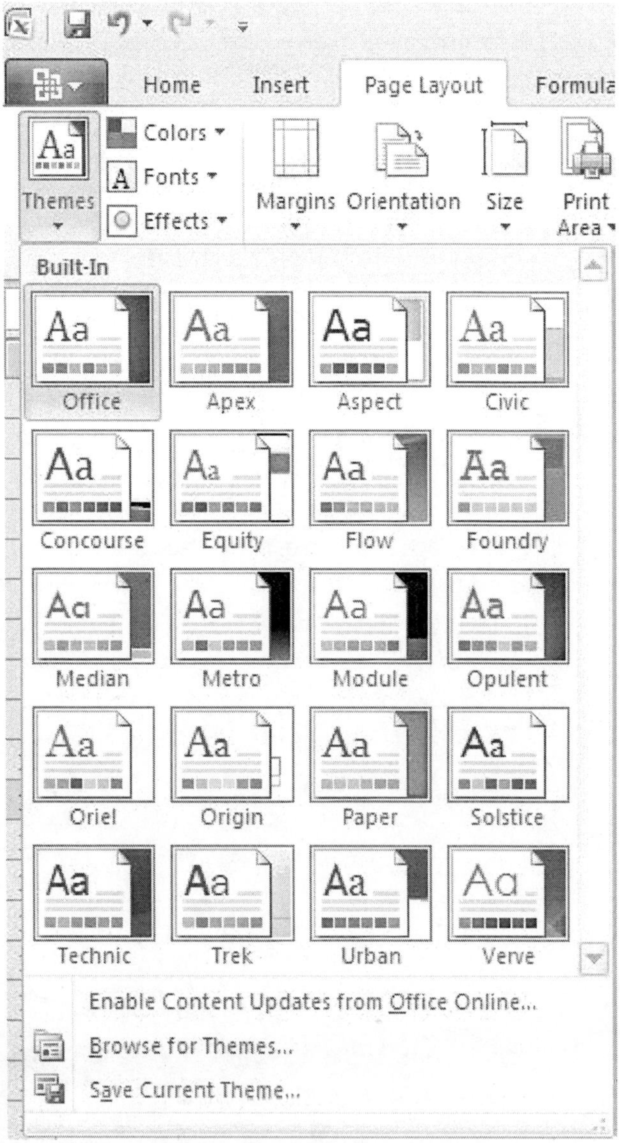

Do one of the following:

- On the Page Layout tab, in the Themes group, click Themes.
- To apply a predefined document theme, click the document theme that you want to use under Built-In.
- To apply a custom document theme, click the document theme that you want to use under Custom.
- Custom is available only if you created one or more custom document themes.
- If a document theme that you want to use is not listed, click Browse for Themes to find it on your computer or a network location.

Customize a Document Theme

To customize a document theme, you start by changing the colors, the fonts, or the line and fill effects that are used. Changes that you make to one or more of these theme components immediately affect the styles that you have applied in the active document. If you want to apply these changes to new documents, you can save them as a custom document theme.

Customize the theme colors

Theme colors contain four text and background colors, six accent colors, and two hyperlink colors. The colors in the Theme Colors button represent the current text and background colors. The set of colors that you see next to the Theme Colors name after you click the Theme Colors button represent the accent and hyperlink colors for that theme. When you change any of these colors to create your own set of theme colors, the colors that are shown in the Theme Colors button and next to the Theme Colors name will change accordingly.

Customize the theme fonts

Theme fonts contain a heading font and a body text font. When you click the Theme Fonts button, you can see the name of the heading font and body text font that is used for each theme font below the Theme Fonts name. You can change both of these fonts to create your own set of theme fonts.

Select a set of theme effects

Theme effects are sets of lines and fill effects. When you click the Theme Effects button , you can see the lines and fill effects that are used for each set of theme effects in the graphic that is displayed with the Theme Effects name. Although you cannot create your own set of theme effects, you can choose the one that you want to use in your own document theme.

Save a document theme

Any changes that you make to the colors, the fonts, or the line and fill effects of a document theme can be saved as a custom document theme that you can apply to other documents.

Add or Remove a Sheet Background

In Microsoft Office Excel, you can use a picture as a sheet background for display purposes only. A sheet background is not printed, and it is not retained in an individual worksheet or in an item that you save as a Web page. Because a sheet background is not printed, it cannot be used as a watermark. You can, however, mimic a watermark by inserting a graphic in a header or footer.

Add a sheet background

1. Click the worksheet that you want to display with a sheet background. Make sure that only one worksheet is selected.
2. On the Page Layout tab, in the Page Setup group, click Background.
3. Select the picture that you want to use for the sheet background, and then click Insert.
4. The selected picture is repeated to fill the sheet.

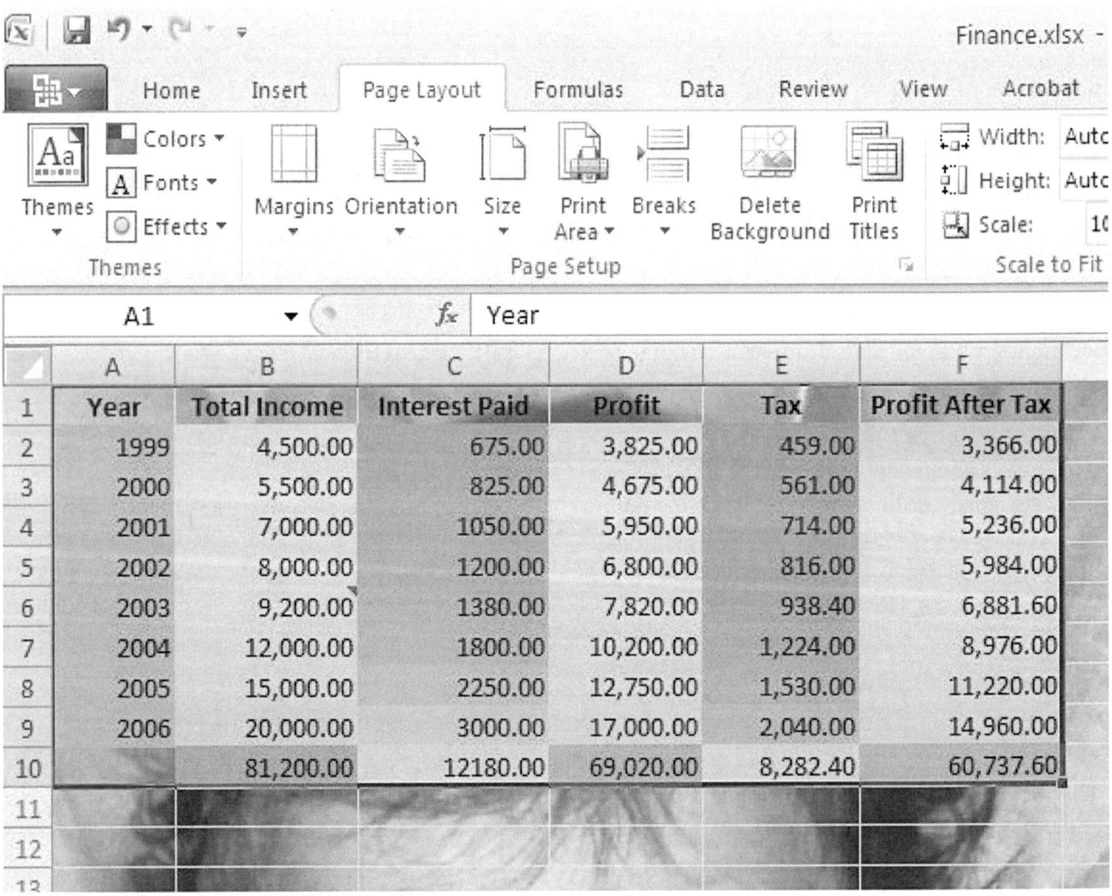

	A	B	C	D	E	F
1	Year	Total Income	Interest Paid	Profit	Tax	Profit After Tax
2	1999	4,500.00	675.00	3,825.00	459.00	3,366.00
3	2000	5,500.00	825.00	4,675.00	561.00	4,114.00
4	2001	7,000.00	1050.00	5,950.00	714.00	5,236.00
5	2002	8,000.00	1200.00	6,800.00	816.00	5,984.00
6	2003	9,200.00	1380.00	7,820.00	938.40	6,881.60
7	2004	12,000.00	1800.00	10,200.00	1,224.00	8,976.00
8	2005	15,000.00	2250.00	12,750.00	1,530.00	11,220.00
9	2006	20,000.00	3000.00	17,000.00	2,040.00	14,960.00
10		81,200.00	12180.00	69,020.00	8,282.40	60,737.60
11						
12						

Remove a sheet background

1. Click the worksheet that is displayed with a sheet background. Make sure that only one worksheet is selected.
2. On the Page Layout tab, in the Page Setup group, click Background.

Convert Text to Columns

You can convert text to columns in Excel by using the Wizard called Convet Text to Columns. For this select the text which you want to convert and select the wizard from Data menu and Text to Columns from Data Tools tab. Rest is easy. Just follow the three steps.

Protect Worksheet or Workbook Elements

To prevent a user from accidentally or deliberately changing, moving, or deleting important data, you can protect certain worksheet (worksheet: The primary document that you use in Excel to store and work with data. Also called a spreadsheet. A worksheet consists of cells that are organized into columns and rows; a worksheet is always stored in a workbook.) or workbook elements, with or without a password.

Workbook and worksheet element protection should not be confused with workbook-level password security. Element protection cannot protect a workbook from users who have malicious intent.

Protect Worksheet Elements

1. Select the worksheet that you want to protect.
2. To unlock any cells or ranges that you want other users to be able to change, do the following:
1. Select each cell or range that you want to unlock.
2. On the Home tab, in the Cells group, click Format, and then click Format Cells.
3. On the Protection tab, clear the Locked check box, and then click OK.
3. To hide any formulas that you don't want to be visible, do the following:
1. In the worksheet, select the cells that contain the formulas that you want to hide.
2. On the Home tab, in the Cells group, click Format, and then click Format Cells.
3. On the Protection tab, select the Hidden check box, and then click OK.
4. To unlock any graphic objects (such as pictures, clip art, shapes, or Smart Art graphics) that you want users to be able to change, do the following:
1. Hold down CTRL and click each graphic object that you want to unlock.
2. This displays the Picture Tools or Drawing Tools, adding the Format tab.

   You can also use the Go To command to quickly select all of the graphic objects in a worksheet. On the Home tab, in the Editing group, click Find & Select, and then click Go To. Click Special, and then click Objects.
3. On the Format tab, in the Size group, click the Dialog Box Launcher next to Size.

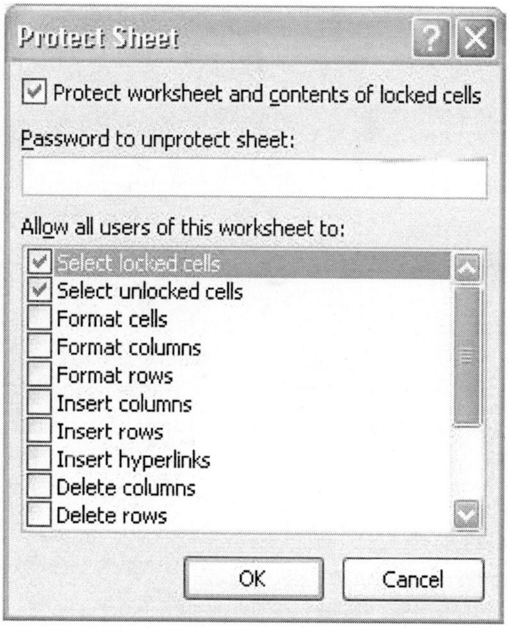

4. On the Properties tab, clear the Locked check box, and if present, clear the Lock text check box. You don't need to unlock buttons or controls for users to be able to click and use them. You can unlock embedded charts, text boxes, and other objects created with the drawing tools that you want users to be able to modify.
5. On the Review tab, in the Changes group, click Protect Sheet.
6. In the Allow all users of this worksheet to list, select the elements that you want users to be able to change.

Worksheet elements

Clear this check box	To prevent users from
Select locked cells	Moving the pointer to cells for which the Locked check box is selected on the Protection tab of the Format Cells dialog box. By default, users are allowed to select locked cells.
Select unlocked cells	Moving the pointer to cells for which the Locked check box is cleared on the Protection tab of the Format Cells dialog box. By default, users are allowed to select unlocked cells, and they can press the TAB key to move between the unlocked cells on a protected worksheet.
Format cells	Changing any of the options in the Format Cells or Conditional Formatting dialog boxes. If you applied conditional formats before you protected the worksheet, the formatting continues to change when a user enters a value that satisfies a different condition.
Format columns	Using any of the column formatting commands, including changing column width or hiding columns (Home tab, Cells group, Format button).
Format rows	Using any of the row formatting commands, including changing row height or hiding rows (Home tab, Cells group, Format button).
Insert columns	Inserting columns.
Insert rows	Inserting rows.
Insert hyperlinks	Inserting new hyperlinks (hyperlink: Colored and underlined text or a graphic that you click to go to a file, a location in a file, a Web page on the World Wide Web, or a Web page on an intranet. Hyperlinks can also go to newsgroups and to Gopher, Telnet, and FTP sites.), even in unlocked cells.
Delete columns	Deleting columns. Note If Delete columns is protected and Insert columns is not also protected, a user can insert columns that he or she cannot delete.
Delete rows	Deleting rows. Note If Delete rows is protected and Insert rows is not also protected, a user can insert rows that he or she cannot delete.
Sort	Using any commands to sort data (Data tab, Sort & Filter group). Note Users can't sort ranges that contain locked cells on a protected worksheet, regardless of this setting.
Use AutoFilter	Using the drop-down arrows to change the filter on ranges when AutoFilters are applied. Note Users cannot apply or remove AutoFilters on a protected worksheet, regardless of this setting.
Use PivotTable reports	Formatting, changing the layout, refreshing, or otherwise modifying PivotTable reports or creating new reports. Edit objects Doing the any of the following:

	• Making changes to graphic objects—including maps, embedded charts, shapes, text boxes, and controls—that you did not unlock before you protected the worksheet. For example, if a worksheet has a button that runs a macro, you can click the button to run the macro, but you cannot delete the button. • Making any changes, such as formatting, to an embedded chart. The chart continues to be updated when you change its source data. • Adding or editing comments.
Edit scenarios	Viewing scenarios that you have hidden, making changes to scenarios that you have prevented changes to, and deleting these scenarios. Users can change the values in the changing cells, if the cells are not protected, and add new scenarios.

Functions in Excel

As mentioned earlier, functions are ready-made formulas which can be recalled and used while working in Excel. Here is the complete list of functions, alongwith some examples.

Financial Functions

DB	Returns the depreciation of an asset for a specified period using the fixed-declining balance method.
DDB	Returns the depreciation of an asset for a specified period using the double-declining balance method or some other method you specify.
FV	Returns the future value of an investment.
IPMT	Returns the interest payment for an investment for a given period.
IRR	Returns the internal rate of return for a series of cash flows.
ISPMT	Returns the straight-loan payment interest.
MIRR	Returns the internal rate of return where positive and negative cash flows are financed at different rates.
NPER	Returns the number of periods for an investment.
NPV	Returns the net present value of an investment based on a series of periodic cash flows and a discount rate.
PMT	Returns the periodic payment for an annuity.
PPMT	Returns the payment on the principal for an investment for a given period.
PV	Returns the present value of an investment.
RATE	Returns the Interest rate per period of an annuity.
SLN	Returns the straight-line depreciation of an asset for one period.
SYD	Returns the sum-of-years digits depreciation of an asset for a specified period.
VDB	Returns the depreciation of an asset for a specified or partial period using a declining balance method.

Logical Functions

AND	Returns TRUE if all its arguments are TRUE.
FALSE	Returns the logical value FALSE.
IF	Specifies a logical test to perform.
NOT	Reverses the logic of its argument.
OR	Returns TRUE if any argument is TRUE.
TRUE	Returns the logical value TRUE.

Text Functions

BAHTTEXT	Converts a number to text (bath).
CHAR	Returns the character specified by the code number.
CLEAN	Removes all nonprintable characters from text.
CODE	Returns a numeric code for the first character in a text string.
CONCATENATE	Joins several text items into one text item.
DOLLAR	Converts a number to text, using currency format.
EXACT	Checks to see if two text values are identical.
FIND	Finds one text value within another (case-sensitive).
FIXED	Formats a number as text values are identical.
LEFT	Returns the leftmost characters from a text value.
LEN	Returns the number of characters in a text string.
LOWER	Converts text to lowercase.
MID	Returns a specific number of characters from a text string starting at the position you specify.
PROPER	Capitalizes the first letter in each word of a text value.
REPLACE	Replaces characters within text.
REPT	Repeats text a given number of times.
RIGHT	Returns the rightmost characters from a text value.
SEARCH	Finds one text value within another (not case-sensitive).
SUBSTITUTE	Substitutes new text for old text in a text string.
T	Converts its arguments to text.
TEXT	Formats a number and converts it to text.
TRIM	Removes spaces from text.
UPPER	Converts text to uppercase.
VALUE	Converts a text argument to a number.

Date and Time Functions

DATE	Returns the serial number of a particular date.
DATEVALUE	Converts a date in the form of text to a serial number.
DAY	Converts a serial number to a day of the month.
DAYS360	Calculates the number of days between two dates based on a 360-day year.
HOUR	Converts a serial number to an hour.
MINUTE	Converts a serial number to a minute.
MONTH	Converts a serial number to a month.
NOW	Returns the serial number of the current date and time.
SECOND	Converts a serial number to a second.
TIME	Returns the serial number of a particular time.
TIMEVALUE	Converts a time in the form of text to a serial number.
TODAY	Returns the serial number of today's date.
WEEKDAY	Converts a serial number to a number that represents a day of the week.
YEAR	Converts a serial number to a year.

Lookup and Reference Functions

ADDRESS	Returns the number of areas in a reference.
AREAS	Chooses a value from a list of values.
CHOOSE	Chooses a value or action to perform from a list of values, based on an index number.
COLUMN	Returns data stored in a PivotTable.

COLUMNS	Returns the number of columns in an array or reference.
GETPIVOTDATA	Extracts data stored in a PivotTable
HLOOKUP	Looks in the top row of an array and returns the value of a cell in the same column, in the row that you specify.
HYPERLINK	Creates a shortcut or jump that opens a document stored on a network server, an intranet, or the internet.
INDEX	Uses an index to choose a value from a reference or array.
INDIRECT	Returns a reference indicated by a text value.
LOOKUP	Looks up values in a one-row or one-column vector or array.
MATCH	Looks up values in a reference or array and returns its relative position in the array.
OFFSET	Returns a reference offset from a given reference.
ROW	Returns the row number of a reference.
ROWS	Returns the number of rows in a reference.
RTD	Retrieves real-time data from a program that supports COM automation.
TRANSPOSE	Returns the transpose of an array.
VLOOKUP	Looks in the first column of an array and moves across the row to return the value of a cell in the column you specify.

Math and Trigonometric Functions

ABS	Returns the absolute value of a number.
ACOS	Returns the arccosine of a number.
ACOSH	Returns the inverse hyperbolic cosine of a number.
ASIN	Returns the arcsine of a number.
ASINH	Returns the inverse hyperbolic sine of a number.
ATAN	Returns the arctangent of a number.
ATAN2	Returns the arctangent from x- and y- coordinates.
ATANH	Returns the inverse hyperbolic tangent of a number.
CEILING	Rounds a number up to the nearest integer or to the nearest multiple of significance.
COMBIN	Returns the number of combinations for a given number of objects.
COS	Returns the cosine of a number.
COSH	Returns the hyperbolic cosine of a number.
DEGREES	Converts radians to degrees.
EVEN	Rounds a number up to the nearest even integer.
EXP	Returns e raised to the power of a given number.
FACT	Returns the factorial of a number.
FLOOR	Rounds a number down, toward zero.
INT	Rounds a number down to the nearest integer.
LN	Returns the natural logarithm of a number.
LOG	Returns the logarithm of a number to a specified base.
LOG10	Returns the base-10 logarithm of a number.
MDETERM	Returns the matrix determinant of an array.
MINVERSE	Returns the matrix inverse of an array.
MMULT	Returns the matrix product of two arrays.
MOD	Returns the remainder from division.
ODD	Rounds a number up to the nearest odd integer.
PI	Returns the value of p (pi) to 15 digits.
POWER	Returns the result of a number raised to a power.

PRODUCT	Multiplies its arguments.
RADIANS	Converts degrees to radians.
RAND	Returns a random number between 0 and 1.
ROMAN	Converts an arabic numeral to roman, as text.
ROUND	Rounds a number to a specified number of digits.
ROUNDDOWN	Rounds a number down, toward zero.
ROUNDUP	Rounds a number up, away from zero.
SIGN	Returns the sign of a number.
SIN	Returns the sine of the given angle.
SINH	Returns the hyperbolic sine of a number.
SQRT	Returns a positive square root.
SUBTOTAL	Returns a subtotal in a list or database.
SUM	Adds its arguments.
SUMIF	Adds the cells specified by a given criteria.
SUMPRODUCT	Returns the sum of the products of corresponding array components.
SUMSQ	Returns the sum of the squares of the arguments.
SUMX2MY2	Returns the sum of the difference of squares of corresponding values in two arrays.
SUMX2PY2	Returns the sum of the sum of squares of corresponding values in two arrays.
SUMXMY2	Returns the sum of squares of differences of corresponding values in two arrays.
TAN	Returns the tangent of a number.
TANH	Returns the hyperbolic tangent of a number.
TRUNC	Truncates a number to an integer.

Statistical Functions

AVEDEV	Returns the average of the absolute deviations of data points from their mean.
AVERAGE	Returns the average of its arguments.
AVERAGEA	Returns the average of its arguments, including numbers, text, and logical values.
BETADIST	Returns the cumulative beta probability density function.
BETAINV	Returns the inverse of the cumulative beta probability density function.
BINOMDIST	Returns the individual term binomial distribution probability.
CHIDIST	Returns the one-tailed probability of the chi-squared distribution.
CHIINV	Returns the inverse of the one-tailed probability of the chi-squared distribution.
CHITEST	Returns the test for independence.
CONFIDENCE	Returns the confidence interval for a population mean.
CORREL	Returns the correlation coefficient between two data sets.
COUNT	Counts how many numbers are in the list of arguments.
COUNTA	Counts how many values are in the list of arguments.
COUNTBLANK	Counts the number of blank cells within a range.
COUNTIF	Counts the number of non blank cells within a range that meet the given criteria.
COVAR	Returns covariance, the average of the products of paired deviations.
CRITBINOM	Returns the smallest value for which the cumulative binomial distribution is less than or equal to a criterion value.
DEVSQ	Returns the sum of squared of deviations.
EXPONDIST	Returns the exponential distribution.
FDIST	Returns the F probability distribution.
FINV	Returns the inverse of the F probability distribution.
FISHER	Returns the Fisher transformation.

FISHERINV	Returns the inverse of the Fisher transformation.
FORECAST	Returns a value along a linear trend.
FREQUENCY	Returns a frequency distribution as a vertical array.
FTEST	Returns the result of an F-test.
GAMMADIST	Returns the gamma distribution.
GAMMAINV	Returns the inverse of the gamma cumulative distribution.
GAMMALN	Returns the natural logarithm of the gamma function, G(x).
GEOMEAN	Returns the geometric mean.
GROWTH	Returns values along an exponential trend.
HARMEAN	Returns the harmonic mean.
HYPGEOMDIST	Returns the hypergeometric distribution.
INTERCEPT	Returns the intercept of the linear regression line.
KURT	Returns the kurtosis of a data set.
LARGE	Returns the kth largest value in a data set.
LINEST	Returns the parameters of a linear trend.
LOGEST	Returns the parameters of an exponential trend.
LOGINV	Returns the inverse of the lognormal distribution.
LOGNORMDIST	Returns the cumulative lognormal distribution.
MAX	Returns the maximum value in a list of arguments.
MAXA	Returns the maximum value in a list of arguments, including numbers, text, and logical values.
MEDIAN	Returns the median of the given numbers.
MIN	Returns the minimum value in a list of arguments.
MINA	Returns the smallest value in a list of arguments, including numbers, text, and logical values.
MODE	Returns the most common value in a data set.
NEGBINOMDIST	Returns the negative binomial distribution.
NORMDIST	Returns the normal cumulative distribution.
NORMSINV	Returns the inverse of the standard normal cumulative distribution.
PEARSON	Returns the Pearson product moment correlation coefficient.
PERCENTILE	Returns the kth percentile of values in a range.
PERCENTRANK	Returns the percentage rank of a value in a data set.
PERMUT	Returns the number of permutations for a given number of objects.
POISSON	Returns the Poisson distribution.
PROB	Returns the probability that values in a range are between two limits.
QUARTILE	Returns the quartile of a data set.
RANK	Returns the rank of a number in a list of numbers.
RSQ	Returns the square of the Pearson product moment correlation coefficient.
SKEW	Returns the skewness of a distribution.
SLOPE	Returns the slope of the linear regression line.
SMALL	Returns the kth smallest value in a data set.
STANDARDIZE	Returns a normalized value.
STDEV	Estimates standard deviation based on a sample.
STDEVA	Estimates standard deviation based on a sample, including numbers, text, and logical values.
STDEVP	Calculates standard deviation based on the entire population.
STDEVPA	Calculates standard deviation based on the entire population, including numbers, text, and logical values.

STEYX	Returns the standard error of the predicted y- value for each x in the regression.
TDIST	Returns the Student's t-distribution.
TINV	Returns the inverse of the Student's t-distribution.
TREND	Returns values along a linear trend.
TRIMMEAN	Returns the mean of the interior of a data set.
TTEST	Returns the probability associated with a Student's t-test.
VAR	Estimates variance based on a sample.
VARA	Estimates variance based on a sample, including numbers, text, and logical values.
VARP	Calculates variance based on the entire population.
VARPA	Calculates variance based on the entire population, including numbers, text, and logical values.
WEIBULL	Returns the Weibull distribution.
ZTEST	Returns the two-tailed P-value of a z-test.

Database Functions

DAVERAGE	Returns the average of selected database entries.
DCOUNT	Counts the cells that contain numbers in a particular field of records that match specified criteria in a database.
DCOUNTA	Counts non blank cells in a particular field of records that match specified criteria in a database.
DGET	Extracts a single record from a database that matches the specified criteria.
DMAX	Returns the maximum value from selected database entries.
DMIN	Returns the minimum value from selected database entries.
DPRODUCT	Multiplies the values in a particular field of records that match the criteria in a database.
DSTDEV	Estimates the standard deviation based on a sample of selected database entries.
DSTDEVP	Calculates the standard deviation based on the entire population of selected database entries.
DSUM	Sums the values in a particular field for all records that match the specified criteria.
DVAR	Estimates variance based on a sample from selected database entries.
DVARP	Calculates variance based on the entire population of selected database entries.

Information Functions

CELL	Returns information about the formatting, location, or contents of a cell.
ERRORTYPE	Returns a number corresponding to an error type.
INFO	Returns information about the current operating environment.
ISBLANK	Returns TRUE if the value is blank.
ISERR	Returns TRUE if the value is any error value expect #N/A.
ISERROR	Returns TRUE if the value is any error value.
ISLOGICAL	Returns TRUE if the value is a logical value.
ISNA	Returns TRUE if the value is the #N/A error value.
ISNONTEXT	Returns TRUE if the value is non text.
ISNUMBER	Returns TRUE if the value is a number.
ISREF	Returns TRUE if the value is reference.
ISTEXT	Returns TRUE if the value is text.
N	Returns a value converted to a number.
NA	Returns the error value #N/A.
TYPE	Returns a number indicating the data type of a value.

CHAPTER 5

Introduction to Microsoft PowerPoint 2013

Introduction

Want to make a presentation in a hurry! This is an ideal program of the same. Make sophisticated slide shows and professional looking electronic presentations. It also allows you to add charts, tables and pictures for make the presentation look alive.

Creating Presentation from Template

Most of the office 2013 software have ready made outputs called Templates. This is true in the case of PowerPoint 2013 too. Let us see how it can be used to create a presentation.

1. Select New from the Office button.
2. Select Installed Themes and then select any one of the available templates. I have chosen Take a tour.

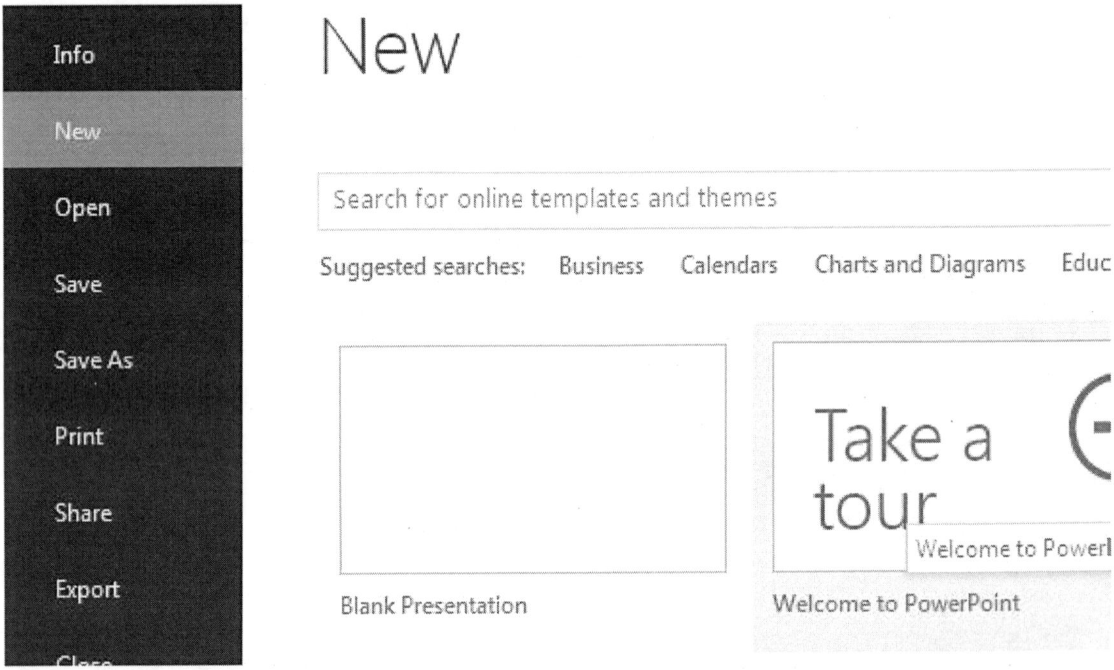

3. Click at Create to start with the presentation.
4. The first slide with the Introduction to PowerPoint 2013 appears on the screen.

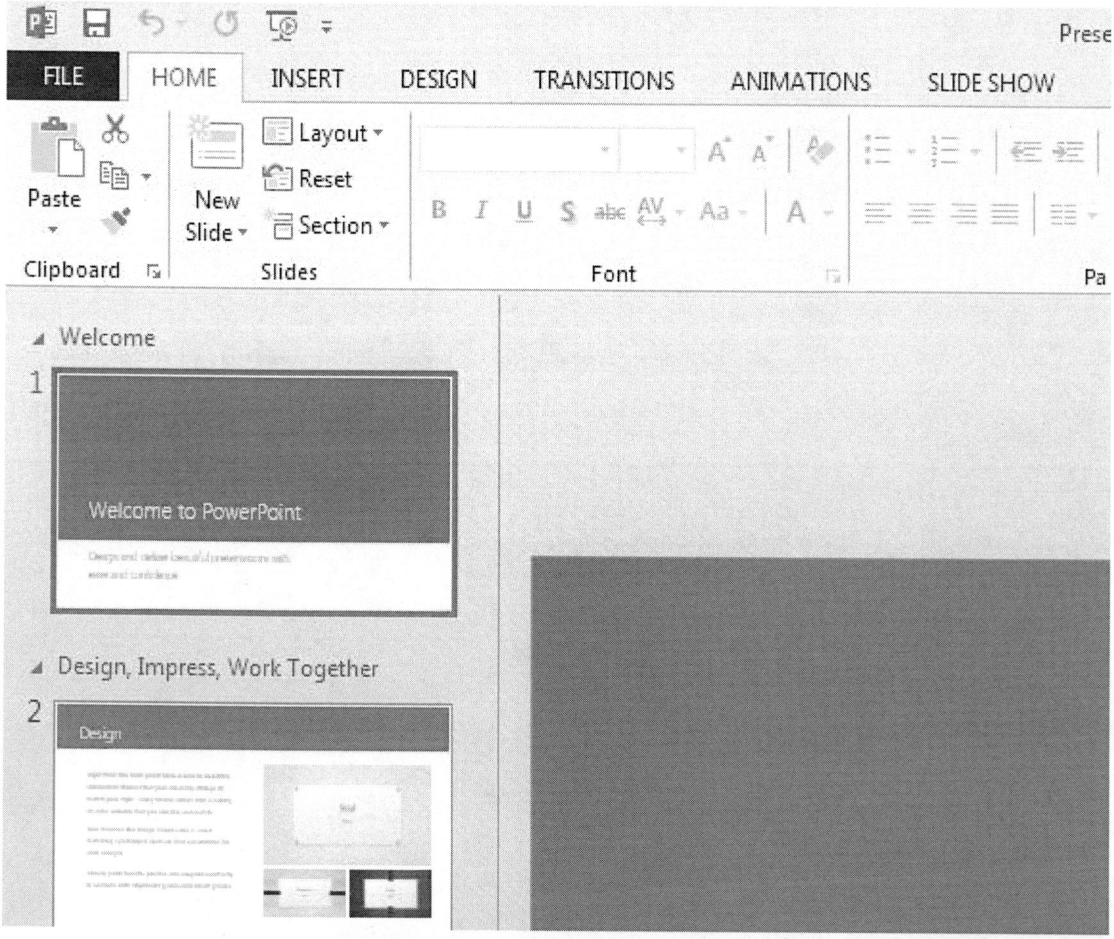

5. As you will that on the left panel 5 slides have been created and are thus numbered from 1 to 5.
6. You can see any one of them by just clicking at it. I am showing here the slide numbers 3 and 18.

Creating a New Presentation

Another method of creating presentation is by using the option of New presentation using the Blank presentation option. You can select an option of text and graphics to make show on the screen.

1. Select New from the Office button.
2. Select Blank presentation and click Create.
3. A new slide is shown on the screen.

PowerPoint Views

There are different ways of looking at the presentations. These are called the views. There are as many as 5 different views in which you can see your presentation. They are:

Outline view: It displays only the text of the presentation in the outline form, allowing you to work easily with the content.

Impress

The improved Presenter View has new tools to keep you in control. The new Auto-Extend instantly applies the right settings for you, so you can focus on speaking instead of your display.

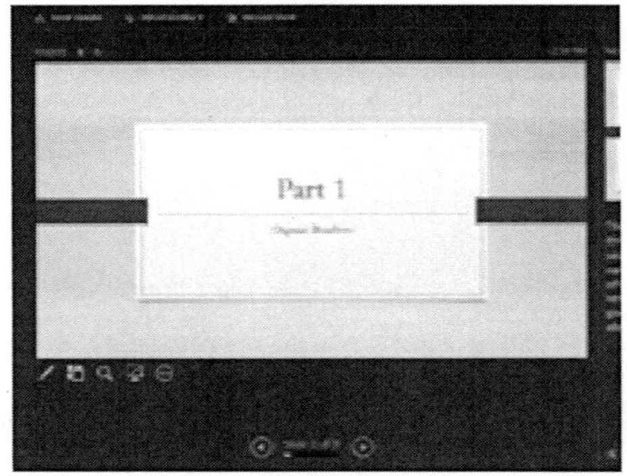

Slide zoom – Help focus your audience on your ideas. Just click to zoom in and out on a specific diagram, chart or graphic.

Slide Navigator – A feature that enables the user to visually browse for and navigate to other slides without leaving Slide Show view. Your audience only sees the slide you're presenting.

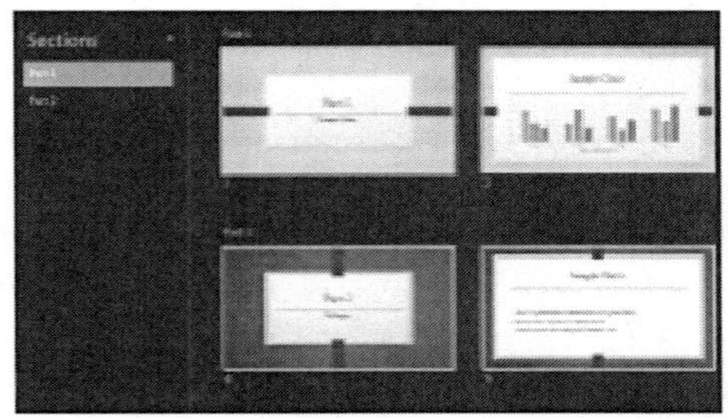

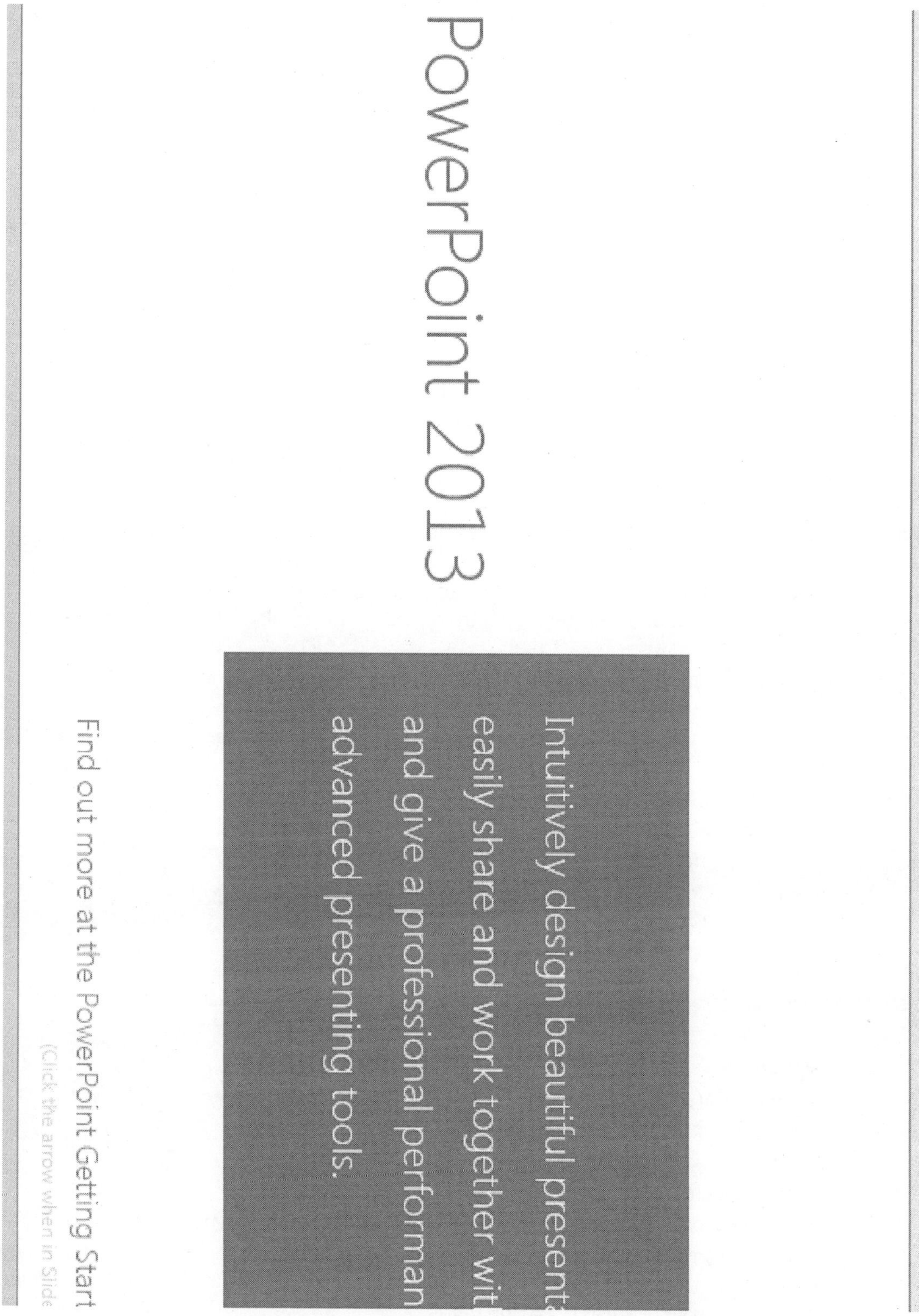
PowerPoint 2013
Intuitively design beautiful presenta
easily share and work together wit
and give a professional performan
advanced presenting tools.
Find out more at the PowerPoint Getting Start
(Click the arrow when in Slide

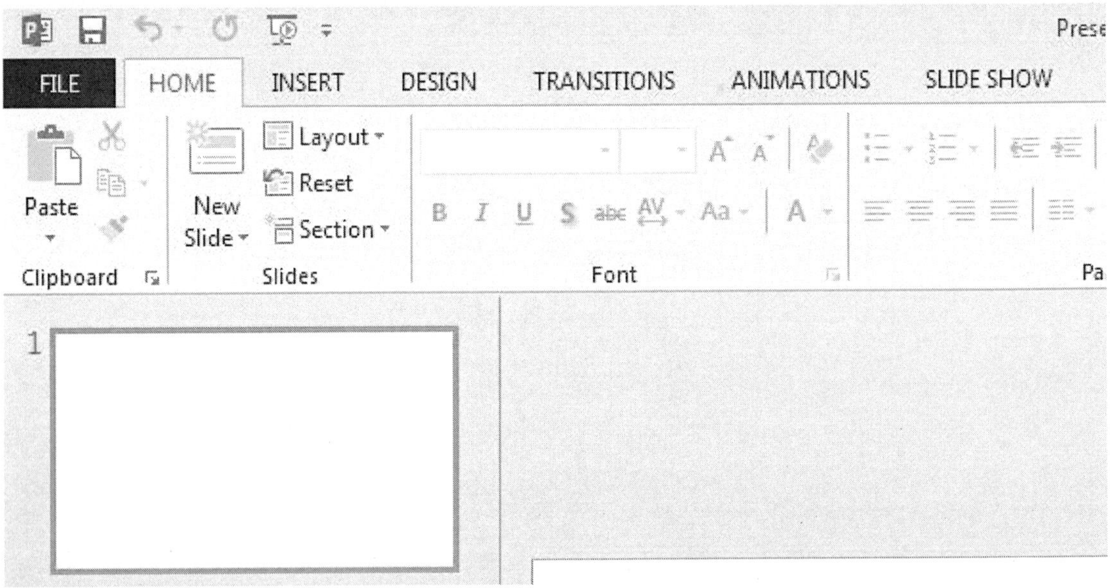

Normal view: It displays 3 panes that show the outline, the slide, and an area which you can enter speaker's notes.

Slide Sorter view: It displays thumbnail views of your slides so that you can reorganize the slides and change the overall look of the presentation. In this view you can also add and edit the transition effects for the slide show.

Slide Show view: It displays the presentation one slide at a time in sequence as an automatic slide show.

Notes Page view: It is available only from the view menu, lets you enter and edit speaker's notes for the presenter.

Points to Remember

1. Each view shows a different aspect of the same presentation.
2. You can switch from one view to another at any time.
3. Right-click in Slide Sorter view or click the button at lower left corner of the current slide to display the Slide Show shortcut menu.

Entering the Text

Let us create another presentation which has more of text. Here, we will add the text as per the following:

1. Create a new presentation which has only text in the slide.
2. Type the name Adobe Corporation in the title bar.
3. In the next box, type the name of the famous software of the company called PageMaker.
4. Pressing enter would lead you to another sub heading.
5. Type here the next heading, Photoshop.
6. Similarly press enter and type Illustrator.
7. Now we come to adding text in between the main headings, i.e., sub-headings.
8. Place your cursor at the end of the first heading, i..e., after PageMaker and press Enter. A new heading with 2 will appear. Just press Tab to get the bulleted text format. Type here the first line of your tabbed matter, which is Version 6.5.

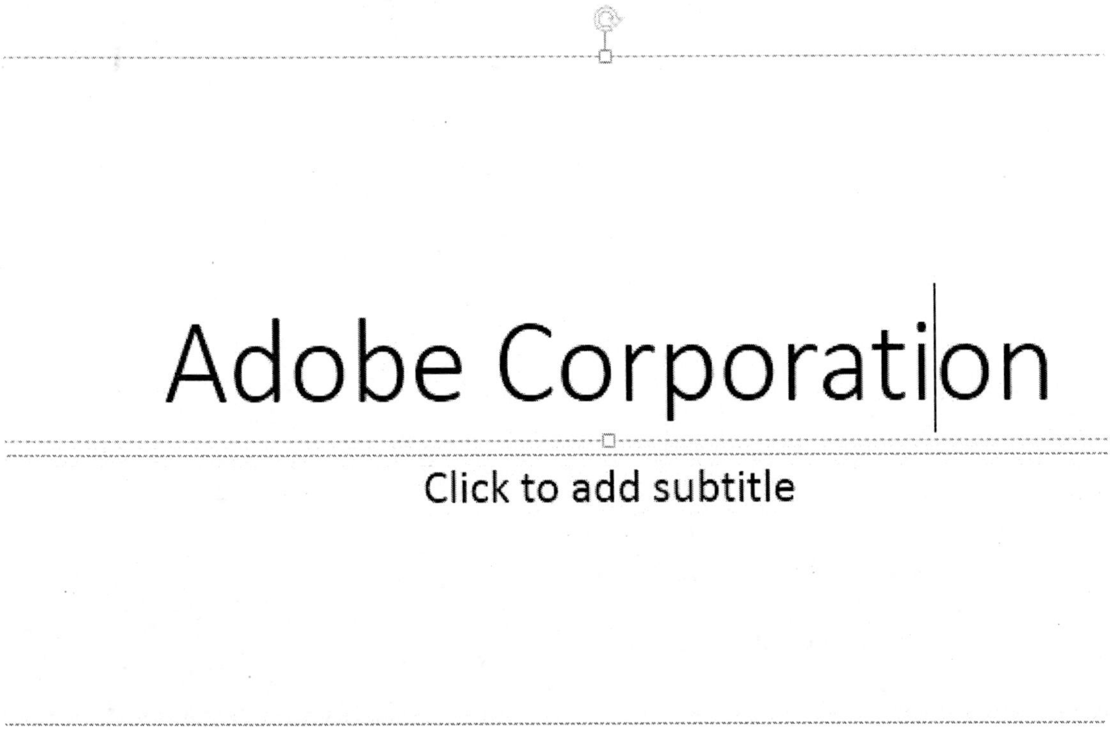
Adobe Corporation
Click to add subtitle

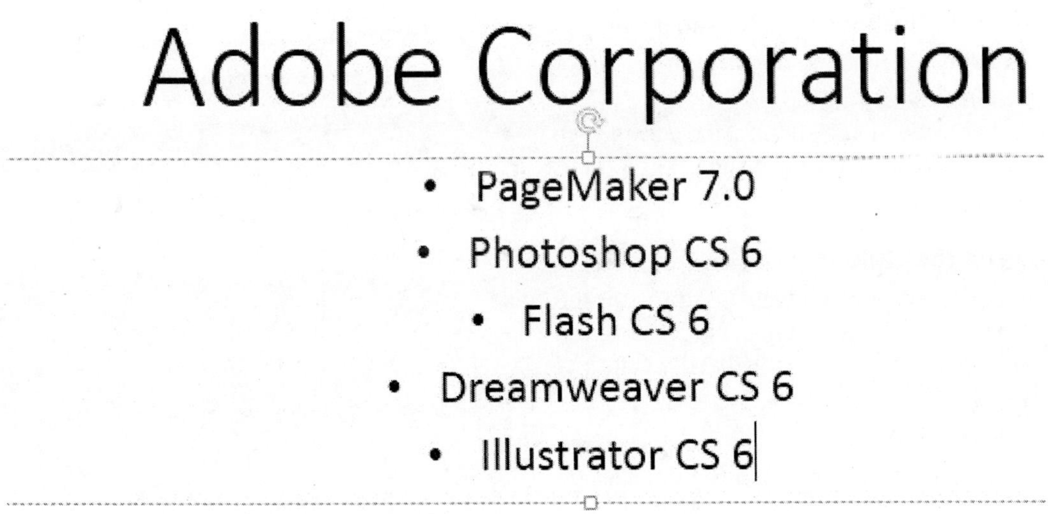
Adobe Corporation
• PageMaker 7.0
• Photoshop CS 6
• Flash CS 6
• Dreamweaver CS 6
• Illustrator CS 6

9. Press enter again to get the new line and type version 7.0.
10. You can thus type the date in the steps required by you.
11. All these slides are shown here.
12. Next obvious step would be change the data, read on.

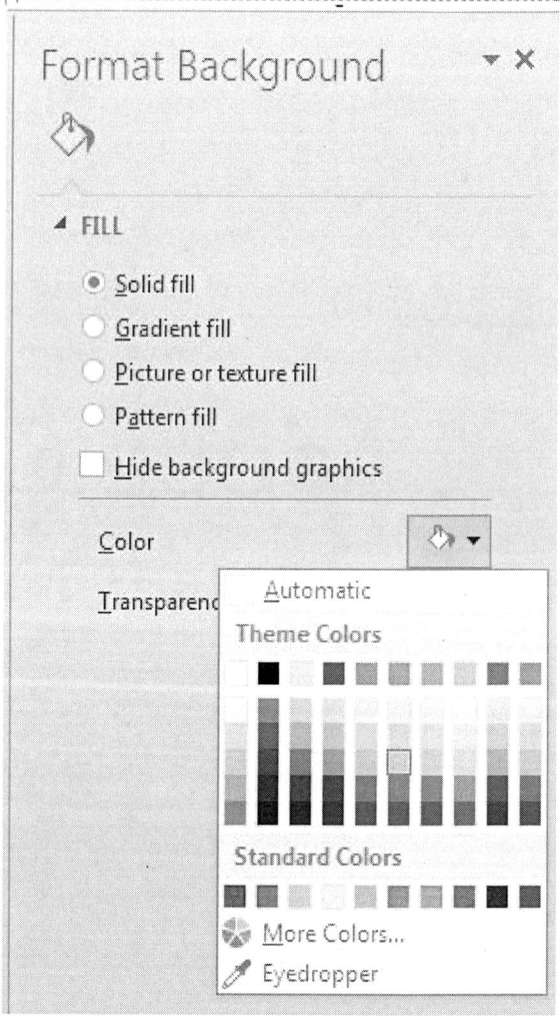

Moving the Text

You can move up or down a particular heading for reorganizing. For this do the following:

1. Highlight the text you want to move.
2. With text highlighted drag the text up or down.
3. Leave the mouse button at the place where you feel like placing the text.
4. The text will be moved there.

Changing the Colour

The colour schemes are always used to suit the atmosphere. So it depends where the presentation is going to be. Depending upon that the colour of the presentations are selected.

To Change the Colours

1. Select Background Styles from Design menu.
2. Background dialog box appears, as shown next.

3. Select whether you want to Fill slide with colours or have a picture as the background.
4. Under Fill, select Gradient fill.
5. Click at Preset colors, it will show you the various options of gradients.
6. Select one of them.
7. In the meanwhile the same colour combination would be applied to the slide and can be seen at the background.
8. Click Ok to make the changes in the slide, as shown below.

To change a slide background picture

1. From the Desing menu, choose background styles option.
2. The Format Background dialog box is displayed.
3. Under Picture, select the picture you want to have as background.
4. Click Apply button to apply the change to the current slide or click Apply to All to apply change to all the slides.

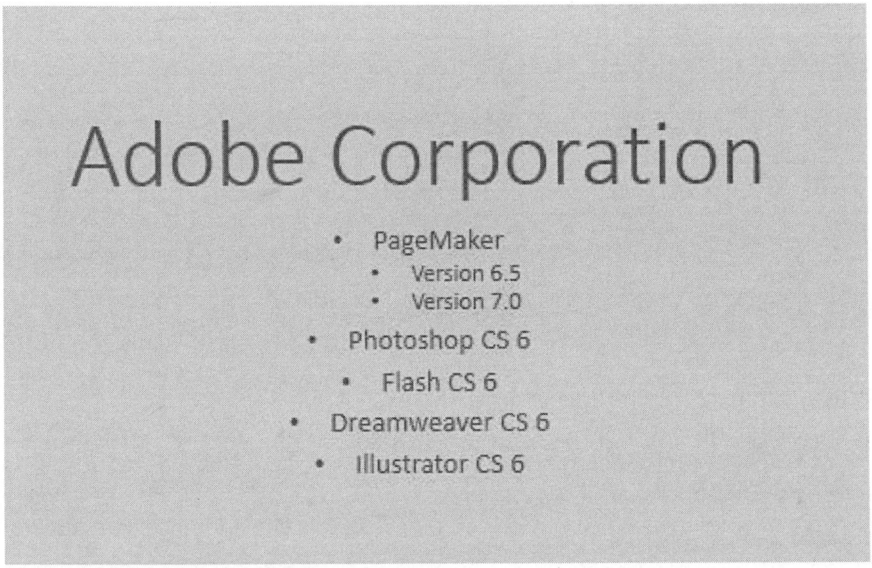

Adding Graphics to a Slide

You can add effects to your slide by adding the various types of graphics to it. Such graphics can be informative, such as a chart that displays sales results; or they can be decorative, such as a cartoon smiley face that emphasizes the presentation's good news.

The three common types of graphics you can add to a PowerPoint slide include:

- **Picture files**: Includes clip art images as well as images you may have stored on your hard disk, such as photographs from your digital camera.
- **Charts**: Displays bar, column, line, pie, and other types of charts.
- **WordArt**: Displays text as colourful tex.

Adding Picture to the Presentation

1. Click a slide to which you want to add a picture.
2. Click the Insert tab.

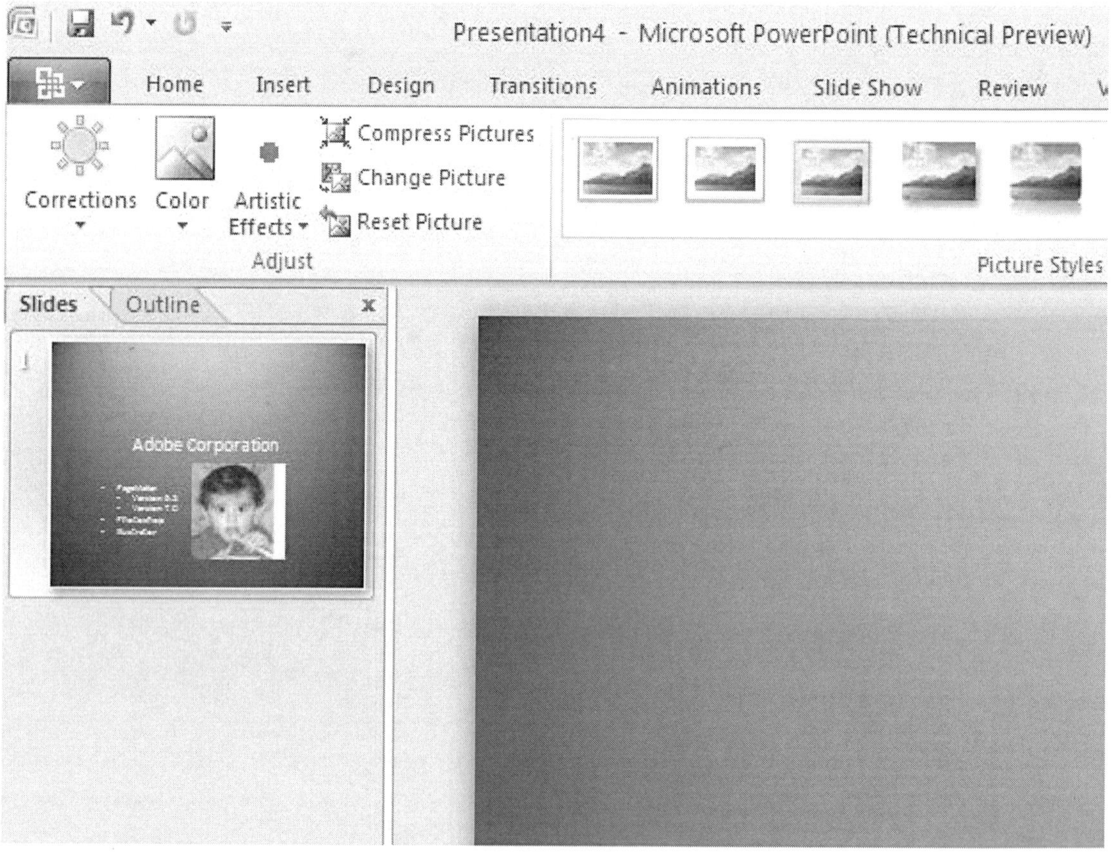

3. Click the Picture icon in the Images group.
4. Click the picture file you want and then click Open.

Adding Clip Art on a Slide

Clip Art consists of drawings that come with PowerPoint. To add a clip art image to a slide, follow these steps.:

1. Click a slide to which you want to add a click art.
2. Click the Insert tab.
3. Click the Clip ARt icon in the Illustrations group.
4. Click in the Search For text box and type a word that describes the type of image you want to find.
5. Click Ok.
6. Click the clip art image you want to use.

Adding from WordArt

WordArt is an independent program which allows you to create text in a presentable form and this text can be used in slides then. This is how it is done.

1. Click the slide to which you want to add WordArt.
2. Click the Insert Tab.

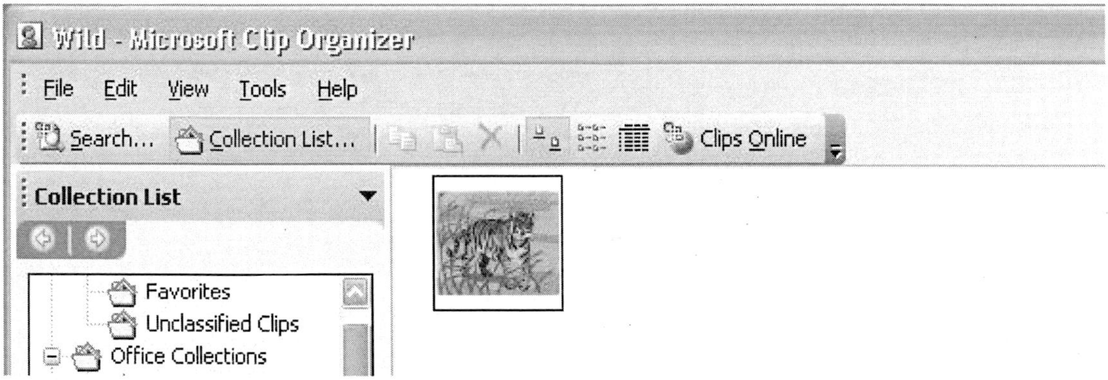
Wild - Microsoft Clip Organizer
File Edit View Tools Help
Search... Collection List... Clips Online
Collection List
Favorites
Unclassified Clips
Office Collections

Presentation4 - Microsoft PowerPoint (Technical Preview)
Home Insert Design Transitions Animations Slide Show Review
Table
Picture Clip Art Pane Screenshot Photo Album
Shapes SmartArt Chart
Hyperlink Action
Text Box
Tables Images Illustrations Links
Slides Outline
Adobe Corporation
Adobe

3. Click the WordArt icon in the Text group.
4. Click a WordArt style to use.
5. Click in the WordArt text box and type text.

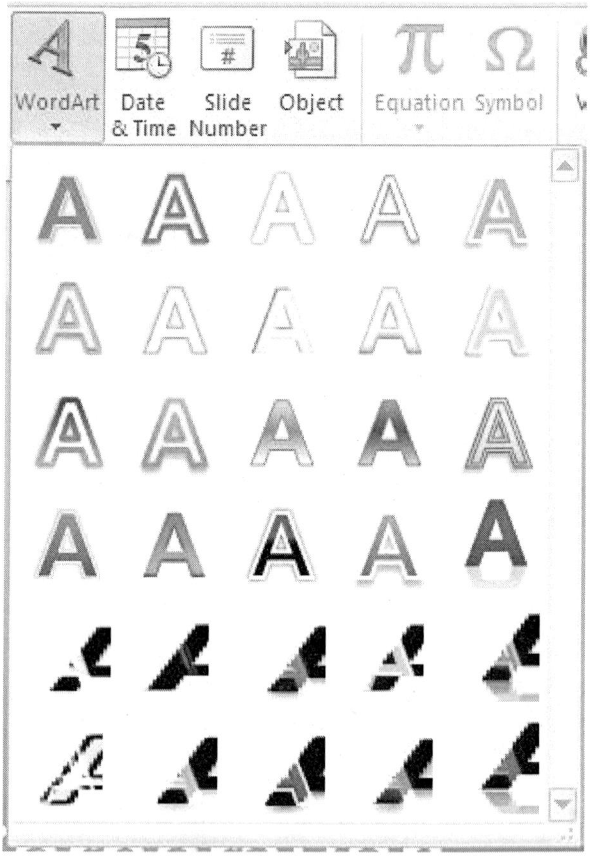

Reordering Slides

As you see from the view, each slide is numbered. These number belong to their order of display. This order can be changed at any point of time in the presentation.

To Change the Order of the Slides:

1. Click with the mouse the slide whose position you want to change.
2. Pressing the mouse button drag the slide to a new position.
3. A vertical line appears to indicate where the slide will drop when you release the mouse button.
4. Releasing the mouse button will drop the slide at the right place.

Points to Remember

1. You can select several slides to move by drawing a selection box around the group of slides and then dragging the group to the new position.
2. You can also select several slides by holding down the Shift key and selecting the first and last slides in the series.
3. To gather slides from different parts of a presentation, hold down the Ctrl key as you click each slide. Drag any one slide in the group to a new point in the presentation. All the selected slides will appear in sequence and in the same relative order at new position.

Duplicating Slides

You can duplicate selected slides in Slide Sorter view and see the effect on the flow of slides immediately.

To Duplicate a slide or slides:

1. Select the slide or slides you want to duplicate.
2. Press Ctrl + D to duplicate the slide.
3. Slide would be duplicated.

Deleting Slides

You can delete the selected slides in Slide Sorter view and see that the numbering of other slides change immediately.

To delete a slide or slides:

1. Select the slide or slides you want to delete.

2. Press right mouse button to get the sub menu.
3. Select Delete slide to delete the slide.

Adding a Movie to a Slide

PowerPoint slides can also display a movie. When you store a movie on a slide, you can resize its size and move it anywhere on your slide. As soon as your slide appears, you hae the option of having the movie play automatically or wait until you click the mouse first.

PowerPoint can use movies stored in common Windows view formats such as AVI, MPEG, ASF (streaming video), and WMV files. If your movie is stored in a different file format, such as QuickTime, you have to convert the file first before you can add it to a PowerPoint presentation.

To add a movie to a slide, follow these steps:

1. Click the slide to which you want to add a movie.
2. Click the Insert tab.
3. Click the Movie icon in the Media Clips group.

   The Insert Movie dialog box appears.

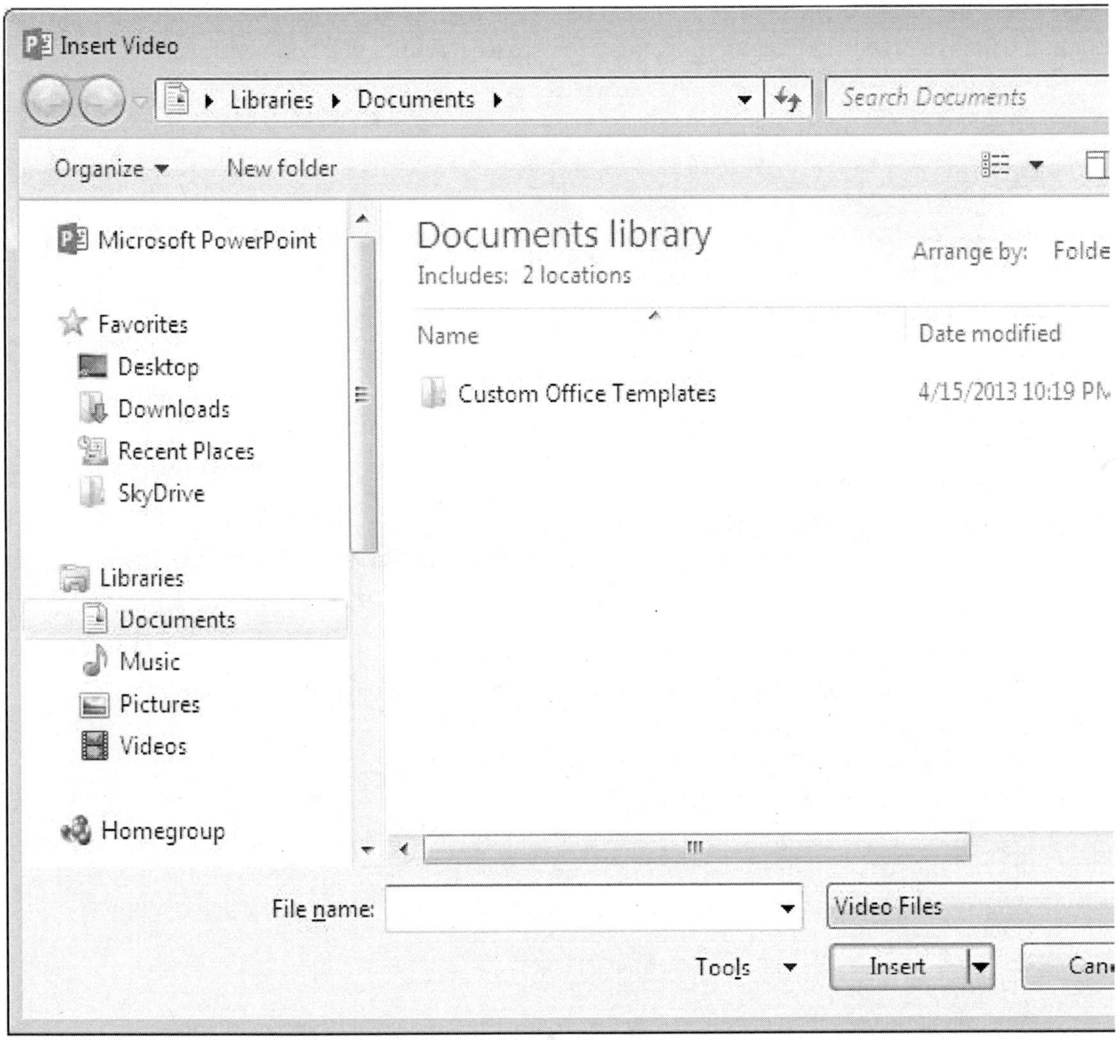

4. Click the movie file you want to add and then click Ok.

   PowerPoint displays a box on your slide where your movie will appear along with a dialog box, asking whether you want the movie to play automatically or when you click the mouse.
5. Clikc Automatically or When clicked.
6. Move the mouse pointer over the movie.

   The mouse pointer turns into a long-way pointing arrow.
7. Hold down the left mouse button and drap (move) the mouse to place the movie where you want it to appear on the slide.
8. Move the mouse pointer over one corner of the movie until the mouse pointer turns into a two-way pointing arrow.
9. Hold down the left mouse button and drag (move) the mouse to resize the movie.

Adding Sound

You can add sounds to the transition effects and to the preset animation. You can also add audio to your presentation by inserting files from the Clip Art Gallery or from other folders available to you.

PowerPoint can use audio files stored in common formats such as AIFF, MIDI, MP3, and WAV file. If your audio file is stored in a different file format, such as Real Audio, you will have to convert the file first before you can add it to a PowerPoint presentation.

To Add an Audio File

1. Select the slide where you want to put this audio.
2. Click the Insert tab.
3. Click the downward-pointing arrow underneath the Sound icon to the Media Clips group.
4. Choose Sound from File

   The Insert Sound dialog box appears.
5. Click the audio file you want to add and thne click Ok.

   PowerPoint adds you audio file to the currently displayed slide (reprresent as a horn icon) and displays a dialog box, asking whether you want the sound to play automatically or when you click the mouse.
6. Click Automatically or When Clicked.

   PowerPoint displays your audio file as a sound icon on your slide. You may want to move the sound icon on your slide so it doesn't obscure part of your slide.

Adding Slide Transitions

These effects can be of the form of wipes, splits, dissolves, etc., which you usually see in the film show. For this you have to work in the Slide Sorter view.

When creating a transition, you need to define the following:

- The actual visual appearance of the transition.
- The speed of the transition (Slow, Medium, or Fast).
- Any sound effects you want to play during the transition (these can get really annoying, so use them sparingly)
- When to display the transition (after a certain time period or when you click the mouse).

To Add a Transition View

1. Click a slide (in the Slide or Outline view pane).

   Any transition you choose will end by displaying the slide you choose in this step.

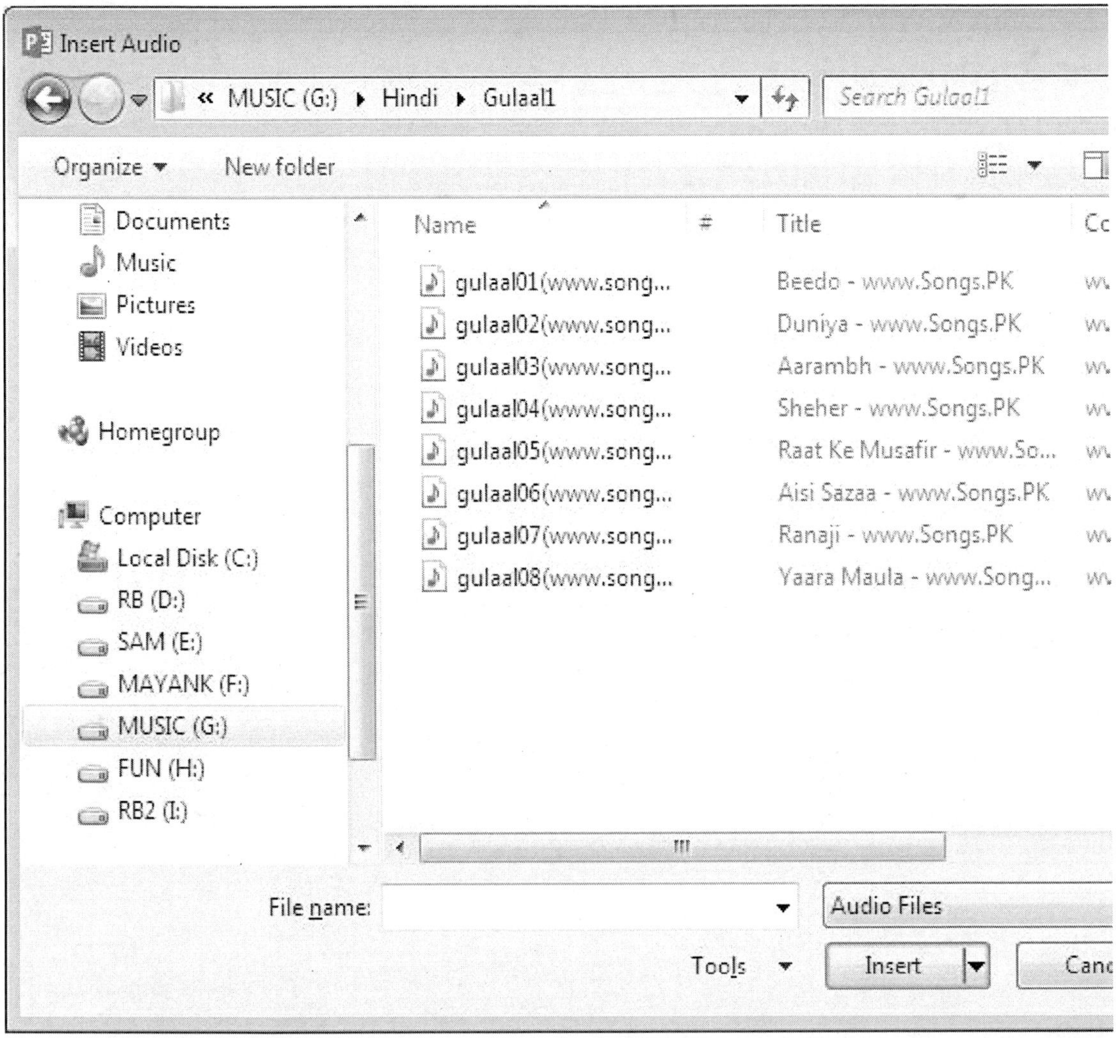

2. Click the Animations tab.

   PowerPoint displays the different animation.
3. Click the More button of the Transition To This Slide group.

   A pull-down menu appears listing all the different transitions available. If you move the mouse over the a transition, PowerPoint shows you what that transition will look like on your chosen slide.
4. Click the transition you want.
5. Click in the Transition Sound list box and choose a sound, such as Cash Register or Drum Roll.
6. Click in the Transition Speed list box and choose a speed (Slow, Medium, or Fast).
7. Select the Automatically After or the On Mouse Click check box.

   If you select the Automatically After check box, you have to specify a time in the Automatically After text box for the slide to wait before running the transition.

   You can select both the On Mouse Click and Automatically After check boxes, so the slide transition waits until you click the mouse or until a certain amount of time passes.

8. Click Apply to All to apply your transition to every slide in your presentation.

Adding Text Transitions

Besides animating how your slides appear and disappear you can also add transitions to your text boxes or graphics so they fly or drop into place across a slide.

Use text transitions sparingly becaust eht transitions can get distracting when people just want to read your presentation without having to watch letters zoom around the screen.

To Create a simple text ransition, follow these steps:

1. Click a text box or picture on a slide.
   PowerPoint displays handles around your chosen item.
2. Click the Animations tab.
3. Click the Animate list box in the Animations group.
   A list of different animation schemes appear.
4. Click an animation, such as Fly In or Wipe.
   PowerPoint animates your text so you can see how it looks.

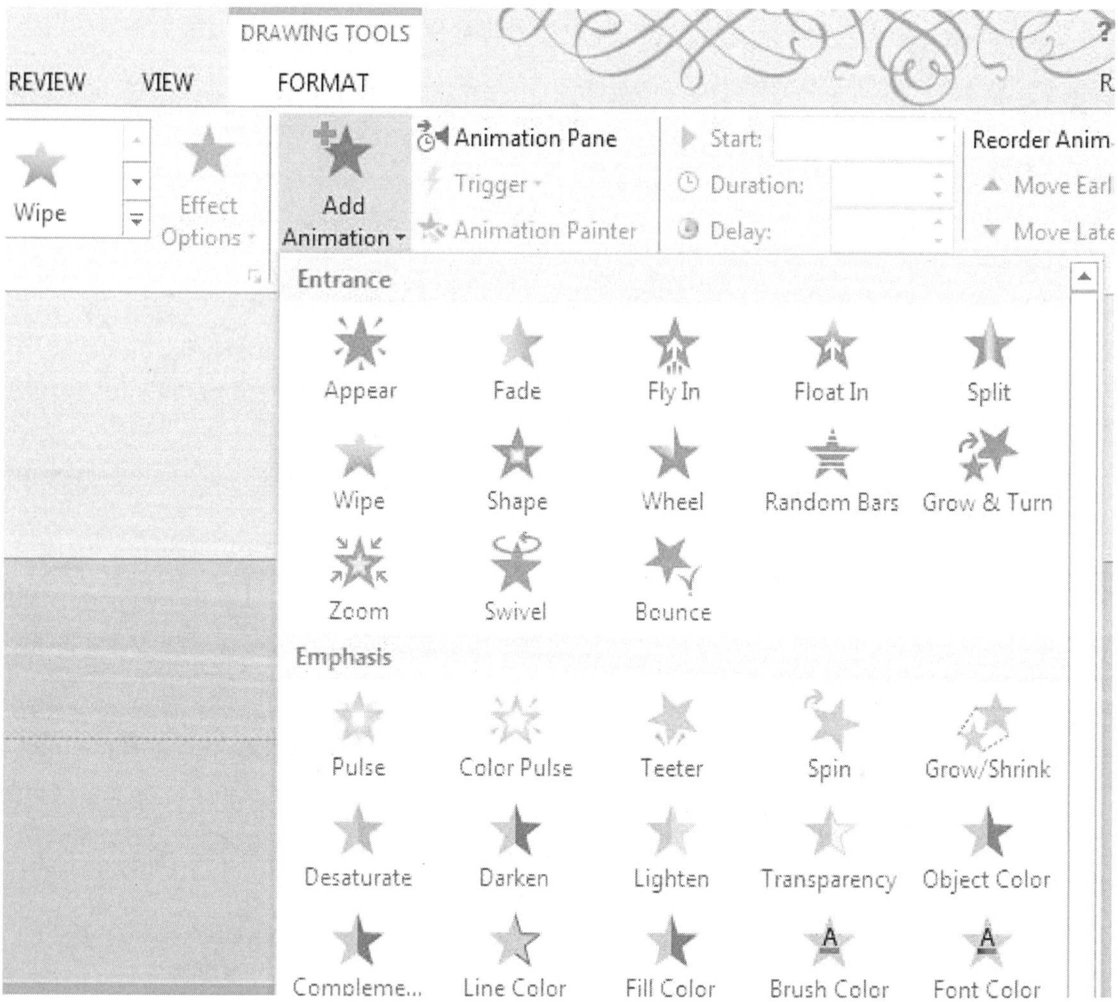

Viewing a Presentation

After you finish arranging your slides, adding transitions, and adding hyper links, you are ready to test how your entire presentation looks. To view your entire presentation, follow these steps:

1. Click the Slide Show tab.
2. Click the From Beginning icon in the Start Slide Show group.

   PowerPoint displays the first slide of your presentation.
3. Choose one of the following:

- Click the mouse or press the spacebar to view the next slide.
- Press Esc to exit your presentation.

  If you have a large presentation consisting of 300 slides, you may not want ot view the first 290 slides just to test how your last 10 slides look. To avoid this problem, PowerPoint lets you choose to view your presentation starting with any slide.

  To view your presentation starting with a slide other than the first one, follow these steps:

1. Click the Slide Show tab.
2. Click the From Current Slide icon in the Start Slide Show group. PowerPoint displays the currently displayed slide.
3. Choose one of the following:

- Click the mouse or press the spacebar to view the next slide.
- Press Esc to exit your presentation.

Making Slide Shows

This effect shows all the hard work you have put in making the slides. It shows one slide after another, stopping in between for a set time on either the monitor of your screen or on the projector which may have been attached to your computer. It is also possible to add animated effects on the slides and show them in a sophisticated manner. It is also possible to add audio, video, narration, music, etc., to your slides.

To arrange the order of a custom slide show, follow these steps:

1. Click the Slide Show tab.
2. Click the the Custom Slide Show icon in the Start Slide Show group.

   A pull down menu appears.
3. Choose Custom Shows.

   The Custom Shows dialog box appears.
4. Click New.

   The Define Custom Show dialog box appears.
5. Click in the Slide Show Name text box and type a name for your custom slide show.
6. Clcik a slide in the Slides in Presentation list box and then click the Add button.

   This tells PowerPoint which existing slides you want to resuse in your custom slide show.
7. Repeat Step 6 for each slide you want to include in your custom slide show.
8. Click a slide in the Slides in Custom Show list box and click the Up or Down arrow button to rearrange their order.
9. Repeat Step 8 for each slide you want to rearrange in your custom slide show.

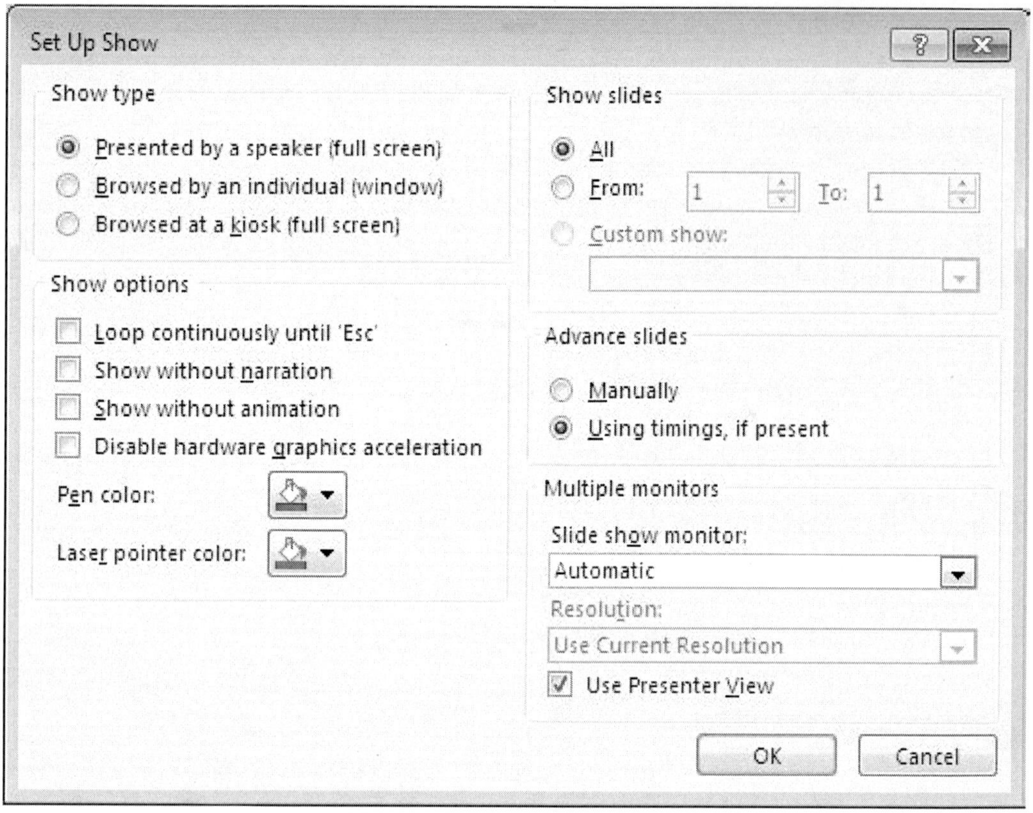

10. Click Ok.

    The Custom Shows dialog box appears again.

11. Click the name of your custom slide show and then click Show.

    PowerPoint shows your new, customized presentation.

To present a custom slide show, follow these steps:

1. Click the Slide Show tab.
2. Click the Custom Slide Show icon in the Start Slide Show group.

   A pull-down menu appears that lists the names of all the custom slide shows you have created.

3. Click the name of the custom slide show you want to view.
4. Choose one of the following:

- Click the mouse or press the spacebar to view the next slide.
- Press Esc to exit your presentation.

Hiding a Slide

PowerPoint can hide a slide, which lets you keep your slide but not display it during a presentation. Hiding a slide can be expecially handy when you need to create a custom slide show and need a slide show but not the original presentation (or vice versa).

To hide a slide, followthese steps:

1. Click the slide that you want to hide (in Slide or Outline view).
2. Click the Slide Show tab.
3. Click the Hide Show icon in the Set Up group.

   PowerPoint dims your selected slide.

   To unhide a slide, just repeat the above three steps.

Notes, Handouts and Masters for Presentation

There are three important tools for your presentation. These tools are:

Notes Pages

These pages are like the script for your presentation. In this script you have an image of slides along with the words you want to deliver for the specific slide.

Handouts

These printed pages are the hard copies of the presentation slides which you can distribute to your audience.

Master

These are control elements of a slide like the title master which controls appearance of the title on all the slides.

Using Notes Pages

Notes Pages act like a cheat sheet for your presentation. You would write the text you want to read without letting the audience know that you are reading during the course of a presentation for each slide.

Printing Handouts

You can print your entire presentation in the form of handouts. These handouts are used to distribute among the audience in advance. You can also print specific slides, notes pages or outline pages.

For this do the following:

1. Open the presentation you want to print.
2. Click the Office button and Print.
3. The Print dialog box appears.
4. In the Print what: box, click the item you want to print.
5. If you select Handouts, you can then select a number of slides per page and whether the order should be horizontal or vertical,
6. Select any other options you want to apply.

7. After applying the option in the handouts section, click OK.

Handouts Master

The Handouts Master can be used to modify your Handout format.

For this do the following:

1. Click the View menu, highlight Master and choose Handout Master. The Handout Master appears.
2. In the Handout Master view, you can select the two slide per page, three slides per page or the six slides per page formats by clicking on the Handout Master toolbar as shown.
3. To apply any changes to the Handout Master, just follow the procedure as for the Notes master.
4. Save the presentation file to save any changes you make to the Handout Master.
5. You cannot change the position of the slide images on the Handout Master.
6. There is no notes text placeholder on the Handout Master.

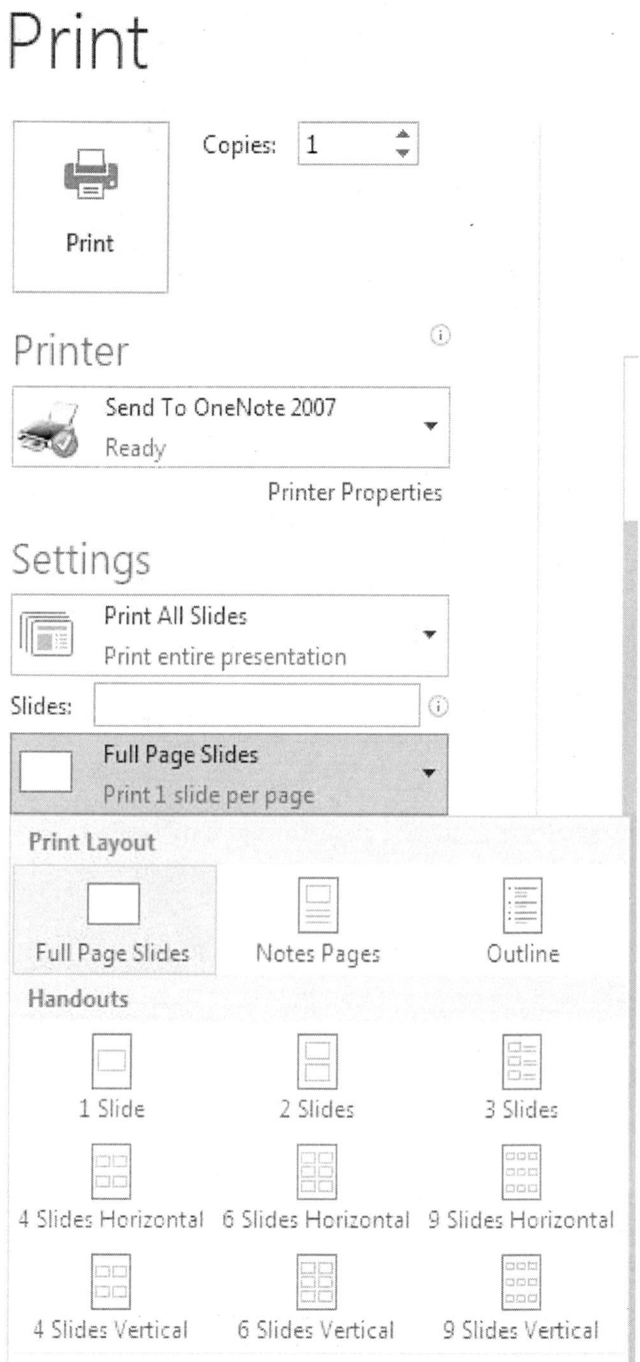

CHAPTER 6

Introduction to Microsoft Access 2010

Introduction

A software to take care of most of your database requirements. It allows you to store and organize information in sets of tables, which can be displayed in the form of columns and rows to look like a table or an index card. What's more it allows you to perform calculations and find for you simple statistics like totals and averages. It allows you to sort the data in any form and extract the required information based on the key given by you.

Creating a Database

Creating database with a Wizard is probably the easiest and fastest method of creating a database where you have to fill up some information and the database is ready for you. It not only creates Tables for you but all the Forms, Reports, etc., connected with it are done too.

Creating Database using the Wizard

Access can create a blank database or a database using one of many templates available from the Microsoft Web site. No matter how you create a database, you will likely need to modify it to customize it for the type of data you want.

To create a blank database, follow these steps:

1. Click the Info button and choose New.

   The Getting Started with Microsoft Access screen appears.

2. Click the Blank Database icon.

   The file name text box appears in the right corner of the screen.

3. Type a descriptive filename for your database.

   You may want to click the Browse icon to specify a different folder or drive to store your database.

4. Click Create.

   Access displays a blank table and an Add New Field text box. Displaying your database in rows and columns in Datasheet view.

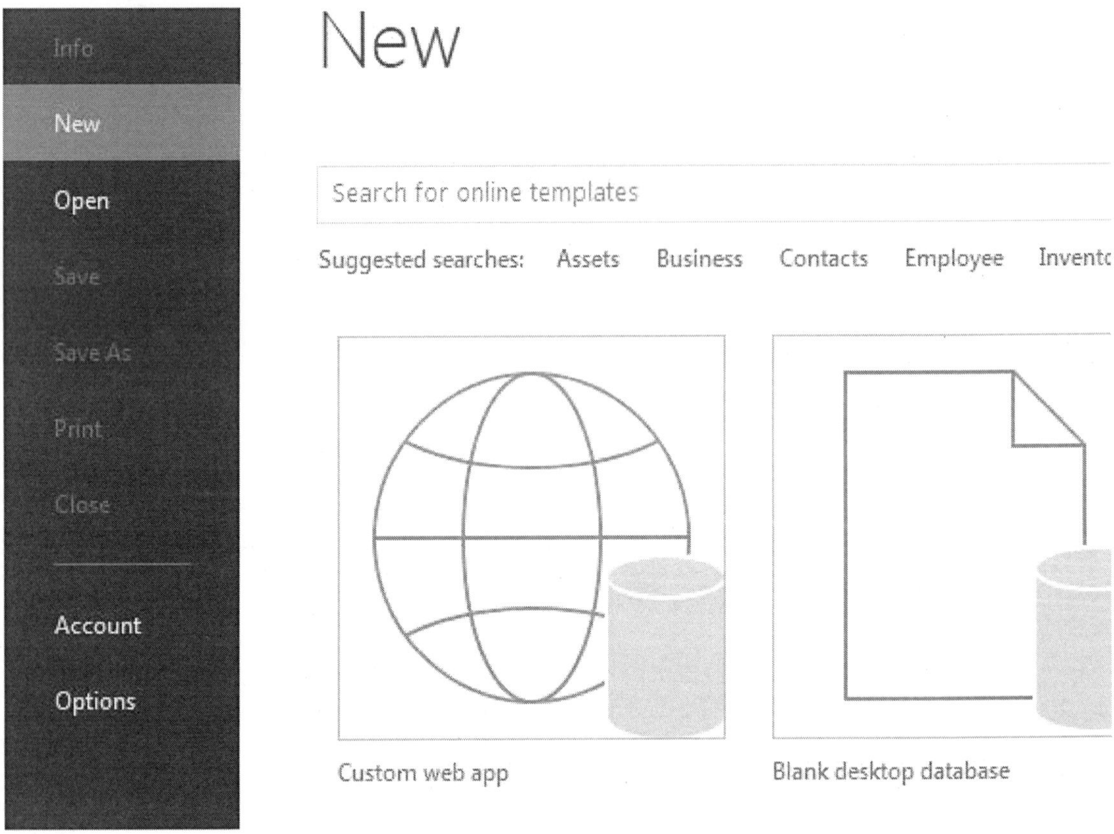

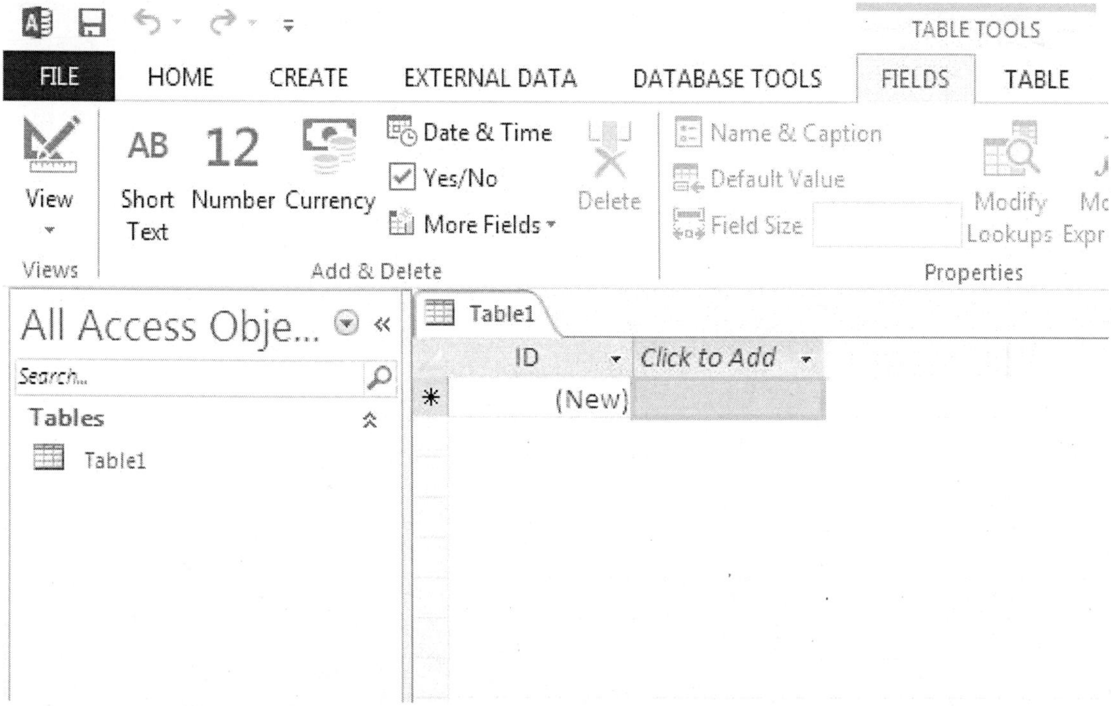

Creating Database using the Template

Just like it's easier to copy someone else's work, it's easier to use an existing database templates and modify it for your own needs. You need an Internet connection to retrieve any database templates from the Microsoft Web site.

To create a database file from a template, follow these steps:

1. Click the Info button and choose New.

   The Getting Started with Microsoft Access screen appears.

2. Click a category under the From Microsoft Office Online categroy such as Business or Education or choose Local Templates.

   A list of available templates appear.

3. Click a template. Access displays a default name in the File Name text box in the bottom right corner of the screen.

4. Type a descriptive name for your database in the File Name text box and then click Create.

   Access displays your database in rows and columns (Datasheet View).

   On the next page, see the database of Project Management.

Working with Fields of Database

After you have created a database and it has given you a database in the Datasheet View. It becomes apparent that you add fields, name them and then fill up the data in them (or import it).

Naming a Field

If you create a database from scratch, Access displays generic field names such as Field1. If you create a database from a template, you will see the descriptive field names, but you may still want to rename the fields to something else.

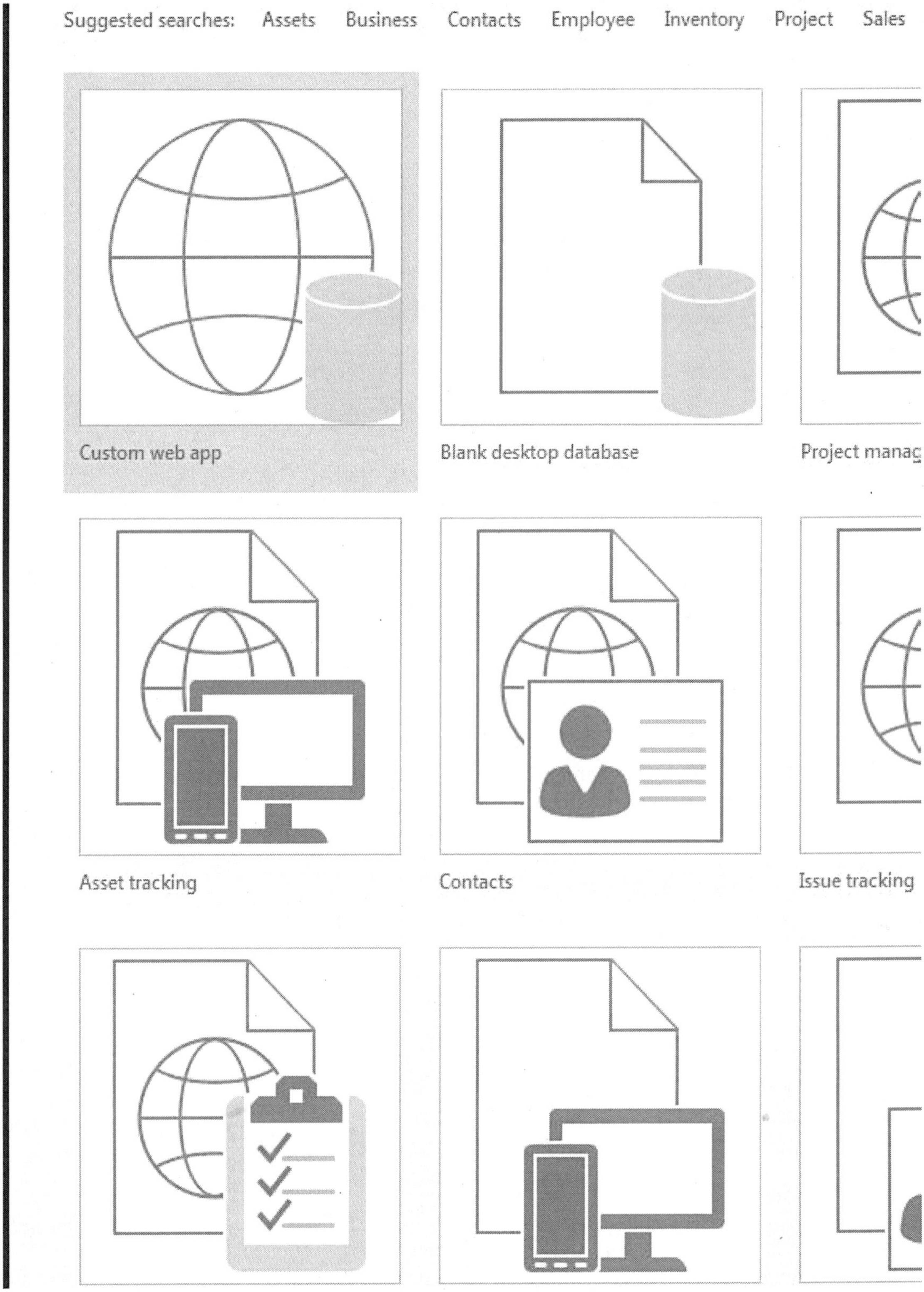
Suggested searches: Assets Business Contacts Employee Inventory Project Sales
Custom web app
Blank desktop database
Project manag
Asset tracking
Contacts
Issue tracking

To rename a field, follow these steps:

1. Click the Info Button and then choose Open.
   The Open dialog box appears.
2. Click the Access database file you want to modify and then click Open.
   Access displays your chosen database.
3. In the All Tables pane on the left of the screen, double-click the table that contains the fields you want to rename.
   Access displays the Datasheet view of your database.
4. Click the Datasheet tab.
5. Click the field (column head) that you want to rename.
6. Click the Rename icon in the Fields & Columns group.
   Access highlights the field name.
7. Type a new name for your field and then click outside the field name when you are done.

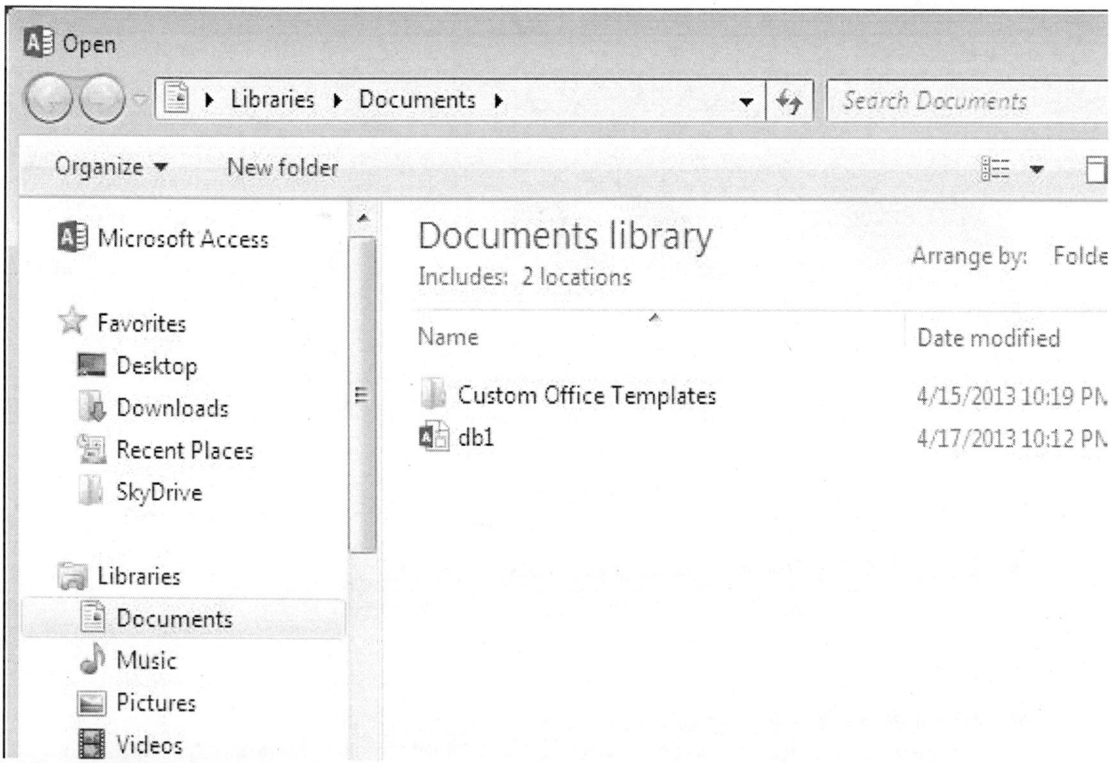

Adding/Deleting a Field

Sometimes you may need to add a field to make room to store new information. Other times, you may want to delete a field that you don't really want after all.

To add a field to a database table, follow these steps:

1. Click an existing field in your database table.
2. Click the Datasheet tab.
3. Click the Insert button in the Fields & Columns group.
   Access inserts a new field (column) in your database table.

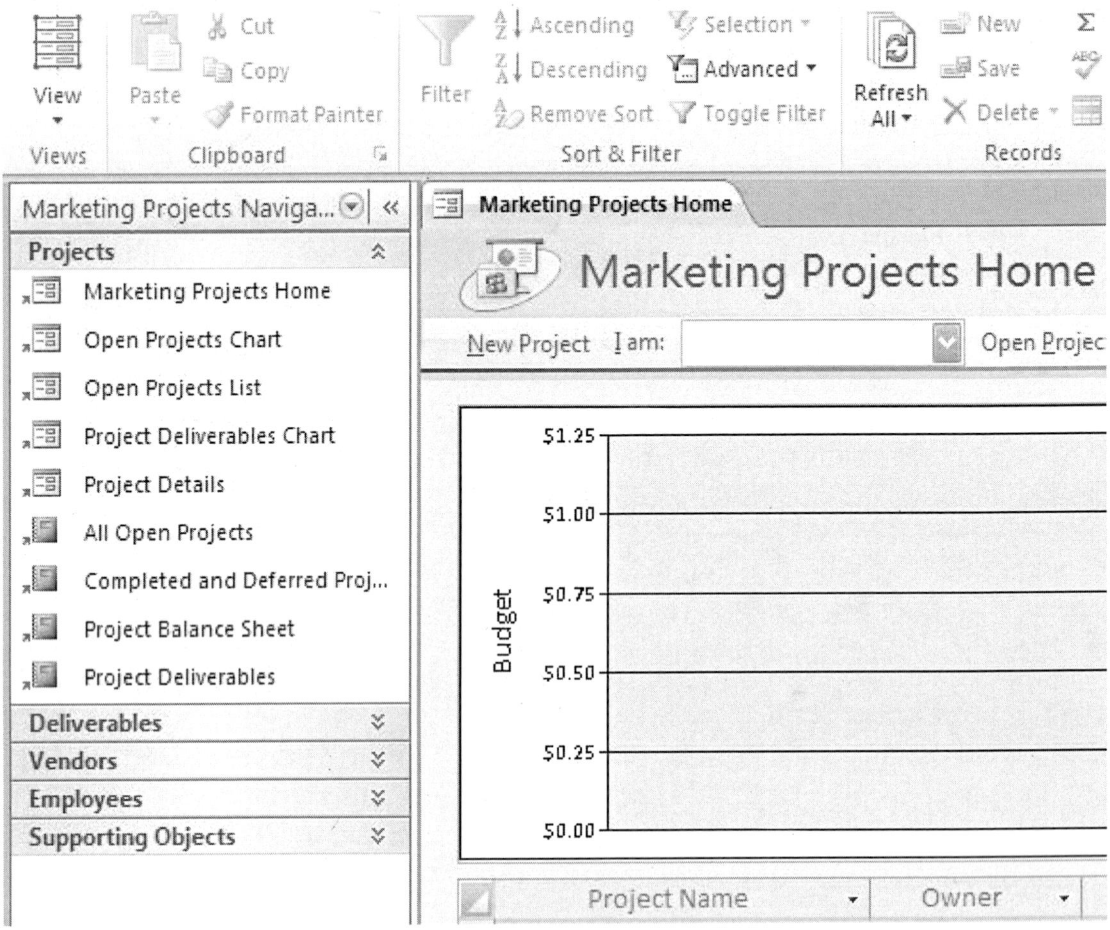

To delete a field from a database table, follow these steps:

1. Click the field you want to delete.

   Access highlights the entire column in your database table.
2. Click the Datasheet tab.
3. Click the Delete button in the Fields & Columns group.

   A dialog box appears, asking whether you want to permanently delete all the data in the field.

   If you delete a field, you also delete any data that may be stored in the field. Depending on how much data you have stored, you could wipe out a lot of information by deleting a signle field, so be careful.
4. Click Yest (or No).

   If you click Yes, Access deletes your chosen field.

Setting the Type and Size of a Field

The type of a field defines the type of data the field can hold (numbers, text, dataes, and so on), and the size of a field defines the amount of data the field can hold (no numbers larger than 250 digits, any text string fewer than 120 characters, and so on).

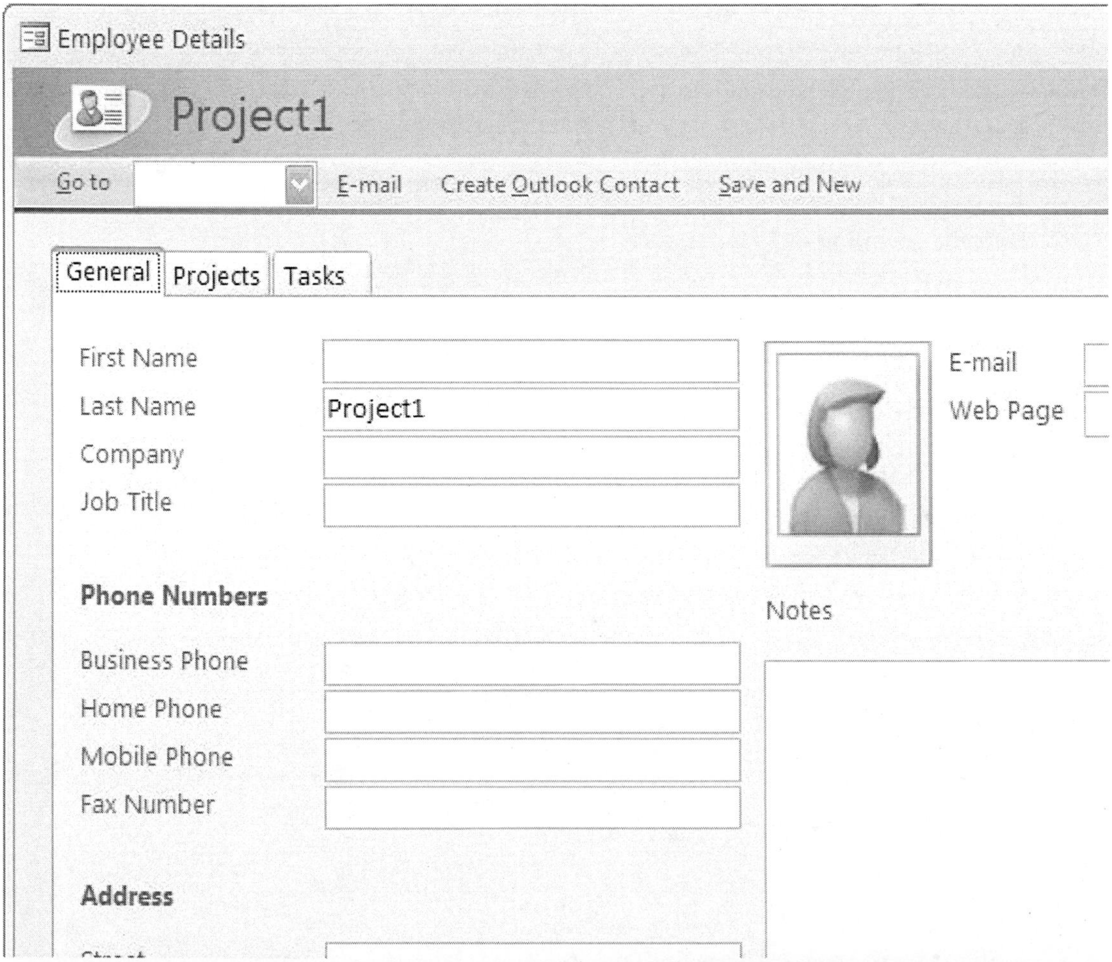

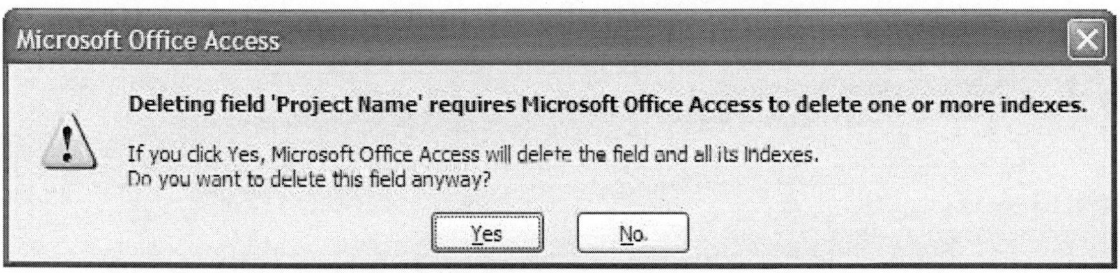

To define the type and amount of a data a field can store, follow these steps:

1. Click the Home or Datasheet tab.
2. In the All Tables pane on the left of the screen, double-click the table that contains the fields you want to define.

   Access displays the Datasheet view of your table.
3. Click the downward-pointing arrow underneath the View icon, which appears in the Views group.

   A pull down menu appears.

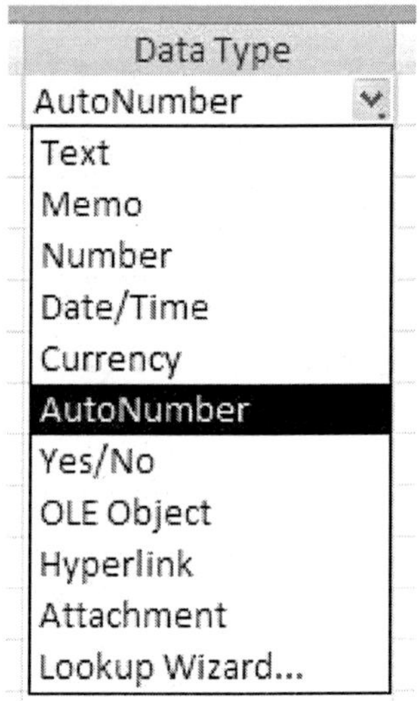

4. Click Design View.
   Access displays the Design view of your database table.
5. Click in the Field Name column and edit an existing filed name.
   If you click in a blank row, you can add a field to a database table.
6. Click in the Data Type column.
   A downward-pointing arrow appears.
7. Click the downward-pointing arrow.
   A pull-down menu appears, listing all the different types of data you can define to store in a field.
8. Choose a data type, such as Number, Text or Data/Time. Access displays a General tab that contains different options for modifying your chosen data type.
9. Click one of the data type options, such as Format or Input Mask, listed under the General tab.
   Sometimes you have to type a value directly into a data type option. Other time a pull-down menu appears, from which you can choose an option.
10. Repeat Step 9 for each data type option you want to modify.

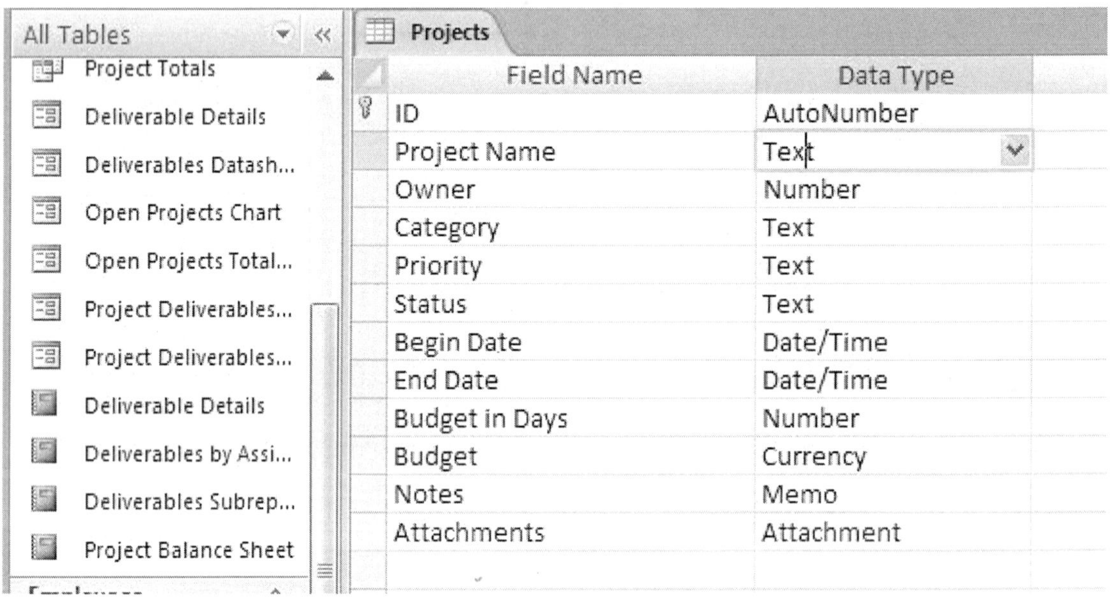

Creating a Form

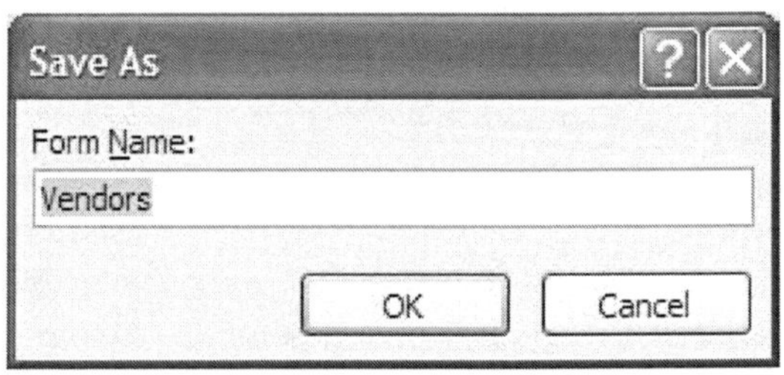

The biggest problem with Datasheet view is that it can be confusing to find a field for a specific record. Because most people are familiar with paper forms or index cards that arrange related data (fields) on a page, Access offers you Form view. Form view simply displays the fields of a single record onscreen. To use Form view, you must first create a form and arrange your fields on that form. After you create a form, you can add, edit and view data through that form.

General | Lookup

Display Control	Combo Box
Row Source Type	Table/Query
Row Source	SELECT [Employees Extended].ID, [Employees Extended].[Employee Name]
Bound Column	1
Column Count	2
Column Heads	No
Column Widths	0";2"
List Rows	16
List Width	2"
Limit To List	Yes
Allow Multiple Values	No
Allow Value List Edits	Yes
List Items Edit Form	Employee Details
Show Only Row Source V	No

Creating a Form

The simplest way to create a form to let Access desing one for you, which you can modify.

To create a form quickly, follow these steps:

1. Click the Office Button and then choose Open.

   The Open dialog box appears.
2. Click the Access database file you want to add or edit data. Then click Open.

   Access displays your chosen database.
3. In the All Tables pane on the left of the screen, double-click a table.

   Access displays the Datasheet view of your database.
4. Click the Create tab.
5. Click the Form icon in the Forms group.

   Access creates a form. Notice that the form name automatically uses the name of the database table you choose in Step 3.
6. Click the Office Button and then choose Save (or click the Save icon on the Quick Access toolbar).

   The Save As dialog box appears, asking you to type a name for your form.
7. Type a descriptive name for your form in the Form Name text box and then click Ok.

   Acess displays your form's name underneath the All Tables pabe. The next time you open this database and want to view the form, you can double-click the form's name in the left pane.

Searching a Database

The simplest type of search ooks for a specific record. To search for a record, you need to know the data stored in at least one of its fields, such as a phone number and e-mail address. The more information you already know, the more likely Access will find the one record you want. If you search for all records that contain the first name, Access could find dozens of records. But, if you feed in the name and surname, your search would narrow down to just few records.

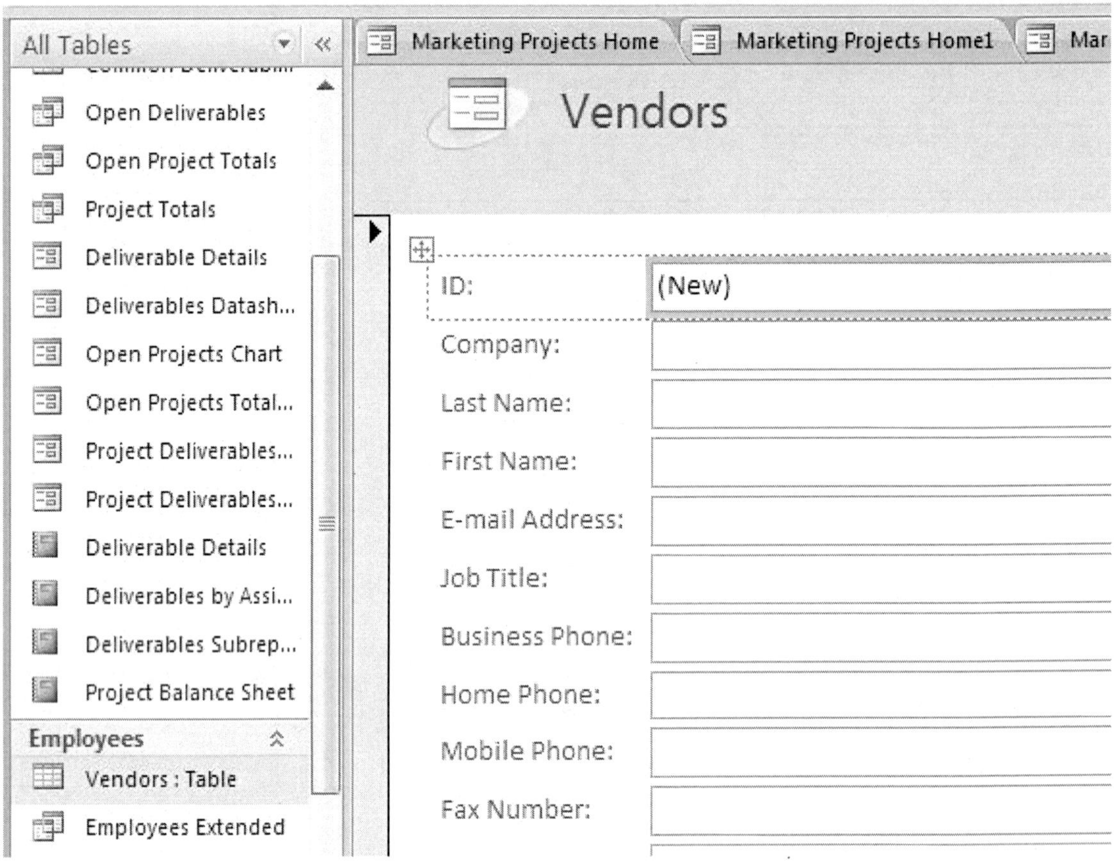

To search for a specific record in a database table, follow these steps:

1. In the All Tables pane on the left of the screen, double-click the name of the databse table you want to search.

   Access displays the Datasheet view of your database.
2. Click the Home tab.
3. Click the Find icon in the Find group.

   The Find and Replace dialog box appears.
4. Click in the Find What text box and type in the data you know is stored in the record in the record you want to find.

   For example, if you want to find the phone number of a person but you know only that person's last name in the Find What text box.
5. Click the Look In list box and choose the name of the entire databse table.
6. Click in the Match list box and choose one of the following:
   - Any Part of Field: The Find What text can appear in any part of a field.
   - Whole Field: The Find What text is the only text stored in a field.
   - Start of Field: The Find What text can be only at the beginning of a field.
7. Click in the Search list box and choose one of the following:.
   - Up: Searches from the record where the cursor appears, up to the beginning of the database table.

- Down: Searches from the record where the cursor appears, down to the end of the database table.
- All: Searches the entire database table.

8. Click Find Next.
9. Repeat Step 8 to search for more records that might contain the text you typed in Step 4.
10. Click Cancel or the Close button.

Creating a Query

A query is nothing more than a saved version of your sort or filter criteria. By saving the particular sort or filter criteria as a query, you can select that query by name later.

Creating a Simple Query

If your databse table contains dozens of different fields, you may find it confusing to make sense of all your information. As an aid, a simple query strips away fields so you see only the fields containing data you want to see, such as a person's name and phone number but not her hire date or employee number.

To create a query, follow these steps:

1. Click the Create tab.
2. Click the Query Wizard icon in the Other group.
   The New Query dialog box appears.
3. Click Simple Query Wizard and then click Ok.
   The Simple Query Wizard dialog box appears.
4. Click a field name listed in the Available Fields box and then click the > button.
   Access displays your chosen filed in the Selected Fields box.

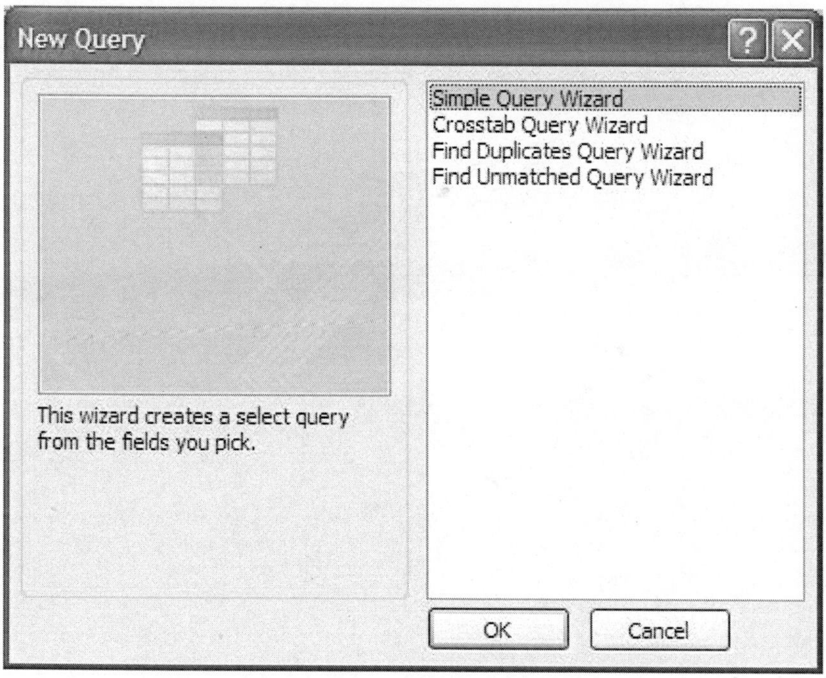

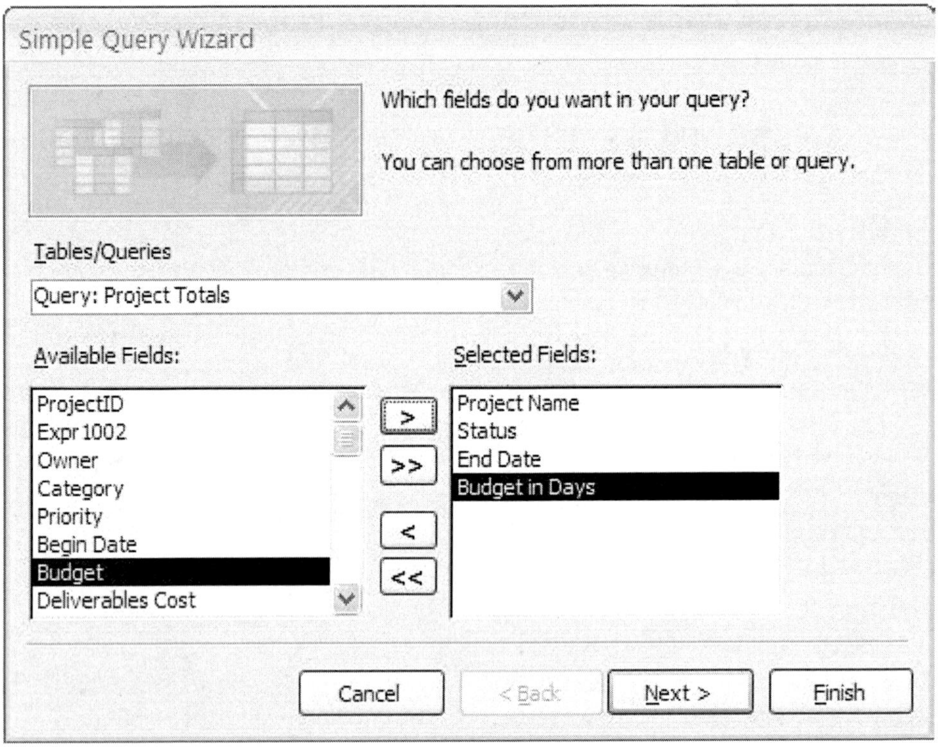
Simple Query Wizard
Which fields do you want in your query?
You can choose from more than one table or query.
Tables/Queries
Query: Project Totals
Available Fields:
ProjectID
Expr1002
Owner
Category
Priority
Begin Date
Budget
Deliverables Cost
Selected Fields:
Project Name
Status
End Date
Budget in Days
Cancel
< Back
Next >
Finish

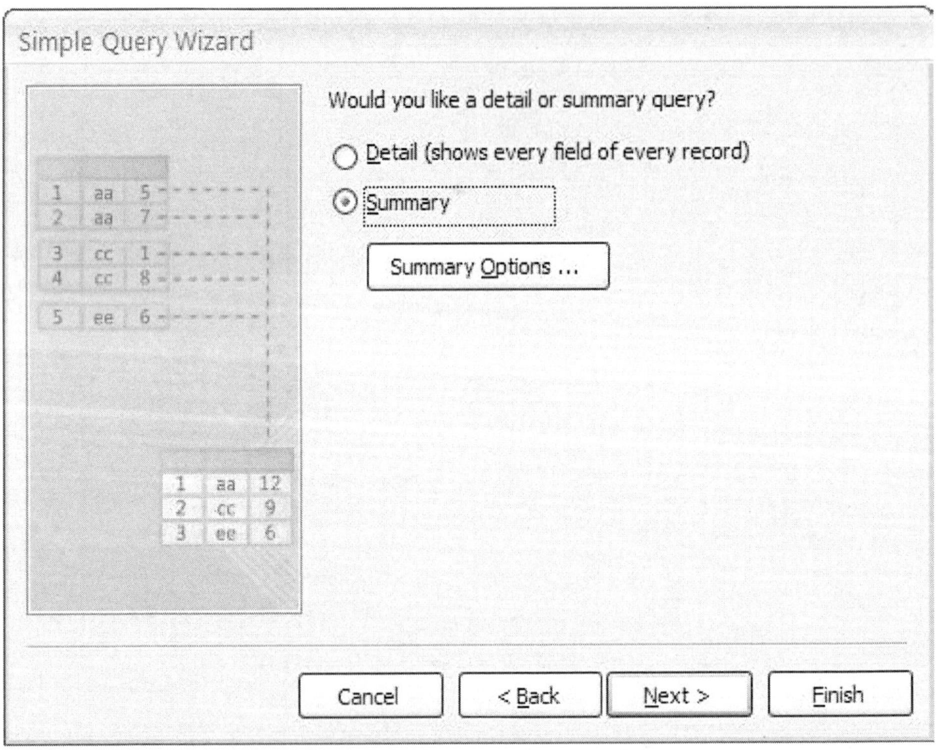
Simple Query Wizard
Would you like a detail or summary query?
Detail (shows every field of every record)
Summary
Summary Options ...
Cancel
< Back
Next >
Finish

5. Repeat Step 4 for each field you want to use in your query.
6. Click Next.

   Another dialog box appears. This dialog box asks whether you want to display a Detail or Summary (shows numerical information such as the total number of records found, the average value, and the minimum/maximum value) view of your data.
7. Select the Detail or Summary radio button and then click Next.

   Another dialog box appears, asking you to type a descriptive name for your query.
8. Click to the text box, type a descriptive name for your query, and then click Finish.
9. Click the Office Button and then choose Save to save your query.

Creating a Crosstab Query

A crosstab query lets you combine tow or more fields to calculate and display a calculation based on a third field. For example, if your database contains the names of salespeople and the products they sold, you can use those two fields to create a crosstab that tells you how much each salesperson sold of each product.

To create a crosstab query, you need to identify three types of fields.

- One to three fields to identify each record (such as the First Name and Last Name fields)
- A single field to dsiplay specific data from each record (such as the Product field, which displays the actual product names like Nails, Barbed Wire, and Screws)
- A crosstab field that dsiplays a calculate result (such as Sales)

To create a crosstab query, follow these steps:

1. Click the Create tab.
2. Click the Query Wizard icon in the Other group.

   The New Query dialog box appears.
3. Click Crosstab Query Wizard and then click Ok.

   The Crosstab Query Wizard dialog box appears.
4. Click a database table and then click Next.

   Another Crosstab Query Wizard dialog box appears that asks for between one and three fields to identify each row (record).
5. Click a field in the Available Fields box and then click the > button to move your chosen field to the Selected Fields box.
6. Repeat Step 5 for each additional field you want to include.
7. Click Next.

   Another dialog box appears, asking for a single field to use to crosstabular data with the fields you choose in Steps 5 and 6.
8. Click a field name and then click Next.
9. Click a field that contains numerical data and then click a matematical function that you want Access to calculate, such as Sum, Avg., or Count.
10. Click Next.

    Another dialog box appears.
11. Type a descriptive name for your query in the text box at the top of the dialog box and then click Finish.
12. Click the Office Button and choose Save to save your query.

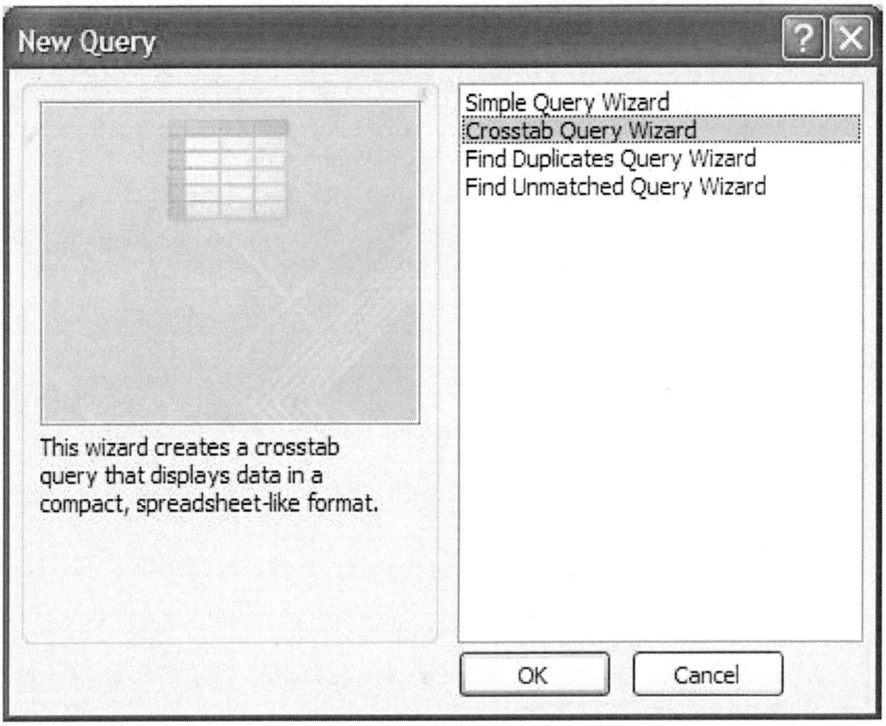
New Query
Simple Query Wizard
Crosstab Query Wizard
Find Duplicates Query Wizard
Find Unmatched Query Wizard
This wizard creates a crosstab query that displays data in a compact, spreadsheet-like format.
OK
Cancel

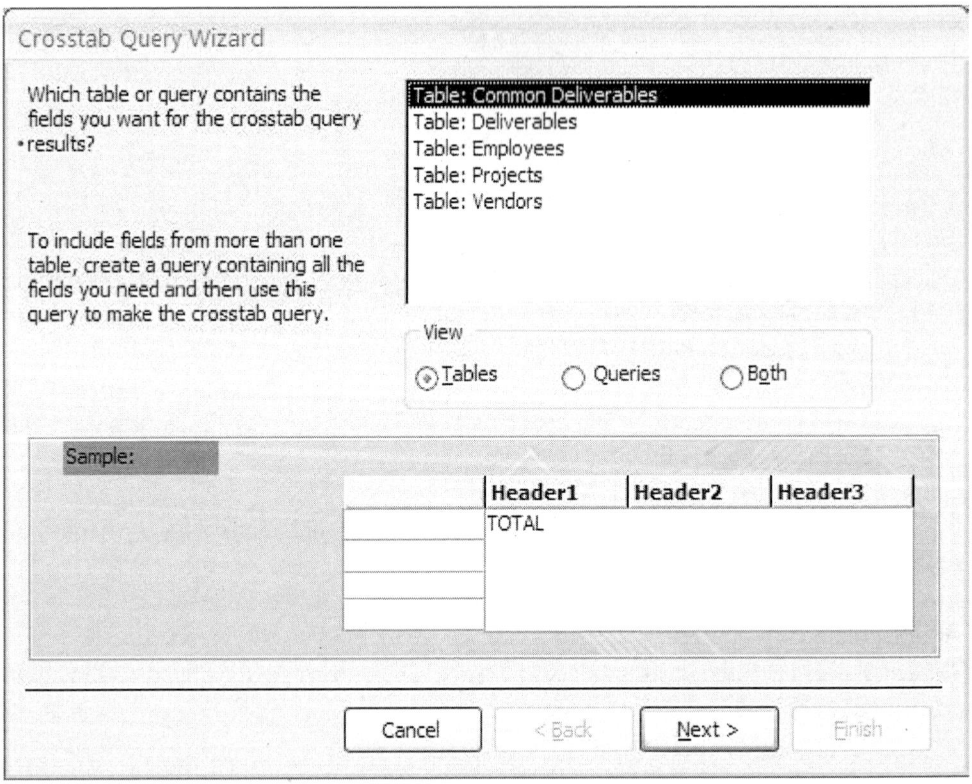
Crosstab Query Wizard
Which table or query contains the fields you want for the crosstab query results?
To include fields from more than one table, create a query containing all the fields you need and then use this query to make the crosstab query.
Table: Common Deliverables
Table: Deliverables
Table: Employees
Table: Projects
Table: Vendors
View
Tables
Queries
Both
Sample:
Header1
Header2
Header3
TOTAL
Cancel
< Back
Next >
Finish

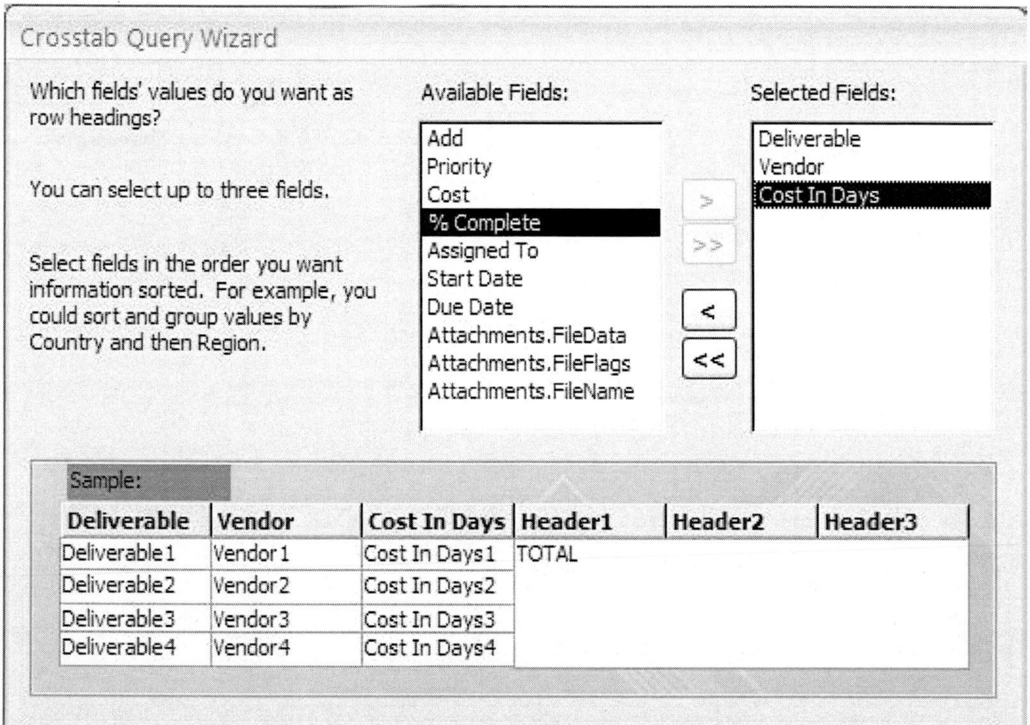
Crosstab Query Wizard
Which fields' values do you want as row headings?
You can select up to three fields.
Select fields in the order you want information sorted. For example, you could sort and group values by Country and then Region.
Available Fields:
Add
Priority
Cost
% Complete
Assigned To
Start Date
Due Date
Attachments.FileData
Attachments.FileFlags
Attachments.FileName
Selected Fields:
Deliverable
Vendor
Cost In Days
Sample:
Deliverable
Vendor
Cost In Days
Header1
Header2
Header3
Deliverable1
Vendor1
Cost In Days1
TOTAL
Deliverable2
Vendor2
Cost In Days2
Deliverable3
Vendor3
Cost In Days3
Deliverable4
Vendor4
Cost In Days4

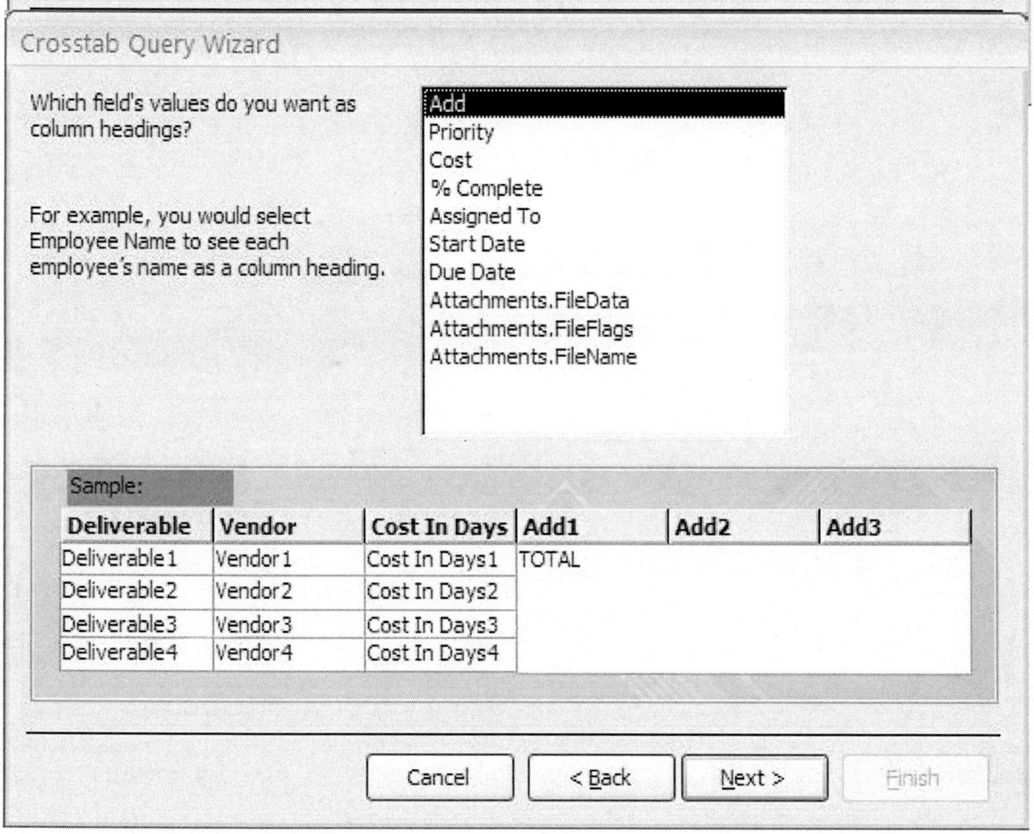
Crosstab Query Wizard
Which field's values do you want as column headings?
For example, you would select Employee Name to see each employee's name as a column heading.
Add
Priority
Cost
% Complete
Assigned To
Start Date
Due Date
Attachments.FileData
Attachments.FileFlags
Attachments.FileName
Sample:
Deliverable
Vendor
Cost In Days
Add1
Add2
Add3
Deliverable1
Vendor1
Cost In Days1
TOTAL
Deliverable2
Vendor2
Cost In Days2
Deliverable3
Vendor3
Cost In Days3
Deliverable4
Vendor4
Cost In Days4
Cancel
< Back
Next >
Finish

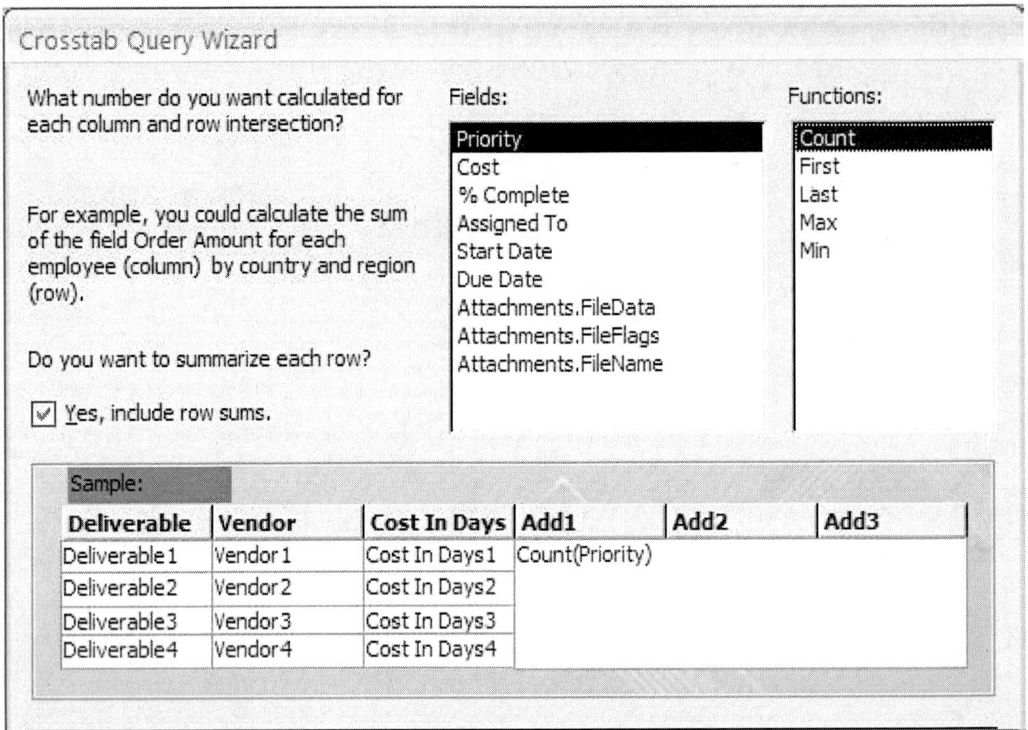
Crosstab Query Wizard
What number do you want calculated for each column and row intersection?
For example, you could calculate the sum of the field Order Amount for each employee (column) by country and region (row).
Do you want to summarize each row?
Yes, include row sums.
Fields:
Priority
Cost
% Complete
Assigned To
Start Date
Due Date
Attachments.FileData
Attachments.FileFlags
Attachments.FileName
Functions:
Count
First
Last
Max
Min
Sample:
Deliverable
Vendor
Cost In Days
Add1
Add2
Add3
Deliverable1
Vendor1
Cost In Days1
Count(Priority)
Deliverable2
Vendor2
Cost In Days2
Deliverable3
Vendor3
Cost In Days3
Deliverable4
Vendor4
Cost In Days4

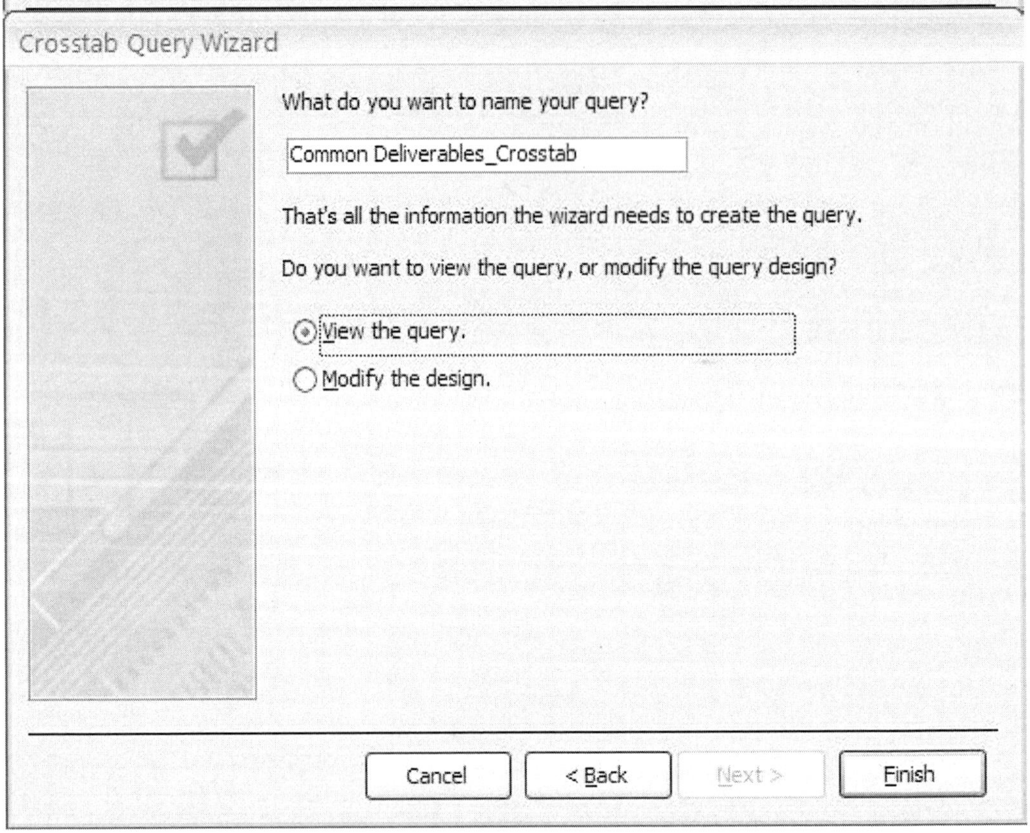
Crosstab Query Wizard
What do you want to name your query?
Common Deliverables_Crosstab
That's all the information the wizard needs to create the query.
Do you want to view the query, or modify the query design?
View the query.
Modify the design.
Cancel
< Back
Next >
Finish

Creating a Report

Each software has its own method of giving the output in the form of a print out, which can either be on printer or on screen. Access also has the same. But for this you have to first create a report design and then send it either to printer or monitor.

Creating Report using Wizard

The easiest way to create a report is to use the Report Wizard, which guides you step by step through arranging and selecting which data to print on a report along with sorting your data at the same time.

To use the Report Wizard, follow these steps:

1. Click the Create tab.
2. Click the Report Wizard icon in the Reports group.
   The Report Wizard dialog box appears.
3. Click in the Tables/Queries list box and choose the table or query that contains the data you want to print in a report.

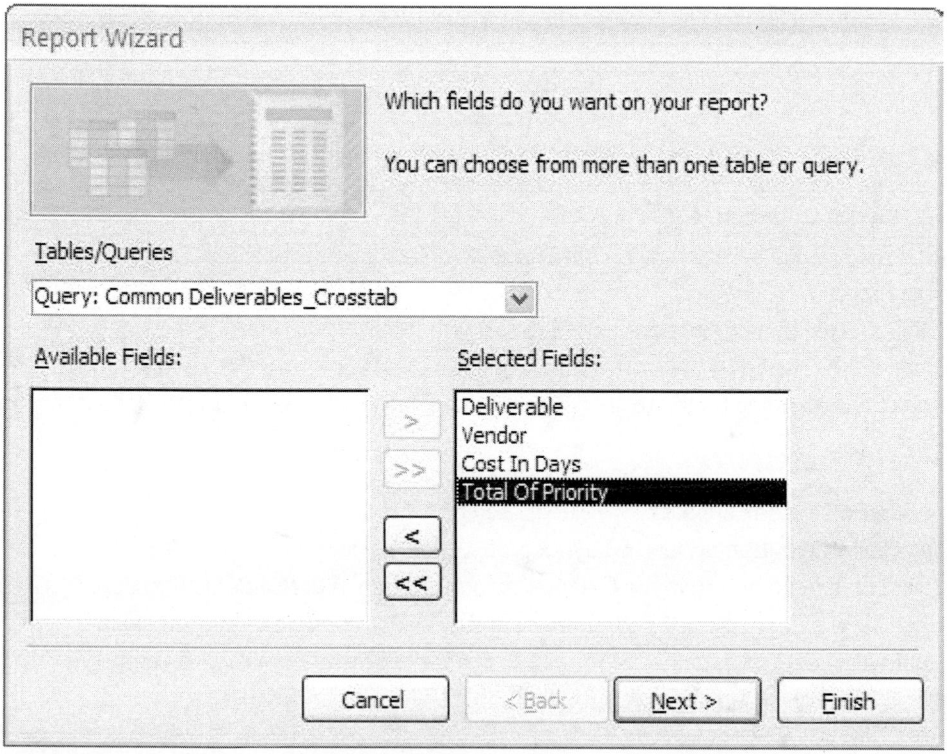

4. Click a field in the Available Fields box and then click this > button. Report this step for each additional field you want to display in your report.
5. Click Next.
   Another dialog box appears, asking whether you want to group your data by a speecific field such as Last Name or Employee Number.
6. Click a field name displayed in the box and then click the > button. Repeat this step for each additional field you want to use to group your data on the report.
7. Click Next.
   Another dialog box appears, asking you to choose up to four fiels to use for sorting your data in

your report.

8. Click in a list box and choose a field to sort your data.

   Data will be sorted by the order chosen here for each additional field you sort on.
9. Click the Ascending button to change the soring criteria from Ascending to Descending and vice versa.
10. Click Next.

    Another dialog box appears.
11. Select a radio button under the Layout group, such as Stepped or Outline.
12. Select on a radio button in the Orientation group, such as Portrait or Landscape.
13. Click Next.

    Another dialog box appears, asking you to choose a style for your report. The preview to the left will give you an indication of what the printed report will look like.
14. Click Next.

    Another dialog box appears, asking you for a descriptive name for your report.
15. Type a descriptive name for your report and then click Finish.

    Access displays your report.
16. Right-click the Report tab.

    A pop-up menu appears.
17. Click Close.

    A dialog box appears.
18. Click Yes.

    Access saves your report for future use and removes it from view.

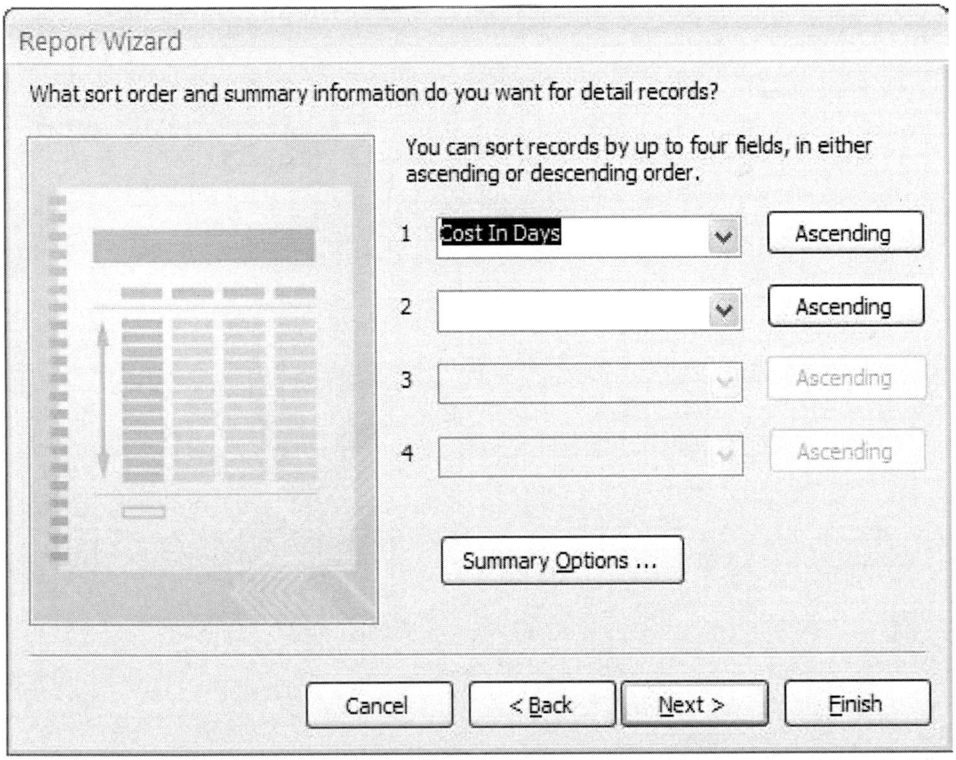
Report Wizard
What sort order and summary information do you want for detail records?
You can sort records by up to four fields, in either ascending or descending order.
1 Cost In Days
Ascending
2
Ascending
3
Ascending
4
Ascending
Summary Options ...
Cancel
< Back
Next >
Finish

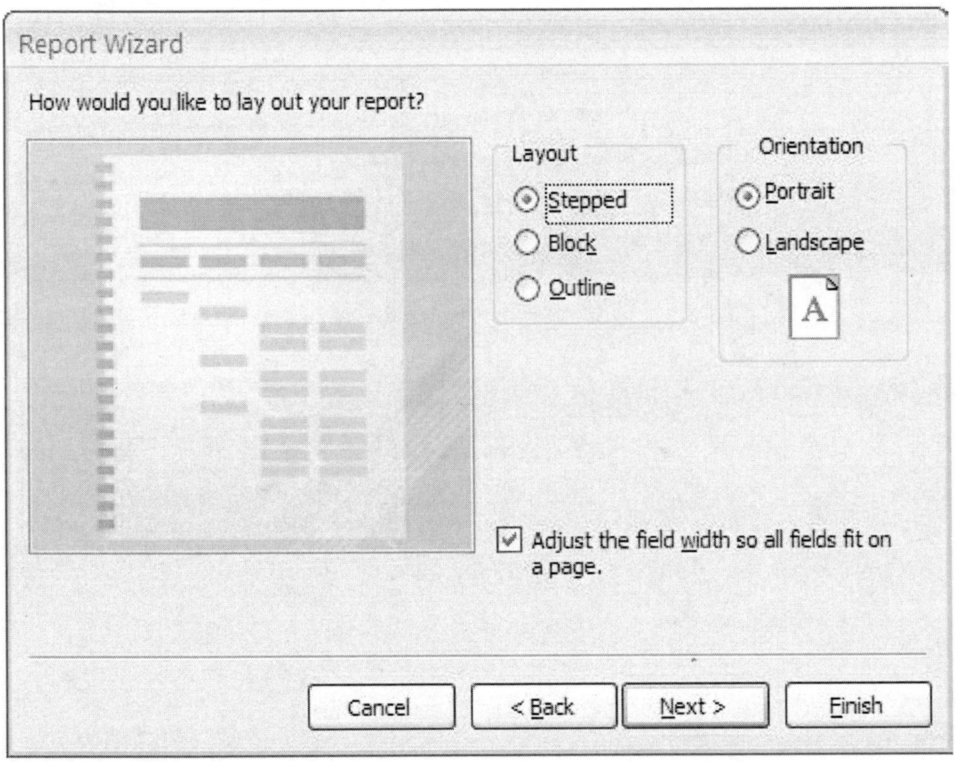
Report Wizard
How would you like to lay out your report?
Layout
Stepped
Block
Outline
Orientation
Portrait
Landscape
A
Adjust the field width so all fields fit on a page.
Cancel
< Back
Next >
Finish

Report Wizard
What style would you like?
Title
Label above Detail
Control from Detail
Civic
Concourse
Equity
Flow
Foundry
Median
Metro
Module
None
Northwind
Office
Opulent
Oriel
Origin
Cancel
< Back
Next >
Finish

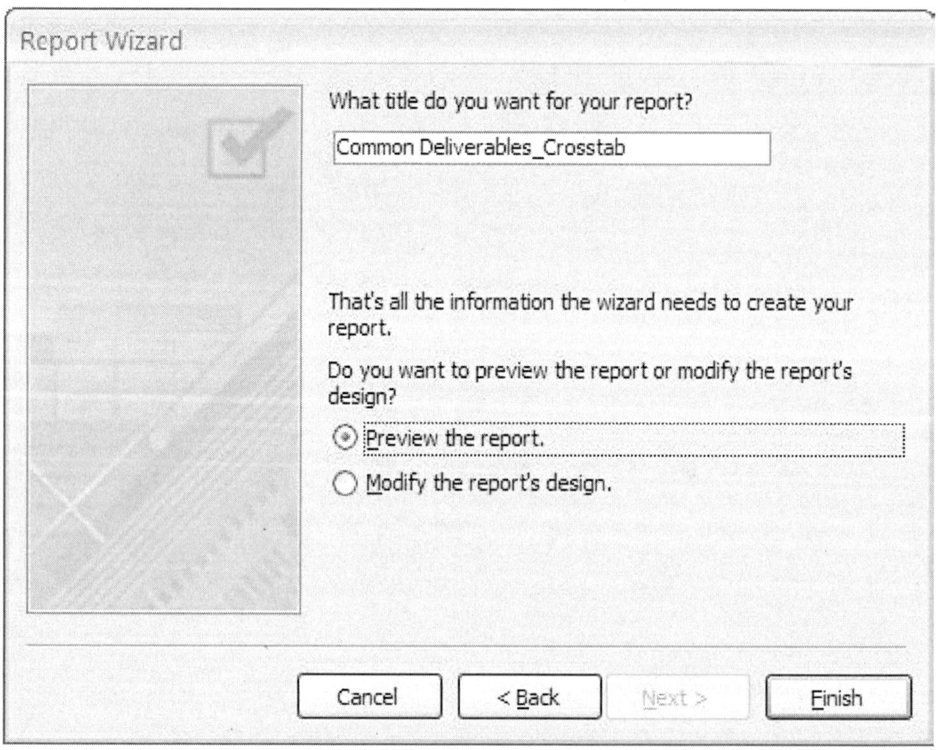
Report Wizard
What title do you want for your report?
Common Deliverables_Crosstab
That's all the information the wizard needs to create your report.
Do you want to preview the report or modify the report's design?
Preview the report.
Modify the report's design.
Cancel
< Back
Next >
Finish

CHAPTER 7

Other Software of Microsoft Office 2013

Introduction

Publisher 2013 Microsoft's answer to the various other publishing software available in the market like PageMaker. It allows you to create invitations, design business-cards, and letter-heads, make your own calenders, produce newsletter, etc.

OneNote 2013 used to gather information during meetings, brainstorming sessions, interviews, and more. The notes you create can include text, drawings, images, and audio recordings. OneNote uses a freeform page layout, so you can place and move information wherever you want.

InfoPath 2013 helps you collect and work with data by using dynamic, online forms that have a familiar Office interface. Based on the Extensible Markup Language (XML), InfoPath makes it easy to create and use robust forms to more effectively gather and share information throughout your organization.

Microsoft Office Publisher 2013

Publisher is included in higher-end editions of Microsoft Office, reflecting Microsoft's emphasis on the application as an easy-to-use and less expensive alternative to the "heavyweights," with a focus on the small business market where firms do not have dedicated design professionals available to make marketing materials and other documents. However, it has a relatively small share of the desktop publishing market, which is dominated by Adobe InDesign and QuarkXPress. Publisher has historically been less well liked among high-end commercial print shops, compared with other desktop publishing applications.

Publisher's proprietary file format (.pub) is unsupported by almost all other applications, including other Microsoft products, although Corel Draw X4 features "open only" support, and there is an ongoing work on converter for LibreOffice with support for 97—2013 versions of the PUB file format. As such, Publisher is generally recognized to be of limited functionality where multiple-user electronic editing or dissemination is concerned. Adobe's PageMaker software saves files with a .pub extension but the two files are incompatible and unrelated. Publisher supports numerous other file formats, including the Enhanced Metafile (EMF) format which is supported on Windows platforms. The Microsoft Publisher trial version can be used to view .pub files beyond the trial period.

Make greeting cards

1. Pick a template
2. Start Publisher, click Built-in > Greeting Cards.
3. Scroll through the predesigned greeting card publications. When you find one that you like, click it to see a larger image preview.
4. Under Customize and Options, you can modify many design elements before you open the publication:
   - Under Customize, click the color scheme and font scheme that you want.
   - Under Customize, click the business information set that you want, or create a new one.
   - Under Options, select the page size that you want, such as Half-page side fold or Quarter-page top fold.
   - Under Options, select the layout that you want.

   If you use a template that you downloaded from Office Online, you cannot customize the design until you open the publication.
5. Click Create.

If you don't see a design that you like, you can search for additional greeting card templates on Office.com by returning to the New page and entering **greeting card** in the Search online templates search box and pressing ENTER.

Personalize your card

Make global design changes

You might want to make changes that affect the entire publication. For example, you might want to try other color or font schemes. You can make such changes at any time, but it is best to do it before you insert the text and pictures.

Do either of the following:

- To try a different color scheme, on the Page Design tab, click the color scheme that you want. If you hover over the color schemes you'll immediately see how your greeting card will look if you choose the color scheme.
- To try a different font scheme, on the Page Design tab, click Fonts, and then choose the font scheme that you want.

Work with the pictures

- Replace the placeholder pictures with your own pictures
- Right-click the placeholder picture, click Change Picture > Change Picture.
- In the Insert Picture dialog, either click Browse to find pictures on your own computer or on your local network, or search for pictures on Office.com or from Bing.
- Repeat, as needed, for other pictures in your publication.

Add a new picture

On the Insert tab, click either Pictures on my PC or Online Pictures.

Browse you own computer, or search Office.com or Bing for images, and click Insert.

Work with the text

- Replace the placeholder text with your own message
- Select the placeholder text, and then type your own message.

Add new text

- On the Insert tab, click Draw Text Box.
- In your card, point to where you want one corner of the text to appear, and then click and drag diagonally until you have a box that is the size that you want. Click inside the box and type your text.

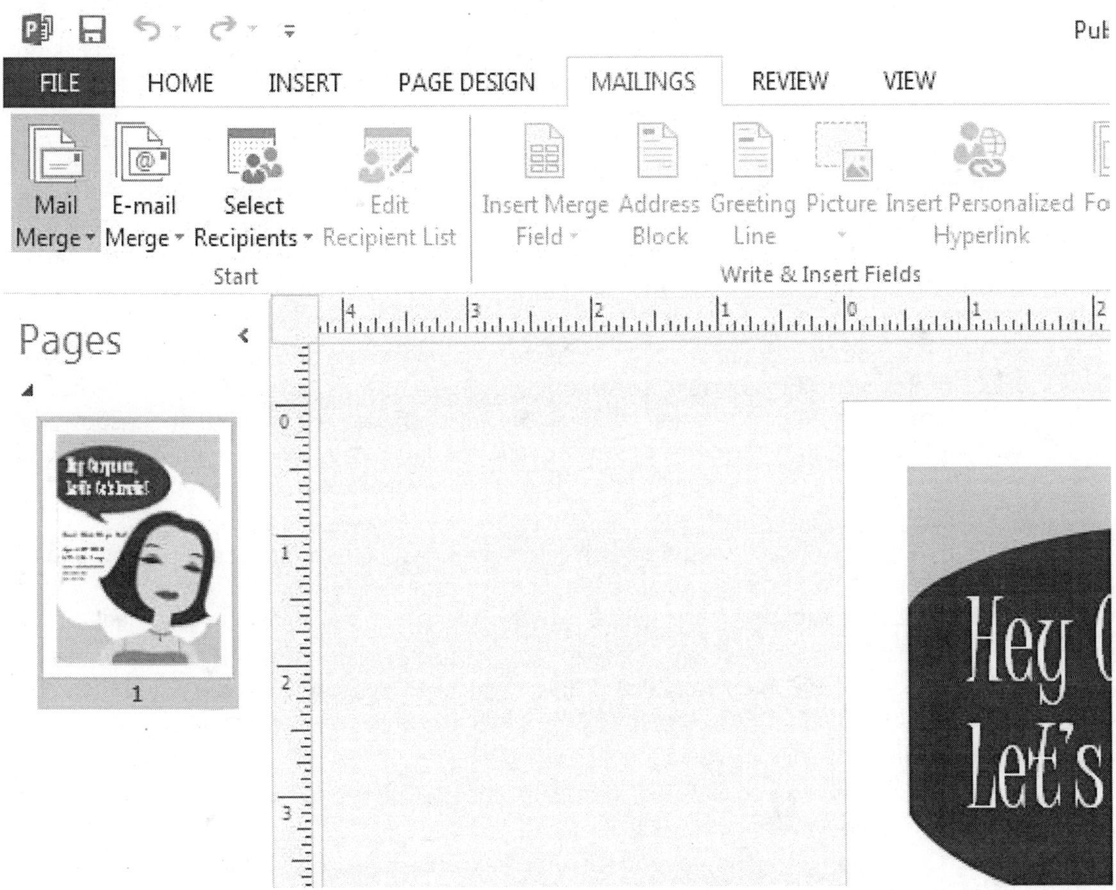

Replace the placeholder text with a verse

- In the Page Design tab click Options.
- Under Category, click the message category that you want. Under Available messages, click the message that you want, preview the two parts of the message on the right, and then click OK.

Microsoft Office InfoPath 2013

Microsoft Office InfoPath is a software application for designing, distributing, filling and submitting electronic forms containing structured data. According to one of its inventors, a key architectural design decision was "to adhere to the XML paradigm of separating the data in a document from the formatting." Thus the product features a WYSIWYG form design area in which the various controls (dropdowns, text boxes, etc.) are bound to data fields represented separately as a hierarchical tree view of folders and data fields. A patent filed in 2000 by Adriana Neagu, Jean Paoli and others describes the technology as "authoring XML using DHTML views and XSLT."

Microsoft initially released InfoPath as part of Microsoft Office 2003 family. In summer 2013, Microsoft released a new version that split InfoPath into two applications: InfoPath Designer 2013 is used to create forms and define data structures, and InfoPath Filler 2013 is used to fill out and submit forms.

Features

- Rules apply specific actions when triggered by button clicks or changing values in the form. They can change the values of fields in the data source, submit to and query databases, display messages, open and close forms, and switch to different views of the form.
- Data Validation tests the validity of input into fields by comparing the input to patterns, checking for the correct data type (such as a string or an integer), and in other customizable ways.
- Conditional Formatting can be used to change the appearance or visibility of objects based on values in the form.
- InfoPath has many different ActiveX Controls, all of which have a value bound to a field in the form's data source. Common controls include list boxes, radio buttons, text boxes, buttons, and check boxes. Info Path also uses controls such as Calculated Values, which display the result of xPath expressions, and sections, which are containers for other controls. InfoPath also includes repeating fields and sections, which can store many different values.
- XPath Expressions and Functions can be used to calculate values by applying functions to the value of fields in the form, such as "concat(string(field1 + field2), "#;", field3)" (the concatenation of the sum of two fields, the string "#;", and the value of another field). XPath functions for manipulation of strings, simple mathematical operations, and many other operations are included in InfoPath. In addition, data can be filtered (select individual values from a repeating field or database).
- InfoPath supports Connections to External Datasources. SQL, Microsoft Access, and SharePoint databases can be connected to and submitted in the form. Because of InfoPath's superior user experience and ease of data entry, it is often preferable to manipulate databases through it.
- JScript, Visual Basic, C#, and other languages can be used to extend InfoPath's capabilities by adding custom HTML taskpanes, iterating through data, using Active Directory, and generally accomplishing tasks that are impossible in the InfoPath design environment.
- SharePoint integration (see Integration with SharePoint).
- User Roles can customize a user's experience by changing views or using conditional formatting based on the identity of the user.
- InfoPath's formatting capabilities and user interface are similar to Microsoft Word 2003 and 2013, depending on version.

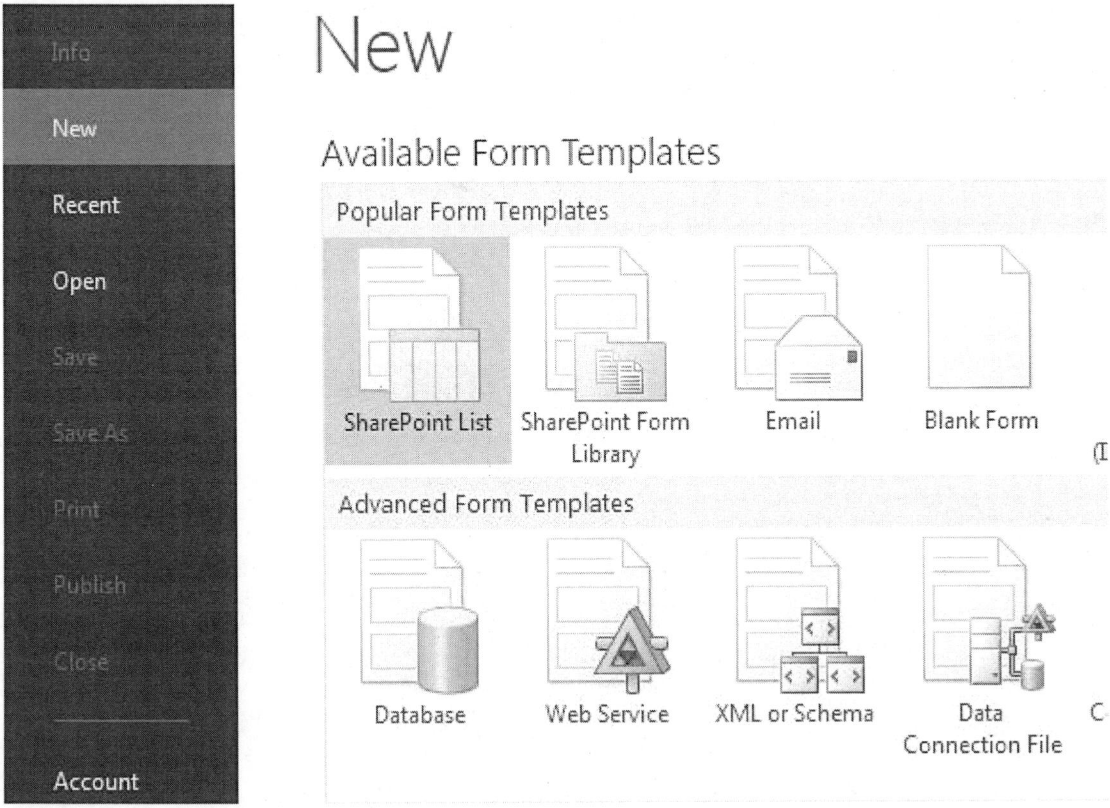

Usage

InfoPath is used to create forms to capture information and save the contents as a file on a PC or on a web server when hosted on SharePoint. InfoPath can be used to access and display data from divergent sources (web services, XML, databases, other forms) and have rich interactive behaviors based on Rules, Conditions and Actions. An InfoPath form requires the client to have InfoPath Filler or InfoPath Designer installed, or by viewing the form in a browser when hosted on SharePoint. InfoPath is mostly used in business rather than by individuals, as it is a collaboration tool used to gather data from multiple individuals in a structured method, and to deploy requires either a SharePoint host and/or individual licensed Filler copies. InfoPath forms can be viewed on mobile devices if viewed from a browser (hosted on SharePoint) or by using a third-party product.

To run as a Web browser form, the file needs to be uploaded to a server running InfoPath Forms Services. The advantage of this is the client doesn't need InfoPath, just a Web browser. The form can then be set up to be e-mailed when completed or its fields can be added directly to a SharePoint list.

Microsoft Office OneNote 2013

With OneNote, you can jot down ideas generated in a meeting session, sketch your original vision, record your interviews and assemble material from your online reference sources.

You can enter original notes by typing on a keyboard. Your virtual notebook works much like a physical one – your notes are organized on pages and in sections. But you can also mark and highlight your notes as well as rearrange them, search them and create Microsoft Outlook tasks from them – try that with a physical notebook!

For your convenience, OneNote automatically saves your notes at regular intervals, so you don't have to stop working to save. Simply close OneNote at the end of a session and when you open it again, all your notes – in all the sections and all the pages – are there for you to continue your work.

Getting Started with OneNote

As usual I would show how you can start with OneNote and make your own notes for future use. Here I am making plans for the World Book Fair and what sort of activities to be taken up there.

Follow the following steps for this:

1. Click the Start button, point to All Programs, point to Microsoft Office and then click Microsoft OneNote 2013.

   OneNote 2013 opens with two sections: General, on the blue tab and Meetings on the green tab.
2. On the General section, click the Title box at the top of the page and type World Book Fair.
3. In the body of the page, directly below the title, click the shaded area and type **What we would like to do**.
4. Press enter and type Meet all the publishers.
5. Press enter and type Select the books to be purchased.
6. Press enter and type Pick up catalog of competitors.
7. Select the first line, what we'd like to present and on the Formatting toolbar, click the Bold button.
8. Select the remaining three lines of text on the page and on the Formatting toolbar, click the Bullets button.
9. At this stage your screen would look like the one shown on the next page.
10. Near the top of the window, click the Meetings section tab.

    OneNote 2013 displays the Meetings section of the notebook. This is where you'll record your notes during a meeting with the various publishers.
11. Click the Title box and type Planning Session.
12. Click in the body of the page, type Stall Decoration.
13. Press the down key and type Arrange books category wise.
14. Press enter and type Arrange banners.
15. Press enter and type Arrange posters.
16. Select the three lines you just typed and on the Formatting toolbar, click the Bullet button.
17. On the File menu, click Exit.

OneNote closes. Your notes are saved as you crate them, so there's no need to save them when you close the program.

Adding Drawings and Images

To make your notes look more presentable, add the drawings, pictures or images. This can be done like this:

1. Click the Start button, point to All Programs, point to Microsoft Office and then click Microsoft OneNote 2013.

   OneNote 2013 opens, showing the Meetings section because that section was active when you closed OneNote.
2. Click the General section tab and click the blank area below the text on the page.

3. On the Insert menu, click Picture.
   The Insert Picture dialog box appears.
4. Click at the picture you want to insert. OneNote inserts the image into your notes, as shown here.
5. On the Standard toolbar, click the Pen button and move your mouse pointer over the note page. Your mouse pointer becomes a small colored dot.
6. In any blank area of the note page, drag the shape of a square with mouse pointer. Don't worry about making your lines straight – this is a rough sketch!
7. Click the down arrow to the right of the Pen button and click another color.
8. Position the mouse pointer over one edge of the square you just drew and drag the pointer to divide the square into two sections. This section can be any size or shape you 'd like – this will represent the layout for your exhibition booth.
9. On the Standard toolbar, click the Selection Tool button.
10. Click in the larger portion of your exhibition booth drawing and type main visitor area.
11. Click the smaller portion of the booth and type demo area.
12. See how we have drawn the various portions of the stall.

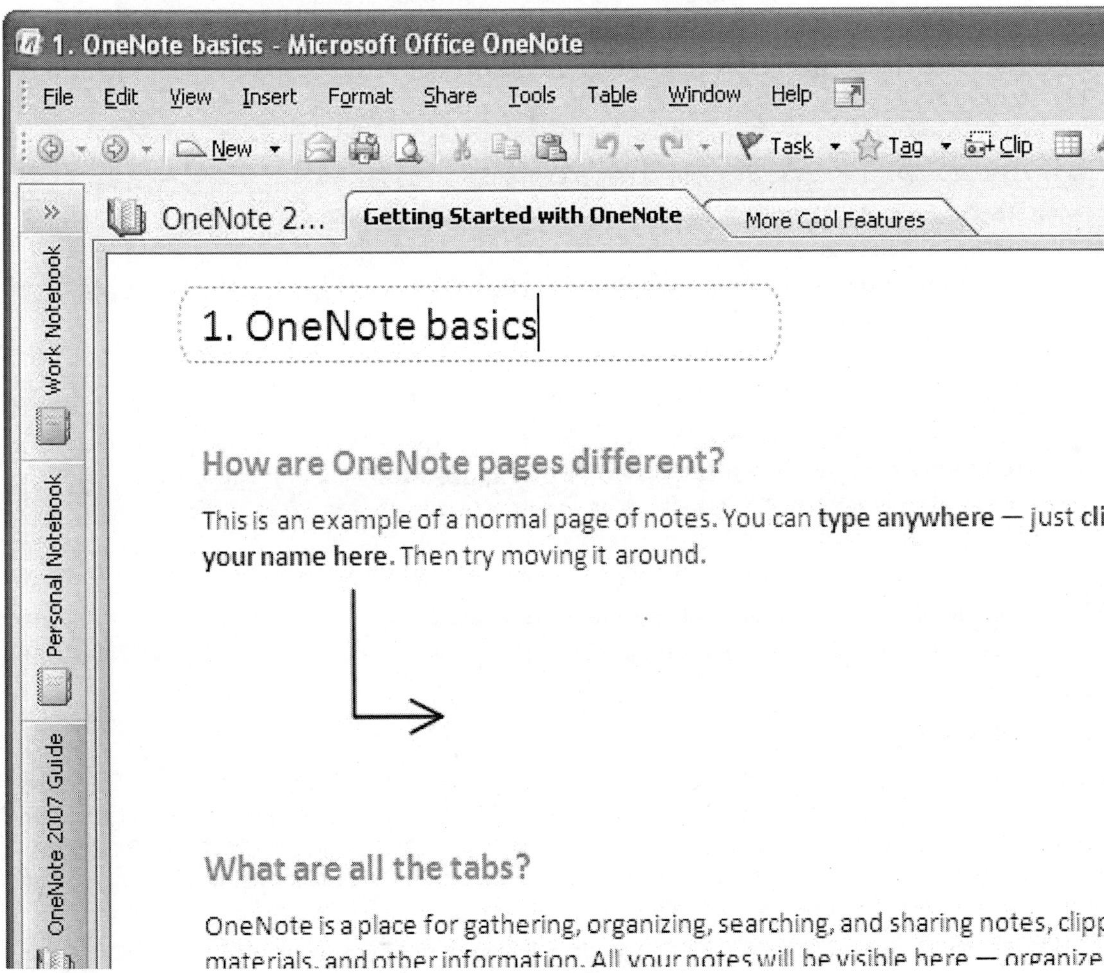

Organizing Notes into Sections and Folders

As you work with OneNote over time, you might collect notes about a wide variety of topics and your virtual notebook could get disorganized. To help you keep track of them, you can divide your notebook into sections and folders. Sections can contain one or more pages or groups of pages. Folders can contain pages, sections or other folders.

Be sure to start OneNote before beginning this exercise.

1. On the Insert menu, click New Section.
   OneNote creates a new section as a tab at the top of the note page. Ready for you to name.
2. Type World Book Fair as the section name and press enter.
3. Right-click the new section tab, point to Section Color on the shortcut menu and click Magenta.
4. In the Title box, type Publisher Here.
5. On the Insert menu, click the New Folder.
   OneNote creates a new folder as a tab at the top of the note page, ready for you to name.
6. Type Books Displayed as the folder name and press enter.
7. Right-click the World Book Fair section tab and click Move on the shortcut menu.
   The Move Section to dialog box appears, as shown on the next page.
8. In the Move section to list, select the Meetings folder and click Move.
9. The World Book Fair section is no longer visible because it is contained within the Meetings folder.
10. Click the Meetings tab. The Meetings folder opens, displaying the World Book Fair tab.
11. Click the down arrow to the right of the folder name.
    The drop-down list shows all the sections and folders in your notebook.
12. In the list, click Meetings.
13. The Meetings section is displayed and the Event Planning folder again appears as a tab at the top of the page.
14. Close One Note.

Remember

With OneNote you can do the following:

- You can easily take notes made up of typed text, handwritten text, images, Web clippings, drawings and sound recordings.
- You take notes on pages and can group pages with related content.
- You can organize pages into sections and sections into folders.
- You can rearrange your notebook by moving notes and pages.
- OneNote automatically saves your notebook at regular intervals and each time you close the program.

Microsft SkyDrive

SkyDrive (officially Microsoft SkyDrive, previously Windows Live SkyDrive and Windows Live Folders) is a file hosting service that allows users to upload and sync files to a cloud storage and then access them from a Web browser or their local device. It is part of the Windows Live range of online services and allows users to keep the files private, share them with contacts, or make the files public. Publicly shared files do not require a Microsoft account to access.

The service offers 7 GB of free storage for new users. Additional storage is available for purchase. Users who signed up to SkyDrive prior to April 22, 2012 could opt-in for a limited time offer of 25 GB of free storage upgrade. The service is built using HTML5 technologies, and files up to 300 MB can be uploaded via drag and drop into the web browser, or up to 2 GB via the SkyDrive desktop application for Microsoft Windows and OS X.

Features

Office Web Appls: Microsoft added Office Web Apps support to SkyDrive in its "Wave 4" update allowing users to upload, create, edit, and share Microsoft Office documents directly within a Web browser. Users can create, view and edit Word, Excel, PowerPoint and OneNote documents within the Web browser. In addition, Office Web Apps on SkyDrive also allow multiple users to simultaneously co-author Excel directly within the web browser, and co-author OneNote documents with another web user or the desktop application. Users can also view the version history of Office documents stored on SkyDrive.

Integration with Microsoft Office: Users of recent versions of Microsoft Office (for Microsoft Windows or OS X) can use the desktop applications to simultaneously edit the same section of documents stored on SkyDrive. Changes are synchronized when users save the document, and where conflicts occur, the saving user is given the selection to choose which version to keep. This is a collaborative real-time editing suite, as multiple users can use combinations of desktop applications and web apps to edit a document.

Format support: SkyDrive supports viewing of Portable Document Format (PDF) as well as Open Document Format (ODF), an XML-based file format supported in a number of word processing apps including Microsoft Office, OpenOffice, and Corel's WordPerfect. SkyDrive's search function does not support search within PDF documents, however.

Document embedding: SkyDrive allows users to embed their Office documents (Word, Excel and PowerPoint) onto other web pages. These embedded documents allow anyone who visits these web pages to interact with them, such as browsing an embedded PowerPoint slideshow, or perform calculations within an embedded Excel spreadsheet.

Email integration: SkyDrive integrates with Outlook.com which allows users to:

- Directly upload Office documents and photos within Outlook.com, store them on SkyDrive, and share them with other users.
- Directly save Office documents within Outlook.com to SkyDrive, and view or edit these documents directly within the web browser
- Edit Office documents within the web browser using Office Web Apps, and reply directly back to the sender with the edits made

Share on social networks: SkyDrive integrates with social networks such as Facebook, Twitter and LinkedIn to enable users to quickly share their files with their contacts on these social networks. SkyDrive maintains an access control list of all users granted permission to view or edit the files, including those users on social networks.

Bing integration: SkyDrive integrates with Bing's Save & Share feature, allowing users to save search histories into a SkyDrive folder.

Windows Live Groups integration: Each group within Windows Live Groups is provided with 5 GB of storage space on SkyDrive to be shared between the group members. Group members are allowed to access, create, modify and delete files within the group's SkyDrive folders, along with the other functionalities that SkyDrive provides.

Location and people tagging: SkyDrive supports geo-location data for photos uploaded onto the service, and will automatically display a map of the tagged location. SkyDrive also allows users to tag people on the photos uploaded onto the service via the web interface or via Windows Photo Gallery.

Photo slideshows: Photos uploaded onto SkyDrive can be played as an automatic slideshow.

Download as .zip file: Entire folders can be downloaded as a single .zip file with SkyDrive. For a single download, there is a limit of 4GB or 65,000 files (whichever comes first).

Recycle bin: When users delete any files on SkyDrive, the service will allow the user to undo the action and restore the deleted file from the recycle bin back to the original folder. Items in the recycle bin do not count against the user's SkyDrive storage limit. All items stored in the recycle bin are kept for a minimum of 3 days and a maximum of 30 days. If the content in a user's recycle bin exceeds 10% of the user's storage limit (e.g. 0.7GB for a user with a total of 7GB SkyDrive storage limit), SkyDrive will delete the oldest content from the recycle bin (provided that the files have been in the recycle bin for at least 3 days).

CHAPTER 8

Keyboard Shortcuts of Microsoft Office 2013

Introduction

Shortcut keys are key combinations that start commands. For example, you can press CTRL+O to open a file and CTRL+S to save a file, which is the same result as choosing Open and Save from the File menu. .

Microsoft Office Basics

Action	Shortcut
Switch to the next window.	ALT+TAB
Switch to the previous window.	ALT+SHIFT+TAB
Close the active window.	CTRL+W or CTRL+F4
Restore the size of the active window after you maximize it.	ALT+F5
Move to a task pane from another pane in the program window (clockwise direction). You may need to press F6 more than once.	F6
Move to a task pane from another pane in the program window (counterclockwise direction).	SHIFT+F6
When more than one window is open, switch to the next window.	CTRL+F6
Switch to the previous window.	CTRL+SHIFT+F6
Maximize or restore a selected window.	CTRL+F10
Copy a picture of the screen to the Clipboard.	PRINT SCREEN
Copy a picture of the selected window to the Clipboard.	ALT+PRINT SCREEN
Move from an open dialog box back to the document, for dialog boxes such as Find and Replace that support this behavior.	ALT+F6
Move to the next option or option group.	TAB
Move to the previous option or option group.	SHIFT+TAB
Switch to the next tab in a dialog box.	CTRL+TAB
Switch to the previous tab in a dialog box.	CTRL+SHIFT+TAB
Move between options in an open drop-down list, or between options in a group of options.	Arrow keys
Perform the action assigned to the selected button; select or clear the selected check box.	SPACEBAR
Select an option; select or clear a check box.	ALT+ the letter underlined in an option
Open a selected drop-down list.	ALT+DOWN ARROW
Select an option from a drop-down list.	First letter of an option in a drop-down list
Close a selected drop-down list; cancel a command and close a dialog box.	ESC
Run the selected command.	ENTER
Move to the beginning of the entry.	HOME
Move to the end of the entry.	END
Move one character to the left or right.	LEFT ARROW or RIGHT ARROW
Move one word to the left.	CTRL+LEFT ARROW
Move one word to the right.	CTRL+RIGHT ARROW
Select or unselect one character to the left.	SHIFT+LEFT ARROW
Select or unselect one character to the right.	SHIFT+RIGHT ARROW
Select or unselect one word to the left.	CTRL+SHIFT+LEFT ARROW
Select or unselect one word to the right.	CTRL+SHIFT+RIGHT ARROW
Select from the insertion point to the beginning of the entry.	SHIFT+HOME
Select from the insertion point to the end of the entry.	SHIFT+END

Use the Open and Save As dialog boxes

Action	Shortcut
Display the Open dialog box.	CTRL+F12 or CTRL+O
Display the Save As dialog box.	F12
Go to the previous folder.	ALT+1
Up One Level button: Open the folder one level above the open folder.	ALT+2
Delete button: Delete the selected folder or file.	DELETE
Create New Folder button: Create a new folder.	ALT+4

Views button: Switch among available folder views.	ALT+5
Display a shortcut menu for a selected item such as a folder or file.	SHIFT+F10
Move between options or areas in the dialog box.	TAB
Open the Look in list.	F4 or ALT+I
Update the file list.	F5

Undo and redo actions

Cancel an action.	ESC
Undo an action.	CTRL+Z
Redo or repeat an action.	CTRL+Y

Access and use task panes and galleries

Move to a task pane from another pane in the program window. (You may need to press F6 more than once.)	F6
When a menu is active, move to a task pane. (You may need to press CTRL+TAB more than once.)	CTRL+TAB
When a task pane is active, select the next or previous option in the task pane.	TAB or SHIFT+TAB
Display the full set of commands on the task pane menu.	CTRL+SPACEBAR
Perform the action assigned to the selected button.	SPACEBAR or ENTER
Open a drop-down menu for the selected gallery item.	SHIFT+F10
Select the first or last item in a gallery.	HOME or END
Scroll up or down in the selected gallery list.	PAGE UP or PAGE DOWN
Close a task pane	
Press F6 to move to the task pane, if necessary.	Press CTRL+SPACEBAR.
Use the arrow keys to select Close, and then press ENTER.	

Access and use smart tags

Display the shortcut menu for the selected item.	SHIFT+F10
Display the menu or message for a smart tag or for the AutoCorrect Options button or the Paste options button . If more than one smart tag is present, switch to the next smart tag and display its menu or message.	ALT+SHIFT+F10
Select the next item on a smart tag menu.	DOWN ARROW
Select the previous item on a smart tag menu.	UP ARROW
Perform the action for the selected item on a smart tag menu.	ENTER
Close the smart tag menu or message.	ESC

Change the keyboard focus without using the mouse

Another way to use the keyboard to work with Ribbon programs is to move the focus among the tabs and commands until you find the feature that you want to use. The following table lists some ways to move the keyboard focus without using the mouse.

Select the active tab of the Ribbon and activate the access keys.	ALT or F10. Press either of these keys again to move back to the document and cancel the access keys.
Move to another tab of the Ribbon.	F10 to select the active tab, and then LEFT ARROW or RIGHT ARROW
Hide or show the Ribbon.	CTRL+F1

Action	Shortcut
Display the shortcut menu for the selected command.	SHIFT+F10 Move the focus to select each of the following areas of the window:
Move the focus to each command on the Ribbon, forward or backward, respectively.	TAB or SHIFT+TAB
Move down, up, left, or right, respectively, among the items on the Ribbon.	DOWN ARROW, UP ARROW, LEFT ARROW, or RIGHT ARROW
Activate the selected command or control on the Ribbon.	SPACEBAR or ENTER
Open the selected menu or gallery on the Ribbon.	SPACEBAR or ENTER
Activate a command or control on the Ribbon so you can modify a value.	ENTER
Finish modifying a value in a control on the Ribbon, and move focus back to the document.	ENTER
Get help on the selected command or control on the Ribbon. (If no Help topic is associated with the selected command, a general Help topic about the program is shown instead.)	F1

Quick reference for Microsoft Office Word

Action	Shortcut
Create a nonbreaking space.	CTRL+SHIFT+SPACEBAR
Create a nonbreaking hyphen.	CTRL+HYPHEN
Make letters bold.	CTRL+B
Make letters italic.	CTRL+I
Make letters underline.	CTRL+U
Decrease font size one value.	CTRL+SHIFT+<
Increase font size one value.	CTRL+SHIFT+>
Decrease font size 1 point.	CTRL+[
Increase font size 1 point.	CTRL+]
Remove paragraph or character formatting.	CTRL+SPACEBAR
Copy the selected text or object.	CTRL+C
Cut the selected text or object.	CTRL+X
Paste text or an object.	CTRL+V
Paste special	CTRL+ALT+V
Paste formatting only	CTRL+SHIFT+V
Undo the last action.	CTRL+Z
Redo the last action.	CTRL+Y
Open the Word Count dialog box.	CTRL+SHIFT+G

Working with documents and Web pages

Create, view, and save documents

Action	Shortcut
Create a new document of the same type as the current or most recent document.	CTRL+N
Open a document.	CTRL+O
Close a document.	CTRL+W
Split the document window.	ALT+CTRL+S
Remove the document window split.	ALT+SHIFT+C
Save a document.	CTRL+S

Find, replace, and browse through text

Action	Shortcut
Find text, formatting, and special items.	CTRL+F
Repeat find (after closing Find and Replace window).	ALT+CTRL+Y
Replace text, specific formatting, and special items.	CTRL+H

Go to a page, bookmark, footnote, table, comment, graphic, or other location.	CTRL+G
Switch between the last four places that you have edited.	ALT+CTRL+Z
Open a list of browse options. Press the arrow keys to select an option, and then press ENTER to browse through a document by using the selected option.	ALT+CTRL+HOME
Move to the previous edit location.	CTRL+PAGE UP
Move to the next edit location.	CTRL+PAGE DOWN

Switch to another view

Switch to Print Layout view.	ALT+CTRL+P
Switch to Outline view.	ALT+CTRL+O
Switch to Draft view.	ALT+CTRL+N

Outline view

Promote a paragraph.	ALT+SHIFT+LEFT ARROW
Demote a paragraph.	ALT+SHIFT+RIGHT ARROW
Demote to body text.	CTRL+SHIFT+N
Move selected paragraphs up.	ALT+SHIFT+UP ARROW
Move selected paragraphs down.	ALT+SHIFT+DOWN ARROW
Expand text under a heading.	ALT+SHIFT+PLUS SIGN
Collapse text under a heading.	ALT+SHIFT+MINUS SIGN
Expand or collapse all text or headings.	ALT+SHIFT+A
Hide or display character formatting.	The slash (/) key on the numeric keypad
Show the first line of body text or all body text.	ALT+SHIFT+L
Show all headings with the Heading 1 style.	ALT+SHIFT+1
Show all headings up to Heading n.	ALT+SHIFT+n
Insert a tab character.	CTRL+TAB

Print and preview documents

Print a document.	CTRL+P
Switch in or out of print preview.	ALT+CTRL+I
Move around the preview page when zoomed in.	Arrow keys
Move by one preview page when zoomed out.	PAGE UP or PAGE DOWN
Move to the first preview page when zoomed out.	CTRL+HOME
Move to the last preview page when zoomed out.	CTRL+END

Review documents

Insert a comment.	ALT+CTRL+M
Turn change tracking on or off.	CTRL+SHIFT+E
Close the Reviewing Pane if it is open.	ALT+SHIFT+C

Full Screen Reading view

Some screen readers may not be compatible with Full Screen Reading view.

Go to beginning of document.	HOME
Go to end of document.	END
Go to page n.	n, ENTER
Exit reading layout view.	ESC

References, footnotes, and endnotes

Mark a table of contents entry.	ALT+SHIFT+O
Mark a table of authorities entry (citation).	ALT+SHIFT+I

Mark an index entry.	ALT+SHIFT+X
Insert a footnote.	ALT+CTRL+F
Insert an endnote.	ALT+CTRL+D

Work with Web pages

Insert a hyperlink.	CTRL+K
Go back one page.	ALT+LEFT ARROW
Go forward one page.	ALT+RIGHT ARROW
Refresh.	F9

Edit and move text and graphics

Delete one character to the left.	BACKSPACE
Delete one word to the left.	CTRL+BACKSPACE
Delete one character to the right.	DELETE
Delete one word to the right.	CTRL+DELETE
Cut selected text to the Office Clipboard.	CTRL+X
Undo the last action.	CTRL+Z
Cut to the Spike.	CTRL+F3

Copy and move text and graphics

Open the Office Clipboard	Press ALT+H to move to the Home tab, and then press F,O.
Copy selected text or graphics to the Office Clipboard.	CTRL+C
Cut selected text or graphics to the Office Clipboard.	CTRL+X
Paste the most recent addition to the Office Clipboard.	CTRL+V
Move text or graphics once.	F2 (then move the cursor and press ENTER)
Copy text or graphics once.	SHIFT+F2 (then move the cursor and press ENTER)
When text or an object is selected, open the Create New Building Block dialog box.	ALT+F3
When the building block — for example, a SmartArt graphic — is selected, display the shortcut menu that is associated with it.	SHIFT+F10
Cut to the Spike.	CTRL+F3
Paste the Spike contents.	CTRL+SHIFT+F3
Copy the header or footer used in the previous section of the document.	ALT+SHIFT+R

Insert special characters

A field	CTRL+F9
A line break	SHIFT+ENTER
A page break	CTRL+ENTER
A column break	CTRL+SHIFT+ENTER
An em dash	ALT+CTRL+MINUS SIGN
An en dash	CTRL+MINUS SIGN
An optional hyphen	CTRL+HYPHEN
A nonbreaking hyphen	CTRL+SHIFT+HYPHEN
A nonbreaking space	CTRL+SHIFT+SPACEBAR
The copyright symbol	ALT+CTRL+C
The registered trademark symbol	ALT+CTRL+R
The trademark symbol	ALT+CTRL+T
An ellipsis	ALT+CTRL+PERIOD
A single opening quotation mark	CTRL+'(single quotation mark), '(single quotation mark)
A single closing quotation mark	CTRL+' (single quotation mark), ' (single quotation mark)

Double opening quotation marks	CTRL+` (single quotation mark), SHIFT+' (single quotation mark)
Double closing quotation marks	CTRL+' (single quotation mark), SHIFT+' (single quotation mark)
An AutoText entry	ENTER (after you type the first few characters of the AutoText entry name and when the ScreenTip appears)

Insert characters by using character codes

Insert the Unicode character for the specified Unicode (hexadecimal) character code. For example, to insert the euro currency symbol (), type 20AC, and then hold down ALT and press X.	The character code, ALT+X
Find out the Unicode character code for the selected character	ALT+X
Insert the ANSI character for the specified ANSI (decimal) character code. For example, to insert the euro currency symbol, hold down ALT and press 0128 on the numeric keypad.	ALT+the character code (on the numeric keypad)

Select text and graphics

Select text by holding down SHIFT and using the arrow keys to move the cursor.

Extend a selection

Turn extend mode on.	F8
Select the nearest character.	F8, and then press LEFT ARROW or RIGHT ARROW
Increase the size of a selection.	F8 (press once to select a word, twice to select a sentence, and so on)
Reduce the size of a selection.	SHIFT+F8
Turn extend mode off.	ESC
Extend a selection one character to the right.	SHIFT+RIGHT ARROW
Extend a selection one character to the left.	SHIFT+LEFT ARROW
Extend a selection to the end of a word.	CTRL+SHIFT+RIGHT ARROW
Extend a selection to the beginning of a word.	CTRL+SHIFT+LEFT ARROW
Extend a selection to the end of a line.	SHIFT+END
Extend a selection to the beginning of a line.	SHIFT+HOME
Extend a selection one line down.	SHIFT+DOWN ARROW
Extend a selection one line up.	SHIFT+UP ARROW
Extend a selection to the end of a paragraph.	CTRL+SHIFT+DOWN ARROW
Extend a selection to the beginning of a paragraph.	CTRL+SHIFT+UP ARROW
Extend a selection one screen down.	SHIFT+PAGE DOWN
Extend a selection one screen up.	SHIFT+PAGE UP
Extend a selection to the beginning of a document.	CTRL+SHIFT+HOME
Extend a selection to the end of a document.	CTRL+SHIFT+END
Extend a selection to the end of a window.	ALT+CTRL+SHIFT+PAGE DOWN
Extend a selection to include the entire document.	CTRL+A
Select a vertical block of text.	CTRL+SHIFT+F8, and then use the arrow keys; press ESC to cancel selection mode
Extend a selection to a specific location in a document.	F8+arrow keys; press ESC to cancel selection mode

Select text and graphics in a table

Select the next cell's contents.	TAB
Select the preceding cell's contents.	SHIFT+TAB
Select an entire table.	ALT+5 on the numeric keypad (with NUM LOCK off)

Move through your document	
One character to the left	LEFT ARROW
One character to the right	RIGHT ARROW
One word to the left	CTRL+LEFT ARROW
One word to the right	CTRL+RIGHT ARROW
One paragraph up	CTRL+UP ARROW
One paragraph down	CTRL+DOWN ARROW
One cell to the left (in a table)	SHIFT+TAB
One cell to the right (in a table)	TAB
Up one line	UP ARROW
Down one line	DOWN ARROW
To the end of a line	END
To the beginning of a line	HOME
To the top of the window	ALT+CTRL+PAGE UP
To the end of the window	ALT+CTRL+PAGE DOWN
Up one screen (scrolling)	PAGE UP
Down one screen (scrolling)	PAGE DOWN
To the top of the next page	CTRL+PAGE DOWN
To the top of the previous page	CTRL+PAGE UP
To the end of a document	CTRL+END
To the beginning of a document	CTRL+HOME
To a previous revision	SHIFT+F5
After opening a document, to the location you were working in when the document was last closed	SHIFT+F5

Move around in a table	
To the next cell in a row	TAB
To the previous cell in a row	SHIFT+TAB
To the first cell in a row	ALT+HOME
To the last cell in a row	ALT+END
To the first cell in a column	ALT+PAGE UP
To the last cell in a column	ALT+PAGE DOWN
To the previous row	UP ARROW
To the next row	DOWN ARROW
One row up	ALT+SHIFT+UP ARROW
One row down	ALT+SHIFT+DOWN ARROW

Insert paragraphs and tab characters in a table	
New paragraphs in a cell	ENTER
Tab characters in a cell	CTRL+TAB

Character and paragraph formatting

Copy formatting

Copy formatting from text.	CTRL+SHIFT+C
Apply copied formatting to text.	CTRL+SHIFT+V

Change or resize the font

The following keyboard shortcuts do not work in Full Screen Reading mode.

Open the Font dialog box to change the font.	CTRL+SHIFT+F
Increase the font size.	CTRL+SHIFT+ >
Decrease the font size.	CTRL+SHIFT+ <
Increase the font size by 1 point.	CTRL+]

Decrease the font size by 1 point.	CTRL+[
Apply character formats	
Open the Font dialog box to change the formatting of characters.	CTRL+D
Change the case of letters.	SHIFT+F3
Format all letters as capitals.	CTRL+SHIFT+A
Apply bold formatting.	CTRL+B
Apply an underline.	CTRL+U
Underline words but not spaces.	CTRL+SHIFT+W
Double-underline text.	CTRL+SHIFT+D
Apply hidden text formatting.	CTRL+SHIFT+H
Apply italic formatting.	CTRL+I
Format letters as small capitals.	CTRL+SHIFT+K
Apply subscript formatting (automatic spacing).	CTRL+EQUAL SIGN
Apply superscript formatting (automatic spacing).	CTRL+SHIFT+PLUS SIGN
Remove manual character formatting.	CTRL+SPACEBAR
Change the selection to the Symbol font.	CTRL+SHIFT+Q
View and copy text formats	
Display nonprinting characters.	CTRL+SHIFT+* (asterisk on numeric keypad does not work)
Review text formatting.	SHIFT+F1 (then click the text with the formatting you want to review)
Copy formats.	CTRL+SHIFT+C
Paste formats.	CTRL+SHIFT+V
Set the line spacing	
Single-space lines.	CTRL+1
Double-space lines.	CTRL+2
Set 1.5-line spacing.	CTRL+5
Add or remove one line space preceding a paragraph.	CTRL+0 (zero)
Align paragraphs	
Switch a paragraph between centered and left-aligned.	CTRL+E
Switch a paragraph between justified and left-aligned.	CTRL+J
Switch a paragraph between right-aligned and left-aligned.	CTRL+R
Left align a paragraph.	CTRL+L
Indent a paragraph from the left.	CTRL+M
Remove a paragraph indent from the left.	CTRL+SHIFT+M
Create a hanging indent.	CTRL+T
Reduce a hanging indent.	CTRL+SHIFT+T
Remove paragraph formatting.	CTRL+Q
Apply paragraph styles	
Open Apply Styles task pane.	CTRL+SHIFT+S
Open Styles task pane.	ALT+CTRL+SHIFT+S
Start AutoFormat.	ALT+CTRL+K
Apply the Normal style.	CTRL+SHIFT+N
Apply the Heading 1 style.	ALT+CTRL+1
Apply the Heading 2 style.	ALT+CTRL+2
Apply the Heading 3 style.	ALT+CTRL+3

Close the Styles task pane

If the Styles task pane is not selected, press F6 to select it. Use the arrow keys to select Close, and then press ENTER.	Press CTRL+SPACEBAR.

Insert and edit objects

Insert an object	Press ALT, N, J, and then J to open the Object dialog box.

Mail Merge and Fields

Perform a mail merge

You must be on the Mailings tab to use these keyboard shortcuts.

Preview a mail merge.	ALT+SHIFT+K
Merge a document.	ALT+SHIFT+N
Print the merged document.	ALT+SHIFT+M
Edit a mail-merge data document.	ALT+SHIFT+E
Insert a merge field.	ALT+SHIFT+F

Work with fields

Insert a DATE field.	ALT+SHIFT+D
Insert a LISTNUM field.	ALT+CTRL+L
Insert a PAGE field.	ALT+SHIFT+P
Insert a TIME field.	ALT+SHIFT+T
Insert an empty field.	CTRL+F9
Update linked information in a Microsoft Office Word source document.	CTRL+SHIFT+F7
Update selected fields.	F9
Unlink a field.	CTRL+SHIFT+F9
Switch between a selected field code and its result.	SHIFT+F9
Switch between all field codes and their results.	ALT+F9
Run GOTOBUTTON or MACROBUTTON from the field that displays the field results.	ALT+SHIFT+F9
Go to the next field.	F11
Go to the previous field.	SHIFT+F11
Lock a field.	CTRL+F11
Unlock a field.	CTRL+SHIFT+F11

Language bar

Handwriting recognition

Switch between languages or keyboard layouts.	Left ALT+SHIFT
Display a list of correction alternatives.	+C
Turn handwriting on or off.	+H
Turn Japanese Input Method Editor (IME) on 101 keyboard on or off.	ALT+ ~
Turn Korean IME on 101 keyboard on or off.	Right ALT
Turn Chinese IME on 101 keyboard on or off.	CTRL+SPACEBAR

Function key reference

Function keys

Get Help or visit Microsoft Office Online.	F1
Move text or graphics.	F2
Repeat the last action.	F4
Choose the Go To command (Home tab).	F5
Go to the next pane or frame.	F6
Choose the Spelling command (Review tab).	F7
Extend a selection.	F8
Update the selected fields.	F9
Show KeyTips.	F10

Go to the next field.	F11
Choose the Save As command (Microsoft Office Button).	F12

SHIFT+Function key

Start context-sensitive Help or reveal formatting.	SHIFT+F1
Copy text.	SHIFT+F2
Change the case of letters.	SHIFT+F3
Repeat a Find or Go To action.	SHIFT+F4
Move to the last change.	SHIFT+F5
Go to the previous pane or frame (after pressing F6).	SHIFT+F6
Choose the Thesaurus command (Review tab, Proofing group).	SHIFT+F7
Shrink a selection.	SHIFT+F8
Switch between a field code and its result.	SHIFT+F9
Display a shortcut menu.	SHIFT+F10
Go to the previous field.	SHIFT+F11
Choose the Save command (Microsoft Office Button).	SHIFT+F12

CTRL+Function key

Choose the Print Preview command (Microsoft Office Button).	CTRL+F2
Cut to the Spike.	CTRL+F3
Close the window.	CTRL+F4
Go to the next window.	CTRL+F6
Insert an empty field.	CTRL+F9
Maximize the document window.	CTRL+F10
Lock a field.	CTRL+F11
Choose the Open command (Microsoft Office Button).	CTRL+F12

CTRL+SHIFT+Function key

Insert the contents of the Spike.	CTRL+SHIFT+F3
Edit a bookmark.	CTRL+SHIFT+F5
Go to the previous window.	CTRL+SHIFT+F6
Update linked information in an Office Word 2013 source document.	CTRL+SHIFT+F7
Extend a selection or block.	CTRL+SHIFT+F8, and then press an arrow key
Unlink a field.	CTRL+SHIFT+F9
Unlock a field.	CTRL+SHIFT+F11
Choose the Print command (Microsoft Office Button).	CTRL+SHIFT+F12

ALT+Function key

To do this	Press
Go to the next field.	ALT+F1
Create a new Building Block.	ALT+F3
Exit Office Word 2013.	ALT+F4
Restore the program window size.	ALT+F5
Move from an open dialog box back to the document, for dialog boxes such as Find and Replace that support this behavior.	ALT+F6
Find the next misspelling or grammatical error.	ALT+F7
Run a macro.	ALT+F8
Switch between all field codes and their results.	ALT+F9
Maximize the program window.	ALT+F10
Display Microsoft Visual Basic code.	ALT+F11

ALT+SHIFT+Function key

Go to the previous field.	ALT+SHIFT+F1
Choose the Save command (Microsoft Office Button).	ALT+SHIFT+F2

Display the Research task pane.	ALT+SHIFT+F7
Run GOTOBUTTON or MACROBUTTON from the field that displays the field results.	ALT+SHIFT+F9
Display a menu or message for a smart tag.	ALT+SHIFT+F10
CTRL+ALT+Function key	
Display Microsoft System Information.	CTRL+ALT+F1
Choose the Open command (Microsoft Office Button).	CTRL+ALT+F2

Microsoft Excel

Ctrl combination shortcut keys

Key	*Description*
Ctrl+Shift+(	Unhides any hidden rows within the selection.
Ctrl+Shift+)	Unhides any hidden columns within the selection.
Ctrl+Shift+&	Applies the outline border to the selected cells.
Ctrl+SHIFT_	Removes the outline border from the selected cells.
Ctrl+Shift+ ~	Applies the General number format.
Ctrl+Shift+$	Applies the Currency format with two decimal places (negative numbers in parentheses).
Ctrl+Shift+%	Applies the Percentage format with no decimal places.
Ctrl+Shift+^	Applies the Exponential number format with two decimal places.
Ctrl+Shift+#	Applies the Date format with the day, month, and year.
Ctrl+Shift+@	Applies the Time format with the hour and minute, and AM or PM.
Ctrl+Shift+!	Applies the Number format with two decimal places, thousands separator, and minus sign (-) for negative values.
Ctrl+Shift+*	Selects the current region around the active cell (the data area enclosed by blank rows and blank columns). In a PivotTable, it selects the entire PivotTable report.
Ctrl+Shift+:	Enters the current time.
Ctrl+Shift+"	Copies the value from the cell above the active cell into the cell or the Formula Bar.
Ctrl+Shift+Plus (+)	Displays the Insert dialog box to insert blank cells.
Ctrl+Minus (-)	Displays the Delete dialog box to delete the selected cells.
Ctrl+;	Enters the current date.
Ctrl+`	Alternates between displaying cell values and displaying formulas in the worksheet.
Ctrl+'	Copies a formula from the cell above the active cell into the cell or the Formula Bar.
Ctrl+1	Displays the Format Cells dialog box.
Ctrl+2	Applies or removes bold formatting.
Ctrl+3	Applies or removes italic formatting.
Ctrl+4	Applies or removes underlining.
Ctrl+5	Applies or removes strikethrough.
Ctrl+6	Alternates between hiding objects, displaying objects, and displaying placeholders for objects.
Ctrl+8	Displays or hides the outline symbols.
Ctrl+9	Hides the selected rows.
Ctrl+0	Hides the selected columns.
Ctrl+A	Selects the entire worksheet. If the worksheet contains data, Ctrl+A selects the current region. Pressing Ctrl+A a second time selects the current region and its summary rows. Pressing Ctrl+A a third time selects the entire worksheet.When the insertion point is to the right of a function name in a formula, displays the Function Arguments dialog box.Ctrl+Shift+A inserts the argument names and

	parentheses when the insertion point is to the right of a function name in a formula.
Ctrl+B	Applies or removes bold formatting.
Ctrl+C	Copies the selected cells. Ctrl+C followed by another Ctrl+C displays the Clipboard.
Ctrl+D	Uses the Fill Down command to copy the contents and format of the topmost cell of a selected range into the cells below.
Ctrl+F	Displays the Find and Replace dialog box, with the Find tab selected. Shift+F5 also displays this tab, while Shift+F4 repeats the last Find action.Ctrl+Shift+F opens the Format Cells dialog box with the Font tab selected.
Ctrl+G	Displays the Go To dialog box. F5 also displays this dialog box.
Ctrl+H	Displays the Find and Replace dialog box, with the Replace tab selected.
Ctrl+I	Applies or removes italic formatting.
Ctrl+K	Displays the Insert Hyperlink dialog box for new hyperlinks or the Edit Hyperlink dialog box for selected existing hyperlinks.
Ctrl+N	Creates a new, blank workbook.
Ctrl+O	Displays the Open dialog box to open or find a file. Ctrl+Shift+O selects all cells that contain comments.
Ctrl+P	Displays the Print dialog box. Ctrl+Shift+P opens the Format Cells dialog box with the Font tab selected.
Ctrl+R	Uses the Fill Right command to copy the contents and format of the leftmost cell of a selected range into the cells to the right.
Ctrl+S	Saves the active file with its current file name, location, and file format.
Ctrl+T	Displays the Create Table dialog box.
Ctrl+U	Applies or removes underlining. Ctrl+Shift+U switches between expanding and collapsing of the formula bar.
Ctrl+V	Inserts the contents of the Clipboard at the insertion point and replaces any selection. Available only after you have cut or copied an object, text, or cell contents.
Ctrl+W	Closes the selected workbook window.
Ctrl+X	Cuts the selected cells.
Ctrl+Y	Repeats the last command or action, if possible.
Ctrl+Z	Uses the Undo command to reverse the last command or to delete the last entry that you typed. Ctrl+Shift+Z uses the Undo or Redo command to reverse or restore the last automatic correction when AutoCorrect Smart Tags are displayed.

Function keys

Key	***Description***
F1	Displays the Microsoft Office Excel Help task pane. Ctrl+F1 displays or hides the ribbon.Alt+F1 creates a chart of the data in the current range.Alt+Shift+F1 inserts a new worksheet.
F2	Edits the active cell and positions the insertion point at the end of the cell contents. It also moves the insertion point into the Formula Bar when editing in a cell is turned off. Shift+F2 adds or edits a cell comment.Ctrl+F2 displays the Print Preview window.
F3	Displays the Paste Name dialog box. Shift+F3 displays the Insert Function dialog box.
F4	Repeats the last command or action, if possible. Ctrl+F4 closes the selected workbook window.
F5	Displays the Go To dialog box. Ctrl+F5 restores the window size of the selected workbook window.
F6	Switches between the worksheet, ribbon, task pane, and Zoom controls. In a worksheet that has been split (View menu, Manage This Window, Freeze Panes, Split Window command), F6 includes the split panes when switching between panes and the ribbon

	area. Shift+F6 switches between the worksheet, Zoom controls, task pane, and ribbon.Ctrl+F6 switches to the next workbook window when more than one workbook window is open.
F7	Displays the Spelling dialog box to check spelling in the active worksheet or selected range. Ctrl+F7 performs the Move command on the workbook window when it is not maximized. Use the arrow keys to move the window, and when finished press Enter, or Esc to cancel.
F8	Turns extend mode on or off. In extend mode, Extended Selection appears in the status line, and the arrow keys extend the selection. Shift+F8 enables you to add a nonadjacent cell or range to a selection of cells by using the arrow keys.Ctrl+F8 performs the Size command (on the Control menu for the workbook window) when a workbook is not maximized.Alt+F8 displays the Macro dialog box to create, run, edit, or delete a macro.
F9	Calculates all worksheets in all open workbooks. Shift+F9 calculates the active worksheet.Ctrl+Alt+F9 calculates all worksheets in all open workbooks, regardless of whether they have changed since the last calculation.Ctrl+Alt+Shift+F9 rechecks dependent formulas, and then calculates all cells in all open workbooks, including cells not marked as needing to be calculated.Ctrl+F9 minimizes a workbook window to an icon.
F10	Turns key tips on or off. Shift+F10 displays the shortcut menu for a selected item.Alt+Shift+F10 displays the menu or message for a smart tag. If more than one smart tag is present, it switches to the next smart tag and displays its menu or message.Ctrl+F10 maximizes or restores the selected workbook window.
F11	Creates a chart of the data in the current range. Shift+F11 inserts a new worksheet.Alt+F11 opens the Microsoft Visual Basic Editor, in which you can create a macro by using Visual Basic for Applications (VBA).
F12	Displays the Save As dialog box.

Other useful shortcut keys

Key	***Description***
Arrow Keys	Move one cell up, down, left, or right in a worksheet. Ctrl+ARROW KEY moves to the edge of the current data region (data region: A range of cells that contains data and that is bounded by empty cells or datasheet borders.) in a worksheet.Shift+ARROW KEY extends the selection of cells by one cell.Ctrl+Shift+ARROW KEY extends the selection of cells to the last nonblank cell in the same column or row as the active cell, or if the next cell is blank, extends the selection to the next nonblank cell.Left Arrow or Right Arrow selects the tab to the left or right when the ribbon is selected. When a submenu is open or selected, these arrow keys switch between the main menu and the submenu. When a ribbon tab is selected, these keys navigate the tab buttons.Down Arrow or Up Arrow selects the next or previous command when a menu or submenu is open. When a ribbon tab is selected, these keys navigate up or down the tab group.In a dialog box, arrow keys move between options in an open drop-down list, or between options in a group of options.Down Arrow or Alt+Down Arrow opens a selected drop-down list.
Backspace	Deletes one character to the left in the Formula Bar. Also clears the content of the active cell.In cell editing mode, it deletes the character to the left of the insertion point.
Delete	Removes the cell contents (data and formulas) from selected cells without affecting cell formats or comments. In cell editing mode, it deletes the character to the right of the insertion point.
End	Moves to the cell in the lower-right corner of the window when SCROLL LOCK is turned on. Also selects the last command on the menu when a menu or submenu is visible.Ctrl+End moves to the last cell on a worksheet, in the lowest used row of the rightmost used column. If the cursor is in the formula bar, Ctrl+End moves the cursor to the end of the text. Ctrl+Shift+End extends the selection of cells to the last used cell on the worksheet

(lower-right corner). If the cursor is in the formula bar, Ctrl+Shift+End selects all text in the formula bar from the cursor position to the end—this does not affect the height of the formula bar.

Enter — Completes a cell entry from the cell or the Formula Bar, and selects the cell below (by default). In a data form, it moves to the first field in the next record.Opens a selected menu (press F10 to activate the menu bar) or performs the action for a selected command.In a dialog box, it performs the action for the default command button in the dialog box (the button with the bold outline, often the OK button).Alt+Enter starts a new line in the same cell.Ctrl+Enter fills the selected cell range with the current entry.Shift+Enter completes a cell entry and selects the cell above.

Esc — Cancels an entry in the cell or Formula Bar. Closes an open menu or submenu, dialog box, or message window.It also closes full screen mode when this mode has been applied, and returns to normal screen mode to display the Ribbon and status bar again.

Home — Moves to the beginning of a row in a worksheet. Moves to the cell in the upper-left corner of the window when SCROLL LOCK is turned on.Selects the first command on the menu when a menu or submenu is visible.Ctrl+Home moves to the beginning of a worksheet.Ctrl+Shift+Home extends the selection of cells to the beginning of the worksheet.

Page Down — Moves one screen down in a worksheet. Alt+Page Down moves one screen to the right in a worksheet.Ctrl+Page Down moves to the next sheet in a workbook.Ctrl+Shift+Page Down selects the current and next sheet in a workbook.

Keyboard shortcuts for using the Help window

The Help window provides access to all Office Help content. The Help window displays topics and other Help content.

Open the Help window.	F1
Close the Help window.	Alt+F4
Switch between the Help window and the active program.	Alt+Tab
Go back to Program Name Home.	Alt+Home
Select the next item in the Help window.	Tab
Select the previous item in the Help window.	Shift+Tab
Perform the action for the selected item.	Enter
In the Browse Program Name Help section of the Help window, select the next or previous item.	Tab or Shift+Tab
In the Browse Program Name Help section of the Help window, expand or collapse the selected item.	Enter
Select the next hidden text or hyperlink, including Show All or Hide All at the top of a Help topic.	Tab
Select the previous hidden text or hyperlink.	Shift+Tab
Perform the action for the selected Show All, Hide All, hidden text, or hyperlink.	Enter
Move to the previous Help topic (Back button).	Alt+Left Arrow or Backspace
Move to the next Help topic (Forward button).	Alt+Right Arrow
Scroll small amounts up or down within the current Help topic.	Up Arrow, Down Arrow
Scroll larger amounts up or down within the current Help topic.	Page Up, Page Down
Change whether the Help window appears connected to (tiled) or separate from (untiled) the active program.	Alt+U
Display a menu of commands for the Help window. This requires that the Help window is the active focus. (Click in the Help window.)	Shift+F10
Stop the last action (Stop button).	Esc
Refresh the window (Refresh button).	F5
Print the current Help topic. Note If the cursor is not in the current Help topic, press F6 and then press Ctrl+P.	Ctrl+P

Change the connection state.	F6, and then click Down Arrow
Type text in the Type words to search for box.	F6, and then click Down Arrow
Switch among areas in the Help window; for example, switch between the toolbar, Type words to search for box, and Search list.	F6
In a Table of Contents in tree view, select the next or previous item.	Up Arrow, Down Arrow
In a Table of Contents in tree view, expand or collapse the selected item.	Left Arrow, Right Arrow

Keyboard shortcuts for Microsoft Office basics

Display and use windows

Switch to the next window.	Alt+Tab
Switch to the previous window.	Alt+Shift+Tab
Close the active window.	Ctrl+W or Ctrl+F4
Restore the size of the active window after you maximize it.	Ctrl+F5
Move to a task pane from another pane in the program window (clockwise direction). You may need to press F6 more than once. Note If pressing F6 doesn't display the task pane that you want, try pressing Alt to place focus on the menu bar or the Ribbon, and then press Ctrl+Tab to move to the task pane.	F6
Move to a pane from another pane in the program window (counterclockwise direction).	Shift+F6
When more than one window is open, switch to the next window.	Ctrl+F6
Switch to the previous window.	Ctrl+Shift+F6
When a document window is not maximized, perform the Move command (on the Control menu for the window). Use the arrow keys to move the window, and, when finished, press Esc.	Ctrl+F7
When a document window is not maximized, perform the Size command (on the Control menu for the window). Press the arrow keys to resize the window, and, when finished, press Esc.	Ctrl+F8
Minimize a window to an icon (works for only some Microsoft Office programs).	Ctrl+F9
Maximize or restore a selected window.	Ctrl+F10
Copy a picture of the screen to the Clipboard.	Print Screen
Copy a picture of the selected window to the Clipboard.	Alt+Print Screen

Change or Resize the Font

Change the font.	Ctrl+Shift+F
Change the font size.	Ctrl+Shift+P
Increase the font size of the selected text.	Ctrl+Shift+ >
Decrease the font size of the selected text.	Ctrl+Shift+ <

Move around in text or cells

Move one character to the left.	Left Arrow
Move one character to the right.	Right Arrow
Move one line up.	Up Arrow
Move one line down.	Down Arrow
Move one word to the left.	Ctrl+Left Arrow
Move one word to the right.	Ctrl+Right Arrow
Move to the end of a line.	End
Move to the beginning of a line.	Home
Move up one paragraph.	Ctrl+Up Arrow
Move down one paragraph.	Ctrl+Down Arrow

Move to the end of a text box.	Ctrl + End
Move to the beginning of a text box.	Ctrl + Home
In Microsoft Office PowerPoint, move to the next title or body text placeholder. If it is the last placeholder on a slide, this will insert a new slide with the same slide layout as the original slide.	Ctrl + Enter
Repeat the last Find action.	Shift + F4

Move around in and work in tables

Move to the next cell.	Tab
Move to the preceding cell.	Shift + Tab
Move to the next row.	Down Arrow
Move to the preceding row.	Up Arrow
Insert a tab in a cell.	Ctrl + Tab
Start a new paragraph.	Enter
Add a new row at the bottom of the table.	Tab at the end of the last row

Access and use task panes

Move to a task pane from another pane in the program window. (You may need to press F6 more than once.) Note If pressing F6 doesn't display the task pane that you want, try pressing Alt to place focus on the menu bar, and then press Ctrl + Tab to move to the task pane.	F6
When a menu or toolbar is active, move to a task pane. (You may need to press Ctrl + Tab more than once.)	Ctrl + Tab
When a task pane is active, select the next or previous option in the task pane.	Tab or Shift + Tab
Display the full set of commands on the task pane menu.	Ctrl + Down Arrow
Move among choices on a selected submenu; move among certain options in a group of options in a dialog box.	Down Arrow or Up Arrow
Open the selected menu, or perform the action assigned to the selected button.	Spacebar or Enter
Open a shortcut menu; open a drop-down menu for the selected gallery item.	Shift + F10
When a menu or submenu is visible, select the first or last command on the menu or submenu.	Home or End
Scroll up or down in the selected gallery list.	Page Up or Page Down
Move to the top or bottom of the selected gallery list.	Ctrl + Home or Ctrl + End
Open the Research task pane. Note This keyboard shortcut does not work in Microsoft Office PowerPoint or Microsoft Office SharePoint Designer.	Alt + Click

Access and use smart tags

Display the menu or message for a smart tag. If more than one smart tag is present, switch to the next smart tag and display its menu or message.	Alt + Shift + F10
Select the next item on a smart tag menu.	Down Arrow
Select the previous item on a smart tag menu.	Up Arrow
Perform the action for the selected item on a smart tag menu.	Enter
Close the smart tag menu or message.	Esc

Press Ctrl + Tab repeatedly to select the toolbar or task pane that you want.

Use dialog boxes

Action	Shortcut
Move to the next option or option group.	Tab
Move to the previous option or option group.	Shift+Tab
Switch to the next tab in a dialog box.	Ctrl+Tab
Switch to the previous tab in a dialog box.	Ctrl+Shift+Tab
Move between options in an open drop-down list, or between options in a group of options.	Arrow keys
Perform the action assigned to the selected button; select or clear the selected check box.	Spacebar
Open the list if it is closed and move to that option in the list.	First letter of an option in a drop-down list
Select an option; select or clear a check box.	Alt+ the letter underlined in an option
Open a selected drop-down list.	Alt+Down Arrow
Close a selected drop-down list; cancel a command and close a dialog box.	Esc
Perform the action assigned to a default button in a dialog box.	Enter

Use edit boxes within dialog boxes

An edit box is a blank box in which you type or paste an entry, such as your user name or the path to a folder.

Action	Shortcut
Move to the beginning of the entry.	Home
Move to the end of the entry.	End
Move one character to the left or right.	Left Arrow or Right Arrow
Move one word to the left.	Ctrl+Left Arrow
Move one word to the right.	Ctrl+Right Arrow
Select or cancel selection one character to the left.	Shift+Left Arrow
Select or cancel selection one character to the right.	Shift+Right Arrow
Select or cancel selection one word to the left.	Ctrl+Shift+Left Arrow
Select or cancel selection one word to the right.	Ctrl+Shift+Right Arrow
Select from the insertion point to the beginning of the entry.	Shift+Home
Select from the insertion point to the end of the entry.	Shift+End

Use the Open and Save As dialog boxes

Action	Shortcut
Go to the previous folder.	Alt+1
Up One Level button: open the folder up one level above the open folder.	Alt+2
Search the Web button: close the dialog box and open your Web search page.	Alt+3
Delete button: delete the selected folder or file.	Alt+3
Create New Folder button: create a new folder.	Alt+4
Views button: switch among available folder views.	Alt+5
Tools button: show the Tools menu.	Alt+L
Display a shortcut menu for a selected item, such as a folder or file.	Shift+F10
Move between options or areas in the dialog box.	Tab
Open the Look in list.	F4 or Alt+I
Refresh the file list.	F5

Work with shapes in a SmartArt graphic

Action	Shortcut
Select the next element in a SmartArt graphic.	Tab
Select the previous element in a SmartArt graphic.	Shift+Tab
Select all shapes.	Ctrl+A
Remove focus from the selected shape.	Esc
Nudge the selected shape up.	Up Arrow
Nudge the selected shape down.	Down Arrow
Nudge the selected shape left.	Left Arrow

Nudge the selected shape right.	Right Arrow
Edit text in the selected shape.	Enter or F2
Delete the selected shape.	Delete or Backspace
Cut the selected shape.	Ctrl+X or Shift+Delete
Copy the selected shape.	Ctrl+C
Paste the contents of the Clipboard.	Ctrl+V
Undo the last action.	Ctrl+Z

Move and resize shapes in a SmartArt graphic

Enlarge the selected shape horizontally.	Shift+Right Arrow
Reduce the selected shape horizontally.	Shift+Left Arrow
Enlarge the selected shape vertically.	Shift+Up Arrow
Reduce the selected shape vertically.	Shift+Down Arrow
Rotate the selected shape to the right.	Alt+Right Arrow
Rotate the selected shape to the left.	Alt+Left Arrow

Work with text in a SmartArt graphic

Move one character to the left.	Left Arrow
Move one character to the right.	Right Arrow
Move up one line.	Up Arrow
Move down one line.	Down Arrow
Move one word to the left.	Ctrl+Left Arrow
Move one word to the right.	Ctrl+Right Arrow
Move one paragraph up.	Ctrl+Up Arrow
Move one paragraph down.	Ctrl+Down Arrow
Move to the end of a line.	End
Move to the beginning of a line.	Home
Move to the end of a text box.	Ctrl+End
Move to the beginning of a text box.	Ctrl+Home
Cut selected text.	Ctrl+X
Copy selected text.	Ctrl+C
Paste selected text.	Ctrl+V
Undo the last action.	Ctrl+Z
Delete one character to the left.	Backspace
Delete one word to the left.	Ctrl+Backspace
Delete one character to the right.	Delete
Delete one word to the right.	Ctrl+Delete
Promote the selected text.	Alt+Shift+Right Arrow
Demote the selected text.	Alt+Shift+Left Arrow
Check the spelling (not available in Microsoft Office Word 2013).	F7

Apply character formatting

Open the Font dialog box.	Ctrl+Shift+F or Ctrl+Shift+P
Increase the font size of the selected text.	Ctrl+Shift+ >
Decrease the font size of the selected text.	Ctrl+Shift+ <
Switch the case of selected text (lower case, Title Case, Upper Case).	Shift+F3
Apply bold formatting to the selected text.	Ctrl+B
Apply an underline to the selected text (not available in Office Word 2013).	Ctrl+U
Apply italic formatting to the selected text.	Ctrl+I
Apply subscript formatting to the selected text.	Ctrl+Equal Sign
Apply superscript formatting to the selected text.	Ctrl+Shift+Plus Sign
Adjust the superscript/subscript offset up.	Ctrl+Alt+Shift+ >

Adjust the superscript/subscript offset down.	Ctrl+Alt+Shift+<
Remove all character formatting from the selected text.	Ctrl+Spacebar

Copy text formatting

Copy formatting from the selected text.	Ctrl+Shift+C
Paste formatting to the selected text.	Ctrl+Shift+V

Apply paragraph formatting

Center a paragraph.	Ctrl+E
Justify a paragraph.	Ctrl+J
Left align a paragraph.	Ctrl+L
Right align a paragraph.	Ctrl+R
Demote a bullet point.	Tab or Alt+Shift+Right Arrow
Promote a bullet point.	Shift+Tab or Alt+Shift+Left Arrow

Use the Text pane

Merge two lines of text.	Delete at the end of the first line of text
Display the shortcut menu.	Shift+F10
Switch between the Text pane and the drawing canvas.	Ctrl+Shift+F2
Close the Text pane.	Alt+F4
Switch the focus from the Text pane to the border of the SmartArt graphic.	Esc
Open the SmartArt graphics Help topic.	Ctrl+Shift+F1

Microsoft PowerPoint

Display and use windows

Switch to the next window.	ALT+TAB
Switch to the previous window.	ALT+SHIFT+TAB
Close the active window.	CTRL+W or CTRL+F4
Restore the size of the active window after you maximize it.	CTRL+F5
Move to a task pane from another pane in the program window (clockwise direction). You may need to press F6 more than once. Note If pressing F6 doesn't display the task pane that you want, try pressing ALT to place focus on the menu bar or Ribbon and then pressing CTRL+TAB to move to the task pane.	F6
Move to a pane from another pane in the program window (counterclockwise direction).	SHIFT+F6
When more than one window is open, switch to the next window.	CTRL+F6
Switch to the previous window.	CTRL+SHIFT+F6
When a document window is not maximized, perform the Move command (on the Control menu for the window). Use the arrow keys to move the window and when finished, press ESC.	CTRL+F7
When a document window is not maximized, perform the Size command (on the Control menu for the window). Press the arrow keys to resize the window and when finished, press ESC.	CTRL+F8
Minimize a window to an icon (works for only some Microsoft Office programs).	CTRL+F9
Maximize or restore a selected window.	CTRL+F10

Copy a picture of the screen to the Clipboard.	PRINT SCREEN
Copy a picture of the selected window to the Clipboard.	ALT+PRINT SCREEN

Change or resize the font

Change the font.	CTRL+SHIFT+F
Change the font size.	CTRL+SHIFT+P
Increase the font size of the selected text.	CTRL+SHIFT+ >
Decrease the font size of the selected text.	CTRL+SHIFT+ <

Move around in text or cells

Move one character to the left.	LEFT ARROW
Move one character to the right.	RIGHT ARROW
Move one line up.	UP ARROW
Move one line down.	DOWN ARROW
Move one word to the left.	CTRL+LEFT ARROW
Move one word to the right.	CTRL+RIGHT ARROW
Move to the end of a line.	END
Move to the beginning of a line.	HOME
Move up one paragraph.	CTRL+UP ARROW
Move down one paragraph.	CTRL+DOWN ARROW
Move to the end of a text box.	CTRL+END
Move to the beginning of a text box.	CTRL+HOME
In Microsoft Office PowerPoint, move to the next title or body text placeholder. If it is the last placeholder on a slide, this will insert a new slide with the same slide layout as the original slide.	CTRL+ENTER
Repeat the last Find action.	SHIFT+F4

Find and replace

Open the Find dialog box.	CTRL+F
Open the Replace dialog box.	CTRL+H
Repeat the last Find action.	CTRL+F4

Move around in and work in tables

Move to the next cell.	TAB
Move to the preceding cell.	SHIFT+TAB
Move to the next row.	DOWN ARROW
Move to the preceding row.	UP ARROW
Insert a tab in a cell.	CTRL+TAB
Start a new paragraph.	ENTER
Add a new row at the bottom of the table.	TAB at the end of the last row

Access and use task panes

Move to a task pane from another pane in the program window. (You may need to press F6 more than once.) Note If pressing F6 doesn't display the task pane that you want, try pressing ALT to place focus on the menu bar and then pressing CTRL+TAB to move to the task pane.	F6
When a menu or toolbar is active, move to a task pane. (You may need to press CTRL+TAB more than once.)	CTRL+TAB
When a task pane is active, select the next or previous option in the task pane, respectively.	TAB, SHIFT+TAB

Display the full set of commands on the task pane menu.	CTRL+DOWN ARROW
Move among choices on a selected submenu; move among certain options in a group of options in a dialog box.	DOWN ARROW or UP ARROW
Open the selected menu, or perform the action assigned to the selected button.	SPACEBAR or ENTER
Open a shortcut menu; open a drop-down menu for the selected gallery item.	SHIFT+F10
When a menu or submenu is visible, select the first or last command, respectively, on the menu or submenu.	HOME, END
Scroll up or down in the selected gallery list, respectively.	PAGE UP, PAGE DOWN
Move to the top or bottom of the selected gallery list, respectively.	HOME, END
Close a task pane.	CTRL+SPACEBAR, C
Open the Clipboard.	ALT+H, F, O

Access and use smart tags

Display the menu or message for a smart tag. If more than one smart tag is present, switch to the next smart tag and display its menu or message.	ALT+SHIFT+F10
Select the next item on a smart tag menu.	DOWN ARROW
Select the previous item on a smart tag menu.	UP ARROW
Perform the action for the selected item on a smart tag menu.	ENTER
Close the smart tag menu or message.	ESC

Use dialog boxes

Move to the next option or option group.	TAB
Move to the previous option or option group.	SHIFT+TAB
Switch to the next tab in a dialog box.	CTRL+TAB
Switch to the previous tab in a dialog box.	CTRL+SHIFT+TAB
Open a selected drop-down list.	ALT+DOWN ARROW
Open the list if it is closed and move to an option in the list.	First letter of an option in a drop-down list
Move between options in an open drop-down list, or between options in a group of options.	Arrow keys
Close a selected drop-down list; cancel a command and close a dialog box.	ESC
Perform the action assigned to the selected button; select or clear the selected check box.	SPACEBAR
Select an option; select or clear a check box.	ALT+ the letter underlined in an option
Perform the action assigned to a default button in a dialog box.	ENTER

Use edit boxes within dialog boxes

An edit box is a blank in which you type or paste an entry, such as your user name or the path to a folder.

Move to the beginning of the entry.	HOME
Move to the end of the entry.	END
Move one character to the left or right, respectively.	LEFT ARROW, RIGHT ARROW
Move one word to the left.	CTRL+LEFT ARROW
Move one word to the right.	CTRL+RIGHT ARROW
Select or cancel selection one character to the left.	SHIFT+LEFT ARROW
Select or cancel selection one character to the right.	SHIFT+RIGHT ARROW
Select or cancel selection one word to the left.	CTRL+SHIFT+LEFT ARROW
Select or cancel selection one word to the right.	CTRL+SHIFT+RIGHT ARROW
Select from the cursor to the beginning of the entry.	SHIFT+HOME
Select from the cursor to the end of the entry.	SHIFT+END

Use the Open and Save As dialog boxes

Go to the previous folder.	ALT+1
Up One Level button: Open the folder up one level above the open folder.	ALT+2
Delete button: Delete the selected folder or file.	ALT+3 or DELETE
Create New Folder button: Create a new folder.	ALT+4
Views button: Switch among available folder views.	ALT+5
Tools button: Show the Tools menu.	ALT+L
Display a shortcut menu for a selected item, such as a folder or file.	SHIFT+F10
Move between options or areas in the dialog box.	TAB
Open the Look in list.	F4 or ALT+I
Refresh the file list.	F5

Microsoft Access 2013

General shortcut keys

Open a new database	CTRL+N
Open an existing database	CTRL+O
Exit Office Access 2013Access	ALT+F4

Printing and saving

Print the current or selected object	CTRL+P
Open the Print dialog box from Print Preview	P or CTRL+P
Open the Page Setup dialog box from Print Preview	S
Cancel Print Preview or Layout Preview	C or ESC
Save a database object	CTRL+S or SHIFT+F12
Open the Save As dialog box	F12

Using a combo box or list box

Open a combo box	F4 or ALT+DOWN ARROW
Refresh the contents of a Lookup field list box or combo box	F9
Move down one line	DOWN ARROW
Move down one page	PAGE DOWN
Move up one line	UP ARROW
Move up one page	PAGE UP
Exit the combo box or list box	TAB

Finding and replacing text or data

Open the Find tab in the Find and Replace dialog box (Datasheet view and Form view only)	CTRL+F
Open the Replace tab in the Find and Replace dialog box (Datasheet view and Form view only)	CTRL+H
Find the next occurrence of the text specified in the Find and Replace dialog box when the dialog box is closed (Datasheet view and Form view only)	SHIFT+F4

Working in Design view

Switch between Edit mode (with insertion point displayed) and Navigation mode in a datasheet. When working in a form or report, press ESC to leave Navigation mode.	F2
Switch to the property sheet (Design view in forms and reports in both Access databases and Access projects)	F4
Switch to Form view from form Design view	F5
Switch between the upper and lower portions of a window (Design view of queries, and the Advanced Filter/Sort window)	F6

Action	Shortcut
Cycle through the field grid, field properties, Navigation Pane, access keys in the Keyboard Access System, Zoom controls, and the security bar (Design view of tables)	F6
Open the Choose Builder dialog box (Design view window of forms and reports)	F7
Open the Visual Basic Editor from a selected property in the property sheet for a form or report	F7
Switch from the Visual Basic Editor back to form or report Design view	SHIFT+F7 or ALT+F11

Editing controls in form and report Design view

Action	Shortcut
Copy the selected control to the Clipboard	CTRL+C
Cut the selected control and copy it to the Clipboard	CTRL+X
Paste the contents of the Clipboard in the upper-left corner of the selected section	CTRL+V
Move the selected control to the right (except controls that are part of a layout)	RIGHT ARROW or CTRL+RIGHT ARROW
Move the selected control to the left (except controls that are part of a layout)	LEFT ARROW or CTRL+LEFT ARROW
Move the selected control up	UP ARROW or CTRL+UP ARROW
Move the selected control down	DOWN ARROW or CTRL+DOWN ARROW
Increase the height of the selected control	SHIFT+DOWN ARROW
Increase the width of the selected control Note If used with controls that are in a layout, the entire layout is resized	SHIFT+RIGHT ARROW
Reduce the height of the selected control	SHIFT+UP ARROW
Reduce the width of the selected control Note If used with controls that are in a layout, the entire layout is resized	SHIFT+LEFT ARROW
Toggle the Navigation Pane	F11
Cycle between open windows	CTRL+F6
Restore the selected minimized window when all windows are minimized	ENTER
Turn on Resize mode for the active window when it is not maximized; press the arrow keys to resize the window	CTRL+F8
Display the Control menu	ALT+SPACEBAR
Display the shortcut menu	SHIFT+F10
Close the active window	CTRL+W or CTRL+F4
Switch between the Visual Basic Editor and the previous active window	ALT+F11

Working with Wizards

Action	Shortcut
Toggle the focus forward between controls in the wizard	TAB
Move to the next page of the wizard	ALT+N
Move to the previous page of the wizard	ALT+B
Complete the wizard	ALT+F

Miscellaneous

Action	Shortcut
Display the complete hyperlink address for a selected hyperlink	F2
Check spelling	F7
Open the Zoom box to conveniently enter expressions and other text in small input areas	SHIFT+F2
Display a property sheet in Design view	ALT+ENTER
Exit Access or close a dialog box	ALT+F4
Invoke a Builder	CTRL+F2
Toggle forward between views when in a table, query, form, report, page, PivotTable list, PivotChart report, stored procedure, or Access project (.adp) function. If there are	

additional views available, successive keystrokes will move to the next available view.	CTRL+RIGHT ARROW or CRTL+COMMA (,)
Toggle back between views when in a table, query, form, report, page, PivotTable list, PivotChart report, stored procedure, or .adp function. If there are additional views available, successive keystrokes will move to the previous view. Note CTRL+PERIOD (.) does not work under all conditions with all objects.	CTRL+LEFT ARROW or CRTL+PERIOD (.)

Navigation Pane shortcut keys

Editing and navigating the Object list

Rename a selected object	F2
Move down one line	DOWN ARROW
Move down one window	PAGE DOWN
Move to the last object	END
Move up one line	UP ARROW
Move up one window	PAGE UP
Move to the first object	HOME

Navigating and opening objects

Open the selected table or query in Datasheet view	ENTER
Open the selected form or report	ENTER
Run the selected macro	ENTER
Open the selected table, query, form, report, data access page, macro, or module in Design view	CTRL+ENTER
Display the Immediate window in the Visual Basic Editor	CTRL+G

Work with menus

Show the shortcut menu	SHIFT+F10
Show the access keys	ALT or F10
Show the program icon menu (on the program title bar)	ALT+SPACEBAR
With the menu or submenu visible, select the next or previous command	DOWN ARROW or UP ARROW
Select the menu to the left or right; or, when a submenu is visible, to switch between the main menu and the submenu	LEFT ARROW or RIGHT ARROW
Select the first or last command on the menu or submenu	HOME or END
Close the visible menu and submenu at the same time	ALT
Close the visible menu; or, with a submenu visible, to close the submenu only	ESC

Work in windows and dialog boxes

Using a program window

Switch to the next program	ALT+TAB
Switch to the previous program	ALT+SHIFT+TAB
Show the Windows Start menu	CTRL+ESC
Close the active database window	CTRL+W
Switch to the next database window	CTRL+F6
Switch to the previous database window	CTRL+SHIFT+F6
Restore the selected minimized window when all windows are minimized	ENTER

Using a dialog box

Switch to the next tab in a dialog box	CTRL+TAB

Action	Shortcut
Switch to the previous tab in a dialog box	CTRL+SHIFT+TAB
Move to the next option or option group	TAB
Move to the previous option or option group	SHIFT+TAB
Move between options in the selected drop-down list box, or to move between some options in a group of options	Arrow keys
Perform the action assigned to the selected button; select or clear the check box	SPACEBAR
Move to the option by the first letter in the option name in a drop-down list box	Letter key for the first letter in the option name you want (when a drop-down list box is selected)
Select the option, or to select or clear the check box by the letter underlined in the option name	ALT+letter key
Open the selected drop-down list box	ALT+DOWN ARROW
Close the selected drop-down list box	ESC
Perform the action assigned to the default button in the dialog box	ENTER
Cancel the command and close the dialog box	ESC
Close a dialog box	ALT+F4

Editing in a text box

Action	Shortcut
Move to the beginning of the entry	HOME
Move to the end of the entry	END
Move one character to the left or right	LEFT ARROW or RIGHT ARROW
Move one word to the left or right	CTRL+LEFT ARROW or CTRL+RIGHT ARROW
Select from the insertion point to the beginning of the entry	SHIFT+HOME
Select from the insertion point to the end of the entry	SHIFT+END
Change the size of the selection by one character to the left	SHIFT+LEFT ARROW
Change the size of the selection by one character to the right	SHIFT+RIGHT ARROW
Change the size of the selection by one word to the left	CTRL+SHIFT+LEFT ARROW
Change the size of the selection by one word to the right	CTRL+SHIFT+RIGHT ARROW

Work with the Open, File New Database, and Save As dialog boxes

Action	Shortcut
Go to the previous folder ( )	ALT+1
Open the folder up one level from the open folder (Up One Level button)	ALT+2
Delete the selected folder or file (Delete button)	DEL
Create a new subfolder in the open folder (Create New Folder button)	ALT+4
Switch between Thumbnails, Tiles, Icons, List, Details, Properties, and Preview views	ALT+5
Show the Tools menu (Tools button)	ALT+L

Work with property sheets

Using a property sheet with a form or report

Action	Shortcut
Toggle the property sheet tab	F4
Move among choices in the control drop-down list one item at a time	DOWN ARROW or UP ARROW
Move among choices in the control drop-down list five items at a time	PAGE DOWN or PAGE UP
Move to the property sheet tabs from the control drop-down list	TAB
Move among the property sheet tabs with a tab selected, but no property selected	LEFT ARROW or RIGHT ARROW
With a property already selected, move down one property on a tab	TAB
With a property selected, move up one property on a tab; or if already at the top, move to the control drop-down list	SHIFT+TAB
Toggle forward between tabs when a property is selected	CTRL+TAB

Toggle backward between tabs when a property is selected	CTRL+SHIFT+TAB

Using a property sheet with a table or query

Toggle the property sheet tab	F4
With a tab selected, but no property selected, move among the property sheet tabs	LEFT ARROW or RIGHT ARROW
Move to the property sheet tabs when a property is selected	CTRL+TAB
Move to the first property of a tab when no property is selected	TAB
Move down one property on a tab	TAB
Move up one property on a tab; or if already at the top, select the tab itself	SHIFT+TAB
Toggle forward between tabs when a property is selected	CTRL+TAB
Toggle backward between tabs when a property is selected	CTRL+SHIFT+TAB

Work with the Field List pane

Toggle the Field List pane	ALT+F8
Add the selected field to the form or report detail section	ENTER
Move up or down the Field List pane	UP ARROW or DOWN ARROW
Move to the upper Field List pane from the lower pane	SHIFT+TAB
Move to the lower Field List pane from the upper pane	TAB

Keyboard shortcuts for using the Help window

Select the next hidden text or hyperlink, or Show All or Hide All at the top of a topic	TAB
Select the previous hidden text or hyperlink, or the Browser View button at the top of a Microsoft Office Web site article	SHIFT+TAB
Perform the action for the selected Show All, Hide All, hidden text, or hyperlink	ENTER
Move back to the previous Help topic	ALT+LEFT ARROW
Move forward to the next Help topic	ALT+RIGHT ARROW
Open the Print dialog box	CTRL+P
Scroll small amounts up and down, respectively, within the currently-displayed Help topic.	UP ARROW AND DOWN ARROW
Scroll larger amounts up and down, respectively, within the currently-displayed Help topic.	PAGE UP AND PAGE DOWN
Display a menu of commands for the Help window; requires that the Help window have active focus (click an item in the Help window).	SHIFT+F10

Send e-mail messages

Send the active database object (the object selected in the Navigation Pane) as an e-mail message	ALT+F+E
Open the Address Book from within Outlook	CTRL+SHIFT+B
Check the names in the To, Cc, and Bcc boxes against the Address Book	ALT+K or CTRL+K
Select the next box in the e-mail header or the body of the message when the last box in the e-mail header is active	TAB
Select the previous field or button in the e-mail header	SHIFT+TAB

Keys for working with text and data

Selecting text in a field

Change the size of the selection by one character to the right	SHIFT+RIGHT ARROW
Change the size of the selection by one word to the right	CTRL+SHIFT+RIGHT ARROW
Change the size of the selection by one character to the left	SHIFT+LEFT ARROW
Change the size of the selection by one word to the left	CTRL+SHIFT+LEFT ARROW

Selecting a field or record

Note To cancel a selection, use the opposite arrow key.

Select the next field	TAB

Switch between Edit mode (with insertion point displayed) and Navigation mode in a datasheet. When using a form or report, press ESC to leave Navigation mode.	F2
Switch between selecting the current record and the first field of the current record, in Navigation mode	SHIFT+SPACEBAR
Extend selection to the previous record, if the current record is selected	SHIFT+UP ARROW
Extend selection to the next record, if the current record is selected	SHIFT+DOWN ARROW
Select all records	CTRL+A or CTRL+SHIFT+SPACEBAR

Extending a selection

Turn on Extend mode (in Datasheet view, Extended Selection appears in the lower-right corner of the window); pressing F8 repeatedly extends the selection to the word, the field, the record, and all records	F8
Extend a selection to adjacent fields in the same row in Datasheet view	LEFT ARROW or RIGHT ARROW
Extend a selection to adjacent rows in Datasheet view	UP ARROW or DOWN ARROW
Undo the previous extension	SHIFT+F8
Cancel Extend mode	ESC

Selecting and moving a column in Datasheet view

Select the current column or cancel the column selection, in Navigation mode only	CTRL+SPACEBAR
Select the column to the right, if the current column is selected	SHIFT+RIGHT ARROW
Select the column to the left, if the current column is selected	SHIFT+LEFT ARROW
Turn on Move mode; then press the RIGHT ARROW or LEFT ARROW key to move selected column(s) to the right or left	CTRL+SHIFT+F8

Edit text and data

Note If the insertion point is not visible, press F2 to display it.

Moving the insertion point in a field

Move the insertion point one character to the right	RIGHT ARROW
Move the insertion point one word to the right	CTRL+RIGHT ARROW
Move the insertion point one character to the left	LEFT ARROW
Move the insertion point one word to the left	CTRL+LEFT ARROW
Move the insertion point to the end of the field, in single-line fields; or to move it to the end of the line in multi-line fields	END
Move the insertion point to the end of the field, in multiple-line fields	CTRL+END
Move the insertion point to the beginning of the field, in single-line fields; or to move it to the beginning of the line in multi-line fields	HOME
Move the insertion point to the beginning of the field, in multiple-line fields	CTRL+HOME

Copying, moving, or deleting text

Copy the selection to the Clipboard	CTRL+C
Cut the selection and copy it to the Clipboard	CTRL+X
Paste the contents of the Clipboard at the insertion point	CTRL+V
Delete the selection or the character to the left of the insertion point	BACKSPACE
Delete the selection or the character to the right of the insertion point	DELETE
Delete all characters to the right of the insertion point	CTRL+DELETE

Undoing changes

Undo typing	CTRL+Z or ALT+BACKSPACE

Undo changes in the current field or current record; if both have been changed, press ESC twice to undo changes, first in the current field and then in the current record	ESC

Entering data in Datasheet or Form view

Insert the current date	CTRL+SEMICOLON (;)
Insert the current time	CTRL+SHIFT+COLON (:)
Insert the default value for a field	CTRL+ALT+SPACEBAR
Insert the value from the same field in the previous record	CTRL+APOSTROPHE (')
Add a new record	CTRL+PLUS SIGN (+)
In a datasheet, delete the current record	CTRL+MINUS SIGN (-)
Save changes to the current record	SHIFT+ENTER
Switch between the values in a check box or option button	SPACEBAR
Insert a new line	CTRL+ENTER

Refreshing fields with current data

Recalculate the fields in the window	F9
Requery the underlying tables; in a subform, this requeries the underlying table for the subform only	SHIFT+F9
Refresh the contents of a Lookup field list box or combo box	F9

Keys for navigating records

Navigate in Design view

Switch between Edit mode (with insertion point displayed) and Navigation mode	F2
Toggle the property sheet	F4
Switch to Form view from form Design view	F5
Switch between the upper and lower portions of a window (Design view of macros, queries, and the Advanced Filter/Sort window) Use F6 when the TAB key does not take you to the section of the screen you want.	F6
Toggle forward between the design pane, properties, Navigation Pane, access keys, and Zoom controls (Design view of tables, forms, and reports)	F6
Open the Visual Basic Editor from a selected property in the property sheet for a form or report	F7
Invokes the Field List pane in a form, report, or data access page. If the Field List pane is already open, focus moves to the Field List pane.	ALT+F8
When you have a code module open, switch from the Visual Basic Editor to form or report Design view	SHIFT+F7
Switch from a control's property sheet in form or report Design view to the design surface without changing the control focus	SHIFT+F7
Display a property sheet	ALT+ENTER
Copy the selected control to the Clipboard	CTRL+C
Cut the selected control and copy it to the Clipboard	CTRL+X
Paste the contents of the Clipboard in the upper-left corner of the selected section	CTRL+V
Move the selected control to the right by a pixel along the page's grid	RIGHT ARROW
Move the selected control to the left by a pixel along the page's grid	LEFT ARROW
Move the selected control up by a pixel along the page's grid Note For controls in a stacked layout, this switches the position of the selected control with the control directly above it, unless it is already the uppermost control in the layout.	UP ARROW

Move the selected control down by a pixel along the page's grid Note For controls in a stacked layout, this switches the position of the selected control with the control directly below it, unless it is already the lowermost control in the layout.	DOWN ARROW
Move the selected control to the right by a pixel (irrespective of the page's grid)	CTRL+RIGHT ARROW
Move the selected control to the left by a pixel (irrespective of the page's grid)	CTRL+LEFT ARROW
Move the selected control up by a pixel (irrespective of the page's grid) Note For controls in a stacked layout, this switches the position of the selected control with the control directly above it, unless it is already the uppermost control in the layout.	CTRL+UP ARROW
Move the selected control down by a pixel (irrespective of the page's grid) Note For controls in a stacked layout, this switches the position of the selected control with the control directly below it, unless it is already the lowermost control in the layout.	CTRL+DOWN ARROW
Increase the width of the selected control (to the right) by a pixel Note For controls in a stacked layout, this increases the width of the whole layout.	SHIFT+RIGHT ARROW
Decrease the width of the selected control (to the left) by a pixel Note For controls in a stacked layout, this decreases the width of the whole layout.	SHIFT+LEFT ARROW
Decrease the height of the selected control (from the bottom) by a pixel	SHIFT+UP ARROW
Increase the height of the selected control (from the bottom) by a pixel	SHIFT+DOWN ARROW

Navigate in Datasheet view

Going to a specific record

Move to the record number box; then type the record number and press ENTER	F5

Navigating between fields and records

Move to the next field	TAB or RIGHT ARROW
Move to the last field in the current record, in Navigation mode	END
Move to the previous field	SHIFT+TAB, or LEFT ARROW
Move to the first field in the current record, in Navigation mode	HOME
Move to the current field in the next record	DOWN ARROW
Move to the current field in the last record, in Navigation mode	CTRL+DOWN ARROW
Move to the last field in the last record, in Navigation mode	CTRL+END
Move to the current field in the previous record	UP ARROW
Move to the current field in the first record, in Navigation mode	CTRL+UP ARROW
Move to the first field in the first record, in Navigation mode	CTRL+HOME

Navigating to another screen of data

Move down one screen	PAGE DOWN
Move up one screen	PAGE UP
Move right one screen	CTRL+PAGE DOWN
Move left one screen	CTRL+PAGE UP

Navigate in subdatasheets

Going to a specific record

Move from the subdatasheet to move to the record number box; then type the record number and press ENTER	ALT+F5

Expanding and collapsing subdatasheet

Move from the datasheet to expand the record's subdatasheet	CTRL+SHIFT+DOWN ARROW
Collapse the subdatasheet	CTRL+SHIFT+UP ARROW

Navigating between the datasheet and subdatasheet

Enter the subdatasheet from the last field of the previous record in the datasheet	TAB
Enter the subdatasheet from the first field of the following record in the datasheet	SHIFT+TAB
Exit the subdatasheet and move to the first field of the next record in the datasheet	CTRL+TAB
Exit the subdatasheet and move to the last field of the previous record in the datasheet	CTRL+SHIFT+TAB
From the last field in the subdatasheet to enter the next field in the datasheet	TAB
From the datasheet to bypass the subdatasheet and move to the next record in the datasheet	DOWN ARROW
From the datasheet to bypass the subdatasheet and move to the previous record in the datasheet	UP ARROW

You can navigate between fields and records in a subdatasheet with the same shortcut keys used in Datasheet view.

Navigate in Form view

Going to a specific record

Move to the record number box; then type the record number and press ENTER	F5

Navigating between fields and records

Move to the next field	TAB
Move to the previous field	SHIFT+TAB
Move to the last control on the form and remain in the current record, in Navigation mode	END
Move to the last control on the form and set focus in the last record, in Navigation mode	CTRL+END
Move to the first control on the form and remain in the current record, in Navigation mode	HOME
Move to the first control on the form and set focus in the first record, in Navigation mode	CTRL+HOME
Move to the current field in the next record	CTRL+PAGE DOWN
Move to the current field in the previous record	CTRL+PAGE UP

Navigating in forms with more than one page

Move down one page; at the end of the record, moves to the equivalent page on the next record	PAGE DOWN
Move up one page; at the end of the record, moves to the equivalent page on the previous record	PAGE UP

Navigating between the main form and subform

Enter the subform from the preceding field in the main form	TAB
Enter the subform from the following field in the main form	SHIFT+TAB
Exit the subform and move to the next field in the master form or next record	CTRL+TAB
Exit the subform and move to the previous field in the main form or previous record	CTRL+SHIFT+TAB

Navigate in Print Preview and Layout Preview

Dialog box and window operations

Open the Print dialog box	P (for forms and reports) or CTRL+P (for datasheets, forms, and reports)

Open the Page Setup dialog box (forms and reports only)	S
Zoom in or out on a part of the page	Z
Cancel Print Preview or Layout Preview	C or ESC

Viewing different pages

Move to the page number box; then type the page number and press ENTER	ALT+F5
View the next page (when Fit To Window is selected)	PAGE DOWN or DOWN ARROW
View the previous page (when Fit To Window is selected)	PAGE UP or UP ARROW

Navigating in Print and Layout Preview

Scroll down in small increments	DOWN ARROW
Scroll down one full screen	PAGE DOWN
Move to the bottom of the page	CTRL+DOWN ARROW
Scroll up in small increments	UP ARROW
Scroll up one full screen	PAGE UP
Move to the top of the page	CTRL+UP ARROW
Scroll to the right in small increments	RIGHT ARROW
Move to the right edge of the page	END
Move to the lower-right corner of the page	CTRL+END
Scroll to the left in small increments	LEFT ARROW
Move to the left edge of the page	HOME
Move to the upper-left corner of the page	CTRL+HOME

Navigate in the Database Diagram window in an Access project

Move from a table cell to the table's title bar	ESC
Move from a table's title bar to the last cell you edited	ENTER
Move from table title bar to table title bar, orfrom cell to cell inside a table	TAB
Expand a list inside a table	ALT + DOWN ARROW
Scroll through the items in a drop-down list from top to bottom	DOWN ARROW
Move to the previous item in a list	UP ARROW
Select an item in a list and move to the next cell	ENTER
Change the setting in a check box	SPACEBAR
Go to the first cell in the row, orto the beginning of the current cell	HOME
Go to the last cell in the row, orto the end of the current cell	END
Scroll to the next "page" inside a table, orto the next "page" of the diagram	PAGE DOWN
Scroll to the previous "page" inside a table, orto the previous "page" of the diagram	PAGE UP

Navigate in the Query Designer in an Access project

Any Pane

Move among the Query Designer panes	F6, SHIFT+F6

Diagram Pane

Move among tables, views, and functions, (and to join lines, if available)	TAB, or SHIFT+TAB
Move between columns in a table, view, or function	Arrow keys
Choose the selected data column for output	SPACEBAR or PLUS key
Remove the selected data column from the query output	SPACEBAR or MINUS key
Remove the selected table, view, or function, or join line from the query	DELETE

If multiple items are selected, pressing SPACEBAR affects all selected items. Select multiple items by holding down the SHIFT key while clicking them. Toggle the selected state of a single item by holding down CTRL while clicking it.

Grid Pane

Action	Shortcut
Move among cells	Arrow keys or TAB or SHIFT+TAB
Move to the last row in the current column	CTRL+DOWN ARROW
Move to the first row in the current column	CTRL+UP ARROW
Move to the top left cell in the visible portion of grid	CTRL+HOME
Move to the bottom right cell	CTRL+END
Move in a drop-down list	UP ARROW or DOWN ARROW
Select an entire grid column	CTRL+SPACEBAR
Toggle between edit mode and cell selection mode	F2
Copy selected text in cell to the Clipboard (in edit mode)	CTRL+C
Cut selected text in cell and place it on the Clipboard (in edit mode)	CTRL+X
Paste text from the Clipboard (in edit mode)	CTRL+V
Toggle between insert and overstrike mode while editing in a cell	INS
Toggle the check box in the Output columnNote If multiple items are selected, pressing this key affects all selected items.	SPACEBAR
Clear the selected contents of a cell	DELETE
Remove row containing selected data column from the query Note If multiple items are selected, pressing this key affects all selected items.	DELETE
Clear all values for a selected grid column	DELETE
Insert row between existing rows	INS (after you select grid row)
Add an Or ... column	INS (after you select any Or ... column)

SQL Pane

You can use the standard Windows editing keys when working in the SQL pane, such as CTRL+ arrow keys to move between words, and the Cut, Copy, and Paste commands on the Edit menu.

Note You can only insert text; there is no overstrike mode.

Action	Shortcut
Move the selection from left to right, and then down	The TAB key
Move the selection from top to bottom, and then to the right	ENTER
Select the cell to the left. If the current cell is the leftmost cell, SHIFT+TAB selects the last cell in the previous row.	SHIFT+TAB
Select the cell above the current cell. If the current cell is the topmost cell, SHIFT+ENTER selects the last cell in the previous column.	SHIFT+ENTER
Select the detail cells for the next item in the row area	CTRL+ENTER
Select the detail cells for the previous item in the row area	SHIFT+CTRL+ENTER
Move the selection in the direction of the arrow key. If a row or column field is selected, press DOWN ARROW to move to the first item of data in the field, and then press an arrow key to move to the next or previous item or back to the field. If a detail field is selected, press DOWN ARROW or RIGHT ARROW to move to the first cell in the detail area.	Arrow keys
Extend or reduce the selection in the direction of the arrow key	SHIFT+arrow keys
Move the selection to the last cell in the direction of the arrow key	CTRL+arrow keys
Move the selected item in the direction of the arrow key	SHIFT+ALT+arrow keys
Select the leftmost cell of the current row	HOME
Select the rightmost cell of the current row	END
Select the leftmost cell of the first row	CTRL+HOME
Select the last cell of the last row	CTRL+END
Extend selection to the leftmost cell of the first row	SHIFT+CTRL+HOME

Extend selection to the last cell of the last row	SHIFT+CTRL+END
Select the field for the currently selected item of data, total, or detail	CTRL+SPACEBAR
Select the entire row containing the currently selected cell	SHIFT+SPACEBAR
Select the entire PivotTable view	CTRL+A
Display the next screen	PAGE DOWN
Display the previous screen	PAGE UP
Extend the selection down one screen	SHIFT+PAGE DOWN
Reduce the selection by one screen	SHIFT+PAGE UP
Display the next screen to the right	ALT+PAGE DOWN
Display the previous screen to the left	ALT+PAGE UP
Extend the selection to the page on the right	SHIFT+ALT+PAGE DOWN
Extend the selection to the page on the left	SHIFT+ALT+PAGE UP

Keys for carrying out commands

Display Help topics	F1
Display the shortcut menu for the selected element of the PivotTable view. Use the shortcut menus to carry out commands in the PivotTable view.	SHIFT+F10
Carry out a command on the shortcut menu	Underlined letter
Close the shortcut menu without carrying out a command	ESC
Display the Properties dialog box	ALT+ENTER
Close the Properties dialog box	ALT+F4
Cancel a refresh operation in progress	ESC
Copy the selected data from the PivotTable view to the Clipboard	CTRL+C
Export the contents of the PivotTable view to Microsoft Office Excel 2013	CTRL+E

Keys for displaying, hiding, filtering, or sorting data

Show or hide the expand indicators (and boxes) beside items	CTRL+8
Expand the currently selected item	CTRL+PLUS SIGN (on the numeric keypad)
Hide the currently selected item	CTRL+MINUS SIGN (on the numeric keypad)
Open the list for the currently selected field	ALT+DOWN ARROW
Alternately move to the most recently selected item, the OK button, and the Cancel button in the drop-down list for a field	The TAB key
Move to the next item in the drop-down list for a field	Arrow keys
Select or clear the check box for the current item in the drop-down list for a field	SPACEBAR
Close the drop-down list for a field and apply any changes you made	ENTER
Close the drop-down list for a field without applying your changes	ESC
Turn AutoFilter on or off	CTRL+T
Sort data in the selected field or total in ascending order (A – Z 0 – 9)	CTRL+SHIFT+A
Sort data in the selected field or total in descending order (Z – A 9 – 0)	CTRL+SHIFT+Z
Move the selected member up or left	ALT+SHIFT+UP ARROW or ALT+SHIFT+LEFT ARROW
Move the selected member down or right	ALT+SHIFT+DOWN ARROW or ALT+SHIFT+RIGHT ARROW

Keys for adding fields and totals and changing the layout of a PivotTable view

Keys for working with the Field List pane

Display the Field List pane, or activate it if it is already displayed	CTRL+L
Move to the next item in the Field List pane	Arrow keys
Move to the previous item and include it in the selection	SHIFT+UP ARROW
Move to the next item and include it in the selection	SHIFT+DOWN ARROW
Move to the previous item, but don't include the item in the selection	CTRL+UP ARROW

Move to the next item, but don't include the item in the selection	CTRL+DOWN ARROW
Remove the item from the selection, if the item that has focus is included in the selection, and vice versa	CTRL+SPACEBAR
Expand the current item in the Field List pane to display its contents. Or expand Totals to display the available total fields.	PLUS SIGN (numeric keypad)
Collapse the current item in the Field List pane to hide its contents. Or collapse Totals to hide the available total fields.	MINUS SIGN (numeric keypad)
Alternately move to the most recently selected item, the Add to button, and the list next to the Add to button in the Field List pane	The TAB key
Open the drop-down list next to the Add to button in the Field List pane. Use the arrow keys to move to the next item in the list, and then press ENTER to select an item.	ALT+DOWN ARROW
Add the highlighted field in the Field List pane to the area in the PivotTable view that is displayed in the Add to list	ENTER
Close the Field List pane	ALT+F4

Keys for adding fields and totals

Add a new total field for the selected field in the PivotTable view by using the Sum summary function	CTRL+SHIFT+S
Add a new total field for the selected field in the PivotTable view by using the Count summary function	CTRL+SHIFT+C
Add a new total field for the selected field in the PivotTable view by using the Min summary function	CTRL+SHIFT+M
Add a new total field for the selected field in the PivotTable view by using the Max summary function	CTRL+SHIFT+X
Add a new total field for the selected field in the PivotTable view by using the Average summary function	CTRL+SHIFT+E
Add a new total field for the selected field in the PivotTable view by using the Standard Deviation summary function	CTRL+SHIFT+D
Add a new total field for the selected field in the PivotTable view by using the Standard Deviation Population summary function	CTRL+SHIFT+T
Add a new total field for the selected field in the PivotTable view by using the Variance summary function	CTRL+SHIFT+V
Add a new total field for the selected field in the PivotTable view by using the Variance Population summary function	CTRL+SHIFT+R
Turn subtotals and grand totals on or off for the selected field in the PivotTable view	CTRL+SHIFT+B
Add a calculated detail field	CTRL+F

Keys for changing the layout

Note The following four shortcuts do not work if you press the keys 1, 2, 3, or 4 from the numeric pad of your keyboard.

Move the selected field in the PivotTable view to the row area	CTRL+1
Move the selected field in the PivotTable view to the column area	CTRL+2
Move the selected field in the PivotTable view to the filter area	CTRL+3
Move the selected field in the PivotTable view to the detail area	CTRL+4
Move the selected row or column field in the PivotTable view to a higher level	CTRL+LEFT ARROW

Move the selected row or column field in the PivotTable view to a lower level	CTRL+RIGHT ARROW

Keys for formatting elements in PivotTable view

To use the following shortcuts, first select a detail field or a data cell for a total field. The first seven keyboard shortcuts change the number format of the selected field.

Apply the general number format to values in the selected total or detail field	CTRL+SHIFT+ ~ (tilde)
Apply the currency format, with two decimal places and negative numbers in parentheses, to values in the selected total or detail field	CTRL+SHIFT+$
Apply the percentage format, with no decimal places, to values in the selected total or detail field	CTRL+SHIFT+%
Apply the exponential number format, with two decimal places, to values in the selected total or detail field	CTRL+SHIFT+^
Apply the date format, with the day, month, and year, to values in the selected total or detail field	CTRL+SHIFT+#
Apply the time format, with the hour, minute, and AM or PM, to values in the selected total or detail field	CTRL+SHIFT+@
Apply the numeric format, with two decimal places, thousands separator, and a minus sign for negative values, to values in the selected total or detail field	CTRL+SHIFT+!
Make text bold in the selected field of the PivotTable view	CTRL+B
Make text underlined in the selected field of the PivotTable view	CTRL+U
Make text italic in the selected field of the PivotTable view	CTRL+I

PivotChart view

Keys for selecting items in a chart

Select the next item in the chart	RIGHT ARROW
Select the previous item in the chart	LEFT ARROW
Select the next group of items	DOWN ARROW
Select the previous group of items	UP ARROW

Keys for working with properties and options

Display the Properties dialog box	ALT+ENTER
Close the Properties dialog box	ALT+F4
When the Properties dialog box is active, select the next item on the active tab	The TAB key
When a tab in the Properties dialog box is active, select the next tab	RIGHT ARROW
When a tab in the Properties dialog box is active, select the previous tab	LEFT ARROW
Display a list or palette when a button that contains a list or palette is selected	DOWN ARROW
Display the shortcut menu	SHIFT+F10
Carry out a command on the shortcut menu	Underlined letter
Close the shortcut menu without carrying out a command	ESC

Keys for working with fields

Open the list for the currently selected field	ALT+DOWN ARROW
In the drop-down list for a field, alternately move to the most recently selected item, the OK button, and the Cancel button	The TAB key
In the drop-down list for a field, move to the next item	Arrow keys
In the drop-down list for a field, select or clear the check box for the current item	SPACEBAR
Close the drop-down list for a field and apply any changes you made	ENTER
Close the drop-down list for a field without applying your changes	ESC

Keys for working with the Field List pane

Display the Field List pane, or activate it if it is already displayed	CTRL+L

Move to the next item in the Field List pane	Arrow keys
Move to the previous item and include it in the selection	SHIFT+UP ARROW
Move to the next item and include it in the selection	SHIFT+DOWN ARROW
Move to the previous item, but don't include the item in the selection	CTRL+UP ARROW
Move to the next item, but don't include the item in the selection	CTRL+DOWN ARROW
Remove the item from the selection if the item that has focus is included in the selection, and vice versa	CTRL+SPACEBAR
Expand the current item in the Field List pane to display its contents, or expand Totals to display the available total fields	PLUS SIGN (numeric keypad)
Collapse the current item in the Field List pane to hide its contents, or collapse Totals to hide the available total fields.	MINUS SIGN (numeric keypad)
In the Field List pane, alternately move to the most recently selected item, the Add to button, and the list next to the Add to button	The TAB key
Open the drop-down list next to the Add to button in the Field List pane. Use the arrow keys to move to the next item in the list, and then press ENTER to select an item.	ALT+DOWN ARROW
Add the highlighted field in the Field List pane to the drop area that is displayed in the Add to list	ENTER
Close the Field List pane	ALT+F4

In the Help window

Open the Help window.	F1
Close the Help window	ALT+F4
Switch between the Help window and the active program.	ALT+TAB
Go back to *Program Name* Home.	ALT+HOME
Select the next item in the Help window.	TAB
Select the previous item in the Help window.	SHIFT+TAB
Perform the action for the selected item.	ENTER
In the Browse *Program Name* Help section of the Help window, select the next or previous item, respectively.	TAB or SHIFT+TAB
In the Browse *Program Name* Help section of the Help window, expand or collapse the selected item, respectively.	ENTER
Select the next hidden text or hyperlink, including Show All or Hide All at the top of a topic.	TAB
Select the previous hidden text or hyperlink.	SHIFT+TAB
Perform the action for the selected Show All, Hide All, hidden text, or hyperlink.	ENTER
Move back to the previous Help topic (Back button).	ALT+LEFT ARROW or BACKSPACE
Move forward to the next Help topic (Forward button).	ALT+RIGHT ARROW
Scroll small amounts up or down, respectively, within the currently displayed Help topic.	UP ARROW, DOWN ARROW
Scroll larger amounts up or down, respectively, within the currently displayed Help topic.	PAGE UP, PAGE DOWN
Display a menu of commands for the Help window. This requires that the Help window have the active focus (click in the Help window).	SHIFT+F10
Stop the last action (Stop button).	ESC
Refresh the window (Refresh button).	F5

Print the current Help topic. Note If the cursor is not in the current Help topic, press F6 and then press CTRL+P.	CTRL+P
Change the connection state.	F6, and then press ENTER to open the list of choices
Switch among areas in the Help window; for example, switch between the toolbar and the Search list.	F6
In a Table of Contents in tree view, select the next or previous item, respectively.	UP ARROW, DOWN ARROW
In a Table of Contents in tree view, expand or collapse the selected item, respectively.	LEFT ARROW, RIGHT ARROW

CHAPTER 9

Questions

Introduction

Questions help you in revising the matter read in the various chapters.

ANSWER THE FOLLOWING QUESTIONS

OBJECTIVE TYPE QUESTIONS

1. In word processing, you manipulate _______
   (a) numbers (b) text
2. You can set Left, Right and ______ alignment in word processing.
   (a) Center (b) Justify
   (c) Both
3. Can you spell check you text in word processing?
   (a) Yes (b) No
4. Can you locate a word in word processing?
   (a) No (b) Yes
5. Blinking point which shows your position in the text is called:
   (a) Cursor (b) Blinker
   (c) Position
6. Spacebar is used for :
   (a) giving space (b) deleting space
7. You can start Microsoft Word by using ________ button.
   (a) New (b) Start
   (c) Program
8. For creating a document, you use _____ command at File menu.
   (a) New (b) Open
   (c) Document
9. For saving a document, you need to have ________ for it.
   (a) Name (b) Surname
10. For opening an existing document, you need to give _____ command.
    (a) New (b) Open
    (c) Close
11. You can select the text by:
    (a) Keyboard (b) Mouse
    (c) Both
12. You click at B to make the text
    (a) Bold (b) Italics
    (c) Underline
13. Can you emboss you text?
    (a) Yes (b) No

14. You can change the size of the text from:
    (a) Formatting bar
    (b) Font dialog box
    (c) Both
15. You click at I to make the text
    (a) Bold
    (b) Italics
    (c) Underline
16. You can change the font of the text from
    (a) Formatting bar
    (b) Font dialog box
    (c) Box
17. Colour of the text can be changed:
    (a) Yes
    (b) No
18. You click at U to make the text
    (a) Bold
    (b) Italics
    (c) Underline
19. Word supports alignments like Left, Right, Center and ______
    (a) Justify
    (b) Up
    (c) Down
20. You can change the line and para spacing from ______ dialog box.
    (a) Font
    (b) Paragraph
    (c) Open
21. Header appears at the ______ of the page.
    (a) Top
    (b) Bottom
    (c) Center
22. Footer appears at the ________ of the page
    (a) Top
    (b) Bottom
    (c) Center
23. For printing a document you have to have _________ on.
    (a) Printer
    (b) Monitor
    (c) Scanner
24. Most of the editing tools are available under _____ menu.
    (a) File
    (b) Format
    (c) Edit
25. You can add picture in your document from the _______ menu.
    (a) File
    (b) Edit
    (c) Insert
26. Clip Art is
    (a) Text
    (b) Graphics
    (c) Both

27. Can Text be mingled with Graphics?
    (a) Yes (b) No
28. WordArt is a
    (a) Text (b) Graphic
    (c) Independent program
29. You can set margins by using the dialog box:
    (a) Font (b) Page Setup
    (c) Margins
30. Two main orientations are, Potrait and
    (a) Landscape (b) Photo
    (c) Lying
31. Can you shade your text?
    (a) Yes (b) No
32. Can you put border across your text in the document?
    (a) Yes (b) No
33. Decimal is tab?
    (a) Yes (b) No
34. In text you can find a word and replace it with another word using command ________.
    (a) Find (b) Replace
    (c) None
35. You can insert a table from ________ toolbar.
    (a) Formatting (b) Standard
    (c) Drawing
36. You can align data vertically in a table:
    (a) Yes (b) No
37. Can you insert more rows in a table?
    (a) Yes (b) No
38. Sending of same letter to different people is done by:
    (a) Send (b) Letter
    (c) Mailmerge
39. Headers are put:
    (a) at the top (b) at the bottom
    (c) in the middle
40. You can put page numbers :
    (a) at the top (b) at the bottom
    (c) both places
41. Footers are put:
    (a) at the top (b) at the bottom
    (c) in the middle

42. Table of contents has:
    (a) Page number (b) Marked entry
    (c) both
43. Borders can be shaded:
    (a) Yes (b) No
44. You can have line in between the columns:
    (a) Yes (b) No
45. Index has all marked enteries with page numbers:
    (a) Yes (b) No
46. Word count gives you :
    (a) Numuber of lines (b) Number of words
    (c) Both
47. For opening and closing of the file in Excel you can use which bar.
    (a) Formatting (b) Standard
    (c) Title
48. What are numbered from A to Z, etc?
    (a) Rows (b) Cells
    (c) Columns
49. You can move around the worksheet using which buttons?
    (a) Scroll (b) Logic
    (c) Start
50. For making the text bold in the cell, you use B in which bar.
    (a) Standard (b) Formatting
    (c) Title
51. For getting the short menu on the screen, you click which button of the mouse.
    (a) Right button (b) Left button
    (c) Centre button
52. Charts are created using which option.
    (a) Chart Wizard (b) Pivto Table
    (c) Pie Chart
53. For editing the chart, you ____________ the chart itself.
    (a) Click (b) Delete
    (c) Double click
54. In Excel formula starts with ___________.
    (a) = sign (b) + sign
    (c) - sign
55. In Excel worksheets are given _____ extension.
    (a) .xls (b) .doc
    (c) .bmp

56. In Microsoft Excel, you use _______ for calcualtions.
(a) Formula (b) Row
(c) Cell

57. Formula which can be used directly from the Standard toolbar is
(a) AutoSum (b) Auto
(c) Sum

58. The result of AutoCalculate is shown at ___ bar.
(a) Standard (b) Formatting
(c) Status

59. Sum function needs to have ______ before it.
(a) + (b) –
(c) =

60. To access to any formula in Microsoft Excel, you need to go through _____
(a) Function Wizard (b) File
(c) Formula

61. Anything that is typed in a worksheet appears:
(a) in both the active cell and the formula bar
(b) in the active cell only
(c) nonc of the above

62. The formatting toolbar
(a) is placed just below the Standard toolbar (b) is used to apply common formats
(c) both of above

63. The combination of the column letter and row number for a cell in an Excel worksheet is called a
(a) cell identification number (b) cell reference
(c) cell identity

64. In Excel the simplest way to move data from one location to another is
(a) by menu commands (b) by mouse
(c) by drag and drop method

65. Using borders you
(a) can add lines above, below or to either side of a cell
(b) can add a single line or multiple lines, along one side of a cell or around it.
(c) both a and b above

66. Cell address B$6 in a formula means it is a
(a) relative cell reference (b) absolute cell reference
(c) mixed cell reference

67. A function in Excel
(a) is a ready made formula (b) is a shortcut formula
(c) both of above

68. PowerPoint is used for:
    (a) Word processing (b) Spreadsheets
    (c) Presentations
69. Overhead projections can be created using PoerPoint:
    (a) Yes (b) No
70. AutoContent Wizard creates a
    (a) Document (b) Presentation
    (c) Spreadsheet
71. There is no need to use templates in PowerPoint:
    (a) True (b) False
72. You can view your presentation through various views :
    (a) Yes (b) No
73. You can move your text in the slide, up and down:
    (a) Yes (b) No
74. A slide with background picture can be created in PowerPoint:
    (a) Yes (b) No
75. You can even have textured patterns in the background of a slide:
    (a) Yes (b) No
76. You can add organization format in the form of a :
    (a) Table (b) Chart
    (c) Graphic
77. You can use a picture as a background for a slide:
    (a) Yes (b) No
78. Various alignments available for text formatting in PowerPoint are Left, Right, Center and :
    (a) Justify (b) Natural
    (c) Reverse
79. Various tabs available in PowerPoint are, Left, Right, Center and :
    (a) Comma (b) Decimal
    (c) Full stop
80. Optional command which allows you to preset your errors is called:
    (a) Autoset (b) Autoplay
    (c) Autocorrect
81. Notes pages have on them:
    (a) text (b) graphic
    (c) pictures
82. You can view all slides continuously by using:
    (a) Show (b) Slide show
    (c) Slides

83. You can set tabs using
    (a) Ruler (b) Scale
    (c) Footer
84. For getting information from the database we use :
    (a) Table (b) Query
    (c) Report
85. It consists of various records having data:
    (a) Table (b) Query
    (c) Report
86. For printing the information from the Table we use:
    (a) Table (b) Query
    (c) Report
87. You can create a database using :
    (a) Home panel (b) Wizard
    (c) Programs
88. Main controlling point in Access is:
    (a) Switchboard (b) Home panel
    (c) Edit panel
89. Easy way of creating a Table is by using:
    (a) Wizard (b) Design View
    (c) New
90. A Table is a collection of :
    (a) Queries (b) Data
    (c) Reports
91. Forms are filled with :
    (a) Data (b) Database
    (c) Information
92. The number of forms which you can create from a Table:
    (a) One (b) Many
    (c) None
93. You can modify your report using :
    (a) Wizard (b) AutoFormat
    (c) Printer
94. Report can be created using :
    (a) Wizard (b) AutoFormat
    (c) Printer

ANSWERS TO OBJECTIVE TYPE QUESTIONS

1. b	2. c	3. a	4. b
5. a	6. a	7. b	8. a
9. a	10 b	11. c	12. a
13. a	14. c	15. a	16. c
17. a	18. a	19. a	20. b
21. a	22. b	23. a	24. c
25. c	26. b	27. a	28. c
29. b	30. a	31. a	32. a
33. a	34. b	35. a	36. a
37. a	38. c	39. a	40. c
41. b	42. a	43. a	44. a
45. a	46. c	47. b	48. c
49. a	50. b	51. a	52. a
53. c	54. a	55. a	56. a
57. a	58. c	59. c	60. a
61. a	62. c	63. b	64. c
65. c	66. b	67. c	68. c
69. a	70. b	71. b	72. a
73. a	74. a	75. a	76. b
77. a	78. a	79. b	80. c
81. a	82. b	83. a	84. b
85. a	86. c	87. b	88. a
89. a	90. b	91. a	92. b
93. b	94. a		

SUBJECTIVE TYPE QUESTIONS

Chapter 1 — Introduction to Windows 8

1. What is Windows 8?
2. Describe the various items available on the Desktop of Windows 8?
3. What are the online features of Windows 8?
4. Describe the process of using Windows 8.
5. What are the System Requirements of Windows 8?
6. How would you upgrade to Windows 8?
7. What is Charms Bar?
8. How would you work with Start Screen Apps?

Chapter 2 — Introduction to Microsoft Word 2013

1. Write a short note on the following commands of Microsoft Word.

   Applying Fonts
   Paragraph Setting
   Page Numbering
   Change Case
   Date and Time
   Insert Picture
   Sort
   Bullets and Numbering
   Animate Text
   AutoCorrect
   AutoFormat
   Break, Insert
   Columns
   Comments, Insert
   Table of Contents
   Creating a Table
   Creating an Index
   Drop Cap
   File, Insert
   Find and Replace
   Footnotes and Endnotes
   Header and Footer
   Hyperlinks
   Macro
   Protect Document
   Reveal Formatting
   Send To
   Tabs
   Tracking the Document Changes
   Bookmarks
   Versions
   Word Count
   Zoom
2. How would you save a document file?
3. Which alignments Word 2013 supports?
4. How would you apply various fonts?
5. Describe the process of Spell Checking in Word 2013.
6. What is Thesaurus?

7. What are Styles?
8. Describe the various Borders in Word 2013.
9. How would you close a document file?
10. Describe the various options of saving the document.
11. How would you print your document?
12. Describe the process of mailmerge in Word 2013.

Chapter 3 — Introduction to Microsoft Excel 2013

1. What conventions are used in Excel 2013?
2. How would you create a worksheet?
3. How would you copy a formula?
4. How are decision making formula used?
5. Write a short note on the following commands of Microsoft Excel.

Styles	Functions
AutoCalculate	Sum Function
Average Function	Creating Charts
Auditing	Comments
Outlines	Fitting on a page
Function wizard	Goal seeking
Scenarios manager	Pivot Table
AutoFill	Formatting Numbers and Labels
Applying Themes	Background Themes
Protecting Worksheets	Functions
Adding/Deleting Rows	Inserting Page Breaks
Convert Text to Columns	

Chapter 4 — Introduction to PowerPoint 2013

1. How would you create presentation from Template?
2. Describe the various PowerPoint views.
3. How would you change the background colour of the presentation?
4. How would you add graphics to the slide?
5. Describe the process of reordering the slides.
6. How would you add an animated cartoon to a slide?
7. What are slide transitions?
8. How would you create a Slide Show?
9. How would you pack the presentation?

Chapter 5 — Introduction to Access 2013

1. How would you create a database?
2. Describe the process of creating a database using the wizard.
3. How would you create a database using template?
4. What is a Form?
5. How would you create a Query?
6. How would you create a Report?

Chapter 6 — Other Software of Microsoft Office 2013

1. What is Publisher 2013 used for?
2. What all you can do using InfoPath Forms?
3. What in OneNote 2013 used for?

CHAPTER 10

SHORT QUESTIONS & ANSWERS

Chapter 1 — Introduction to Windows 8

Q.1. What is Windows environment in general ?

Ans. A window is a viewing place on a screen in a computer system which allows multiple viewing as a part of GUI (Graphical User Interface). Basically, a window is a series of OS (Operating Systems) developed, marketed, and sold by IT giant company Microsoft. It releases many versions eventually; each release of Windows version must include an improved support of graphical user interface that allows correspondent users to view files and folders in windows easily.

An IT giant Microsoft introduced operating environment known as Windows on 20th November in the year 1985, as a graphical operating system shell for MS-DOS since, by observing growing lot of interest in graphical user interfaces (GUIs). The first version of Windows released in 1985, which was a just simple graphical user interface provided an extension of Microsoft's existing disk OS (operating system) or MS-DOS. Before Windows introduction to the market, computer systems were using a series of text commands which used for operations.

Windows is growing and most used operating systems for personal computer systems from the past two decades. The beauty of Microsoft Windows is that it is designed for both personal and professional purposes, which makes more convenient for users.

Q.2. What are windows' key benefits and features?

Ans. Following are salient windows' key benefits and features:

1. Windows allows its user to interact with the system (using a keyboard, mouse, microphone, etc.).
2. It controls memory allocation, data storage in a computer system.
3. It controls hardware's incorporated into the computer system such as scanners and printers, etc.
4. Windows control computer access to users for computer's security.
5. An important feature is that it allows multitasking for the user to do several tasks on the computer at once

Q.3. Explain the main purpose of an operating system?

Ans. Operating systems built mainly for two purposes:

1. OS is designed to make sure a computer system performs well by managing all its activities.
2. Operating systems provide an environment for the development of code and execution of programs as well.

Q.4. What Is the Purpose of Microsoft Windows?

Ans. Microsoft Windows is one of the big giants in the market, which provides services as a core of most of desktop and laptop computer systems, with more than 90 percent of running version of windows operating system.

Windows provides a platform for all programs to run on it. Microsoft has started and ruled the market over the last three decades, it always adds more features to improvise user interfaces for easier to use.

Q.5. What are the functions of an operating system?

Ans. Microsoft Windows is a computer operating system in which the programming code is not available to the public.

Operating System (OS) is one of the core software code/programs that run on the computer hardware which makes and helps a user to interact with hardware, and then it can send commands (input) and receive results with respect to inputs provided as output. Its function is to provide a consistent environment for all the software to execute their commands.

Q.6. What is Windows Server?

Ans. Window server is defined as a series of server operating system and it is developed by Microsoft Corporation. This is the common Windows Interview Questions asked in a windows Interview.

Q.7. Explain In windows DNS server what is Primary, Secondary and Stub zone?

Ans. DNS (Domain Name System) Server is a system which makes the process of name resolution in DNS. DNS Servers consists of files known as zone files, it makes and enables them to resolve names to IP addresses and vice versa.

1. **Primary Zone:** In this area, a file will be saved as a normal text file with extension as ".dns"
2. **Secondary Zone:** In this zone, it keeps and maintains a read-only copy data of zone database in another supported DNS server. And also, it provides a backup server to the primary server by supporting fault tolerance and load balancing.
3. **Stub Zone:** This Stub zone consists of a copy of all name servers and SOA records which are used to reduce the DNS search orders.

Q.8. Explain what is the difference between a thread and a computer process?

Ans. There is a lot of difference between a thread and a computer process and some of them are as listed below:

1. **Computer Process**: Computer process is an instance of computer programs which will be executed sequentially (as one by one) by a computer system which helps to run several programs in parallel.
2. **Thread:** A thread is set of several executable programs that work together as a single process. For instance, one thread will send an error message to the user; another will handle error signals while the third thread might be executing the original action of a program.

Q.9. Explain what is the purpose of deploying local DNS servers?

Ans. This is the most popular Windows Interview Questions asked in an interview. A local DNS server provides the fully qualified domain names & local mapping to IP respective addresses. And also to resolve remote requests related to the domains names on a computer network, local DNS servers can provide record information to remote DNS servers.

Q.10. To check TCP/IP configurations and IP connectivity, what are the two command line utilities that can be used?

Ans. **Ipconfig:** ipconfig is the command to check the computer's IP configuration also it can be used to renew the client's IP address (only if it is provided by a DHCP server).

Ping: Ping command is used to check the connection between the local computer and any of the other computer devices on the network.

Q.11. Explain what is the major difference between NTFS (New Technology File System) or FAT (File Allocation Table) on a local server?

Ans. FAT (File Allocation Table) and FAT32 provides security to local users of the computer system, meanwhile NTFS (New Technology File System) provides security for domain users as well as local users. NTFS also provides file-level security which is not possible through FAT32.

Q.12. What is Active Directory?

Ans. Active Directory (AD) is a directory, it is developed by Microsoft which is used to store the objects (ex: User information, Computer, printer, Network information), Active directory also provide to manage computer network effectively with multiple Domain Controllers in different location with Active directory databases which are able to manage/change AD from any Domain Controllers and those will be replicated to all other DC's, centralized Administration with multiple geographical location and authenticates users and computers in a Windows domain.

Q.13. Describe the various items available on the Desktop of Windows 8?

Ans. There are several principal components to Windows desktops: **The Start menu, the Task bar, and the time, which are all located at the bottom of the screen, and the main workspace, which takes up most of your screen.** The workspace is composed of a background, and usually some icons and/or windows.

Q.13. What are the various features added in Windows 8?

Ans. Windows 8 added support for USB 3.0, Advanced Format, near-field communication, and cloud computing. Additional security features were introduced, such as built-in antivirus software, integration with Microsoft SmartScreen phishing filtering, and support for Secure Boot on supported devices.

Q.14. What are the online features of Windows?

Ans. The online features of Windows Page 2

Q.15. Describe the process of using Windows 8.

Ans. Windows 8 provides heavier integration with online services from Microsoft and others. A user can now log into Windows with a Microsoft account, which can be used to access services and synchronize applications and settings between devices. See also bottom paragraph of page 5.

Q.16. What are the System Requirements of Windows 8?

Ans. The system's requirements are given on page 8.

Q.17. How would you upgrade to Windows 8?

Ans. The upgradation process is discussed on page 7,

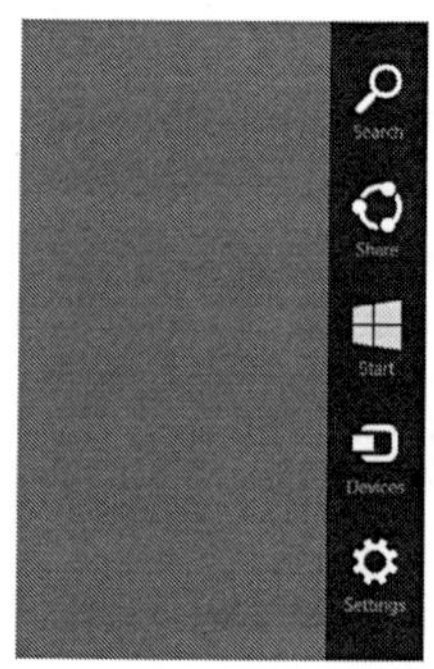

Q.18. What is Charms Bar?

Ans. The **Charms bar** is a toolbar that lets you **access your computer's settings**, along with other options. You can access the Charms bar by hovering the mouse in the **top-right or bottom-right corner**.

The Charms bar contains several icons, which are called **charms**, and each one contains different options:

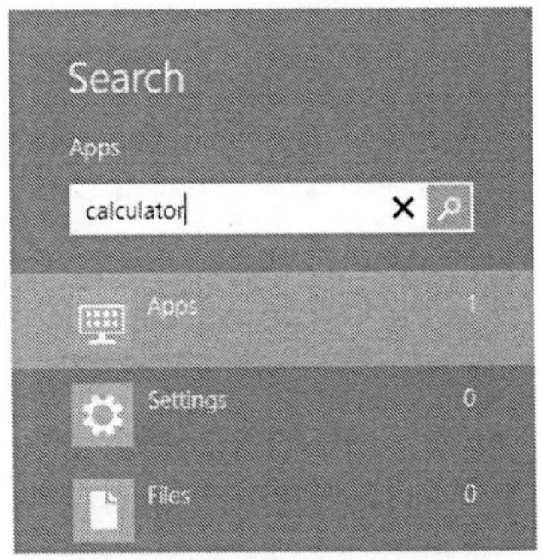

-  **Search:** The Search charm lets you **find apps, files, or settings on your computer**. However, a simpler way to search is to go to the Start screen and type the name of the file or app that you're looking for.

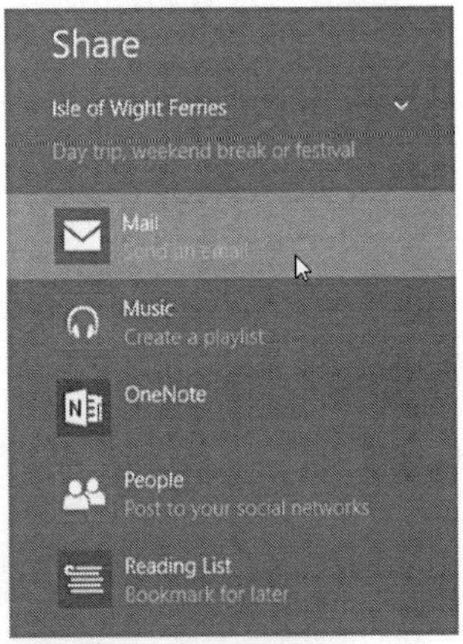

-  **Share:** The Share charm is basically a **copy and paste** feature that is designed to be as convenient as possible. It allows you to "copy" information (such as a photo or web address) and "paste" it into another app. For example, if you're reading an article online, you can **share the address with the Mail app**, which lets you email the article to a friend.

-  **Start:** This switches to the Start screen. If you're already on the Start screen, it will open the most recent app.

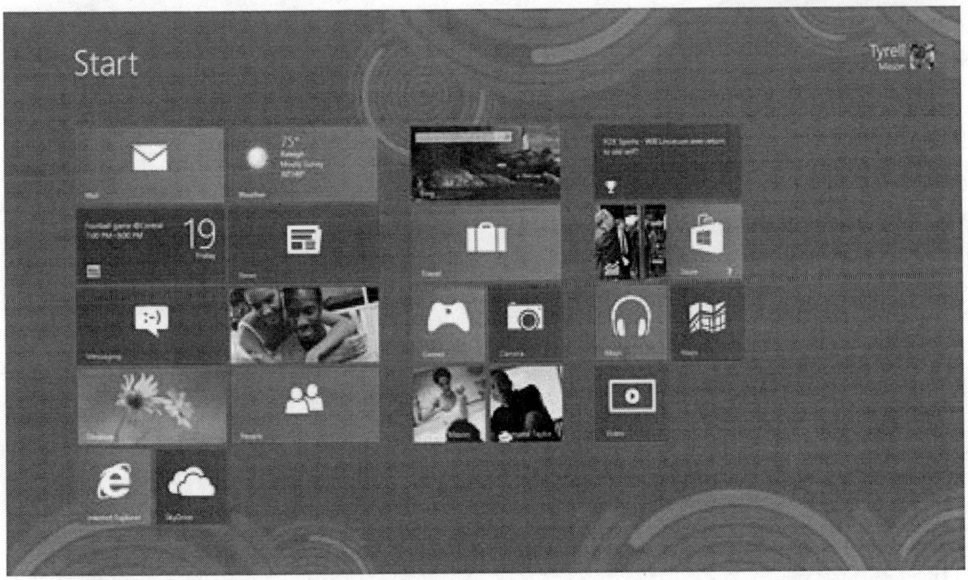

-  **Devices:** This shows any hardware devices that are connected to your computer, such as printers or monitors.

- **Settings:** This lets you access general settings for for the app you're currently viewing. For example, if you're in Internet Explorer, you can go to the Settings charm to access your Internet Options.

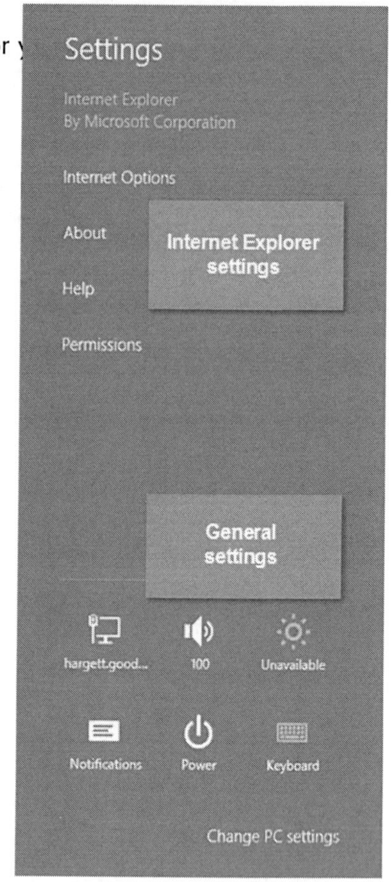

Q.19. How would you work with Start Screen Apps? How did you close Windows 8

Ans. Start screen apps are different from the "classic" Windows apps you may be used to. Apps **fill the entire screen** instead of opening in a window. However, you can still **multi-task** by opening two apps side by side.

To open an app:

- **On the Start screen, locate and click the** app **you want to open.**

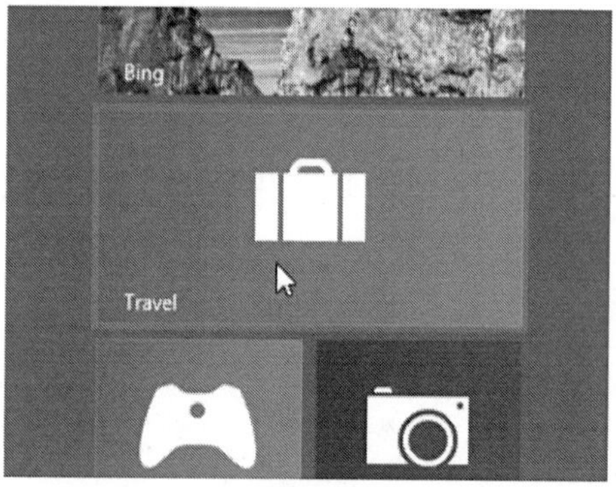

- **The app will open and fill the entire screen.**

- **To close an app:**
  - Hover the mouse at the top of the app. The cursor will change to a hand icon.

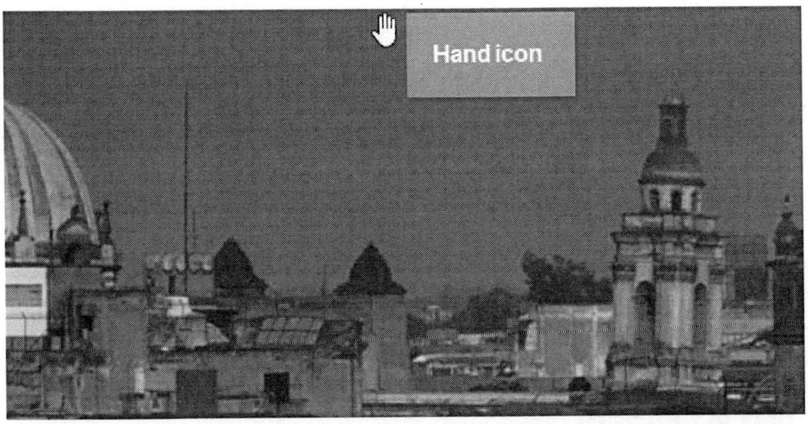

  - Click, hold, and drag the top of the app all the way down to the bottom of the screen and then release. The app will close, and you'll return to the Start screen.

  - **When dragging the app down, it may look like it's "stuck." However, just** keep moving the mouse down **until the cursor gets to the bottom of the screen, and the app will then close.**

Q.20. What is the best feature of Windows 8?

Ans. One great thing about Windows 8 is that **you can literally pin all your most used programs on the Start Menu**. Unlike the previous versions of Windows, your programs are conveniently laid down from the screen. Microsoft also developed a way in which your icons can be live and active.

Chapter 2: Microsoft Office 2013

Q.1. What does Microsoft Office 2013 include?

Ans. All traditional editions of Microsoft Office 2013 contain **Word, Excel, PowerPoint and OneNote** and are licensed for use on one computer. Five traditional editions of Office 2013 were released: Home & Student: This retail suite includes the core applications Word, Excel, PowerPoint, and OneNote etc.

Q.2. What is the advantage of MS Office 2013?

Ans. MS Office 2013 is tablet-friendly, unlike the older versions of Office. Mobile users can use the suite on their tablet without any issues or inconveniences. In MS Office 2013, editing files is easier than ever before. In addition, you can now edit PDF files using Office, which wasn't possible in the past.

Q.3. What's new in Office 2013

Ans. The following features had been added since previous version.

1. Save and share files in the cloud. The cloud is like file storage in the sky.
2. Shared meetings. Join online meetings and share PowerPoint slides, Word documents, Excel spreadsheets, and OneNote notes.
3. More choices for getting started.
4. Improved Save As and Open.
5. Easier file sharing.

Q.4. What is the main use of MS Office?

Ans. Microsoft Office is a suite of applications designed to **help with productivity and completing common tasks on a computer**. You can create and edit documents containing text and images, work with data in spreadsheets and databases, and create presentations and posters.

Q.5. On how many devices or computers MS Office is licensed to be installed?

Ans. Office 2013 licence only allows Office 2013 to be installed on **one computer at a time**, that is the licenced computer. You can transfer the licence to a new computer but you must uninstall your office from the old computer before you install it on the new computer

Q.6. What are the minimum system requirements for Office 2013?

Ans. The following are the minimum system requirements for Office 2013.

1. Operating system: Windows 7 or newer.
2. Memory (RAM): 4 GB RAM.
3. Hard Disk: 3.0 GB available.
4. Display: Graphics hardware acceleration requires a DirectX10 graphics card and a 1024 x 576 or higher resolution monitor.

Q.7. What are the 5 functions of Microsoft Office?

Ans. It contains a word processor (Word), a spreadsheet program (Excel) and a presentation program (PowerPoint), an email client (Outlook), a database management system (Access), and a desktop publishing app (Publisher)

Q.7. How to edit PDF document in 2013?

Ans. To edit PDF document in 2013,

1. Click the file menu
2. Click on Open icon
3. Select the PDF file from your local disk
4. Select the file and click Open
5. When word displays the informational dialog, click ok
6. If word display, the protected view bar at the top of the document, click enable editing
7. You can edit PDF file now with word, once file is edited you can save it as PDF or in Word format

Chapter 3 — Introduction to Microsoft Word 2013

Introduction of Word 2013?

Microsoft Word 2013 is **a word-processing program that is used to create professional-looking documents such as reports, resumes, letters, memos, and newsletters**. It includes many powerful tools that can be used to easily create and edit documents, and collaborate with others

Q.1. What is Microsoft Word Application ?

Ans. Microsoft Word is a **word processing** application that allows you to create a variety of **documents**, including letters, resumes, and more. In this lesson, you'll learn how to navigate the Word interface and become familiar with some of its most important features, such as the **Ribbon**, **Quick Access Toolbar**, and **Backstage view**.

Q.2. What is the extension of an MS Word file?

Ans. An MS Word file is always saved with the extension of .doc or .docx.

1. Write a short note on the following commands of Microsoft Word

Q.3. What do we mean by font and how to select and Apply a particular Fonts?

Ans. The word font refers to a set of printable or displayable typography or text characters in a specific style and size. Font styles are used in both print and digital text. To change the font:

1. Select the text you want to modify. Selecting text to modify.
2. On the Home tab, click the drop-down arrow next to the Font box. A menu of font styles will appear.
3. Move the mouse over the various font styles. A live preview of the font will appear in the document. ...
4. The font will change in the document.

Q.4. Why Page Numbering is needed and applied in text document?

Ans. **Page numbers can be used to automatically number each page in your document**. They come in a wide range of number formats and can be customized to suit your needs. Page numbers are usually placed in the header, footer, or side margin.

Q.5. Short notes on Date and Time

Ans. Date and time functions operate on a date and time input value and return a string, numeric, or date and time value. On the Insert tab, in the Text group, click Date & Time. In the Date and time dialog box, select the format you want. Select the Update automatically check box. The date is inserted as a field and will update automatically.

Q.6. Short notes on Sort and sorting process.

Ans. Sorting is the processing of arranging the data in ascending and descending order. There are several types of sorting in data structures namely – *bubble sort, insertion sort, selection sort, bucket sort, heap sort, quick sort, radix sort* etc.

Sorting a table in Word

1. Select anywhere in the table.
2. Select Table Tools Layout > Sort.
3. Choose your sort criteria: Select the column you want to Sort by. To sort on a second column, select Then by and select another column. Select Ascending or Descending. ...
4. Select OK.

Q.6. Short notes on Text Animation. What is the use of animation in MS Word?

Ans. The biggest use for animation is for entertainment. Animation is used on the TV, on your phones, and all over the internet. In television, animation is mostly used to occupy children, as is gives them something to laugh about and keep them entertained for long periods of time.

Animating Your Text

1. Select the text you want to animate.
2. Choose Font from the Format menu. Word displays the Font dialog box.
3. Make sure the Text Effects tab is selected.
4. In the Animations list, select the animation effect you want applied to your text. ...
5. Click on OK

Q.7. Short notes on AutoFormat.

Ans. Using this feature can minimize the need to apply changes from the Ribbon. AutoFormat As You Type provides three categories of options: Replace as you type, Apply as you type, and Automatically as you type.The following is the process of applying autoformat feature.

Go to File > Options > Proofing. Select AutoCorrect Options, and then select the AutoFormat As You Type tab. page 69-70.

Q.8. What is meant by the word 'columns' in MS Word?

Ans. Sometimes the information you include in your document is best displayed in columns. The vertical portion is known as column which may be many. Columns can help improve readability, especially with certain types of documents—like newspaper articles, newsletters, and flyers. Word also allows you to adjust your columns by adding column breaks.

Where is columns in MS Word?

On the Page Layout tab, click Columns, then click the layout you want. To apply columns to only part of your document, with your cursor, select the text that you want to format. On the Page Layout tab, click Columns, then click More Columns

Q.9. What is the importance of table of contents in Word?

Ans. The table of contents serves two purposes: It gives users an overview of the document's contents and organization. It allows readers to go directly to a specific section of an on-line document. For creating the Table of Contents of a document : On the References tab, in the Table of Contents group, click Table of Contents, and then click on the table of Contents style that you want which will insert it. A Table of Contents will now appear On the toolbar ribbon, select References. Near the left end, select Insert Table of Contents. (Or select Table of Contents > Insert Table of Contents. The table of contents is inserted, showing the headings and page numbering in your document.

Q.10. What is an index and how is it created in a document or book.

Ans. An index is an alphabetical and detailed listing of topics in a document at its end , with a corresponding page number displayed alongside. An index is typically located at the end of a long document. An index helps readers to navigate long documents and locate specific information they may need.

Inserting an Index Entry

1. Select the text you want to include in the index.
2. Click the References tab.
3. Click the Mark Entry in the Index group.
4. Adjust the index entry's settings and choose an index entry option:
5. Click the Mark or Mark All button.
6. Repeat the process for your other index entries.
7. Click Close when you're done.

Q.11. What do we mean by File, Insert?

Ans. The Insert tab contains various items that you may want to insert into a document. These items include such things as tables, word art, hyperlinks, symbols, charts, signature line, date & time, shapes, header, footer, text boxes, links, boxes, equations and so on.

Go to **Insert > Object**. Select Create from File. Select Browse and choose the file you want to use. Select Insert.

Q.12. What are Footnotes and Endnotes?

Ans. Footnotes appear on the bottom of the page that contains the sentence to which it refers. Endnotes are listed at the end of the paper on separate pages. On the top of the first page, the title "Notes" is centered one inch from the top of the page. See also page 74-75.

Q.13. What is meant by Hyperlinks in the text documents?

Ans. The hyperlink **can be text or graphics**. By using hyperlinks, you can provide information to your readers without repeating the same information on different pages. To add links that jump from one part of a document to another part of the same document, mark the destination and then add a link to it.

Q.14. What is hyperlink explain types of hyperlinks?

Ans. Some of the hyperlinks that are used normally

Text hyperlink – Uses a word or phrase to take visitors to another page, file or document.

- **Image hyperlink** – Uses an image to take visitors to another page, file or document.
- **Bookmark hyperlink** – Uses text or an image to take visitors to another part of a web page.

Q.15. What is protect document in MS Word?

Ans. Before you send a Microsoft Word document to another person for their comments, you can make use of a feature called Document protection. When you protect a document, **the only changes that can be made to it are Tracked changes and Comments.**

How do I protect a document in Word 2013?

1. Click the File tab, then click Info.
2. Click Protect Document, then click Encrypt with Password.
3. Once the Encrypt Document dialog box appears, type in a strong password, and click OK to finish.
4. The Confirm Password dialog box will appear; re-type the password and click OK.
5. Return to the File tab, and Save the document

Q.16. What is the use of tracking changes in word processing?

Ans. Track Changes **enables you to edit a document electronically (on-screen) and then review those changes, by either accepting or rejecting them**. As the name suggests, tracking does not remove the original text from the document; it simply marks it and leaves it in place.Track changes is a feature within most word processing applications that enables a user to keep track of the entire different types of alterations, changes or deletions made to a specific document.

For Review, accept, or reject changes

Click or tap at the beginning of the document**.** On the Review tab, select Track Changes. Select Accept or Reject. As you accept or reject changes, Word will move to the next change.

Q.17. What is version control in Word?

Ans. Version control is **the process by which different drafts and versions of a document or record are managed**. It is a tool which tracks a series of draft documents, culminating in a final version. It provides an audit trail for the revision and update of these finalised versions. Commercial versions of Word are licensed as a standalone product or as a component of Microsoft Office suite of software, which can be purchased either with a perpetual license or as part of a Microsoft subscription.

The first version of Word for Windows was released in 1989. With the release of Windows 3.0 the following year, sales began to pick up and Microsoft soon became the market leader for word processors for IBM PC-compatible computers. Word for Windows is available stand-alone or as part of the Microsoft Office suite.

2003	Microsoft Word 2003	Version 11.0.Included in Office 2003
2006	Microsoft Word 2007	Version 12.0 , Included in Office 2007
2010	Word 2010	Version 14.0, Included in Office 2010;
2013	Word 2013	Version 15.0, Included in Office 2013

Q.18. What is zoom in and zoom out operation?

Ans. When we apply the zoom-in operation, it enlarges the size of text whereas applying the zoom-out operation reduces the size of text. A zoom operation just changes the size of the font on-screen without impacting any other attribute of the document.

To zoom a document in Word by using the buttons in the "Zoom" button group, click the "View" tab in the Ribbon and then look within the "Zoom" button group. To set the document zoom to 100%, click the "100%" button in the "Zoom" button group on the "View" tab of the Ribbon

Q.19. What is paragraph in word 2013?

Ans. Officially, a paragraph is **any chunk of text that ends when you press the Enter key**. So a single character, a word, a sentence, or a document full of sentences is a paragraph, so long as you press the Enter key.\nThe paragraph symbol appears in a document to mark the end of a paragraph.

To specify paragraph formatting options, **click the dialog launcher of a Paragraph group under the Home or the Page Layout tab to bring up the Paragraph dialog box or right click in your text and choose Paragraph from the shortcut menu.**

Q.20. What do we mean by case? How many Change Case options are available in MS Word 2013?

Ans. There's **up to five** choices on the ribbon with a keyboard shortcut to reach it. Alter the upper/lower case of words, phrases or more. 'change case' can become 'Change Case' or 'CHANGE CASE' or even "cHANGE cASE" without retyping. Alt shortcut to reach the ribbon menu.

The Change Case dialog box. Note that the dialog box provides five different ways you can change the capitalization of your text.

These are the choices in the dialog box:

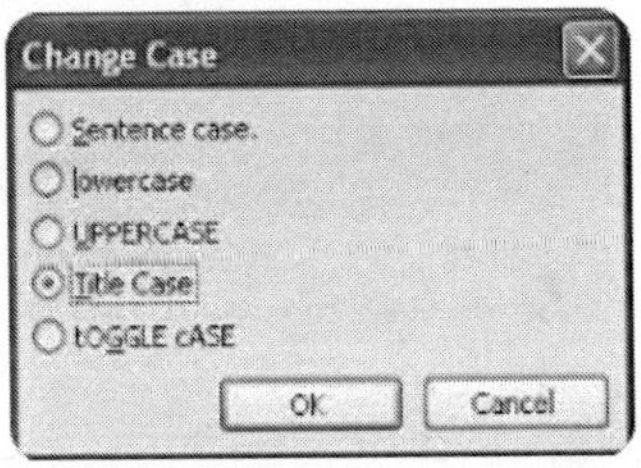

Sentence Case. This option capitalizes the first letter of each sentence in the selection.

Lowercase. ...

Uppercase. ...

Title Case. ...

Toggle Case.

Q.21. How do I insert a picture into Word 2013?

Ans. Whether you want to insert a picture from your computer or find one online, it's easy to add photos in Word. Whether you're working on a hefty research project or a friendly holiday greeting card, adding images to your Word document can really add value to your project.

Select the Insert tab on the Ribbon, then click the Pictures command. The Insert Picture dialog box will appear. Select the desired image file, then click Insert. The image will appear in the document.

Q.22. What are bullets in MS Word 13?

Ans. Different types of bullet symbols are used to specify your points in veery short.Bullet lists identify key items or denote significance when order does not matter. Bullet points are often used in documents and presentations to help organize information and make it easier to read or understand. Bullet example. Bulleted list example.Teachers often use bulleted lists to highlight important pieces of their lessons. Manuals often include numbered lists to assist readers with step-by-step instruction. A bullet is usually a black circle, but it can be any other symbol used to highlight items in a listIn bulleted lists, each paragraph begins with a bullet character. In numbered lists, each paragraph begins with an expression that includes a number or letter and a separator such as a period or parenthesis. The numbers in a numbered list are updated automatically when you add or remove paragraphs in the list. See also page 68.

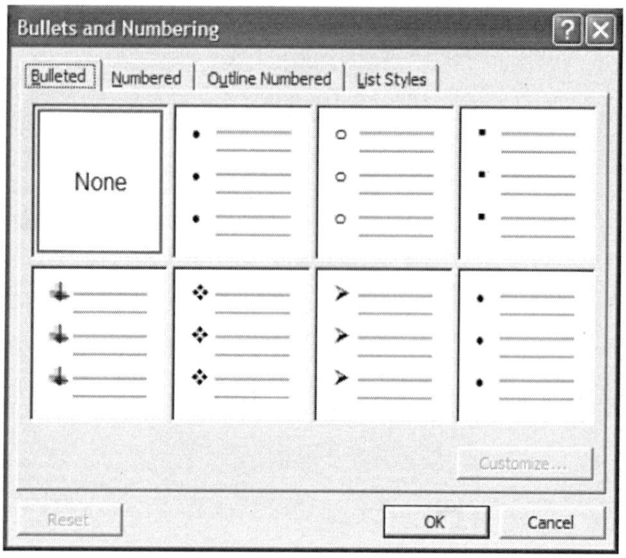

Q.23. What is insert break?

Ans. You can use it to change the number of columns without starting a new page. Even Page Starts the new section on the next even-numbered page. For example, if you insert an Even Page Break at the end of page 3, the next section will start on page 4. Odd Page Starts the new section on the next odd-numbered. Also To insert a section break, click Page Layout, click Breaks, and to find the various section breaks to add.

Q.24. How do you insert a comment in Word 2013?

Ans. Adding a comment to a document is like writing a note in the page's margin. You can use Word's comments feature to add suggestions, notes, or reminders to your documents. Comments appear in boxes at the side of the page. Select the text you want to add a comment to. Click the Review tab.

To add comments:

- Highlight some text, or place the insertion point where you want the comment to appear.

Selecting text.

- From the Review tab, click the New Comment command. Clicking the New Comment command.
- Type your comment

Q.25. Where are the comments on Word?

Ans. In the Comments pane, you can see a single list of all comments in your document, including resolved comments. To switch between the contextual view and the Comments pane, simply click the Comments button in the upper right corner of your Word window.

Q.26. What is a table in Word 2013 and How can you create a table in MS Word 2013?

Ans. A table is a grid of cells arranged in rows and columns. Tables are useful for various tasks such as presenting text information and numerical data. In Word, you can create a blank table, convert text to a table, and apply a variety of styles and formats to existing tables.

Select Insert > Table, and then select Convert Text to Table. To draw your own table, select Insert > Table > Draw Table

Q.27. What is the example of drop cap? How many types of deop caps are ther in MS> Word 2013?

Ans. A drop cap (dropped capital) is a large capital letter used as a decorative element at the beginning of a paragraph or section. The size of a drop cap is usually two or more lines. Drop caps add style or grab a reader's attention. For example: Here is a paragraph that starts using a drop cap letter. As you can see, the first letter of the word "here" is large and helps bring focus to this section Where is drop cap in Word?

The following illustration shows your options for positioning a drop cap

Select the text and go to "Insert > Drop cap" (Windows) or select "Drop Cap" from the Format menu (Mac). Edit your drop cap by going to "Insert > Drop Cap > Drop Cap Options"

There are two types of drop cap: Dropped: Wraps text around the drop cap. In Margin: Isolates drop cap into the left margin.

Q.28. What is the Find and Replace in MS word?

Ans. Find and Replace helps you to find words or formats in a document and can let you replace all instances of a word or format. This is particularly handy in long documents.

- To use Find and Replace, use the shortcut Ctrl + H or navigate to Editing in the Home tab of the ribbon, then choose Replace. or
- Go to Home > Replace.
- Enter the word or phrase you want to replace in Find what.
- Enter your new text in Replace with.

- Choose Replace All to change all occurrences of the word or phrase. ...
- To specify only upper or lowercase in your search, select More > Match case.
- See also page 71.

Q.29. What is header and footer short notes? What is header and footer symbol?

Ans. A header is text that is placed at the top of a page, while a footer is placed at the bottom, or foot, of a page. Typically these areas are used for inserting document information, such as the name of the document, the chapter heading, page numbers, creation date and the like. Headers and footers generally contain additional information such as page numbers, dates, an author's name, and footnotes, which can help keep longer documents organized and make them easier to read. Text entered in the header or footer will appear on each page of the document.See page page 73-74 of this book.

The Header/Footer Symbol button is used to insert a symbol of your choice into the log header or footer. This is typically used to illustrate symbols that will appear in the body of the log. This is a fixed design item with no corresponding data file commands.

Q.30. What is macro in MS Word 2013?

Ans. In Word, you can automate frequently used tasks by creating and running macros. A macro is a series of commands and instructions that you group together as a single command to accomplish a task automatically.

When you have a repetitive series of tasks to perform, you can record those tasks as a macro. Place the cursor where you want to start recording the macro. Click the Record Macro button. The Record Macro window opens, where you can set up the macro's name, description, and triggering mechanism before you record it.

Macros are generally stored in the Normal. dotm template for Word. But the Normal. dotm template also contains many other customizations like styles and autocorrect entries.

Q.31. What is reveal formatting in Word?

Ans. The "Reveal Formatting" pane lets you reveal formatting in Word documents. This pane lets you see the details of text formatting in Word. You can also use it to compare formatting in Word.

To open the "Reveal Formatting" pane in Word, first select the text for which to see the formatting. Then open the "Styles" pane. To open the "Styles" pane in Word, click the "Home" tab in the Ribbon. Then click the "Styles" task pane launcher button in the lower-right corner of the "Styles" button group.

Q.32. What are all the tabs in MS Word in 2013 and how to proves then in practical application?

Ans. It comprises seven tabs; Home, Insert, Page layout, References, Mailing, Review and View. Each tab has specific groups of related commands. It gives you quick access to the commonly used commands that you need to complete a task.

Use tabs in Word 2013?

To set tab stops in Word 2013, do the following:

- On the Home tab, in the Paragraph group, choose Paragraph Settings.

- Click the Tabs button.
- Set the Tab stop position, choose the Alignment and Leader options, and then click Set and OK

Q.33. What is a bookmark in Word 2013?

Ans. A bookmark in Word works like a bookmark you might place in a book: it marks a place that you want to find again easily.

How to Create a Bookmark in Word

- Start by selecting an item or placing your cursor where you want the bookmark.
- Open the Insert tab and click Bookmark in the Links section of the ribbon.
- In the pop-up window, enter a Bookmark name. ...
- Click Add.

Q.34. What is word count in MS word?

Ans. Word counts the number of words in a document while you type. Word also counts pages, paragraphs, lines, and characters. Windows macOSWeb. Play. When you need to know how many words, pages, characters, paragraphs, or lines are in a document, check the status bar Open Word 2013 and write some text. Go to the "Review" tab then "Proofing group". In the Proofing group click on "Word Count". The count of the number of words and the number of characters will be displayed. See also page 73 of this book.

Q.34. How do you save as a document in Word?

Ans. Select the File tab on the top left of the page, afterward locate the Save As button. 2. A Files window should open up after clicking the Save As button. Here you add a name to the file and click Save to save the document.

Q.35. How many types of alignment are there in MS Word 2013?

Ans. By default, Word aligns text to the left margin in new documents. However, there may be times when you want to adjust text alignment to the center or right. Select the text you want to modify. On the Home tab, select one of the four alignment options from the Paragraph group. There are 4 types of text alignments which are left-aligned, center-aligned, right-aligned, and justified.

Q.36. How do I change the font in Word 2013?

Ans. To use your favorite font in Word all the time, set it as the default. Go to Format > Font > Font. + D to open the Font dialog box. Select the font and size you want to use.

To change the font:

- Select the text you want to modify. Selecting text to modify.
- On the Home tab, click the drop-down arrow next to the Font box. A menu of font styles will appear.
- Move the mouse over the various font styles. A live preview of the font will appear in the document.
- The font will change in the document

Q.37. Describe the process of Spell Checking in Word 2013.

Ans. Spell check identifies and corrects misspelled words. It also allows you to search a document yourself for words you know you've misspelled. In Microsoft Word, spell check options, like spelling and grammar may be found under the 'review' tab and 'proofing' window. See also page 62.

Q.38. Which option will you use to check Grammar in a Word 2013 document?

Ans. From the Proofing group on the Review tab, select Spelling & Grammar . Microsoft Word will look for spelling and grammar errors starting from the location of your cursor in the document. You then have the following options: Ignore.

Q.39. How is thesaurus used in word 2013?

Ans. Thesaurus is a tool, which is used in MS Word or Microsoft Word to search for synonyms and synonyms for a particular selected word. Thesaurus in Ms Word helps writers to find exact and suitable words to express their idea

Using the thesaurus, you can look up synonyms (different words with the same meaning) and antonyms (words with the opposite meaning). thesaurus is a book that lists words or phrases that mean the same thing or almost the same thing–a book of synonyms. Some thesauruses list words in alphabetical order, just like a dictionary; however, many don't. They have an index at the front, with instructions of how to use the index to find the word you want.See Page 64 also.

Q.40. What are Styles?

Ans. In Word, a style is a collection of formatting instructions. You use styles to format the paragraphs in your document. So you would use the "Title" style for your title, "Body Text" style for body text, "Caption" style for the picture captions, and "Heading 1" for the major headings. Style sets include a combination of title, heading, and paragraph styles. Style sets allow you to format all elements in your document at once instead of Built-in styles are combinations of formatting characteristics that you can apply to text to quickly change its appearance. For example, applying the Heading 1 style might make text bold, Arial, and 16 point, and applying the Heading 2 style makes text bold, italic.

Q.41. Describe the various Borders in Word 2013. How many types of borders are there in MS Word?

Ans. Microsoft Word allows you to add various different types of borders in your document, such as *colorful border, text border, picture border, paragraph border, and custom border.*

Adding a border to some text

- Select a word, line, or paragraph.
- Go to Home > Borders, and then open the menu of border choices.
- Choose the type of border you want.
- See also page 64-65

Q.42. How do I close an existing document in Word?

Ans. Closing a Document in Word 2013

- Choose File > Close to close your document without exiting. Choose File > Exit to close your document and exit. If you exit, you perform the same procedures for saving the document as with the Close operation.

Q.43. Describe the various options of viewing and saving the document.

Ans. Word provides different ways you can view your documents, depending on your particular needs. The major views available in Word are Print Layout, Full Screen Reading, Web Layout, Outline, and Draft. (In Word 2013 the Full Screen Reading view was renamed the Read Mode view.For saving a file you have to use **Save** or **Save as** command. In the later you have the option for choosing the type of file format such as PDF etc.

Save command

- Use the keyboard shortcut Ctrl+S. Go to File > Save on the Menu bar.
- Click the Save icon on the Standard toolbar. Using the Save command will overwrite the last saved version of the file.
- We can save the document in Microsoft word in 2 ways:
- By clicking File on the top left corner and then click save as after that browse the location where exactly you want to save on your computer.
- By just pressing Ctrl + S and then browse the location where you want to save.

Q.44. How do I print my Word document?

Ans. Follow following steps to Print a Document

Click the File tab.

- Also you can examine the print preview on the right side of the screen to ensure the document appears correct.
- Select the correct printer by clicking the Printer list arrow and selecting it from the list
- **Click Print.**

Q.45. What is mail merge explain step by step?

Ans. To do this, follow these steps:

- Click Edit individual letters.
- In the Merge to New Document dialog box, select the records that you want to merge.
- Click OK. ...
- Scroll to the information that you want to edit, and then make your changes.
- Print or save the document just as you would any regular document
- Also see Page 76-78.

Chapter 4 — Introduction to Microsoft Excel 2013

Q.1. What conventions are used in Excel 2013?

Q.2. How would you create a worksheet?

Ans. See pages 81-96 of this book.

Q.3. How would you copy a formula?

Ans. See pages 81 on ward.

Q.4. How are decision making formula used?

Ans. See pages 92-96.

Q.5. Write a short note on the following commands of Microsoft Excel

Ans.

- Styles–see page 96.
- AutoCalculate See page 98.
- Average Function. See page 98.
- Auditing a workbook. See page 100.
- Outlines. See page 103.
- Function wizard. See page 104-105.
- Scenarios manager -See pages 105-107.
- AutoFill- See page 109.
- Applying Themes-See pages 112-114.
- Protecting Worksheets-See pages 115-116.
- Adding/Deleting Rows-See page 111.
- Convert Text to Columns-See page 116.
- Functions-See pages 96-97 and then 117-122.
- Sum Function-See pages 98-99.
- Creating Charts-See pages 99-100.
- Comments-See pages 102-103.
- Fitting on a page-See pages 103-104.
- Goal seeking-See page 105.
- Pivot Table-See pages 108-109.
- Formatting Numbers and Labels See pages 110-111.
- Applying Themes-See pages 112-114.
- Inserting and removing Page Breaks-See pages 115-116

Chapter 5 — Introduction to PowerPoint 2013

Q.1. How would you create presentation from Template?

Ans. See pages 124 onward of this book.

Q.2. Describe the various PowerPoint views.

Ans. See pages 125-128 of this book.

Q.3. How would you change the background colour of the presentation?

Ans. See pages 130-131 of this book.

Q.4. How would you add graphics to the slide?

Ans. See pages 131-134 of this book.

Q.5. Describe the process of reordering the slides.

Ans. See pages 134 of this book.

Q.6. What are the text transitions?

Ans. See pages 138 of this book. See pages 139-140 of this book

Q.7. How would you create a Slide Show?

Ans. See pages 139-140 of this book.

Q.8. How would you pack the presentation?

Ans. Use PowerPoint's Pack And Go Wizard

- Add password protection to a file
- Select File > Info.
- Select Protect Presentation > Encrypt with Password.
- In the Password box, enter the password you'd like to use. Select OK.
- PowerPoint prompts you to confirm the password by entering it once more.
- Save the file to ensure the password takes effect.
- Alternatively With the presentation open, select File | Pack and Go.
- Follow along with the wizard. ...
- When you've finished selecting all the necessary options, make sure there's a disk in the destination drive, if necessary click Finish.

Chapter 6 – Introduction to Access 2013

Q.1. How would you create a database?

Ans. See page 144 of this book.

Q.2. Describe the process of creating a database using the wizard.

Ans. See page 144 of this book.

Q.3. How would you create a database using template?

Ans. See page 145 of this book.

Q.4. What is a Form?

Ans. See pages 150-151 of this book.

Q.5. How would you create a Query?

Ans. See pages 153-154 of this book.

Q.6. How would you create a Report?

Ans. See pages 159-162 of this book.

Chapter 7 – Other Software of Microsoft Office 2013

Q.1. What is Publisher 2013 used for?

Ans. See pages 164-166 of this book.

Q.2. What all you can do using InfoPath Forms?

Ans. See pages 166-167 of this book.

Q.3. What in OneNote 2013 used for?

Ans. See pages 169-170 of this book.

Q.4. What is Microsoft Skydrive used for?

Ans. See pages 170-172 of this book.